# JIM

**The Life and Work of James Griffiths:
A Hero of the Welsh Nation and an Architect of the
British Welfare State**

# JIM

## The Life and Work of James Griffiths:
## An Architect of the Welfare State

**D. Ben Rees**

Foreword by Dr Huw Edwards, BBC, London

Modern Welsh Publications, Allerton, Liverpool

# Contents

8   Jim and his wife, Winnie and two of the children, Jeanne and Harold.

9   Amanwy (David Rees Griffiths), brother of Jim .

10 Aneurin Bevan, a great friend of Jim addressing a meeting at Shotton, Deeside in support of Eirene White, MP for Flintshire East

11  Jim and his niece Mrs May Harries of Ammanford

12 Jim with Colonel H.S.Lee at the tea party in Ipoh, India on 30-5-1950.

13 Jim and Dr Edith Summerskill, MP   on a tour of Israel

14 Jim on his tour of India

15 Jim presenting a prize to Honourable Mr Vasey of the 21 Club of Nairobi in Kenya.

16 Jim Griffiths on the platform of the National Eisteddfod of Wales when it was held in Llanelli in 1962

17 Jim Griffiths celebrating with members of a Choir on the Eisteddfod field

18 The popular politician celebrating a choral success at the National Eisteddfod of Wales

19 A conversation on the Eisteddfod field between Hywel D. Roberts of Cardiff, Jim and Ifor Bowen Griffith of Caernarfon

20 Cliff Prothero, Regional Secretary for the Labour Party in Wales preparing the microphone for the orator

21 Three well known eisteddfodwyr, Sir Albert Jones Evans (Cynan), Sir David Hughes Parry and Sir T.H. Parry Williams on   the platform of the National Eisteddfod of Wales while Jim addressed the large audience.

22 Jim at the opening of a new factory in his constituency.

23 Cledwyn Hughes who followed Jim as Secretary of State for Wales in 1966

24  Bryn Villa, Betws today, the old house was the birthplace of James Griffiths

*Cyflwynedig i fy annwyl Meinwen a'r meibion gofalus Dafydd a Hefin a'u teuluoedd*

# Foreword

James Griffiths should feature prominently in any serious history of British Labour politics. He was a natural leader, firmly rooted in the trade union world of the coal mines of south Wales. He was a working-class hero who rose to become a cabinet minister and the first Secretary of State for Wales. In a very real sense, devolved modern Wales is a product of the pioneering work done by Jim Griffiths half a century ago.

D. Ben Rees has blended his deep knowledge of the Labour movement with his evident admiration for James Griffiths to produce an intriguing portrait. He is to be warmly congratulated for introducing this (largely-forgotten) Labour statesman to a new audience. Students of the Blair, Brown, Miliband and Corbyn projects will appreciate some striking parallels. Internal Labour politics in the days of Attlee, Gaitskell and Wilson could be every bit as sharp and divisive as the twenty-first century kind.

The narrative flows fluently from Griffiths' origins in Ammanford, in the Welsh-speaking heartland of Carmarthenshire, to Llanelli (where he served as the town's MP for 34 years), Westminster (where he served in Cabinet under Attlee and Wilson), and beyond (as Secretary of State for the Colonies).

Ben Rees provides valuable insights at many points, but the analysis of Griffiths' rejection of the Liberal tradition and his embracing of Labour is especially fascinating. Griffiths was a loyal child of the chapel and his early political journey was much more difficult than people might realise today. The Nonconformist establishment was virtually an extension of Lloyd George's Liberal Party: only the brave or foolhardy would 'rebel' by backing the 'upstart' Labour Party with its 'dangerous' views and (frequently) anti-chapel stance.

Yet, as Ben records, it took courage for Jim Griffiths, as a young man, to express publicly his dismay at the scorn regularly spat from chapel pulpits by preachers whose dislike of Labour outweighed their Christian instincts – or their basic common sense, for that matter. Griffiths accused them of alienating young people and reminded them that a campaign to improve the welfare of working people (the very people sitting in the pews) was hardly a perverse venture.

There are some surprising revelations, including the tale of one unpleasant episode between the normally placid Griffiths and his long-standing agent Douglas Hughes (one of the most influential Welsh Labour fixers of his day) about a union march in Llanelli. It is hardly a significant affair, but the imperial tone of Griffiths' letters conveys all the force of a powerful man determined to protect his good reputation.

Arguably the most interesting section for today's students of politics is the creation of the Welsh Office (at a time when the forces of Welsh nationalism were gathering strength) and the re-shaping of Welsh politics in the 1960s. Jim Griffiths, as Ben explains, had been a consistent opponent of the campaign for a Welsh Parliament, but he fully realised that the democratic imbalance between Westminster and Wales needed to be addressed or Plaid Cymru's performance would surely become a very real threat to Labour.

The answer, despite vigorous opposition from some Welsh Labour MPs, was the establishment by Harold Wilson of the Welsh Office in April 1965. This was not only Labour's answer to the Plaid threat, but also its response to the wider campaign for a Welsh Parliament. That campaign had been led by Lady Megan Lloyd George (her father had been a prominent Home Rule supporter in his early days) and backed by able Labour MPs including Cledwyn Hughes.

Indeed, Hughes was the clear choice of many to be the first Secretary of State for Wales. Instead, as Ben explains, Wilson opted for the 74-year-old 'elder statesman' Jim Griffiths, whose previous experience in Cabinet and as Labour's deputy leader made him a very compelling figure.

The remarkable story of James Griffiths takes us all the way from the origins of British Labour to the origins of devolved Wales. Ben Rees has crafted a highly readable and authoritative account of the life and times of one of Wales' greatest statesmen.

**Huw Edwards**
**2019**

# Introduction

Since I was a young child in rural Cardiganshire (now known as Ceredigion), I was aware of two outstanding Welsh politicians – Aneurin Bevan and James Griffiths – who both played an important role in all our lives as a result of their efforts to create the Welfare State, which became a reality between 1945 and 1950. We felt that of the two statesmen, James Griffiths was 'one of us' as he spoke Welsh and came from Betws, in neighbouring Carmarthenshire, whose community closely reflected my home village of Llanddewi Brefi. Bevan, however, was not a Welsh speaker and Tredegar, his home town, not only seemed so far away to people like us who could not afford the luxury of a motor car but its Welshness was very different. Also, due to his close proximity and deep understanding of my part of Wales, James Griffiths never missed an opportunity to visit Cardiganshire at election times, and he would fill the largest halls with his oratory and his socialist fervour.

When I was a student in Aberystwyth I came to know him personally, to correspond with him and to admire his commitment to Wales. I also appreciated his support for our student magazine, *Aneurin*, which meant so much to us. I still remember the thrill of reading his memoir, *Pages from Memory*, but felt rather disappointed that he had not done himself justice. In my view, his remarkable life – from a boy miner in the Amman Valley to the Cabinet, as Minister for the Colonies, and later the first ever Minister for Welsh Affairs – deserved much greater attention and recognition. James Griffiths had also achieved success as Minister of Pensions, Chairman of the Labour Party, Deputy Leader of the Labour Party and a first-rate MP for Llanelli from 1936 to 1970.

Over the years it became more and more obvious that if anyone deserved a biography, he did, and in 2009 when I had the opportunity of looking at his archive in the National Library of Wales, I had no hesitation in taking on the challenge. The people of Wales, Britain and the Commonwealth, owe him a great debt of gratitude.

The life and work of James Griffiths is indeed a romantic saga. We must remember he was born to a large family at Betws, near Ammanford. His father, William Griffiths, a blacksmith and larger-than-life character, was steeped in the issues of the day. He hero-worshipped W.E. Gladstone and later Tom Ellis and David Lloyd George, and was a loyal member of the local Welsh independent chapel in Ammanford, the Christian Temple. Meanwhile, Griffiths' mother, Margaret, cared for her four sons and three daughters, never forgetting the two infant children she lost. Due to the family's financial circumstances, the seven surviving children were all working by the age of 13, and so never progressed to secondary school. As such, their only means of education was the local elementary school and the chapel.

When he began his working life as a 13-year-old miner, Jeremiah became known as James, and by the time he became President of the South Wales Miners' Federation he was simply known as 'our Jim'. At the beginning of his working life he experienced the 1904-5 Religious Revival and the new theology associated with Reverend R.J. Campbell, as well as the extraordinary impact of Keir Hardie as the prophet of Socialism. His conversion from Liberalism to Socialism had taken place by 1908, the year he lost his eldest brother Gwilym in a mining accident and nearly lost his talented, poetic brother David Rees, known by his eisteddfodic name, Amanwy. It was also the year he took responsibility for a new branch of the Independent Labour Party (ILP) in Ammanford. His ILP convictions brought him into the fellowship of a group of young men alienated from the Liberal Party and the chapels which staunchly supported Lloyd George and the Liberal tradition. A pacifist during the First World War, James Griffiths made a name for himself as a left-wing firebrand, greatly admired by George Lansbury and others who visited the socialist citadel called Tŷ Gwyn (White House).

By the time he won a scholarship, through the Miners' Union, to the Central Labour College in London, where he met like-minded miners such as Aneurin Bevan, Ness Edwards, Bryn Roberts and many more, he knew where he stood politically and his ambition was to be a leader of men in the trade union movement. This he achieved through service, ability, charm as well as through the support – through thick and thin – of his young bride, Winifred Rutley from Hampshire, with whom he had four children. He worked as a political agent, then a miners' agent, and finally became Vice President and later President of 'the Fed', the South Wales Miners' Union (SWMU). In a by-election in 1936 he kept Labour's firm grip on Llanelli and proudly served his constituency for the next 34 years, gaining wide respect as a defender of the working-class.

Griffiths achieved much during his political career and it was a fitting tribute that his devotion to his homeland was rewarded when, despite being 74 years of age, he became the first Secretary of State for Wales. He deserved the opportunity and he certainly laid the foundations for the future growth of devolved government in Wales.

To me, Jim Griffiths represents politics at its best, a model for all those who seek and achieve elected office. His fundamental sense of justice instilled by his nonconformist background, his political convictions inspired by Keir Hardie and his personal discipline as exemplified by his life-long adherence to the temperance movement are all inspiring.

I truly hope that I have done justice to one of the most significant figures of 20th century British socialism.

**D. Ben Rees**
**Liverpool**
**2020**

# Acknowledgements

I am grateful to the institutions and individuals – librarians, archivists, politicians and historians –who have been so helpful to me in the preparation of his book.

Naturally I am very indebted to the past and present staff of the National Library of Wales, in particular to Dr J. Graham Jones, who was always encouraging and ready with his advice. I owe a huge debt to Tony Fyler who read and edited my transcript. I have received valuable assistance from Dr Huw Walters, the authority on Amanwy (Jim's brother), and who is knowledgeable on the history of the Amman Valley. My thanks also to Dr Evan James who prepared James Griffiths' family tree for publication in this book.

I benefited greatly from my many conversations and correspondence with Lord Gwilym Prys Davies, a dear and much missed friend of over 50 years, and a most valuable link with the great man himself. He encouraged me throughout the time I have spent preparing this volume and was a font of knowledge on Welsh political history. The notable broadcaster Huw Edwards (a native of Llangennech, near Llanelli) has taken a great interest in this work, read the original Welsh language version and kindly agreed to provide the Foreword for this, the English edition. I'd also like to thank my typist, Mrs Iona Bailey from Swyddffynnon, for her invaluable assistance in producing the manuscript, as well as David Fletcher, Kingsley near Frodsham who were responsible for inserting the photographs with the text. He has been most valuable with his computing skills.  .

I am grateful to others as well, in particular Reverend Derwyn Morris Jones from Swansea for locating photographs from members of the Griffiths family. I also want to thank Sion Wyn Morris, Waterloo, Liverpool for his expertise with the dust jacket, and Sir Deian Hopkin, a Labour historian who was brought up by James Griffiths' agent, Douglas Hughes, and for sharing his knowledge of the Labour Party in the Llanelli area. The grandson of Jim Griffiths David Griffiths has been immensely helpful, so has Nick Thomas-Symonds, Labour MP for Torfaen for reading the whole typescript and making useful insights. Dr Patricia Williams of Liverpool has checked the first two versions as well as the final version before submitting it to the printer Gomer Press at Llandysul in Ceredigion. These are well known printers that I owe a great debt to them. Modern Welsh Publishers responded to the challenge as usual in style. I am also most grateful for the encouragement of a number of Labour party stalwarts who had the honour of representing Llanelli at Westminster and Cardiff Bay respectively, Nia Griffith and Keith Davies and Lee Walters.

My wife Meinwen has been, as usual, hugely supportive. She well remembers the congratulatory telegram James Griffiths sent to our wedding reception in Aberdare on 31 July 1963. She could not have imagined that her husband, 57 years later, would be the author of the first ever biography of that warm-hearted statesman Jim Griffiths who wished us well at the beginning of our partnership together. For the endless love, patience and encouragement she has shown to me and to our sons Dafydd and Hefin and their families while I've researched and written this book, I therefore dedicate it to her and our close knit family with all my heart. And especially as she recovers from her serious injury which kept her in a hospital atmosphere for ten weeks ( July- September 2019 ), while Corvis-19 has kept this book from being published as we depend greatly  as do every publisher in Wales for our distribution  on  the Welsh Book Centre, Glanyrafon Estate, Llanbadarn Fawr, near Aberystwyth, Ceredigion. We acknowledge our   debt to the Welsh Book Council for processing our request for assistance so that the first ever biography of James Griffiths in English can be published.

D.Ben Rees, August 1, 2020.

**Amended details of the James Griffiths' family tree**

**Winifred Rutley died 1982 at Teddington**

**Jeanne Margaret Brandt   b Llanelli 1923. Died 1997 in Sweden**

**Harold Morris Griffiths b Burry Port 1926**

**Sheila Rose Pryce b Ystradgynlais 1928**

**William Arthur b Ystradgynlais 1931**

# James Griffiths' Family Tree

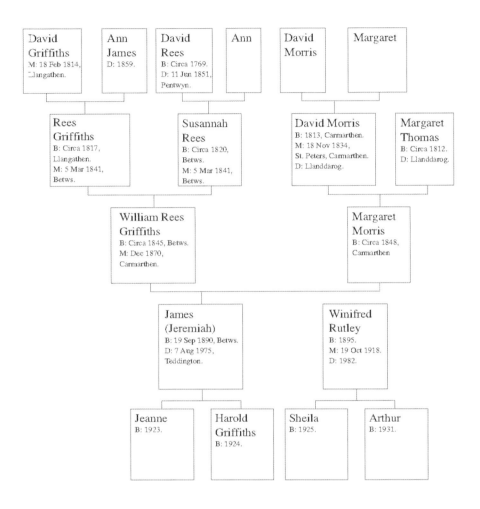

**David Griffiths**
M: 18 Feb 1814, Llangathen.

**Ann James**
D: 1859.

**David Rees**
B: Circa 1769.
D: 11 Jun 1851, Pentwyn.

**Ann**

**David Morris**

**Margaret**

**Rees Griffiths**
B: Circa 1817, Llangathen.
M: 5 Mar 1841, Betws.

**Susannah Rees**
B: Circa 1820, Betws.
M: 5 Mar 1841, Betws.

**David Morris**
B: 1813, Carmarthen.
M: 18 Nov 1834, St. Peters, Carmarthen.
D: Llanddarog.

**Margaret Thomas**
B: Circa 1812.
D: Llanddarog.

**William Rees Griffiths**
B: Circa 1845, Betws.
M: Dec 1870, Carmarthen.

**Margaret Morris**
B: Circa 1848, Carmarthen

**James (Jeremiah)**
B: 19 Sep 1890, Betws.
D: 7 Aug 1975, Teddington.

**Winifred Rutley**
B: 1895.
M: 19 Oct 1918.
D: 1982.

**Jeanne**
B: 1923.

**Harold Griffiths**
B: 1924.

**Sheila**
B: 1925.

**Arthur**
B: 1931.

*Hourglass Tree of David Griffiths*

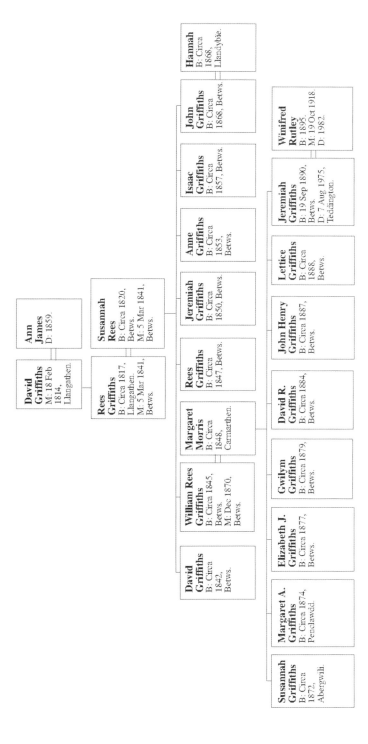

Bryn Villa, Betws today, the old house which was the birthplace of Jim Griffiths.

# 1

## The Roots of the Politician

This is the story of an extremely gifted politician who began his working life as a young miner in the Welsh heartland of Betws in Carmarthenshire and who, in his mature years, contributed immensely to the life of the miners of south Wales and to the political life of the Labour Party. The development of the coal mining industry was largely responsible for the growth of the villages in the industrial region of east Carmarthenshire, from Brynaman to Cross Hands, and down to Llanelli, which was also known as Tinopolis: the capital of the tinplate industry.

At the end of the Victorian era, the Amman Valley as well as the Gwendraeth Valley saw an influx of newcomers who came to seek work in the anthracite coalfield and the developing tinplate industry. Many coal mines were opened in these valleys and these collieries were often given poetic Welsh names, especially in the Gwendraeth Valley and to a lesser extent in the Ammanford area.[1]

In the 30 years between 1870 and 1900, collieries rapidly opened, located on the outskirts of once-rural Carmarthenshire villages such as Betws, Cae'r Bryn, and Pantyffynnon. Indeed, the small rural village of Cross Inn became an important population centre and was renamed Ammanford, or in Welsh, Rhydaman. As recorded in the 1891 census, Ammanford was a thoroughly Welsh-speaking town, as were all the villages surrounding it, and this remained the case for generations: the 1961 census noted that 79% of the population of Betws spoke Welsh.

The Amman Valley was within the anthracite coalfield and Welsh people from north and west Wales, from the slate quarrying areas of Blaenau Ffestiniog in Meirionnydd and from Bethesda in Caernarfonshire, as well as farm workers in Cardiganshire and Pembrokeshire came to live in the expanding villages that grew around the collieries. The colliery in Betws was opened in the 1890s and it was mainly responsible for the growth of the village, which stands across the river Amman from Ammanford.

It was in Betws that James Griffiths was born in 1890.[2] He was named Jeremiah Griffiths, with his childhood friends soon calling him Jerry, and he would only come to be called James later, when he started work as a young collier. Among his friends and admirers in later life he became simply 'our Jim' or 'Jim yr Efail' (Jim of the Smithy/Forge).

He was born at Yr Efail, the home of his parents, on 19 September 1890.[3] It was a beautiful autumn day but within the home there was a great expectation. His mother Margaret knew very well what it all meant having already given birth to eight children. At around nine o'clock the family heard the cry of the new arrival, who had been born into a typical God-fearing Welsh-speaking family where the father, William Rees Griffiths, like most of his contemporaries, ruled with a strong hand. As a strict nonconformist he was not willing, at any time, for his children to misbehave within or outside the home. Shortly after the birth, William gathered the children together to thank God for another addition to the Griffiths family. He and his wife Margaret also agreed that this baby was to be their last. Two brothers had died at birth but the parents were thrilled that their three surviving sons and three daughters had already brought so much joy and happiness, and most of them had already grown up into upstanding young people.

William and Margaret Griffiths were faithful and staunch chapel-goers and gave an Old Testament prophet's name to their newly-born son, with a secret wish that one day he would also be a well-loved preacher in the pulpits of their Welsh Independent denomination, *Yr Annibynwyr Cymraeg* [4] (the Welsh Independents ) an exclusively Welsh-speaking denomination. The newly-born baby was christened at Gellimanwydd chapel (known locally by its English name as the Christian Temple) by its minister, Issac Cynwyd Evans.

William Griffiths was a larger than life character. David John Williams (D. J. Williams, 1885-1970), one of the foremost Welsh language authors of the 20th century, wrote a very memorable portrayal of the young Jeremiah's father in his autobiographical account called *Yn Chwech ar Hugain Oed* (When I was Twenty Six Years Old).[5] D.J. Williams describes him as a man similar in appearance to Joseph Stalin, with dark skin, dark hair and pronounced moustache. After learning his craft as a blacksmith in Ystradgynlais, William Rees Griffiths then worked for a few years in the steel works of Ynyscedwyn, before venturing to a new job on the railway in Dunvant. From there he was promoted to be a station master in Penclawdd and later at Llansamlet before getting a job as a blacksmith at the Glyn-moch Colliery, between Cwmaman and Ammanford, and then opening his own smithy next to his house in the small village of Betws.

His wife Margaret (née Morris) came from the village of Llanddarog near Carmarthen. Her father and her grandfather were handloom weavers, and so was her brother, Sam. The splendid products of the Morris family were well known in the fairs held in Llangyfelach near Swansea, as well as those fairs held in Carmarthen and in Llandeilo.

William Griffiths worked hard as a blacksmith as he had a large family to feed, clothe and care for, and his reputation drew large numbers of customers, such as the local farmers as well as the miners who needed their tools to be sharpened. There was also a social side to the smithy, which became a great attraction to those keen on debate and discussing current affairs and was regarded as a local 'Speaker's Corner'. Griffiths and his brothers had learned the skills of the trade from their father, Rees Griffiths, who was born in Llangathen in 1817, a small village in the heart of the Carmarthenshire countryside. None of William's children, such as young Jeremiah, ever knew Rees Griffiths, but they all remembered his wife – their grandmother – Susannah Rees Griffiths, or '*Mamgu Pontaman*' as she was known, who was born in Betws in 1820 and lived to the grand old age of 95. Her youngest grandson, Jeremiah, heard her tell many colourful and enthralling stories reflecting her hard life but which showed her to be an incredibly strong, determined and energetic woman.[6]

In 1842, Rees and Susannah's eldest son, David Griffiths, was born at Tynycoed, a small farm in Betws where they were living at that time. In 1845 a second son, William Rees Griffiths, was born followed by a third, born in 1847, called Rees after his father. Their fourth son, Jeremiah, was born in 1850, and by 1851 the family had moved to 12 Plas-y-Felin, Betws. Next came their daughter, Anne, born in 1853, and in 1858 another son, Issac, was born. Their sixth and final child, John, followed in 1868.[7] By 1871, however, the family had moved to Pantyffynnon and ten years later they were living at Tŷ Uchaf.

Each one of the sons followed in the footsteps of their father as blacksmiths, a proud record in any family, and were supported by Susannah who would often make the arduous walk from Betws to Merthyr Tydfil to buy supplies of iron, carrying the load on her back. She reminded her grandson Jeremiah of the excellent work of her late husband, telling him: "If you ever go as far as Ynyscedwyn (the Ystradgynlais of today) look at the gates of Sardis (the Welsh Independent Chapel) and you will be proud of your *Dadcu'* (grandfather) who made them with his own hands."[8]

Susannah Rees Griffiths had, in addition to her skill as a storyteller, the gifts of a healer and numerous individuals, especially if they had been scalded or burnt, would walk miles to Betws to receive her herbal medicine. She passed down the secret remedies to her son Jeremiah, who toiled for 50 years in the Emlyn Colliery near the village of Penygroes, and many benefitted from his healing expertise aided by his homemade medicine which came to be known as 'Jerry ointment'.[9]

Despite its reputation as a place of fierce and passionate political debates, William Rees Griffiths maintained complete control as he would not allow any other individual to steal his limelight. Most of those who called in at the smithy would be on his political wavelength anyway – respectable chapel-going Liberals in the Gladstonian tradition – and many were members of the same local Welsh Independent chapel, led by Isaac Cynwyd Evans.[10] Occasionally, though, the smithy would attract the 'awkward squad' such as Rhys Jenkins of Gilfach, whose appearance resembled the American politician Abraham Lincoln. He was tall, thin and spoke carefully, though he had no good words for those he called *y crachach*, a Welsh term commonly used to describe snobbish folk who see themselves as superior to everybody else.[11]

William Rees Griffiths was an out-and-out Liberal, and a convinced nonconformist due to his his Welsh Independent background. His heroes were William Ewart Gladstone, Tom Ellis and David Lloyd George, in that order, and he received two weekly papers, both Welsh language publications, namely *Llais Llafur* (The Voice of Labour), published in the Swansea Valley town of Ystalyfera, and *Tarian y Gweithiwr* [The Worker's Shield] which was published in Aberdare, in the Cynon Valley. Griffiths had become a key figure in the village by the end of the Victorian era and in his obituary, written by William Evans, a fellow Liberal, it was noted that, 'He was a clean-living family.man. He had three things which I greatly admired: he was faithful in his chapel, he was caring of his family and consistent at his calling.'

In 1898 the poet-miner John Harries (Irlwyn) wrote a poem about the village of Betws and referred at the end of a verse to the 'smithy of William Griffiths' which 'keeps our feet in good shape'.[12] Young Jeremiah witnessed a great deal of passion in the conversations and debates in the smithy, especially during the Boer War (1899-1902), and a great deal of sympathy was expressed with the leadership given by David Lloyd George. A large number of Welshmen responded favourably to Lloyd George who sympathised with the Calvinistic Boer farmers of southern Africa. In 1900, the imperialist Liberal MP William Pritchard Morgan lost his seat in Merthyr to the socialist Keir Hardie, largely due to Morgan's support of the Boer War.

Differences of opinion over the war had created tension and disagreements amongst the Liberal supporters who participated in the debates at the smithy in Betws, as some agreed with David Lloyd George who was against Britain's involvement whilst others supported William Pritchard Morgan, who was in favour. The lively debate continued when the Balfour Education Act of 1902 became a topic of conversation and in particular on the injustice of expecting nonconformists to pay tax to support the educational provision of the Church of England schools. A rally and a protest meeting were organised at Ammanford and a young Jeremiah had the opportunity of listening to the finest platform speaker of his day, David Lloyd George, addressing the crowd.[13]

It was not the only large gathering he witnesed in Ammanford; he remembered the Reverend William Hezekiah Williams, known as Watcyn Wyn, returning as the conquering hero from the 1893 World's Fair in Chicago after winning the bardic chair – for an ode in the Welsh language – at the Eisteddfod held in the city.[14] Both Lloyd George and Watcyn Wyn enthralled the young boy.

As well as international matters such as the Boer War, the miners who often came to the smithy and discussed their industrial struggles ensured that Jeremiah quickly became aware of matters much closer to home and he grew to admire them greatly. He also got to know many of them as, usually on a Saturday, along with his brothers, he would call on the homes of the miners to collect their payments for the work that his father had done on their tools, their shoes and garden implements.

Young Jeremiah was educated in two schools: the local Board School located in Betws, and the Sunday School in the Christian Temple in Ammanford. The headmaster of the Board School, John Lewis, hailed from the village of Llanarth in Cardiganshire and was a staunch Anglican.[15] He was in charge of the school for 42 years from 1871 to 1912, and despite being a Welsh speaker, the children of the smithy never heard him speaking Welsh within the confines of the school. The Welsh language was effectively banished from all schools in Wales after the 1870 Forster Act and, under John Lewis, every child was forced to learn the English national anthem as quickly as possible.

In the last year of young Jeremiah's schooling, however, a new teacher, Rhys Thomas, joined the staff. Unlike Lewis, who had not given music any significance in the life of the school, Thomas was a Welshman steeped in the traditional culture of Betws and as the conductor of the local brass band, soon formed a school choir. Jeremiah was thus given an opportunity in his last few months at school to be a member of the choir, which he thoroughly enjoyed. The new teacher also spoke Welsh on every occasion and was proud that he and his brother, the Reverend John Thomas of Soar Welsh Independent Chapel in Merthyr Tydfil, had been thoroughly immersed in the life and culture of their native village. In Merthyr, John Thomas was a highly respected and popular minister of religion but it was his brother Rhys who would be the formative influence on the Griffiths children.

The chapel was an equally important influence for the young Jeremiah and his siblings, with morning and evening worship, the Sunday School in the afternoon and the twice weekly Band of Hope.[16] The first Band of Hope of the week was held at five o'clock on Sunday afternoons when members met to prepare for the different Christian festivals and especially for the many services held during the Christmas season. The Band of Hope was a highly-valued meeting which conveyed to the children of the 1890s the values of temperance.[17] This message was embedded in the mind and life of young Jeremiah and he became a staunch teetotaller for the rest of his life.

In his adult life, James Griffiths always paid homage to his upbringing in the Sunday School and the Band of Hope, and in particular, the influence of the local station master, John Evans, who presided at the meetings.[18] Evans had an amazing ability to communicate with the children, and he always commanded respect from them. His first sentence at the beginning of the Band of Hope was always "*Nawr, 'te, mhlant i*" (Now then, my children). The children heroworshipped him, and every Sunday afternoon and weeknight meeting began with the well-known children's hymn, *Mae Iesu Grist yn derbyn plant bychain fel nyni* (Jesus Christ accepts small children like us). He taught them to participate in debate and public speaking, and gave them a great deal of confidence as well as warning about the evils of alcohol and the need for temperance. In his early days, Jeremiah admired the advice and charm of John Evans, and when Evans died on 5 November 1918 at the early age of 46, Griffiths paid him a fulsome tribute in the local weekly newspaper which reflects the gentle nature of Griffiths himself. It is a sincere, charming tribute to a man who influenced him greatly, Jeremiah praised his lost mentor:

> *What a wonderful way he had with us children. How potent his influence upon us. He had but to raise his hand and he would transform a vestry full of rowdy children like unto an angelic host singing the praise of that Saviour of children whose Love and Spirit, John Evans had partaken so richly.*[19]

Then he adds:

> *And we believed him and sang for him, because in our childlike way we felt that it was true, this story of Jesus, for was it not John Evans who told us? And we knew he loved us.*

The charisma and the influence of Evans remained with Griffiths into later life.

*Gone are the sermons we heard in those days, few of the exhortations remain, but the memory of John Evans and his Band of Hope remains as a sweet, ennobling influence in our lives.'* [20]

At the end of every Band of Hope meeting, their hero John Evans would recite the verse:

*Dare to be a Daniel,*
*Dare to stand alone!*
*Dare to have a purpose firm!*
*Dare to make it known.*[21]

At home in Betws, Jeremiah enjoyed a great deal of freedom. During the school's summer holidays he played with his contemporaries on Betws mountain. Sometimes he would go for a long ride on his bicycle, following his brother David – better known by his bardic name of Amanwy – and his cousin Camber Griffiths, and on other occasions he would enjoy swimming in the river Amman. He had tremendous regard for and enjoyed the company of his two elder brothers, Gwilym and Amanwy. Gwilym was also highly regarded by D.J. Williams, who knew Gwilym well, and always referred to him as 'one of the best and most able lads that I ever met in my time as a miner.'

Jeremiah was particularly sad when, in 1900, Amanwy and some of his friends wandered as far as the mining valleys of Monmouthshire for a few months to seek employment in the coal mines. This was a regular occurrence when the anthracite collieries in west Wales had to lay off miners, especially in the summer months due to a lack of orders. Amanwy and his friends found work in the collieries of Abertillery and Abercarn, and enjoyed their stay at the Six Bells Colliery, where they met a number of Welsh speakers who had migrated to the Monmouthshire valleys from the slate quarrying town of Llanberis in Snowdonia.
Sport also meant a great deal to Jeremiah, in particular rugby and cricket. He became Secretary of the Betws Boys Rugby Club in 1906, which was excellent practice for all the responsibility that was to come to him as a young lad. When Amanwy came back from Abertillery, Jeremiah was 13 and on the threshold of earning his living as a collier.[22] There is no doubt that seeing his friends and his brothers as miners created in Jeremiah a longing for the same calling.[23] His father hoped that after a year's experience in the colliery he would then make an application for a place at the local Welsh nonconformist academy in the town of Ammanford, known as Gwynfryn,[24] which had been established by the poet preacher Watcyn Wyn, to train young men for the Christian ministry in Welsh nonconformity. The Gwynfryn Academy was an important educational institution, in particular in south Wales, and annually attracted some 60 to 80 young men from the Welsh nonconformist denominations in the basic skills needed as communicators of the Christian Gospel. .[25]

In addition to sport, Jeremiah also developed a lifelong interest in reading but found it difficult to understand his parents' opposition to him reading the weekly comics that were sold locally. Years later he recalled his rebellion:

*And so we braved wrath - took our pennies to the paper shop, where we exchanged them for brightly coloured little magazines, and hey, presto, we were soon lost in the adventures of Jack, Sam and Pete.* [26]

This was the beginning of his lifelong passion for reading, which would have probably seen him do well if he had entered Llandeilo Grammar School. One of his classmates from Betws Board School had been accepted at Llandeilo and Jeremiah was extremely impressed with the school colours, especially the cap and the blazer, but he never expressed any disappointment. The only words he wrote on the subject were:

*My father had his own plan for me. To the coal-mine for a year or so, and then to colliers' boy.*[27]

Jeremiah loved his strict but happy childhood in the house next to the smithy in the heart of the village of Betws, and there was no disagreement on his part with what his father had decided for him as far as his future was concerned. It gave him confidence and convictions, and a heritage he called on to guide his trade union and political career.

**Notes and References**

1. Ioan Matthews 'Maes y Glo Carreg ac Undeb y Glowyr 1872-1925', in *Cof Cenedl Cymru VIII, Ysgrifau ar Hanes Cymru*, Ed. Geraint H. Jenkins (Llandysul, 1983), p. 139; NLW Eirene White Papers A 200/24 F2/10. Eirene White described the village of Betws in the *Manchester Evening News* in these words: 'It was a wholly Welsh community, in thought and speech, where the two signs of a snob were to speak in English, except to strangers, and to wear a collar and tie, except on Sundays'. According to James Griffiths, the poet-preacher Watcyn Wyn was responsible for renaming Cross Inn as Rhydaman in Welsh and Ammanford in English. He states: 'A lovable man, a noble character, and the founder of our community. For when "Cross Inn" and Betws were joined together, it was Watcyn Wyn who provided the name of our town: Rhydaman - Ammanford', 'He christened Cross Inn Rhydaman', *South Wales Guardian*, 22 June 1972. (I am grateful to Dr Huw Walters for sending me a copy of this article).
2. The Griffiths family has a family tree on the internet but there are some discrepancies as far as the census returns are concerned. See also, William Evans, 'William Griffiths y Gof', *The Amman Valley Chronicle*, 16 February 1928, and 'Betws' Grand Old Man', ibid., 9 February 1928. William Rees Griffiths was one of seven children, six boys and one girl.
3. W.W. Price, *The Biographical Index of W.W. Price*, Aberdare, NLW 20-1.
4. It is difficult to envisage, in the early 21st century, the hold nonconformity had on Welsh-speakers through its chapels and its activities. Also on the adherents of the 1904-5 Revival: 'It was a good time for the churches of the mining valleys in the years at the beginning of this century. They had no trouble to fill the largest chapels on a Sunday. Indeed if you were not there at least a quarter of an hour to twenty minutes before the beginning of the service you would have little chance of a seat. Most people also had a great deal of seriousness as the shadows of the South African War had not completely disappeared from their consciences. One felt a great deal of sincerity in the services of the sanctuary'. It is no wonder that William and Margaret Griffiths had given their youngest son the name of an Old Testament prophet. This was a tradition in religious families between 1890 and 1930. 'By the dawn of the twentieth century Christianity in Wales seemed in an

invincible position', See R. Tudur Jones, *Ffydd ac Argyfwng Cenedl: Hanes Crefydd yng Nghymru 1890-1914*, Volume 1, Prysurdeb a Phryder (Swansea, 1981), pp. 25-63.

5. D.J. Williams, *Yn Chwech ar Hugain Oed* (Llandysul, 1959), p. 165.

6. James Griffiths, *Pages rom Memory* (London, 1969), p.3.

7. 1961 Census.

8. James Griffiths, *Pages from Memory*, p. 3.

9. Amanwy, *Gweinidog fy Ieuenctid: Canmlwyddiant Geni y Parchedig Isaac Cynwyd Evans (18451945)*, Christian Temple, Ammanford (Ammanford, 1945), pp. 1-24.

10. 'Efail William Griffiths y Betws', *Amman Valley Chronicle*, 14 June 1945 (with thanks to Dr Huw Walters for sending me a copy of this article).

11. D. J. Williams, *Yn Chwech ar Hugain Oed*, p. 165. William Evans gives a similar tribute to the one given by D. J. Williams. See William Evans, 'William Griffiths y Gof, y Betws', *Amman Valley Chronicle*, 16 February 1928.

12. NLW, Amanwy Papers, where we find a copy of the poem written by John Harries (Irlwyn).

13. James Griffiths, *Pages from Memory*, op. cit., pp.5-6. This, according to the politician, was his introduction to the world of politics: 'This carried us out of the smithy to the road to march to the demonstration at Ammanford where the great man himself – David Lloyd George – was the orator. So it was that I began my training in politics, demonstrations and all that goes to the making of a politician – on the way from one "parliament" to another.'

14. The earliest recollection he has, as a boy of three years of age turning out to welcome Watcyn Wyn home after winning the chief poetry prize at the Eisteddfod Fawr y Byd (The Great World Eisteddfod) held as part of the World Fair in Chicago. He states: 'One of my earliest recollections is of the day when Watcyn Wyn returned triumphantly from the World Fair at Chicago. We marched from our school at Betws and set out for Cross Inn to join the throng of villagers and I think that every person in the neighbourhood was in the procession as we carried the bard to his home at Gwynfryn. The Welsh community in USA had organised a "Welsh National Eisteddfod" in connection with the World Fair – as our Bard, Watcyn Wyn had won the Chair. It was a notable triumph for a notable character'. See James Griffiths, 'He christened Cross Inn Rhydaman', South Wales Guardian, 22 June, 1972.

15. NLW, Amanwy Papers. 'A tribute to John Lewis.'

16. Derwyn Morris Jones, 'Teyrnged i James Griffiths a draddodwyd yn ei angladd yn Christian Temple, Rhydaman, brynhawn Mercher, Awst 13' (A tribute to James Griffiths delivered at his funeral in Christian Temple, Ammanford, Wednesday afternoon, August 13), *Y Tyst*, 18 September 1975, pp.5-6. He mentions his debt to the Band of Hope, Sunday School and The Young People Society, where he was trained in the art of public speaking and his debt to the chapel and the nonconformist Christianity which was such an integral part of his early roots.

17. James Griffiths, *Pages from Memory*, p. 6. When he heard of the death of John Evans, he said: 'And now, I am told John Evans is dead. No! No! No! John Evans can never die. He lives: a quiet formative influence in the lives of hundreds of those who, like me, had the privilege of his charming influence in our childhood'. See James Griffiths, 'A Tribute', *Amman Valley Chronicle*, 7 November 1918.

18. NLW, James Griffiths Papers A 5/1. A leaflet of the funeral of John Evans, New Road, Ammanford who died 5 November 1918 at the age of 46. He was the stationmaster at Ammanford and Secretary of the Welsh Independent Chapel of Christian Temple as well as being a deacon, organist and superintendent of the Band of Hope and the Children's Sunday School. He was a hero of Jeremiah (James) Griffiths in his childhood and his youth. He was a beautiful character, a noble soul, and possessed with a generous heart according to Griffiths. He ministered at Christian Temple with great zeal and faithfulness amongst the children. Griffiths kept his funeral leaflet

safely, indeed the only leaflet found in his personal archives at the NLW. 'One result of the memory of John Evans was a lifelong adherence to Temperance beliefs.' See James Griffiths, 'A Tribute', *Amman Valley Chronicle*, 7 November 1918.

19. James Griffiths, 'A Tribute', ibid.

20. Ibid.

21. James Griffiths, *Pages from Memory*, p.7.

22. I realised on 20 January 2012 that the Carmarthenshire Archives do not hold any minutes from the Board School in Betws during the period that James Griffiths was a pupil, or minutes from the Llandeilo County School for 1903-4. Because of this I have failed to get any official report on James Griffiths as a pupil in Betws, or on whether his father got in touch at all with the school in Llandeilo.

23. James Griffiths was not the only one to feel the necessity of working in the colliery because his brothers and friends were already employed. Hugh Bevan (son of a miner) mentions how he in the village of Saron, near Ammanford, regarded mining as his ambition. He mentions in his autobiography how he listened, in the early hours of the morning, while in his bed, to the sound of the heavy boots of miners, who worked in the collieries of Rhos, Y Wernos, Parc, Saron, Betws, Yr Emlyn, Caerbryn, Pantffynnon, Pont-y-clerc a Phencae, walking past his home. He felt that he was becoming a miner himself, but in fact he became a distinguished lecturer in the Department of Welsh at the University in Swansea. See Hugh Bevan, *Morwr Cefn Gwlad* (Llandybie, 1971), p. 30. We must heed the words of Joseph Keating, from the Aberdare valley, in his autobiography, *My Struggle for Life* (London, 1916), a forgotten classic from the south Wales coalfield, describing the influence of his brothers on him and how he decided to follow them to the colliery: 'Two of my brothers were in the pits already. All the boys in school looked forward with longing to the day when they would be allowed to begin work. Release from boredom of school might have influenced them; but my happiness was not so much in leaving school as in the idea of actually going to work underground. We saw the pit boys coming home in their black clothes, with black hands and faces, carrying their food boxes, drinking tins, and gauze-lamps. They adopted an air of superiority to mere schoolboys. Life began to be worth living when once they had gone down.' pp. 37-8.

24. NLW T.E. Nicholas papers. He has reminiscences of the Gwynfryn Academy where he had been a student.

25 The plan that William Rees Griffiths had for his youngest son was a year working in the colliery before then entering the local academy, Ysgol Gwynfryn, which prepared young men for the nonconformist ministry. Amanwy mentions a number of boys who had done exactly what his father had in mind for Jeremiah. They were all names of repute in nonconformist circles of the twentieth century: J.T. Job, W. Crwys Williams, Peter Hughes Griffiths and John Gwili Jenkins who became a tutor at the academy. See NLW, Amanwy Papers.

26. James Griffiths, *Pages from Memory*, p. 11.

27 James Griffiths, *Pages from Memory*, p. 7. If James Griffiths had entered the Welsh Independent

ministry, the author D. J. Williams would have heard him as one of the outstanding pulpit orators, and who comments in his autobiography, *Yn Chwech ar Hugain Oed*, op. cit., p.166: 'On Jim, Right Honourable James Griffiths, Deputy Leader of the Labour Party afterwards, he was only a young lad who had given up playing marbles and was starting to wear long trousers, and I do not have many more recollections of him than he has of me. And from then till today (1959) he and myself walked entirely different paths to each other.'

# 2

# Life at the Coalface

In his memoirs, *Pages from Memory*, James Griffiths mentions the deep sense of loneliness he experienced at the end of the Easter holidays when he returned to school and knowing that all his school friends in Betws had left for the world of work and responsibility.[1] The boys from the mountain had stayed on their family farmsteads to give a helping hand and earn a living, the boys from the village had decided either on the life of a collier or to be employed at the tinplate works, leaving only one lad from the Betws Board School to pursue a different way of life by opting the world of learning at for Llandeilo Grammar School.

Seeing his old school friends now all working and living in an entirely different world to himself left Griffiths feeling lonely and detached.[2] They all wore long trousers and neck scarfs, and many had Cinderella cigarettes dangling from their mouths. Their talk, as they walked together over the Betws bridge to enjoy themselves on the square of Ammanford, was of their daily toil and the ups and downs of working life. In his pocket, the schoolboy James Griffiths had a penny to spend, while in the pockets of the young miners and tin workers you would find at least sixpence, and these growing differences between them proved immensely painful to him.

His whole family were now part of the world of work except him. Three of his brothers still lived at home; two of them were miners, and the eldest worked in the tinworks. The next brother to him, John, or Sioni as he was affectionately called, persuaded James to make a definite break with his schooldays with the promise of work underground. Sioni worked in the mine as a *crwtyn glo* (boy collier) under the supervision of John Davies, an experienced miner who originated from rural Cardiganshire like James Griffiths' old head teacher, John Lewis.[3] Davies was well thought of and admired in the Betws colliery but he needed a young lad to assist him. James Griffiths was delighted with the invitation he received and with no hesitation at all he decided to accept the offer.

Griffiths' mother bought cloth from her brother Sam, the weaver, in order to make him a brand new shirt and a strong pair of moleskin trousers to wear at the coalface, while his father prepared heavy nailed boots as well as a strong leather belt and a pair of 'yorks' to tie under his knees. Then, at 6am on a Monday morning in June 1904, James and his brother Sioni left their home to walk to *Gwaith Isa'r Betws* (The Lower Betws Colliery). He knew that he had to firstly call into the office to meet Picton, 'the gaffer', because every new miner had to sign a contract, an agreement between themselves and the Ammanford Colliery Company Limited. Then he was expected to call into the lamp room, where he had strict instructions from the Lampman to remember his colliery lamp number: 317. Proudly holding the lamp in his hand, the young lad walked on to what was known as the 'spake', and down the slant to the double parting of the little coal vein to John Davies' stall which was the third up the 'heading'. As James and Sioni eventually approached the coalface, they hung-up their coats and waistcoats and started work, and it was still only 7am.

His task was to pour the coal cut by Davies into the 'curling box', before carrying it to the tram and emptying the coal inside. After getting the coal into the tram he was expected to return for another load and to continue backwards and forwards all day. In the course of the morning's work, Sioni explained to him what the various mining tools were all about: the two mandrels, *Cam a Cwt*; the sledge and wedge; the hatchet and bar, and then the most hated tool of all, the *Tro-wr*, which was used to bore holes in the coal. It left distinct marks on the groin because of the way in which it was handled.

It was a long day for the novice miner, though it soon proved enjoyable when break-time came and he met the other young miners from the other stalls on the 'heading'. Together they ate their bread and butter and cheese, with a tomato for 'afters', washed down with pearl-barley water. When half past four in the afternoon arrived, James and Sioni were free to leave the coalface and walk to the double parting, joining the adult colliers on their way to the top of the colliery. The first day had gone exceedingly well.

Waiting for James at home was a feast his mother had prepared for him and his brothers – *cawl cig a tatws* (meat and potato soup), followed by rice pudding and a mug of tea. Then, as the youngest of the family on his first day as a worker, James was given the special favour of jumping the queue for the bath tub, and after washing away the coal dust and drying himself, he was soon on his way to join his friends at Cae'r Ynys, the nearby playing field near the river Amman, for a game of cricket.[4] That evening he was once again one of them and could now speak of life at the coalface as an equal.[5]

On his way home he bought a packet of Cinderella cigarettes for a penny, and when he went to Ammanford on Saturday night he now had sixpence in his pocket, after all he was now earning 1s 3d, plus percentage, for a whole shift. It was good money when it was paid out every fortnight, and James knew that John Davies, a careful and honest collier, gave his young helpers extra money if they were industrious and well behaved and handed on their pay to their mothers.

James Griffiths was a miner during the third phase of the Welsh coal industry, that is between 1850 and 1919.[6] Years later, he wrote about the coal industry in a book entitled *Glo* (Coal), published by the Liverpool-based Brython Press in 1945. In his book, Griffiths explained that in 1893 the total output of coal in Britain was 171 million tons, but by 1913 it had expanded to 1,287 million and the number of miners had grown from 631,000 to 1,106,884.[7] Due to this growth, the population of south Wales, (the old counties of Monmouthshire, Glamorganshire and Carmarthenshire) had expanded due to the thousands of people who had crossed Offa's Dyke to Monmouthshire and Glamorganshire from the west of England and the English Midlands.

It was a different story in Carmarthenshire, however, as  well as the anthracite coal mining valleys – Dulas, Tawe, Amman, and Gwendraeth – which drew its workers from predominantly Welsh speaking west Wales. They did not  experience the same English influx that had been seen in the eastern, steam coal valleys – Ebbw, Rhymney, Taff, Rhondda, Cynon and Ogmore – which became increasingly Anglicised the closer their proximity to the border.

As a result of this varying migration pattern, the villages of the anthracite coalfield in Carmarthenshire maintained their Welsh speaking character, the coalfields of Glamorgan were – during that third phase – a fairly equal mix of Welsh and English, while the character of the Monmouthshire coalfield had quickly become predominantly English-speaking as Aneurin Bevan witnessed in his youth in the town of Tredegar. .

Griffiths often emphasised how the miners in the anthracite coalfield kept their rural Welshness. He fondly recalled the life of these mining valleys with their choirs and nonconformist chapels, the humour of the pubs and the world of boxing, the comradeship of the coalface, and how all this produced a warm environment in spite of the harsh conditions in the collieries.

The constant dangers at the coalface and the tragedies experienced by the colliers, knitted the inhabitants together, with a strong nonconformist faith and total loyalty to the miners' union, 'the Fed', being heavily involved in all the industrial disputes.[8] For the inhabitants of those valleys, the reality of grinding industrial toil combined with an energetic and full social life produced a special atmosphere and real comradeship across the coalfield.

This was especially true in the cultural life of the chapels and their various gatherings, from the religious services on a Sunday, including the Sunday School, to the busy schedule for young and old on week nights. This closely reflected the nature of Wales' rural heartland, where many people's social life usually centred on the nonconformist chapel.

Three nonconformist institutions had huge significance to Griffiths' family.
Firstly the annual, large-scale preaching services known as *Y Cyrddau Mawr*. Secondly the festivals – closely involved with the Sunday School – movement that arose in the vanguard of nonconformity, such as the temperance festivals, the *Gymanfa Ganu* singing festivals, the children's festivals and the Biblically based *Cymanfa Bwnc*, where adults and children were catechised on the contents of scripture. Thirdly, the *eisteddfod* tradition, which had its locally based penny readings as well as the chapel *eisteddfod* and the *eisteddfodau* held on a village or district basis. The climax of all this was the *Eisteddfod Genedlaethol* (National Eisteddfod) then held at the beginning of September (now held during the first week of August). Of the three institutions, *Y Cyrddau Mawr* and it's six-monthly equialvent held the utmost significicace to the Griffiths family.

An unique form of celebratory preaching,[9] *Y Cyrddau Mawr* used everyday language and a popular style, with an easily understandable message and was delivered with superb emotional oratory. It has more or less disappeared from contemporary Welsh pulpits, but in its day, especially when Griffiths was a teenager, it was hughly popular. The visiting guest preacher, like modern-day performers on tour, used heartrending metaphors, with plenty of pathos and emotion, to inspire and motivate the congregations to repent and dedicate their lives to the Christian way of life. This kind of preaching reached its climax in the late Victorian era, but it still occurred in the younger days of James Griffiths.

The most fervent Baptist preacher of the inter-war generation was Reverend Jubilee Young, who served for many years in Llanelli, and was one of the last of these outstanding pulpit orators. Each Welsh nonconformist denomination had their own unique oratorical preachers; men who made a huge spiritual impact on congregations and ensured that those who heard them would discuss their message long after they had left the chapel. Griffiths was always grateful for having experienced these unique preaching meetings, and also praised the debating society at Christian Temple where he claimed to have served his apprenticeship as a public speaker.

One effect of the chapel life and its culture on him was the desire to learn and explore new ideas. In his memoirs, he mentions how the most serious-minded cultured miners enjoyed reading. Most miners' homes had, at some time or another, experienced poverty, but some of the miners felt that the poorest of all hearths were those that had no books. James learnt, in the fraternity of the colliery, what life really should consist of. Most miners who he met as a 13year-old had no time for adults who had no passion for books, learning or Welsh culture. Nor did they have time for men who were mean and forgot to help their needy comrades in their communities.[10] Selfishness was frowned upon in mining circles, and solidarity mean everything. The question that determined every debate was: 'Is he a man of principle?' It was an ingrained belief that no one should ever take advantage of someone else, and a miner should be loyal to, and supportive of, his fellow workers in the union and refrain from being a lackey to the colliery manager – and especially to the colliery owner. The miner was expected to have his priorities: to support his wife and children and be prepared to make sacrifices in support of his chapel, his closeknit community and 'the Fed'. This largely sums up the philosophy and expectations of most miners that James Griffiths knew during his adolescence in Betws and Ammanford.

Griffiths, in his publication *Glo*, also underlines the fact that most of the collieries in Carmarthenshire were small compared with those in the neighbouring coalfield of Glamorganshire. As a rule, these anthracite collieries employed some 200-300 men and boys. There were exceptions, such at Gwauncae–Gurwen colliery which had over a thousand miners working in the colliery, but the smaller workforces in west Wales meant that most of the miners who worked in the same colliery knew each other by name: no one was a stranger, and most were on personal terms with each other.

Most of the villages in east Carmarthenshire were predominately inhabited by mining families. This had the effect of setting the miner at the centre of all political, cultural, religious and sporting activities. The Miners' Eight-Hour Day Committee, in its final report in 1907, spelt out the uniqueness of mining communities as well as the solidarity of the men with each other:

> *This sense of solidarity is perhaps largely due to the fact that, unlike other families in the mining villages, the men shared the good and bad times of their employment at the colliery such as, during an economic downturn, the universal short week's working in preference to the fear of the dismissal of individual miners.*[11]

In his book called *Glo*, James Griffiths stresses that Welsh people, especially in the post-Second World War era, should not be ignorant of the world of the miner and his constant problems.[12] In the inter-war years, before the days of nationalisation, if a miner overslept and turned up late for work he would be severely penalised and lose a whole day's pay, even if he had only been an hour late. Those harsh terms of employment meant, for many, that it was unusual to be paid a full wage at the end of the week.[13]

Prior to its nationalisation in 1947, Griffiths believed that the competitive market forces of mining were irrational. There was no other industry, he argued, which had survived on such insecurity as the collieries did and, as coal mining dominated the Welsh economy, its irrationality had an adverse impact on commerce and society as a whole. The inevitable industrial disputes and the outbreak of any serious conflict – with periods of unemployment and the hooter informing the colliers, 'No work tomorrow' – inflicted disproportionate hardship to the mining communities, and Welsh society in general.

In the anthracite coalfield, most of the mine owners belonged to old local Welsh families who had deep roots in the communities and were involved in the religious and social life of the pit villages. Moreover, many of them were elders and deacons in the Welsh nonconformist chapels, which usually ensured a more stable relationship.

The mining industry totally dominated society across the coalfield, with the fortunes of the colliery and the miner-led social, sporting and religious activities of the pit villages overshadowed everything. The work, though, was dirty, hard and monotonous. It meant long hours, hasty meals, and incredibly unhealthy conditions underground. The dust was a constant menace, as was the exposure to heat, with the threat of death from flooding or explosions never far from the colliers' thoughts. The frequent and, on many occasions, fatal accidents took their toll on young and old miners alike, who sought mental or physical distractions from their day-to-day existence. James Griffiths found solace in reading, comics at first, before graduating to the world of books. It kept him sane. He admits in a letter to the local valley paper:

> *Perhaps, had we read Samuel Smiles, we would have been greater successes; but success is poor stuff for a lad whose daily grind is monotonous and whose eternal Mondays follow each other so rapidly. We wanted colour, adventure – life. These were denied us in reality; what better than to seek for them in romance, even in the poor stuff that our elders contemptuously call Penny Dreadfuls?*[14]

The shift at the colliery meant long hours – at least from six in the morning to five in the afternoon, with only Saturday afternoon and Sunday above ground – which deprived James and Sioni, and all their contemporaries, of daylight for much of the year and giving them shallow and pale complexions. Sunday was a day of rest and for most it meant chapel or church involvement. When David Lloyd George criticised the colliery owners in 1909, he described vividly the dangerous environment of the miners in their tasks:

*Have you been down a coal mine? I went down one the other day. You could see the pit props bent and twisted and sundered. Sometimes they give way and there is mutilation and death. Yet when the Prime Minister and I knock on the doors of these great landlords and say to them, "Here, you know these poor fellows who have been digging up royalties at the risk of their lives, some of them are old and have survived the perils of their trade and are broken and can earn no more. Won't you give something towards keeping them out of the workhouse?" they scowl at us. They retort "You thieves". If this is an indication of the view taken by these great landlords, of their responsibility to the people who, at the risk of life, create their wealth, then I say the day of reckoning is at hand.*[15]

Writing in *Glo*, James Griffiths explains that the miners had to live with a complicated pay structure in return for the hard, heavy, dirty work they undertook. It depended on the coal seam, and very few understood how the final wage packet was made up because there were different pay scales for different tasks: one scale was paid for cutting a ton of coal and putting it into the tram; and there was another price for cutting the stone above or below the seam; and yet another rate for placing a post of wood to keep up the roof. There were between 20 and 40 different rates of pay and often only half of them would be included on the wage packet.

Determined to right the wrongs of the pay rates, the young collier from Betws became, in time, an expert on this complex system. For at least 11 years he took a leading role in setting the pay rate, a task which demanded a great deal of patience as well as considerable intellectual ability. His apprenticeship proved beneficial when he became a miners' agent and then Vice President and later the President of 'the Fed'. It was at Betws that he learned how to cope with all the demands on a miners' leader, and where he understood the frustration of miners who were working hard for a fluctuating wage.

Griffiths never complained about those colliery officials who operated the owners pay rates, as we learn, from the prose of D.J. Williams, who describes an Englishman who was appointed as an official with the company. When D.J. Williams approached him to see if he could be given a better opportunity, the official replied: "Thee-can-have-the-money-whenever-thee-likes-now, – thisminute-if-thee-want-it."[16] Williams seized his opportunity and left *Gwaith Isa'r Betws* (Lower Betws Colliery) for another colliery which was being opened at Pantyffynnon, but Griffiths does not say anything of the obnoxious bully with his strong northern English accent. He was fortunate, though, for he had the well-liked miner, John Davies, to look after his interests. Griffiths was also an entirely different person in outlook to the gifted D.J. Williams, as he always saw the best in everyone. Despite his more generous disposition, however, the tender-hearted Griffiths stayed at *Gwaith Isa* for only a year before returning to *Gwaith Ucha* where he remained – except for a few months in 1914 when he worked at the Pantyffynnon colliery – for the rest of his working life as a miner.

Summer, and the annual family holiday in Cardiganshire – especially in the area around the seaside town of Aberaeron – brought Griffiths and his brother's happiness and a welcome break from the toil of the coalfield. At the beginning of August they usually travelled by train from Tirydail, Ammanford, to Lampeter and then by coach and horse on the last stage to the coast, staying for a fortnight at the home of Marged Jones, who provided bed and breakfast accommodation.

In those days many mining families spent their holidays at Llanwrtyd, while the Welsh middle classes enjoyed the spa in Llandrindod, both in Radnorshire, but it was Cardiganshire that the Griffiths family loved, and it was there, in September 1904, that a religious revival began which enriched and influenced the lives of the family and hundreds of thousands more across Wales.[17]

At the chapel in Blaenannerch, near Cardigan, an ex-miner and young ministerial student called Evan Roberts was converted and became the celebrity of the revival. Soon Griffiths' family came to know of the revival leaders, ministers such as the Reverend John Thickens, of Aberaeron, and his nephew, Joseph Jenkins of New Quay, the famous veteran preacher Evan Phillips of Newcastle Emlyn and, above all, Evan Roberts himself. Even though young James always had his reservations,[18] the religious revival influenced his family, and he wrote extensively about it.[19] In *Pages from Memory*, he mentions its impact, as well as its failings, and fully understood that powerful spiritual influences had descended on his family, the communities of the Amman valley, and upon the Welsh nation.[20]

**Notes and References**

1. James Griffiths, *Pages from Memory*, p. 8. One finds relevant material in the Amanwy Papers in the NLW, namely 'Anerchiad ar bentre'r Betws' [An address on the village of Betws], pp.113; 'Diwylliant fy mro', [The Culture of my Parish], p.1-10, a 'Troi yn ôl hanes Betws' [Looking back, the history of Betws].
2. NLW, James Griffiths Papers. The historian Kenneth O. Morgan uses his baptismal name in his entry on him in the DNB. See Kenneth O. Morgan, 'Griffiths, Jeremiah (1890-1975)', *Oxford Dictionary of National Biography* (Oxford, 2004).
3. James Griffiths, *Pages from Memory*, p.8.
4. Neil Evans and Dot Jones, 'A Blessing for the Miner's Wife: the campaign for Pithead Baths in the South Wales Coalfield, 1908-1950', *Llafur* 6 (3) 1994, p.7. The hard physically exacting life was the daily routine of Griffiths' mother and every miner's mother. Minnie Pallister, Brynmawr, says of a miner's wife/mother: 'She gets up about 5 o'clock and gets their breakfast and sends them off to work. The men soil everything when dressing for the pit as the small coal and dust flies all over the place. Then after the man has bathed she begins to clear up again, and his working clothes have to be attended to'. See 'A Blessing for the Miner's Wife', p. 18.
5. James Griffiths, 'Rufus Adams', *Amman Valley Chronicle* and *East Carmarthen News*, 24 November 1949 (I am grateful to Dr Huw Walters for showing me this tribute).
6. James Griffiths, *Glo* [Coal] (Cyfres Pobun), (Liverpool, 1945), p.16. Dr Thomas Jones mentions this Welsh language book to his daughter Eirene (later Labour MP): 'I've got Jim Griffiths' book on *Glo* – very lively despite lots of figures'. See NLW, Eirene White Papers, A 200/24 F2/10; a letter dated 22 April 1945.
7. Ibid., *Glo*, p.15. James Griffiths does not describe the work of the miner as one finds in many autobiographies of ex-miners. Take, for example, the volume of Joseph Jones, *A Portrait of my Father: William Jones* (Peterborough, 2008). He was a native of Mostyn, Flintshire, but

William Jones spent his working life as a miner in Carlton, near Barnsley. On p.41 his son describes his father's daily work at the coalface: 'It is a dreadful job these fellows do. Judged by ordinary standards it is a superhuman job. They are not only shifting vast quantities of coal, they are doing it in a position which trebles the work. They have to remain kneeling all the time, otherwise they'd hit the roof.'

8. According to Emeritus Professor Ieuan Gwynedd Jones: 'There can be no such thing as an individual collier: there can only be communities of colliers, all inter-dependent, breathing the same inadequate air, relying upon their joint skills, all subject to the same instantaneous disaster'. See Paul H. Ballard and Erastus Jones (editors), *The Valley Call* (Ferndale, 1975), p.63. When criticising the colliery owners of south Wales in 1909, David Lloyd George uttered the words which reinforces the description of the dangerous environment of the colliers. See Roy Hattersley, *David Lloyd George: The Great Outsider* (London, 2010), p. 254.

9. D. Ben Rees, 'Pregethu Dathliadol', *Pregethu a Phregethwyr* (Denbigh, 1997), pp.37-45; Amanwy, 'Colofn Cymry'r Dyffryn', *Amman Valley Chronicle* and *East Carmarthen News*, 23 December 1942, p. 2 and p. 18.

10. James Griffiths, *Pages from Memory*, p.6.

11. NLW, James Griffiths Papers. The owners of the collieries were not the only people associated with mining which were integral to the life of the chapels. These were trade unionists who supported the emerging Labour Party who were active from one Sunday to another. Among the Labour MPs of the inter-war years elected to Parliament were deacons from Welsh Baptist and Welsh Independent chapels, such as: Will John, MP for Rhondda West from 1920 to 1950; William Jenkins MP for Neath from 1922 to 1945; and Charles Edwards MP for Bedwellty 1918-1950. See J. Graham Jones, 'Welsh politics between the wars: the personnel of Labour', *Transactions of the Honourable Society of Cymmrodorion* (1983), pp. 179-80.

12. James Griffiths, *Glo*, p.17.

13. Ibid., p.18.

14. James Griffiths, Letter to the Editor, *Amman Valley Chronicle*, 23 March 1923.

15. Roy Hattersley, *David Lloyd George: The Great Outsider*, p. 254.

16. D. J. Williams, *Yn Chwech ar Hugain Oed*, p. 163.

17. NLW, Amanwy Papers, see 'Cerddetwr', 'Colofn Cymry'r Dyffryn', *Amman Valley Chronicle* and *East Carmarthen News*, 31 July 1941, p. 2. For Joseph Jenkins (1861-1929), see Robert Ellis, *Doniau a Daniwyd* (Llandybïe, 1959), pp. 41-5. There is no doubt that Joseph Jenkins was a significant figure in the preparation for the Religious Revival in Cardiganshire. See Huw Roderick, 'A fire of shavings: The 1904 Revival in Cardiganshire', *Ceredigion*, Vol. XV, No. 1, 2005, pp.107-138. Amanwy mentions him preaching at the Welsh Calvinistic Methodist Chapel in Elim, Tirydail: 'Indeed, for he was more than a master because we never heard anyone treating his subject so brilliantly, as he did'. See NLW, Amanwy Papers. For John Thickens (1865-1952), see *Yearbook of the Calvinistic Methodists* (1954), pp. 232-3; for Evan Phillips (1829-1912), see J. J. Morgan, *Evan Phillips* (Mold, 1930); for Evan Roberts (1878-1951), see Sidney Evans and Gomer M. Roberts (Eds.), *Cyfrol Coffa Diwygiad 1904-1905* (Caernarfon, 1954), pp. 1-118.

18. James Griffiths, *Pages from Memory*, p.13: 'What we needed was a religion which would change society, and a political faith with a vision of a new social order'. Though, on the other hand, James Griffiths should have acknowledged on the same page the skills he received from his chapel upbringing and in the various meetings he attended in the Christian Temple which proved of immense value to him. I insert a valuable assertion from a contemporary Member of Parliament for the Aberavon constituency: 'For that generation which grew up in the first three decades of the twentieth century, the place of worship was also the place where individual skills

of organisation, expression, public speaking, and debate as well as collectivist values were all developed and ultimately taken into the new increasingly secular world of the local communities'. See Hywel Francis, 'Language, Culture and Learning: The experience of a valley community', *Llafur*, 6(3), 1994, p. 88.

19. James Griffiths, *Pages from Memory*, p.11: 'All that I have are the memories of a boy who had just started work, of how everything seemed to be suddenly different. There were services down the mine, in which the gaffer took part, and our home was turned into a chapel'.

20. Ibid  Evan Roberts was not an intellectual or a great orator, and he was severely rebuked by many, such as the Revd. Peter Price of Dowlais, for his emphasis on emotional conversion. James Griffiths was not among his zealous followers. On p.16 of *Pages from Memory*, he states, 'For a year or two it transformed life in the valleys, then it seemed to fade out, leaving behind a void which was later filled by another kind of revival, as I shall come to relate'. However, in west Wales within the anthracite coalfield, one has to admit that the chapels kept their influence well into the second half of the 20th century, and James Griffiths appreciated the contribution of nonconformity to the Labour movement. See J. Griffiths, *The Labour Government – A Record of Achievement* (London, 1961), p.7, and Huw Walters, *Canu'r Pwll a'r Pulpud* (Denbigh, 1987), p. 242. The Revival influenced the behaviour of the miners in the manner in which they treated the horses that worked underground, and in their personal conversations and religious meetings held underground in the collieries. See Cyril E. Gwyther, *The Valley Shall Be Exalted* (London, 1949), p.40; Mabel Bickerstaff, *Something Wonderful Happened* (Liverpool, 1954), pp. 75-6.

# 3

# A Religious Revival and Political Conversion

It was James Griffiths' brother Amanwy who first came into contact with the young Revivalist, Evan Roberts of Loughor, who was brought up by Welsh Calvinistic Methodists.[1] In 1904, intriguiged by reports of the extraordinary ministry of Roberts and the Revival published in the *Western Mail*, Amanwy travelled by train from Ammanford to Gorseinon with three fellow miners to see and hear the theological student who had become the focus of the Revival. Evan Roberts was not the only Revivalist but he had become the most loved of all the Welsh Revivalists due to his mining background and the *Western Mail*, in particular, as well as the mining communities of Wales, came to regard him as the figurehead of the movement sweeping the country. Three of the four miners who travelled from Ammanford were not enthusiasts for the Revival. In fact they were quite cynical: they felt that the so-called spiritual awakening and the burgeoning religious enthusiasm would soon fade. However they felt an affinity with Evan Roberts as one who knew what a miner's life was all about.

Ammanford was deserted when they left that day and there were very few people around when they arrived in Gorseinon. The four colliers then walked to Brynteg, the town's Welsh Independent chapel and were completely surprised when, as they entered the chapel, they heard seven young men simultaneously praying aloud. Amanwy and his friends sat silently, watching and listening, exchanging glances of wonder at what they were witnessing. Around three o'clock, when the large congregation were singing a popular Welsh hymn, Evan Roberts entered the chapel and walked to the '*sêt fawr*' (large seat) where the local religious leaders sat beneath the pulpit. He knelt under the pulpit and at least a dozen other young people followed suit immediately. Amanwy recalled that the sense of peace and contentment that descended upon the congregation as well as the very emotional hymn singing that was spellbinding.

The young Revivalist then ascended the pulpit steps and, when he got himself settled, he looked around the whole chapel. According to Amanwy, the physical presence of Evan Roberts, with his 'two dark eyes which were full of strange fire', was stunning. With the congregation totally silent and full of expectation, Roberts slowly turned the pages of the Bible, and said:

> *Collir dagrau yma'r prynhawn yma, na welwn ni mohonynt, fe ddichon ond fe wêl Duw hwynt oll, ac fe'u costrelir hwynt bob un. Nid gwendid ond cryfder yw colli dagrau. Os nad ydych wedi wylo gyda'r Efengyl, mae lle i ofni nad ydych wedi dechrau ei byw yn iawn. Plygwch wrth Ei Groes ef mewn dagrau, ac fe'u costrelir bob un gan angylion Duw.'*

['We shall lose tears here this afternoon, and we will not see them perhaps, but God will see them all and they will be noted. It is no weakness but rather strength to lose tears. If you are not weeping with the Gospel, there is a cause for concern that you have not started living as you should. Kneel by His Cross in tears, and each one of these tears will be recorded by the angels of God.']²

Amanwy felt a spirit of reverence descend upon him and his three friends, and he mentions that there was an 'indescribable atmosphere' in the chapel, a 'strange influence, that weighed on the heart of a person like lead.' He added: 'There was little desire to converse that night. The experiences were sacred and unusual even to be explained to our kith and kin as well as our friends.'³

By the end of that week, Ammanford had experienced the spiritual forces of the Revival, and the Welsh Calvinistic Methodist chapel of Bethany became the focal point, due to its young minister, the Reverend W. Nantlais Williams, being regarded as the town's leading evangelical Calvinist as well as a born again Revivalist.⁴ When Evan Roberts came to Ammanford, all the Griffiths family went to hear him and Gwilym, the eldest son, was completely converted and often mentioned how he would love to stand on the square in Ammanford and explain to the passers-by how his life had been completely changed.⁵ Amanwy also came under the influence of the Revival, though he was not happy with the attitude of many of the zealous converts who criticised their chapel elders, particularly when his own minister, Isaac Cynwyd Evans of the town's Welsh Independent chapel was challenged by some of these converts at a service at Bethany. The experienced Evans, though, held his ground and won over most of the congregation.

James Griffiths was only a young lad of 14, but he was very impressed by Evan Roberts and admits being drawn to him:

> *I do not remember a word of what he said, but I can still see him standing up in the pulpit, tall, with dark hair falling over his face, and the quiet voice reaching the gallery as if he were singing.*⁶

The experience of hearing Evan Roberts preach had a profound and lifelong impact on Griffiths:

> *All that I have are the memories of a boy who had just started work, of how everything seemed to be suddenly different.*⁷

During 1904 and 1905, the Revival had a huge impact across the coalfield and there were even prayer meetings held down the mines – including in Betws where Griffiths' mentor, John Davies, was active in these gatherings – as noted by the Reverend Elvet Lewis, better known by his bardic name Elfed, who wrote an account of the Revival under the title *Christ Among the Miners*,. After two years, however, the Revival suddenly petered out but its legacy within Welsh society, the nonconformist tradition and politics was immense.

In his autobiography, D. J. Williams explained that the disappearance of the Religious Revival phenomenon was due to its shallow emotionalism. However, this cannot be the only reason as emotionalism had been integral to Welsh nonconformity since the Welsh Methodist

Revival of the 18<sup>th</sup> century, and Welsh nonconformity achieved its position of supremacy through a series of religious revivals in which intense individual experiences and conversion, as mentioned by James Griffiths' brothers Gwilym Griffiths and Amanwy, played an important part. At the beginning of the 20<sup>th</sup> century, Welsh nonconformity was facing a spiritual crisis the like of which it had not faced for 40 years. It can be argued, then, as the sociologist C.R. Williams and others have done, that the 1904-5 Religious Revival was a response to a new set of circumstances that were attracting the people of Wales away from their old allegiance to the chapel and its culture.

It was a remarkable example of popular religion. It offered the ordinary people across industrial and rural Wales alike, as well as the Welsh-speaking diaspora, a new lease of life, spiritually. It was their emotions and their religious aspirations that shaped the Revival, and they consciously repudiated the professional ministerial guidance which had only been in existence for decades. The leadership of the chapels passed into the hands of the young people, and the Revival reversed the roles of different groupings within the congregations. A younger generation (generally aged between 15 and 30) now took the lead in the chapels and women, for the first time on a large scale, became extremely prominent.

A foreign observer who visited south Wales during the Revival, J. Roques de Fursac, stated:

> *The Revival was a unifying movement. It did not create a new sect. It did not raise barriers of hate between people. On the contrary, it reunited people with bond of charity – Methodists, Baptists, Congregationalists and Wesleyans have ceased to condemn one another, and in their different chapels, worship the same God ... Evan Roberts preaches a Christianity so wide that it embraces all Christendom ... This is an isolated case of mysticism, not likely to occur again, not even in Wales. The Welsh people are already coming out of their cultural isolation, and it is this cultural isolation which has provided the fundamental conditions necessary for a popular mystical movement of this kind. Already the Welsh middle and upper classes are becoming enlightened and this enlightenment will soon soak down to the lower classes* [8]

This mystical element was an impressive part of the religious phenomena associated with the 1904-5 Revival. The impression given is of a kinder attitude among people towards each other, but even more important was the desire to challenge some fundamental ideas and to welcome the ideas discussed in magazines and newspapers of the day. A miner who met the Frenchman J. Rogues de Fursac in south Wales expressed it well:

> *We believe, he said, that God has said to Man that he shall earn his bread by the sweat of his brow, but we also know that God never said that the worker shall also provide bread for the shareholder who does nothing ... socialism has lost nothing by the Revival, and trade union membership has not suffered in any way.* [9]

De Fursac also stated:

*The young man said that the Revival was essentially popular and democratic and it would probably lead to the workers relying more that ever on unity and a sense of brotherhood.*[10]

The Revival provided two important factors. Firstly, it gave the Welsh nonconformist chapels a new lease of life, a new impetus and enthusiasm and an awareness of contemporary issues.[11] Secondly, as James Griffiths mentioned, Evan Roberts and his young supporters prepared the way for the Labour movement and especially its prophet, Keir Hardie.[12] The Revival had been a turning point, and to Griffiths and many of his mining friends, they had been inspired by the popular movement to consider changing the world for the better. What was needed was a religion that could change society – a political faith with a vision of a different ideology to the capitalist system and to the Liberal establishment which ruled the roost in most Welsh communities.

There were religious leaders who were willing to respond to such a desire for change, including a number of young ordained ministers who accepted the same challenge as James Griffiths. One, in particular, was the Reverend Robert Silyn Roberts, a Calvinistic Methodist minister, based in London from 1901 to 1905.[13] A member of the Fabian Society and a student of Sidney Webb, Silyn Roberts (known in literary circles simply as Silyn) was an inspiration to James Griffiths, especially after the General Election of 1906, when he became a member of the Labour Party.[14] Another layman who taught theology, and was highly thought of by Griffiths and his brothers, was the poet John Gwili Jenkins, who had tutored at the Gwynfryn Academy since 1897, and who was a Christian socialist.[15]

Griffiths also saw changes in his own family, who were staunch Welsh Independents. They began   reading *The Examiner*, the denominational weekly of the Congregationalists in England, and its companion publication, *The Christian Commonwealth*. Both weekly papers introduced a new awareness of the changing world and both had an intriguing feature of importance: the weekly sermon by the minister of the City Temple in London, the Reverend R. J. Campbell.[16] 'These weekly sermons suddenly threw two bombs into our family circle,' noted Griffiths, 'the New Theology and Socialism. This set us all arguing at home, at chapel, and in the mine and mill.'[17]

1908 proved to be an immensely important year for the young James Griffiths and his parents. Firstly, on the morning of Tuesday 28 January 1908,[18] an explosion at the Pantyffynnon colliery claimed the life of his eldest brother, Gwilym, and badly injured David (Amanwy). Griffiths does not mention the tragedy in *Pages from Memory* and so we do not have a first-hand account of how they coped as a family with a loss of one son and the serious injury to another. A perfect illustration, however, as to how well-read the Griffiths family were, was that Gwilym left his large library to his brothers: a collection of English journals, a full set of *The Examiner* and *Great Thoughts*, the work of the Scotsman, Henry Drummond, and several volumes of contemporary English poetry.

During the weeks of recuperation after the explosion, Amanwy was frequently visited and assisted by three literary-minded miners from Pantyffynnon, in particular John Harries

(Irlwyn), a checkweigher, William Jones (known by his bardic name of Gwilym Myrddin), who looked after the lamproom; and William Cathan Davies, a well-read miner who was, like his friends and fellow workers, an enthusiastic follower of and participant in the eisteddfod movement. From these three cultured miners, Amanwy received the Welsh language periodicals, *Cymru* (Wales) edited by Owen M. Edwards, *Geninen* (The Leek), and the influential *Traethodydd* (The Essayist) which had been in existence since 1854.

The second important event took place in May 1908 when James Griffiths and eight of his friends travelled in an old horse-brake to Panteg Welsh Independent chapel in Ystalyfera, where the minister, the Reverend Ben Davies, a native of Cwmllynfell and an ex-miner, had ministered since 1891, and had invited the Reverend R.J. Campbell to speak. A poet and hymn writer, the Reverend Ben Davies was also a staunch supporter of the emerging Labour Party. Panteg Chapel was full to capacity to hear the exciting 'New Theologian' as Campbell was known. He was a striking presence in the pulpit, with his black academic robe, his boyish face, snow white hair and a distinct, quiet voice which carried a comforting message.[19] He appealed enthusiastically for Christians to work together, to create a new order based on morality and Christian ethics. There was also a special plea to Welsh nonconformist members to cut their ties with the Liberal Party. Britain needed a new mission, especially the adaptation of Christian principles to the complex problems of society. If this did not happen, he argued, the chapels and churches would lose out, would fail to communicate with the workers, and might fail to keep in contact with the democratic emphasis expressed in the socialist movement and the newly-born Labour Party.

A few weeks later Griffiths was in the same horse-brake with the same friends –
Harry Arthur, Harri Griffiths, John Henry Matthews, Harri John Davies, Tomi Thomas, Edgar Bassett, David Henry Rees and Tom Dafen Williams – this time going to the Miners' Hall in the village of Gwaun Cae Gurwen. They were on their way to welcome and listen to the Independent Labour Party (ILP) Member of Parliament for Merthyr Tydfil and Aberdare, Keir Hardie.[20] If Reverend R. J. Campbell looked like a seer, Keir Hardie, with his beard, looked like an Old Testament prophet. His address was a powerful supplement to that which they had heard from Reverend Campbell. The message was simple:

> *The Labour movement is an attempt to enable the working class to realise itself, its thoughts and aspirations. At present the 'people' is a formless and shapeless and wiseless mass at best, an infant crying for the light, with no language but a cry. We will change all this by developing the self-respect and manhood of the workers and placing Labour so strongly on its feet that it will be able to stand alone without the aid of crutches, whether those be called Liberal or Conservative.*[21]

The impact of the meetings in Ystalfera and Gwaun Cae Gurwen was to give inspiration to Griffiths to work for the 'new religion', as he called it. They felt a call  to action in favour of the theology of Campbell and the radicalism of Keir Hardie who was so very different to most of the early political leaders of the Labour movement. Hardie had experienced, in his younger days, material poverty, the difficulty of not enjoying simple human rights and then being treated as a troublemaker by officers of the Liberal Party because of his views. He believed in a radical philosophy which would change society and give women and the vulnerable a better chance in life, and he wanted to be their advocate in parliament. Within a week of the Keir Hardie meeting, a branch of the Independent Labour Party had been formed in Ammanford, and before the end of 1908, Griffiths had been elected its secretary.

Keir Hardie had been leader of the ILP from its inception in 1893 until 1899, but then passed on the task to a fellow Scot, Bruce Glasier, a politician who shared Hardie's religious faith. Hardie's ambition was to represent the working classes in parliament, and he succeeded in winning West Ham in 1892, losing it the seat in 1895, and then his second chance came in 1900 in Merthyr. Hardie believed a Welsh-speaking socialist should have fought Merthyr for the ILP but as they were few in number in those days, and hardly anyone had the same influence or passion for socialism as Hardie, so he became the candidate. He argued for Welsh devolution and strongly believed in combining nationalism and socialism. His motto embraced the 'Red Dragon' and the 'Red Flag' and, following his victory he became a hero to many nonconformist ministers and lay people, among them James Griffiths.

As an ILP member, Griffiths felt that they had two goals: firstly to win over the trade unions to the Labour Party, and secondly, to gain a foothold in industrial seats for the ILP and if possible to choose candidates who had the convictions of Keir Hardie. This was the beginning of Griffiths' life as a socialist and he soon came to know many young men and women with a similar outlook.

So, 1908 proved an important milestone in his political life, for he had made a political choice like so many Welsh nonconformists, of combining the theology of Reverend R.J. Campbell and the politics of Keir Hardie,[22] although it is clear that Hardie was the more influential leader as he was a true friend of the miner and the working class. As Reverend T.E. Nicholas, a minister of left-wing views who ministered in the Swansea Valley commented: 'When Keir Hardie came to Merthyr a new period began in the history of Wales. The workers know that he is the best friend that they have seen.'[23] Griffiths decided that it was much more exciting to follow the prophetic voice of Hardie, combining Socialism and Nationalism, rather than following in his father's footsteps as a Liberal.[24] He had come to the conclusion that supporting the Liberal Party was not for him and his socialist friends, noting: 'What we needed was religion which would change society, and a political faith with a vision of a new social order.'[25]

He also acknowledged that the Liberal Party in Wales had achieved huge success in the General Election of 1906. Almost all of Wales was now in the hands of the Liberal Party, just 12 months after the Religious Revival had petered out, with only one constituency now remaining in Tory hands. For Griffiths, the intriguing Welshman within the Liberal administration was David Lloyd George.[26] He was the hero in Griffiths' home after the passing of Gladstone and Tom Ellis, and praised continually as the Welsh wizard who had delivered miracles such as care for the elderly, as well as introducing Old Age Pensions Act in 1908. This was the beginning of the welfare state, which was later enlarged upon by Griffiths and Aneurin Bevan during the 1945-50 Labour Government. Lloyd George may have possessed a radical political manifesto but, to Griffiths he did not combine that with the same passionate religious spirit of Keir Hardie. When, from 1900 to 1903, Lloyd George had the chance to lead the 2,800 striking quarrymen of Bethesda, he did not take advantage of this opportunity as one would have expected from a politician of his radicalism. His voice was not heard either in 1898 when 100,000 miners in the south Wales coalfield were on strike for six months in a dispute over their pay structure.

The brutal truth was that Lloyd George had very little interest in trade unionism, yet the miners in the anthracite coalfield had welcomed him with open arms.[27] The young Lloyd George certainly fought against the Tories and the landed gentry on questions that were of great importance to chapel-goers such as temperance, the right to bury their departed family members in Anglican churchyards, denominational education and the land question.[28] Yet, by the time of the Religious Revival of 1904-5, the 'Disestablishment Question', to end the dominance of the Church of England in Wales, had exhausted the time and energy of the Welsh nonconformists and the Liberal Party who saw this as their overriding priority. In this political and social vacuum, James Griffiths felt the need for a different agenda and, indeed, different values, for himself and his fellow miners. In the sermons of Reverend Campbell published in the weekly magazines that came to his home, and in the political speeches of Keir Hardie, Griffiths had settled on his political home, the Labour movement, one which would inspire him for the rest of his life.

**Notes and References**

1. NLW, Amanwy Papers, 'Fy Atgofion am y Diwygiad' [My memories of the Revival], notes of a lecture. The story is to be found also in Huw Walters, *Cynnwrf Canrif: Agweddau ar Ddiwylliant Gwerin* (Morriston, 2004), pp. 321-4. Also, in the Amanwy Papers, a study of the 1904-5 Revival and its impact on Ammanford, pp.1-29, 'Diwygiad Crefyddol 1904-5 a'i effaith ar Rhydaman'.
2. NLW, Amanwy Papers, 'Fy Atgofion am y Diwygiad' [My memories of the Revival]. Ibid.
3. Ibid.
4. D. J. Williams, *Yn Chwech ar Hugain Oed*, op. cit., pps.151-2. Also, Reverend W. Nantlais Williams refers to the Religious Revival in Ammanford in his autobiography, *O Gopa Bryn Nebo* (Llandysul, 1967), p.61 onwards.
5. Ibid.
6. James Griffiths, *Pages from Memory*, p. 11.
7. Ibid.
8. J. Rogues de Fursac, *Un Movement Mystique Contemporarin; le Reveil Religieux du Pays de Galles, 1904-1005* (Paris, 1907), pp. 183
9. D. Ben Rees, *Chapels in the Valley: A Study in the Sociology of Welsh Nonconformity* (Upton, 1975), p. 156.
10. Ibid.
11. Another viewpoint is given by the Reverend J. H. Howard, in his autobiography, *Winding Lanes* (Caernarfon, 1938), p. 98. Howard mentions that the Revival had weakened the social witness of the chapels.
12. A great deal has been written on the failure of Evan Roberts to be a successful leader of

the Revival due to his physical and mental health. See Noel Gibbard, 'Evan Roberts: The Post Revival Years 1906-51', *The Journal of Welsh Religious History*, Vol.5, 2005, pp.60-76; Iain Murray, *Pentecost Today* (Edinburgh, 1998), p. 159, Gaius Davies, 'Evan Roberts wedi ei ddifa gan y tân' in Noel Gibbard (ed), *Nefol Dân* (Bridgend, 2006), p. 160. It is obvious that R.J. Campbell and Keir Hardie had been much more influential on the young James Griffiths than Evan Roberts. That also is the verdict of Dr Robert Pope. He claims that: 'Hardie had appealed to Griffiths where Roberts had failed to do so. Griffiths related these meetings in terms of conversion experience and he admitted that it profoundly affected the course of his life. He saw socialism as a fulfilment of his faith'. See Robert Pope, *Building Jerusalem: Nonconformity, Labour and Social Questions in Wales 1906-1939* (Cardiff, 1995), p. 103. As a young socialist who later became a member of Plaid Cymru, and then a MP for the University of Wales as a Liberal in 1943, W.J. Gruffydd had no kind word with regard to the impact of the Revival. He said in Welsh (translation): 'Every sane man in Wales condemns the Revival. I do not know what will become of the country, they have gone back at least a century in the worst kind of superstition. I am nearly tempted to emigrate to England at times to forget the country and the language I have been brought up in. What on earth is the reason? Indeed there are only some five people left in Wales who are completely sane'. See Garmon Rhys, 'Plaid, Beirdd a Llenorion', *Golwg*, Vol. 2, no. 48, 10 August 2000, p. 12.

13.	For Silyn, see David Thomas, *Silyn (Robert Silyn Roberts), 1871-1930* (Liverpool, 1956), pps.156; Robert Pope, 'Sosialaeth Silyn', *Codi Muriau Duw: Anghydffurfiaeth ac Anghydffurfwyr Cymru'r Ugeinfed Ganrif* (Bangor, 2005), pp. 112-125; Ffion Mai Thomas, 'R. Silyn Roberts', *Traethodydd*, Vol. XCVII, (1942), pp. 79-94. Ffion Mai Thomas on page 85 maintains that Silyn had completed a period as Councillor in the name of the Independent Labour Party on Merionethshire County Council in the period after the Religious Revival.

14.	James Griffiths heard Silyn a number of times addressing meetings in the Amman Valley. He says, in Welsh (translation): 'His coming had a special significance to us, the young people of south Wales. He was the link that connected the old and the young, and the old had enough hold on us to make us feel that we needed that link to hold on to. Silyn was the link. He preached God and evolution. Silyn was a minister of religion and a socialist. He was our inspiration and our defence. We could tell our parents who were afraid of the new gospel that we spoke so much about, 'But, Silyn Roberts believes like us'. How many godly parents who were concerned and who were reconciled to the socialism of their sons by this knowledge. He was able to link the south Wales of Evan Roberts with the south Wales of Keir Hardie'. See David Thomas, *Silyn*, p. 77.

15.	During the period he taught in Ammanford. J. Gwili Jenkins, led a whole generation of young nonconformists to the ILP, including many of his ministerial students, such as J.T. Job and T.E. Nicholas, and while Amanwy was recuperating from his wounds from the colliery explosion and his grief after his brother Gwilym died in the colliery, Gwili introduced Amanwy to poetry which had socialist fervour, the poets Whitman and Carpenter in particular. See Deian Hopkin, 'Llafur a'r Diwylliant Cymreig 1900-1940', *Transactions of the Honourable Society of Cymmrodorion*, 2000, p. 135. The influence of J. Gwili Jenkins was extremely important on James Griffiths and his brother Amanwy. See J. Beverley Smith, 'John Gwili Jenkins, 1872-1936', *Transactions of the Honourable Society of Cymmrodorion*, 2000, p. 207.

16.	For R. J. Campbell, see Stephen Mayor, *The Churches and the Labour Movement* (London, 1967), pps.72, 209, 233, 241, 292 & 311. For an account of his standpoint, see his volume *A Spiritual Pilgrimage* (London, 1916), pps.184-249 and also *The New Theology* (London, 1907). See also, W. R. C. Hancock, 'R. J. Campbell: Christianity interpreted as Socialism',

*Journal of the United Reformed Historical Society* Vol. 6, No .8 (2001), pps.61927. M. Wynn Thomas has succinctly described his influence in Wales: 'But Campbell's impact on working class Wales was through his seminal books. Highly respected by many of the Welsh chapelgoing workforce, these taught that the essence of the Christian gospel was radical social reform intended to secure justice for all, a reform that could be accomplished only by broadly socialist means.' See, M. Wynn Thomas, *In the Shadow of the Pulpit: Literature and Nonconformist Wales* (Cardiff, 2010), p. 171. However, the Revd. Robert Ellis, Tŷ Croes, near Ammanford disagrees in his autobiography: 'I remember soon after the 19045 Revival that the new theology of R.J. Campbell became popular and its emphasis on the social gospel. I remember the meetings held all over Cwmaman to debate the right to a living wage, the turning away from religion, and the disrespect for spiritual religion'. See Robert Ellis, *Wrth Gofio'r Daith* (Llandybïe, 1963), p. 100. Most of the ministerial students at the United Theological College, Aberystwyth, preparing for the Calvinistic Methodist ministry rejected the appeal of R. J. Campbell. See J. E. Wynne Davies, 'From the Archives', *The Treasury*, November 2012, p.14. 'The student body was, nevertheless, emphatic in its dismissal of Reverend R. J. Campbell's 'New Theology', categorically stating that Wales will have nothing of this "new theology" which is as old as heresy.'

17. James Griffiths, *Pages from Memory*, pp. 11-12.

18. 'Explosion at Ammanford', *South Wales Daily News*, 29 January 1908; see also the coroner's report in the same paper, 12 February and 6 May 1908.

19. James Griffiths, *Pages from Memory*, p. 13.

20. A valuable study of Hardie is Kenneth O Morgan, *Keir Hardie: Radical and Socialist* (London, 1997), pp. 1-343. For Keir Hardie at Gwaun cae Gurwen, see James Griffiths, *Pages from Memory*, p. 24; also Huw T. Edwards, 'Keir Hardie', *Lleufer*, Vol. 12, No. 2, Summer 1956, pp. 68-70.

21. Keir Hardie succeeded in winning young miners to his ranks as he was one of them. That was the reaction of Wil John Edwards in Aberaman in 1900: 'When eventually the chairman called on Keir Hardie to speak my mind flew back to the Heading and Dai Bobby's words "just like one of us". And this, I saw and felt, was simply true, he was indeed just like one of us but, I know, he had in him a power and, to us, a glory which raised him to the skies in our thinking'. Why was Hardie so successful on the miners' platform? We are given the answer, because he was sincere: 'It was Keir Hardie's complete integrity made the more forceful by the fact that he had no oratorical tricks, no desire to mould events or even conditions into points of eloquence: he offered complete sincerity; he was without guile and told the truth and this went to the hearts and minds of even the more ignorant miners in the valleys'. See Wil John Edwards, *From the Valley I Came* (London, 1956), pp. 90-92.

22. It is a surprise to a historian to realise that a sizeable minority of nonconformist ministers were involved with the Labour movement in the years after the Religious Revival of 1904-5. These men became heavily involved; the Reverends R. Silyn Roberts, Tanygrisiau; T. E. Nicholas, Glais; D. D. Walters (Gwallter Ddu); Cenarth; T. Rhondda Williams, Bradford; but one should not forget Daniel Hughes, Pontypool; Rhys J. Huws, Glanaman; E.K. Jones, Brymbo; J.H. Howard, Cwmavon; John Morgan Jones, Merthyr Tydfil; David Pugh, Merthyr; J. Edryd Jones, Garnant; W. Rowland Jones, Merthyr; Herbert Morgan, London; James Nicholas, Tonypandy; W. D. Roderick, Rhiwfawr; T. M. Roderick, Cwmgors; Iona Williams, Llanelli; D.C. Rees, Bridgend; J. Park Davies, Carmarthen; and the layman and theologian, J. Gwili Jenkins, Ammanford. Each one of these leaders belonged to the traditional Welsh nonconformist denominations such as the Baptists, Welsh Independents, Welsh Calvinistic Methodists and Unitarians. There were socialists within the Anglican Church and the

Wesleyan Methodist Church. As Kate Roberts states in one of her literary volumes: 'The young were pleased to call Christ a socialist. Their interest had moved from Christ the Saviour to Christ the Example'. See Kate Roberts, *Traed Mewn Cyffion* (Swansea , 1936), p.92.

23.  Kenneth O. Morgan, *Keir Hardie: Radical and Socialist* (London, 1975), p. 113. See, *Merthyr Pioneer*, 8 April 1911, p. 3.

24.  'But Hardie left Labour's approach to the rival themes of socialism and nationalism essentially unresolved'. See Kenneth O. Morgan, 'Leaders and led in the Labour movement: the Welsh experience', *Llafur*, 6 (3), 1994, pp. 109-119.

25.  NLW, James Griffiths Papers, 'Nonconformity and Socialism'; *Pages from Memory*, p. 13. The new theology of R. J. Campbell became a topic of conversation on the streets of the villages and towns of south Wales. See C.B. Turner, 'Conflicts of faith, religion and Labour in Wales, 1880-1914' in Deian R. Hopkin and C. S. Kealey (eds), *Class, Community and the Labour Movement: Wales and Canada, 1850-1930* (Cardiff, 1989), pp. 67-85.

26.  Like James Griffiths, David Lloyd George was regarded as a possible preacher as he attended three services on a Sunday, and on Wednesday attended another religious meeting at Penymaes Chapel, Cricieth. If his denomination, Disciples of Christ, had a fully paid ministerial structure there is a strong possibility that he would have opted for a religious career. See Thomas Jones, *Lloyd George*, pp. 6-7. Sir Herbert Lewis claims in his diary of 22 December 1904: 'At breakfast this morning, Lloyd George said he regretted that he had not become a preacher. The pulpit, dealing as it did with every phase of human life, offered infinite opportunities for influence and it dealt with matters of eternal consciences. Politics after all, belong to a lower plane, they are concerned with material things.' NLW, Sir Herbert Lewis Papers. For the socialist conversion of Griffiths, see Ioan Aled Matthews, The World of the Anthracite Miner, unpublished University of Wales PhD Thesis, 1995, p.226. On the religious influences on James Griffiths, see *Pages from Memory*, pps.11-18; Richard Lewis, *Leaders and Teachers: Adult Education and the Challenge of Labour in South Wales, 1906-1940* (Cardiff, 1993), pp. 45-6; J. Beverley Smith, 'An Appreciation', in *James Griffiths and His Times* (Ferndale, 1978), pp. 62-4.

27.  Ioan Aled Matthews, *The World of the Anthracite Miner*, p. 209. When Lloyd George visited Seven Sisters in 1911 everything was closed for the day and the miners were given a holiday. Donald McCormick, *The Mask of Merlin: A Critical Study of David Lloyd George* (London, 1963), p. 242. It was no wonder that young socialists believed that a new age was at hand. According to Evan Owen 'there were signs of the breaking of a new dawn'. See the David Thomas Collection in the University of Bangor Archives, CDT/a, (a) 1, 21 November 1910.

"MABON"—RT. HON. WILLIAM ABRAHAM, M.P.

J. KEIR HARDIE, M.P.

# 4

## Pioneering in the Name of Labour

James Griffiths had been nurtured in a home which stressed the principles, ethics and morality of the Liberal Party and accepted its programme, its philosophy and its planning. A photograph of the most successful Liberal Party prime minister, in the Victorian era, W.E. Gladstone and his wife Catherine Gladstone, had pride of place in the living room of the Griffiths' home in Betws. Though the home belonged to working people and their religious allegiance was definitely to the Welsh Independent denomination, the Anglo-Catholic Gladstone had become an icon to William Griffiths and his wife, Margaret.[1]

William Griffiths had travelled from Betws to Swansea to hear Gladstone speak and had been completely bowled over by the Liberal statesman's oratory. For months following, William would tell his friends at the smithy of Gladstone's outstanding qualities as a politician and, by the beginning of the 20th century, William Griffiths felt completely content that the charisma of Gladstone had been inherited by the Welshman, David Lloyd George. He was also proud that the Liberal Party supported two important yet controversial issues: the Disestablishment of the Church of England in Wales and opposition to the Education Act of 1902. These issues came up frequently in the debates that took place at William's smithy, known in Betws as the 'Parliament'.[2] He had strong social views and expected his family to agree with him. As one frequenter of the smithy admits, if you were in his good books 'you could never do anything wrong' but if you disagreed with him, and hardly anyone did, then you were out of favour, in a great deal of trouble, and as far as Betws was concerned, 'a complete outsider'.

In the early part of the twentieth century, however, William Griffiths was confronted with a different brand of politics, which did not appeal to him as much as it did to his sons. As he looked back on this important period in his life, James Griffiths argued that the socialist philosophy of ILP had been able to ally itself with the spirit and the verve of the 1904-5 Religious Revival.[3] In his opinion this new Labour movement, which was to represent the working class, was more than just a protest against poverty, inequality, war and violence; it was a desire for economic stability. The movement was even more than a protest, especially among the miners and workers in heavy industries. It was a critical appraisal against capitalists who allied themselves with the Tory party, and sometimes with the Liberals, who exploited as well as controlled the lives of the ordinary people.[4]

The inspiration for Keir Hardie, Bruce Glasier, Silyn Roberts and many others in the socialist fold came from the teachings of the New Testament, and The Sermon on the Mount formed the crux of their passionate message, but new contemporary meaning and inspiration also came from the speeches of these leaders. This heady mix of what is now regarded as Liberation Theology and socialism shaped the young Griffiths, who encapsulated his beliefs as:

*Socialism is much closer to religion than it is to political propaganda. From the prophets, apostles, the saints, the religious mystics and the heretics rather that from statesmen, economists and political reformers the socialist movement has its example and idealism.*[5]

The period, from 1905 to 1912, is key to the story of James Griffiths and the cause of the ILP. Its been described the period that saw the 'sowing the seed of socialism'.[6] It also gave added impetus to the emerging Labour Party, in 1906, as well as to the trade union movement in east Carmarthenshire, which saw confrontations between the old Liberal order and the younger ILP-inspired socialists in many nonconformist chapels and in the homes of the leaders as well as among the ranks of the officers of the colliery lodges. This was especially true amongst the leaders of a number of these individual collieries in the Amman and Gwendraeth valleys.

William Abraham, known as Mabon, a staunch Liberal, and leader of 'the Fed', had no option but to become a Lib-Lab candidate in the 1906 General Election. Mabon was the great hero of the miners.[7] Established in 1898, the South Wales Miners' Union could boast over 100,000 members during Mabon's tenure as its President. There were three leaders in command of 'the Fed', who kept the union within the fold of the Liberal Party, namely Mabon as president, William Brace as vice president and Tom Richards as the general secretary. When Mabon was elected as MP for the Rhondda in 1885 he was the first miner from south Wales to be elected to the House of Commons, and naturally took the whip and colours of the Liberal Party, whose radical wing he closely identified with, but his greatest affinity was with the world of Welsh culture and the Welsh Calvinistic Methodist chapels. Mabon inspired large gatherings with his oratory and he was completely at home in the pulpit. As he had been blessed with a tenor voice, he often sang to the congregations and, when a nasty confrontation arose in a miners' conference, he would sing a hymn or even the Welsh national anthem to help restore harmony.

He and some of his fellow union leaders were often at loggerheads. In particular he had a bitter disagreement with his vice president, William Brace, a native of Risca in Monmouthshire, who had been elected a miners' agent in 1890. Mabon would often tell the miners of Glamorganshire to ignore Brace as he brought an 'English element' to Welsh trade unionism. The pair even became involved in a bitter legal case in 1893, which Brace lost and was fined the hefty sum of £500. Brace refused to pay the fine, appealed for help from his religious friends in the chapels in Monmouthshire and Mabon dropped the case.

Mabon was widely criticised by many of his more militant co-workers in the Labour movement as being too supportive of the owners of the collieries. One of the most critical observers of Mabon was Keir Hardie, who was the most effective socialist propagandist that the communities of the south Wales valleys had ever seen and where he single-handedly established 30 branches of the ILP within 12 months of his arrival in Glamorganshire. Hardie was the most enthusiastic supporter of these branches and for years he was the editor of the weekly newspaper, *Labour Leader*. He sincerely could not understand the viewpoint of Mabon and the other mining leaders who still supported the Liberal Party, and why they were unable to break off the close relationship despite being representatives of a workforce that resented the Liberal hierarchy? The truth of the matter was that Mabon and his fellow leaders were able to remain aligned to the Liberals because, at that time, the majority of the miners still had faith in the Liberal Party.

The MP for East Carmarthenshire since 1890 had been Abel Thomas, the son of a nonconformist minister, who practised as a barrister. Thomas was not a particularly conscientious MP but he had a strong grip on the electorate, mainly through the support of his political agent, the Reverend Josiah Towyn Jones, minister of the Bethel Welsh Independent chapel in Garnant between 1885 to 1906. Towyn Jones was the secretary of the Liberal Party in the constituency, and to the inhabitants of Ammanford and the whole Amman Valley he was the personification of the values of Welsh nonconformity, as well as the upholder of Liberal causes such as the disestablishment of the Church of England in Wales, and temperance. By 1904 Jones was representing the Amman Valley, as a Liberal, on Carmarthenshire County Council, and he resigned from his pastorate in 1906 to devote his time to solving the denomination's financial problems. Towyn Jones had a great deal of influence within his denomination, and his chapel in Garnant had been a powerhouse for the Religious Revival of 1904-5. The disestablishment of the Church of England in Wales was foremost in his mind and he worked tirelessly on this issue.

However, from 1906 onwards, there were constant rumours that Abel Thomas was going to retire from politics, and some miners in the constituency, such as James Griffiths, argued that his successor should have strong attachment with the working class and the Labour movement. Had not the time come for East Carmarthenshire to follow in the footsteps of Mabon and William Brace and succeed in having a Lib-Lab Member of Parliament? An MP representing the ordinary people of the region or someone from the middle class who at least sympathised and identified with the working classes, as well as supporting the Liberal Government policies would, Griffiths believed, be the ideal candidate. This was, however, not going to happen in East Carmarthenshire for three reasons:

Firstly, the small rural villages such as Ffairfach and Llanwrda were the backbone of the constituency: in other words, it was still very much a rural seat despite the fact that the mining villages – in the Amman, Loughor and Gwendraeth valleys – were increasing their population from year to year. In addition, there were hundreds of voters in the south of the constituency – between Burry Port and Dafen on the outskirts of Llanelli – who worked in the tinplate and the steel industry. While it was true that the largest group of workers in the constituency were employed as coal miners, and two-thirds of East Carmarthenshire's population, which had doubled between 1901 and 1910, lived in urban or semi-urban areas, it was not an industrial constituency such as Rhondda.

Secondly, while this was a constituency where the working-class should have been considered when electing a future MP, this was not going to happen while Towyn Jones had the upper hand. The neighbouring constituency of Gower, however, had realised the need for change. Although the MP in Gower was a Liberal, a change took place in 1906 with the selection of Reverend John Williams, a well-known Baptist preacher and miners' agent as candidate. This choice pleased the trade unions, as well as the most progressive elements among the Liberals, and Williams won the election as a Lib-Lab MP.

The same combination could have been acceptable in East Carmarthenshire, but the anthracite district within the miners' union caused controversy by suggesting David Morgan – who had a long association with the anthracite coalfield and was an admirer of Mabon – as a possible candidate. The son of a Calvinistic Methodist elder, William Morgan, from Tŷ Croes near Ammanford, David Morgan took part in many community activities in the Ammanford area, and was indeed a promising candidate who would, if elected, serve the political needs of the mining community with distinction. Indeed, the editor of the weekly newspaper, *Tarian y Gweithiwr* [The Worker's Shield], described Morgan as a leader who could be depended upon, a moderate trade unionist who was also a Welsh patriot, and the decision reflected the views of the miners in the anthracite coalfield who were regarded as moderates rather than militants: careful and supportive of their communities, as well as being extremely loyal to the Liberal Party.[8] The younger miners, like Griffiths, tended to be much more radical and were regularly regarded by their contemporaries as 'left wingers'. When David Morgan was given the blessing of the miners in 1907, some within the union argued that they had nothing against the sitting MP but that he had no direct experience of their work. Some of them felt that they needed a different kind of MP, one that knew the coalfield.

At a conference called by the miners' leaders – including John James from Cwmgors who was highly regarded and considered as another possible Labour candidate – to discuss tactics and strategy for the forthcoming General Election, to which the other trade unions and co-operative societies in the constituency were invited, the miners soon found themselves under attack. All the other trade unions were up in arms and annoyed with them for choosing a specific candidate before all the options had been discussed with their fellow trade unionists. In contrast to the Rhondda, and despite their decision in 1907 to support the Labour Party, followed by their affiliation to the party a year later, other trade unionists in East Carmarthenshire strongly believed that the miners could not expect to select their own nominee as a prospective parliamentary candidate. For example, the National Union of Railwaymen (NUR) felt that they had an equally as powerful a claim as the miners.

Thirdly, the miners were reluctant to challenge a Liberal politician who had so much support among chapel-goers, and in a constituency where the Liberal establishment was in complete command. Even the local MP, Abel Thomas, was often referred to as a 'friend of the miners'. Though he was still uncertain if he would stand, it was obvious, too, that David Morgan was not going to be successful as a possible candidate in any selection conference arranged by the wider trade union movement.

As the election drew closer, and after travelling to London to discuss his candidature with Labour Party leaders, Morgan was persuaded to withdraw his name, whilst miners' leader John James took the same course of action after receiving a telegram from Arthur Henderson confirming that he shouldn't stand. At the subsequent Liberal constituency selection meeting a letter was read out, stating that a conference of miners were content to give their backing to Abel Thomas, who was ready to stand again. Abel Thomas then read out a personal letter of support from the president of the South Wales Miners' Union stating: 'Go and stand as a candidate and may God help your cause, and in days to come we can look for someone who is worthy to follow your footsteps in East Carmarthenshire.' Mabon had expressed his clear support for Abel Thomas, and his determined opposition to left-wing candidates contesting the 1910 'progressive vote' election.

James Griffiths could not agree with the attitude of Mabon or with the local officers of the mining fraternity in the anthracite district. Among James Griffiths' manuscripts there is an article which discusses the conflict which was beginning to appear between the nonconformist chapels, the Independent Labour Party, and the newly-formed Labour Party of 1906, which was beginning to make itself known in the anthracite coalfield.[9] He could see the inevitable confrontation and argued that there were understandable reasons for the situation, such as the opposition to the Labour movement, and especially to the activities of the ILP from those politically-minded Liberals who were heavily involved in the chapels. The Liberal dominance of the chapels was by now, however, being challenged by more radical theologians such as the London-based Reverend R. J. Campbell who provided great inspiration to Griffiths and others in the ILP.

Campbell's theology had a great deal of appeal to the young men of the mining valleys and reflected the intellectual ferment that was taking place in Britain as a result of scientific discoveries, the evolution theory of Charles Darwin and the political writings and manifestos of Karl Marx and Friedrich Engels. The theological and Biblical revolution that had taken place in Europe, in particular in Germany, had also become of interest to scholars and students in the theological colleges of Wales. The name associated with these new concepts and discussions was that of George Wilhelm Friedrich Hegel (1770-1831), who had been an influence on Karl Marx and also some Welsh theologians and preachers who began to discuss Hegelian philosophy. By the end of the Edwardian era the traditional Calvinism of the Welsh nonconformist denominations was beginning to be superseded by an optimistic Hegelian modernism, associated especially with David Adams (Hawen), a distinguished Welsh Independent minister in Liverpool who embraced Campbell's 'new theology'.[10]

By the 1904-5 Religious Revival, traditional Calvinism was being discarded by a number of Welsh nonconformist ministers. Evan Roberts's grasp of theology was superficial and his emphasis was on the path of reconciliation, kindness and good living, never taking on board the Calvinism of his denomination. Dr Robert Pope has analysed Roberts's theology, indicating clearly that emotion, feeling and emphasis on the work of the Holy Spirit were his constant message to the congregations he addressed during the Religious Revival.[11] To be fair, though, Roberts realised the danger of too heavy an emphasis on feelings and emotion rather than on belief, for he had become, within a few months, a celebrity and people all over Wales expected miracles from the Revivalist. The miners of south Wales gave him support with many attending the services on their way home from the collieries. Many of these miners were given an additional emotional uplift through the preaching of social gospellers who visited the south Wales coalfield. Among these social gospellers were two brothers from the United States of America, Reverend Stitt Wilson and Reverend Ben Wilson. They came to the constituency of East Carmarthenshire and to the mining village of Brynaman where many of the young miners, all of whom were socialists, were thrilled by their message, style, and presence.[12]

At Brynaman, the Rev. Stitt Wilson gave an impressive sermon on Moses, declaring him to be the first Labour leader but unfortunately, as James Griffiths acknowledged in his essay on socialism and nonconformity, a conflict arose between the chapels and the new campaigners. In their Sunday sermons, some of the preachers who visited Ammanford and who had been nurtured as Gladstonian Liberals would attack the Labour movement from the pulpit and created an inevitable rift. They also attacked Griffiths' generation for spending their leisure time playing billiards and attending whist drives and dances.

Griffiths protested against this attitude in 1921, in a letter to the *Amman Valley Chronicle*:

> *When will our pastors and masters spent less time in futile slating of us for our sin of playing billiards, and devote more of their time to something more useful, such as talks on the best books to read? Ah, when? Perhaps they do know; they did not in my youth, and so I waded through the realm of books from Penny Dreadfuls to the treasures of literature.*[13]

Young chapel-goers like Griffiths often felt distressed as they were regarded as representing the younger generation at the Christian Temple, Bethany and Ebenezer. The same criticism of left-wing activism was also expressed within the Sunday School classes, and Griffiths admitted that he and his brothers remained faithful to the Sunday School even in an atmosphere of anti-socialism, which they occasionally experienced at Christian Temple.

Griffiths remembered the atmosphere, and the fallout, from the 1910 by-election in the Mid Glamorganshire constituency, which he saw as an example of the conflict between Welsh nonconformism and socialism. The favoured candidate of the miners was Vernon Hartshorn, a Primitive Methodist brought up in the Pontywaun area of Gwent, who had moved to the Ogmore Valley in Glamorganshire and, from 1905, had been a miners' agent in the Maesteg District. Hartshorn felt that the Labour Party should stand on its own feet, free from the control of the Liberal Party. He failed to be elected to parliament in 1910, but what amazed Griffiths were the tactics and the propaganda of prominent members of the Liberal Party towards a Christian socialist of the calibre of Hartshorn.

The Liberals allowed the Anti-Socialist League to interfere in Maesteg, in the heart of the Mid-Glamorgan constituency, who took great pleasure in insulting the socialists with crude slogans and claimed that socialism was anti-Christian and was as socially dangerous as promiscuity! In the coalfield valleys that would have been intensely shocking – as indeed would the idea of promoting anything dubbed anti-Christian.

One of the most notorious nonconformists and anti-socialists of the period was William Francis (W.F.) Phillips. A native of Penmaenmawr who had spent years among the affluent Welsh communitity of Liverpool, at the Princes Road Calvinistic Methodist chapel in Toxteth during the ministry of the Rev. John Williams, and one of the most colourful Liberals of his time.[14] Under the watchful eye of Willliams, Phillips felt the call of the Welsh Presbyterian ministry and won a scholarship to the University of Wales College in Cardiff where he graduated with a BA. He then gained a BD at the Theological College in Aberystwyth before moving to Jesus College, Oxford for his BLitt. Ordained in 1909, he ministered at three English chapels within the Presbyterian Church of Wales: first at Havelock Street, Newport, then at Tenby and finally at Spellow Lane, Liverpool.

W. F. Philips expended more energy for the Liberal Party than for his own denomination and his commitment to the party was obvious. He fought as a Liberal parliamentary candidate in the 1910 General Election at Gower, where he criticised nonconformists who had deserted the Liberal camp for socialism. He was also in the vanguard of the anti-socialist camp at the Mid Glamorganshire by-election, criticising Hartshorn, and writing to the Welsh press portraying socialism as an enemy of the Christian faith. In 1911, in the Welsh magazine *Genhinen*, he argued that socialism meant social revolution, the elimination of the family and in particular the Royal Family, as well as the curtailing of freedom for the individual. 'God would be exiled from his world and His Son from the life of humanity', Phillips wrote.[15] W. F. Phillips had no respect at all for Christian socialist ministers such as T. E. Nicholas ('Niclas y Glais'); Rev. R. Silyn Roberts; T. M. Roderick, Cwmgors; W. D. Roderick, Rhiwfawr; and J. Gwili Jenkins, calling them 'disciples of Judas Iscariot'. In his opinion, the Christian socialist who ascended to the nonconformist pulpit was nothing less than a traitor to the faith of the chapels. James Griffiths by now realised that Phillips had become a significant voice for Liberal nonconformists, who mocked socialists within the chapels,[16] and was a leading advocate within the Liberal Party and within the Presbyterian Church of Wales, reminding all and sundry of the Labour Party's atheist philosophy.

Phillips came to the Amman Valley, and the mining villages around Ammanford, with the intention of attacking those who had joined the ILP; he sought to create an anti-socialist front among the chapel members who had lifelong allegiance to the Liberal Party. He was not the only minister of religion belonging to the nonconformist denominations to undertake such a campaign and their views can be be read in the Welsh language periodicals of the period.

Phillips also enjoyed a strong following in every Welsh constituency and, among the miners, there were significant leaders who refused to consider choosing parliamentary candidates in the name of Labour in preference to the colours of the Liberal Party. One of these was John Harries (Irlwyn), who later became an Elder at Betws Welsh Calvinist Methodist chapel. Harries was a cultured miner who was also a checkweigher. Later in his life he became a staunch supporter of James Griffiths, but at this period he did not agree with the argument of ILP members who were ready to opt for the miners' leader, David Morgan, or the charismatic John James from Cwmgors. Indeed, neither did the 700 miners at Gelliceidrim Colliery in the Amman Valley who voted against supporting a Labour candidate at the 1910 election, and John James certainly realised that there were other anthracite collieries of the same opinion as the miners of Gelliceidrim.[17] The effective oratory and anti-Labour invective of W.F. Phillips and other propagandists such as Towyn Jones succeeded in confirming the Liberalism of these miners.

There was, though, a small group of miners and progressive individuals – who had read a great deal of contemporary socialist literature – willing to rebel against the local nonconformist, Liberal establishment in the years after the Revival. These young men appreciated the contribution of the weekly newspaper, *Llais Llafur* [The Voice of Labour] which had been established in Ystalfera by the socialist, Ebenezer Rees in 1898.[18] In his younger days, Rees had suffered for his allegiance to the trade union movement and it was something he never forgot. He became an important figure in the Labour movement and *Llais Llafur* was an excellent medium through which to promote the task of establishing branches of the ILP. The paper carried its political message on behalf of socialism, as well as local news from the different communities in Glamorganshire and East Carmarthenshire, and gave a platform to leading Welsh socialists such as David Thomas, Rev. R. Silyn Roberts, R.J. Derfel of Manchester and the poet T. E. Nicholas. It was a tragedy for the Labour cause within the Welsh language press when R. J. Derfel died in 1905, followed by Ebenezer Rees in 1908. Rees' sons, David James Rees and Elwyn Rees, who succeeded him, compromised with regard to the Welsh language input in the paper to maintain sales, even changing its name from *Llais Llafur* to *Labour Voice* in 1915. Also, after 1908, the paper became lukewarm in its support of the ILP.

From 1898 to 1908, though, *Llais Llafur* had been an effective instrument for the emerging ILP and the Labour cause in south Wales. The rival publication, *Tarian y Gweithiwr*, was cautious, supporting the Lib-Lab alliance, and it did not have the same enthusiasm for socialism as had *Llais Llafur* in the days of Ebenezer Rees.

For many of these socialists, the role of the Welsh language in politics was central. John James of Cwmgors believed that it was important for the Labour movement to use the Welsh language on every possible occasion. He tried with others, such as the local politician in Gwaun Cae Gurwen, Dai Dan Davies, to discuss the relevance of Welsh culture to socialism, and by 1911 they believed in the need for the establishment of a Welsh Labour Party. David Thomas, a schoolmaster in the slate-quarrying Nantlle Valley in Caernarfonshire, preached the same message.[19] In a speech at Caernarfon in 1909, Thomas Jones – later to become the friend of four successive British prime ministers between 1916 and 1930 – argued passionately in support of this proposal. Jones, a native of Rhymney in the Monmouthshire coalfield, had put forward a strong case: to him Wales was not England writ small. He argued that the Welsh had their own language, eisteddfod tradition, a strongly-developed working-class culture and a way of life that was distinctively their own. This was a call for the Welsh to examine the relationship between socialism and nationalism and to understand the pivotal role that the Labour Party could play in forging such links.

All these sentiments were shared by Thomas Jones and his fellow Labourites in north-west Wales and by John James and his supporters, including James Griffiths, in the Amman Valley. The difficulty lay, however, in bringing these supporting strands together in a coherent campaign. David Thomas and John James needed the support of Thomas Jones, the outstanding 'TJ', but by now Jones was a Professor of Economics at Queen's University in Belfast and no longer lived in Wales.

The effort to crystallise the vision rested on the shoulders of Thomas, James and Griffiths, but David Thomas had heavy daytime duties as a school teacher, as well as speaking engagements all over Wales. These he fulfilled, in his leisure time, travelling long distances between north-west Wales and the anthracite coalfield as a propagandist for Welsh socialism.[20] In reality, Thomas' activities would have to be somewhat limited as his desire was to set up branches and arrange public meetings for Labour propagandists although he did manage to organise a major conference during the visit of the National Eisteddfod to Carmarthen in August 1911.

The Editorial of *Llais Llafur* in November 1909 had mentioned an obvious deficiency in the structure of the ILP in Wales, specifically the need for a Welsh-speaking organiser for the ILP in south Wales. John James raised the matter at the conference in Carmarthen but nothing came of it. Though a good number, including James Griffiths and the poet T. Gwynn Jones, attended the conference, the end result was rather disappointing. Those who should have been present, like Thomas Jones, were unavoidably absent. Nevertheless, at the Carmarthen conference, resolutions in favour of creating a Welsh ILP were passed, asserting that:

> *The only party that can represent democracy in Wales is the Labour Party, and that the spirit of Welsh nationalism can only find full scope for its political and industrial activities in the policy of nationalisation of the land and the industries of the country. Welsh branches of the ILP should join together to form one division of the ILP known as the Welsh ILP.* [21]

However, the ILP's Westminster leaders were in the main very hostile. Keir Hardie himself advised Welsh branches not to take any action until the British Labour Party had been consulted and had given their decision, but Thomas was opposed to Hardie's views: he considered that only the 'bond of nationality' could unite the ILP movement in Wales. David Thomas had his supporters and in the south Wales coalfield these included the miners' leader, John James from Cwmgors, Idris Davies of Abercraf who was a county councillor, and James Griffiths. All three were present at the important Carmarthen conference. One of the consequences of the campaign was a change in the national organisational structure of the ILP. In 1912, the ILP Annual Conference resolved that 'all branches in Wales and Monmouthshire be organised as a new Division 8 of the ILP.' Later, in 1918, Wales was retained as a separate administrative unit by the reorganised Labour Party.

Griffiths knew very well that the task of winning the industrial areas of Wales over to the ILP would not be easy, for the Liberal Government of 1906-10 was incredibly progressive with a Welsh-speaking Welshman as one of the most significant Liberal politicians of his day: Lloyd George. It was Lloyd George who was responsible for introducing the 1911 Unemployment and Health Insurance Bill, and he took the imaginative step of recruiting a team of lecturers to visit villages and towns to explain how the new measure would work. The Liberal government was also extending basic rights to workers and, in 1908, Griffiths expressed his joy when the Liberal government decided to introduce an eight-hour day for miners as well as establishing local labour exchanges. However, the miners had been very satisfied when the Labour Party forced the Liberals to accept the complete reversal of the Taff Vale Judgement by passing the Trade Disputes Act of 1906.

However, Griffiths belonged to the ILP which was determined to be completely detached from, and independent of, the Liberal Government. After the British miners had officially affiliated with the Labour Party in 1908, some MPs from coalfield constituencies made the difficult decision to turn their backs on old friends in the Liberal Party, so that they could further the interests of the newlyformed Labour Party.

These new recruits were needed to sustain the Labour Party, which was facing a crisis due to the Osborne Judgement, announced in the House of Lords. It centered on a case brought by W.V. Osborne against his trade union, the Amalgamated Society of Railway Servants, when the House of Lords and the government united in declaring all political action by trade unions to be illegal. It thus prevented trade unions from selecting their own candidates, but much more important still, it denied them the opportunity of supporting candidates in the name of either the Labour Party or the Independent Labour Party. This judgement was a serious setback. It struck at the very foundation of the Labour Party's existence, in particular its finances, and generated new conditions that meant Labour competed at the two general elections of 1910 under a serious handicap.

With Labour having no candidate in East Carmarthenshire for the January 1910 general election, members of the ILP branch in Ammanford were furious that the opportunity had passed without a socialist candidate putting the case for their political aspirations. During this period – 1908 to 1911 – the branch had strong convictions along with plenty of enthusiasm and three able and effective members: David George, Edgar Bassett and James Griffiths, but little money.[22] The trio were ably encouraged by two miners, Jack Griffiths from Cwmtwrch and Dai R. Owen from Garnant, who had been trained in the Central Labour College and helped arrange adult education classes in the town; studying Economics and Marxism. Noah Ablett, the Rhondda Marxist, had prepared a textbook for such classes called *Easy Outlines of Economics* which, along with the evening classes, were an inspiration to the ILP members and introduced them to syndicalist ideas from France and the USA.

By the time of the second general election of 1910, the ILP branch in Ammanford decided that they should, after all, have a candidate as they had at least £50 in their fighting fund, and the number of ILP branches in the constituency had now doubled. It was not going to be easy, admitted James Griffiths, noting that every 'chapel vestry was a Liberal Committee Room'.

A pamphlet, prepared by Keir Hardie under the title *Can a Man be a Christian on a Pound a Week?* proved to be the single most important and influential publication of their campaign. Christianity was the basis of Griffiths' politics, rather than syndicalism or Marxism, and a religious conviction he shared with most of his young comrades.

To Griffiths, and many of the early ILP members who shared his dedicated support of the temperance movement, one of the key enemies of the workingclass were the brewers. The Burry Port-based family doctor, Dr J. H. Williams, was one of the most dedicated supporters of temperance in the locality, and was very keen to stand under the colours of the ILP at the forthcoming election. Due to his strong stance for temperance, Dr Williams' candidature enjoyed the enthusiastic backing of a number of socialist ministers of religion in the Amman Valley, in particular W. D. Roderick, B. D. Davies, and the Welsh Independent minister J. Edryd Jones, and he secured the nomination. Dr Williams's supporters worked hard for him, with conviction and enthusiasm, but their efforts were poorly rewarded with a disappointing result: [23]

| | |
|---|---|
| Abel Thomas (Liberal) | 5,825 |
| Mervyn Peel (Conservative) | 2,315 |
| Dr J.H. Williams (Independent Labour Party) | 1,176 |

Despite this, the socialists continued to distribute their literature, arranged political meetings and prepared for their next opportunity, which came earlier than they expected when Abel Thomas died suddenly in July 1912.[24] The Conservatives were quick off the mark for the by-election in re-selecting Mervyn Peel, while miners' leader John James had already been nominated as the Labour candidate for the next general election, expected in 1914. The Liberal Party, however, had two factions competing for the nomination. One of the most important Liberals in the constituency, the Reverend William Davies of Llandeilo who had been a county councillor for years and was regarded as the ultimate political fixer, made it known that his preferred candidate was either the Honourable Roland Phillips or Sir Stafford Howard, both wealthy Whigs, rather than his fellow nonconformist Liberal, the Reverend Josiah Towyn Jones. Though William Davies and Towyn Jones were both well-known ministers of the same – Welsh Independent – denomination, they were political enemies, but William Davies knew that Towyn Jones had a tremendous advantage over his rivals as he was secretary of the constituency party.

Towyn Jones wasted no time and on 24 July, even before the funeral of Abel Thomas, he wrote to William Jones, a well-known Liberal MP in north Wales, to declare clearly that the the next MP for East Carmarthenshire should be able to speak Welsh, and be a long-time resident in the constituency. He warned William Jones, and through him the Liberal hierarchy, that if Sir Stafford Howard was chosen as a parliamentary candidate then he would have to adopt a different course of action, stating: 'I am going to the poll at all costs'.

Towyn Jones knew he had a battle on his hands for the nomination but, being a well-known preacher-politician and popular with both the working-class and the members of the Welsh nonconformist chapels, he was also aware that he had a lot of local support and easily won the nomination. Jones ran a successful campaign and his public meetings had an enthusiastic atmosphere, similar to Revivalist meetings, such as the one in Garnant, where he had ministered for 15 years. The chapel was packed with supporters and, as the meeting closed, everyone stood up to cheer the Liberal candidate.

The Labour camp, though, was in trouble from the start of the campaign with John James having to withdraw his candidature. He did so with charm and humility, realising that it was pointless to disagree with the Labour Party leaders in London who opposed standing a candidate against Towyn Jones. It was a great loss to Welsh politics.

The Labour Party's timidity presented an opportunity for the Independent Labour Party, as James' withdrawal allowed the medical practitioner Dr J.H. Williams to volunteer as a standard bearer for the ILP. Williams' candidature was severely criticised as such in *Tarian y Gweithiwr* due to the trade unions' support for Towyn Jones and he was rebuked, particularly by the miners, for his audacity in standing.

*Llais Llafur* noted that the whole strength of 'the political establishment of Welsh nonconformity' was against Dr Williams and that ministers of religion in the constituency, despite supporting socialism, were unable to support his candidature. The ILP now had very little hope, though their campaigning was given a boost when Nina Boyle, a militant suffragette, came to Ammanford and offered her financial support to the small band of campaigners. James Griffiths struck a bargain with her, and Nina Boyle brought a number of her fellow campaigners, such as Annie Kenney with her Irish charm, to share the election platform. The by-election, though, saw an easy victory for the Liberals:

| | |
|---|---|
| Reverend Josiah Towyn Jones (Liberal) | 6,082 |
| Mervyn Peel (Conservative) | 3,354 |
| Dr J. H. Williams (Independent Labour Party) | 1,089 |

The ILP campaign had been badly organised and poorly supported, with the *Llanelly Mercury* commenting that no 'Labour MP or a Labour leader sent a letter of support to the candidate or made the effort to visit the constituency' during the campaign. The political consequence of standing against the Liberals was noted by James Griffiths, who admitted: 'We brought down upon us the wrath of the Elders of nonconformity for daring to oppose Towyn.'[25] Griffiths' father as well as his contemporaries could not understand how the younger ILP members could support and campaign for a medical man from Burry Port rather than for the icon of the Amman Valley, with the result that, according to James Griffiths: 'We felt that we were unwelcome at the chapel and many young men drifted away.'[26]

It was during this period of electoral conflict, and the inevitable strain between the young socialists and the Welsh nonconformist establishment, that the miners' union began to exert its support for industrial conflict. Strikes over pay had led to the passing of the Coal Mines (Minimum Wage Act) of 1912, and the creation by the new generation of union leaders of an 'unofficial reform movement', underlined in the Noah Ablett-authored pamphlet *The Miners' Next Step*.[27]

The miners' union were also keen to extend educational opportunities for its leading activists and began to provide scholarships for residential courses at Ruskin College, Oxford, but a bitter controversy quickly arose – led by Welsh students, in particular miners Frank Hodges and Noah Ablett, and supported by Ruskin's principal, Dennis Hird – regarding the teaching of Marxist economics, which led to the call for another college for the young leaders of the workingclass.[28] The end result of this bickering was the decision to establish a brand new institution and the beginning of what came to be known as the Central Labour College in London. For the next 18 years, this college trained a large number of talented miners from south Wales, who were given the opportunity of equipping themselves to be potential leaders.[29]

The young band of socialists in Ammanford were by now attracting the attention and financial support of left-wing benefactors such as the flamboyant George Davison, who had made a fortune through his pioneering work with the photographic firm, Kodak.[30] The night Davison visited Ammanford he attended one of the adult education economics classes being run under the auspices of the Central Labour College, and tutored by former Ruskin student D.R. Owen, a miner from Garnant. The class was held in a tiny room belonging to a temperance organisation, and when Davison saw the unsuitable facilities that D.R. Owen had at his disposal, he told the tutor and his students that he would provide them with a much more suitable meeting place.[31] James Griffiths was a student in the class and was absolutely delighted. At that time a large house in Ammanford's High Street, an old vicarage, came up for sale so Davison bought the house adapted it as a centre for the educational and political needs of the young socialists of the area. He also provided them with a well-stocked library of books on socialism, Marxism and anarchism. Davison called the whole building the White House as it was decorated, on his instructions, with a coat of white paint to remind him of his own home on the banks of the River Thames.

The White House (also known locally as *Tŷ Gwyn*) quickly became the centre for socialist activities for the whole of the Amman Valley during the First World War.[32] Educational classes for adults were held there from Monday to Friday and the building was also used for committee meetings. There were get togethers on Saturday nights and then, on Sunday evenings after chapel, there would be a public meeting or a lecture. The group in charge of the White House, the 'Workers Forum', also organised large gatherings to which Christian socialists were invited, such as the Anglican vicar, the Reverend James H. Jenkins of Cilrhedyn, Pembrokeshire; and from the village of Glais in the Swansea Valley, the Welsh Independent minister, the Reverend T. E. Nicholas. Also invited were the Marxists or neo-Marxists, such as Noah Ablett and W. H. Mainwaring from the Rhondda, Dan Griffiths, a schoolmaster in Llanelli, and S. O. Davies, a native of Abercwmboi near Aberdare, but who, during the First World War, was a checkweigher at the Mynydd Mawr Colliery in Tumble. By this time the Workers' Educational Association (WEA) was making its presence felt all over Wales with its remarkably able adult education practitioner, Dr John Thomas, the author of a University of Wales MA thesis on the anthracite coalfield resided in East Carmarthenshire.

The weekend was a time of constant activity at the White House. On Saturday afternoons a market stall shoe trader from Swansea, Harry Evans, would travel to Ammanford to help James Griffiths and his comrades within the ILP in their local campaigning. In his pocket Evans would carry a selection of pamphlets written by Keir Hardie and Philip Snowden, elected as Labour MP for Blackburn in 1906, who was a powerful platform speaker and was popular in the anthracite coalfield. They were also glad to welcome the young journalist W.H. Stevenson from the Swansea Valley, who worked on the socialist weekly *Llais Llafur* and later became the editor of the daily newspaper of the Labour movement, the *Daily Herald*.

James Griffiths also looked forward to the visits and contribution of Johnny Jones from Pontardawe, who had a wonderful command of language, in both song and word. In his addresses he would quote in English from the poetry of William Morris and the American Walt Whitman, and in Welsh from the literary works of T. E. Nicholas. His message, however, never changed from one week to another: to him, socialism was simply the hope of the world. Other visitors included Edgar Chappel from Swansea, later the historian of Whitchurch, Cardiff, who became influential in the life of south Wales, and the local miners' leader, John James, with his inspirational and fiery oratory.

The White House became the refuge of those who were opposed to the First World War,[33] and an iconic focus for the socialists of the ILP, the largest affiliated socialist society to the Labour Party. ILP leaders like Philip Snowden, who worked within the Labour Party, never challenged the so-called unity of the Labour movement by upsetting the party's cautious trade union representatives, and the Labour Representation Committee, established in 1900, had been based on a compromise whereby trade unionists and socialists had agreed to work together under the general banner of Labour. This compromise had not succeeded fully in East Carmarthenshire and, by the time the White House had been established, James Griffiths, as a left-winger, knew that he would be expected to work with the non-socialist right wing of the Labour Party which still had difficulty in discarding their Liberal associations. He was fully aware that building a socialist Labour Party would not be a straightforward and easy task.

**Notes and References**

1. James Griffiths, *Pages from Memory*, p.5.
2. Ibid. 'My father ruled his parliament with the same iron grip with which he held the colliers' tool. I can see the "Stalin" there.'
3. Richard Lewis, *Leaders and Teachers* (Cardiff, 1993), p.45. 'Instead of fighting the orthodox theology within the chapels, many turned their backs on the chapel and even on possible careers as ordained ministers and directed their intellects and energy into the trade union movement and politics, local and national. James Griffiths was profoundly influenced by Campbell's preaching of the social gospel; it seems to have shaped his religious outlook, but it also convinced him that he could best serve God and mankind through the miners' union'.
4. Huw T. Edwards, *Tros y Tresi* (Denbigh, 1956), pp. 57-8. One has to remember that organised religion in the guise of Christianity and all it meant, such as the use of the Welsh language, preserving its culture, listening to sermons, Sunday observance, and temperance was so important in the valleys of Tawe (Swansea), Gwendraeth and Amman, but this did not deter a sizeable number of chapel members from giving their support to the new campaign of the Labour movement and enlisting with the ILP. One can listen to a contemporary historian: 'Clearly the relationship which existed between political and religious belief is complex, and thus the claim that the adoption of socialism or adherence to the SWMF and its counter-culture led automatically

to the abandonment of religion would appear too simplistic'. See Robert Pope, *Building Jerusalem; Nonconformity, Labour and the Social Questions in Wales - 1906-1939*, p.105.

5. NLW James Griffiths Papers E1/13-14, 1908-A Fateful Year; J. Bruce Glasier wrote: 'Socialism! There are those who hate it, there are those who fear it; there are those who doubt it. There are millions who hope for it, rejoice in it and work for it .... Now the movement grows apace in every land, and has become the most formidable political agitation that the world has ever known.' J. Bruce Glasier, *The Meaning of Socialism* (Manchester, 1919), pp. 13-14.

6. Herbert Morgan, 'The Church and Labour – a Symposium', *Welsh Outlook* V, (1918), pp. 95-6, 127-8, 164-6, 198-9.

7. Huw Morris-Jones, 'William Abraham (Mabon, 1842-1922)', *Dictionary of Welsh Bibliography* (London, 1959). Mabon received generous gifts from the anthracite coalfield in 1900, including a gold watch, gold chain, an illuminated address and money. These was presented to him by leaders of the coalfield, such as: Thomas Roberts, Pontyberem; Edwin Phillips, Glyn Neath; John D. Morgan, Gwaun cae Gurwen; and David J. Morgan, Rhos. See NLW MSS 15068 D.

8. Ioan Aled Matthews, *The World of the Anthracite Miner* (PhD University of Wales (Aberystwyth) Thesis, 1995), for the activities of the miners.

9. NLW, James Griffiths Papers. An article on Socialism and Religion.

10. For David Adams, see the biography, in Welsh, by E. Keri Evans and W. Pari Huws, *Cofiant y Parch David Adams* (Liverpool, 1924); W. Eifion Powell, 'Cyfraniad diwinyddol David Adams (1845-1923)', *Y Traethodydd* (1979), pps.162-70.

11. Robert Pope, 'Diwinyddiaeth Cymru a Neges Evan Roberts' in *Codi Muriau Dinas Duw* (Bangor, 2005) pp.37-64.

12. James Griffiths, *Pages from Memory*, p.16.

13. Ibid., pp.18-19.

14. D. Ben Rees, *Dr John Williams, Brynsiencyn, and his Gifts (1853-1921)* (Llangoed, 2009), pp. 17-23.

15. W. F. Phillips, 'Sosialaeth a Christnogaeth', *Y Geninen* (1911), p. 83.

16. According to *Justice*, the organ of the Social Democratic Front, Phillips had the 'mind of a gnat and the soul of a viper'. See also Peter Stead, 'The Language of Edwardian Politics', in Dai Smith (ed), *A People and a Proletariat in Studies in Welsh History 1880-1980* (London, 1980), p.157.

17. The miners' agents John James and S.O. Davies were trained at Gwynfryn School with the intention of entering the nonconformist ministry. See Ioan Matthews, *The World of the Anthracite Miner*, op. cit., p.194.

18. *Llais Llafur* was an essential tool for the Labour movement in the anthracite coalfield, both during the establishment of the Labour Party and to promote ILP activities. For *Llais Llafur*, see Huw Walters, *Canu'r Pwll a'r Pulpud*, pp. 226-7; Robert Pope, 'Facing the Dawn: Socialists, Nonconformists and Llais Llafur 1906-1914', *Llafur*, Vol. 7, No. 3-4, pp. 77-88. South Wales, in particular Carmarthenshire, had no weekly Welsh language newspaper as E. Morgan Humphreys stresses in *Y Wasg Gymraeg* (ed. E. Tegla Davies), (Liverpool, 1944), p. 44.

19. D. Ben Rees, 'David Thomas (1880-1967), Labour Party Pioneer in Wales', *Dictionary of Labour Biography*, Vol. XIII (eds: Keith Gildart and David Howell), (Basingstoke, 2010), pp. 362-372. David Thomas was one of the early devolutionists. He also argued forcefully for Welsh speakers to be involved in the Labour Party. See his booklet, *Llafur a Senedd i Gymru* (Bangor, 1954), p. 6 and 19.

20. D. Ben Rees, 'David Thomas (1880-1967), Labour Party Pioneer in Wales', ibid., p. 363.

21. Ibid., p. 364.

22. James Griffiths, 'Edgar Bassett, A Tribute', *Amman Valley Chronicle*, 27 January 1949; Amanwy, 'Coffa David George y Betws', *Amman Valley Chronicle*, 7 July 1932. I am grateful to Dr Huw

Walters for bringing to my attention these two articles, for both Bassett and George were influential in the Labour Party in Ammanford.

23. James Griffiths gave fewer votes to Abel Thomas and more to Mervyn Peel in *Pages From Memory*, p.17, than they actually received in the December 1910 general election. Not one of the reviewers saw the discrepancy in the reviews of the volume in 1969.

24. James Griffiths, *Pages from Memory*, p. 17.

25. Ibid.

26. Ibid., p. 18.

27. For the background to the *Miners' Next Step*, see David Egan, 'The Unofficial Reform Committee and the Miners Next Step', *Llafur*, Vol. 2, No. 3, 1978, pp. 64-80.

28. Hywel Francis and David Smith, *The Fed: A History of the South Wales Miners in the Twentieth Century*, pp. 20-1.

29. James Griffiths, *Pages from Memory*, p. 20.

30. For George Davison see Brian Coe, 'George Davison: impressionist and anarchist' in Mike Weaver (ed.), *British Photography in the Nineteenth Century* (Cambridge, 1989), pp. 215-41. Amanwy was not at all comfortable with the ideas propounded in the meetings at the White House in Ammanford. When the Centre was opened in October 1913 he noted: 'The socialists of the area moved to their new home Thursday before last, that is to us the Old Rectory. On that occasion these spoke: Davidson, Harlech; D. R. Owen, Garnant; and Jack Griffiths, Cwmtwrch. Woe the day when the ideas that were preached that night will take hold of the *gwerin* [ordinary folk] of Wales'. See Ioan Aled Matthews, *The World of the Anthracite Miner*, p. 282.

31.     D. R. Owen, Garnant, was a vocal member of the Labour movement, a personal friend of James Griffiths, and a member of the Labour Party in Cwmaman from its inception. See 'David Rees Owen: An Appreciation', *Amman Valley Chronicle*, 9 February 1956.

32. T. Brennan, 'The White House', *Cambridge Journal*, January 1954, pp. 243-8; James Griffiths, *Pages from Memory*, pp. 20-1.

33. James Griffiths, *Pages from Memory*, p. 21.

# 5

# War and Marriage

It was a great disappointment to a left-winger and a pacifist of the calibre of James Griffiths, known widely in Ammanford as 'the Agitator', to see Europe heading to war in the summer of 1914.[1]

As a chapel-goer and an ILP member, James Griffiths' pacifism meant a great deal to him, and his own denomination had declared, at its annual gathering in 1913, that 'every war was contrary to the spirit of Christ'.[2] Following the International Socialist Conference of 1907, the ILP, as well as the Labour Party, and indeed the trade unions, had heeded the call to prevent a war with as much moral authority as they could command. After all, Keir Hardie was a committed pacifist and so were many of the other ILP leaders. In 1914, eight years after its formation, the Labour Party was split over its policy towards Germany's invasion of Belgium, with tension and conflict between the socialists in the ILP and the Labourites in the trade unions. The socialists, in the main, were pacifists but the Labourites were ready to follow David Lloyd George, who reluctantly told Welshmen gathered at a meeting in London in November 1914, that 'we are in the war from motives of purest chivalry to defend the weak'.[3]

By the end of August, however, the Labour Party had decided to support the war effort, with a number of left-wingers finally yielding their pacifist position, but Griffiths could not budge on the issue. Saddened by his colleagues' change of view, he was greatly disappointed to see many of his fellow miners volunteering for the conflict, ready to leave the coalfield for the trenches of Flanders to fight for King and Empire, knowing that many would not return alive to the coalfield. Griffiths suffers significant enmity for holding firm to his principles, and even his hero, Keir Hardie, was shouted down for his antiwar stance when he addressed a meeting of miners in his constituency.[4] This took a great personal toll on Hardie who, in 1915, broken-hearted by the tragedy and the lack of unity in the Labour movement, died suddenly.[5] In the subsequent by-election in November 1915, the one-time militant miners' leader from Aberdare in the Cynon Valley, C. B. Stanton, stood as a an Independent Labour candidate on a jingoistic war platform against the miners' nominee James Winstone, the official Labour candidate. Stanton, triumphed with 10,286 votes, a clear majority over Winstone's 6,080 votes.

The loss of Merthyr, the first constituency in Wales to support a Labour candidate, was a heavy blow to Griffiths, as was the news that one of his earlier heroes in the coalfield, Vernon Hartshorn, was a pro-war campaigner. Griffiths explained his frustration thus:

> We, in our own valley, were derided and persecuted as the 'White House gang', the enemies of our country.[6]

He could agree with his friend from north Wales, David Thomas:

*I am conscientiously opposed to everything that destroys human life. I know nothing in the world that is so precious as human life, and I cannot feel justification, under any circumstances, in destroying men's lives for the sake of anything of less value.*[7]

Griffiths stood bravely against the war, as did many of his socialist friends who frequented the White House, but some could not accept pacifism; Griffiths's close friend Edgar Bassett decided to join the army and even fought at the Battle of the Somme.[8] Another supportive member of the White House was Tom Dafen Williams, a native of the village of Llangennech, near Llanelli,[9] who'd moved to the Ammanford area after he had secured a job at the Pantyffynnon Colliery. Called 'Twm Dafen' by his comrades, he was a warm-hearted individual who was as passionate about his rugby as he was the eisteddfod movement, and became a great friend of James Griffiths, who testified to his support as a leading member of the ILP in Ammanford, and later as chairman of the Pantyffynnon Lodge of the South Wales Miners' Union Federation. His laughter and his humour endeared him to the Griffiths family and he called regularly at their home and the smithy, where he tried his best to persuade William Rees Griffiths to leave the Liberal fold and join the Labour camp.

For a time, Tom Dafen Williams used to compete in recitation competitions at local *eisteddfodau,* often travelling to these events with Amanwy, but the Labour Party's agenda soon became his priority. His untimely death, in January 1938 at the age of 50, as a consequence of a mining accident in the Betws colliery, brought sadness to the Griffiths family and a tremendous loss to the Labour Party in the Amman Valley. Amanwy wrote a fine sonnet to Williams' memory under the title, *Hen Arwr* [Old Hero], describing him as an orator with the passion of a prophet who believed in freedom and the rights of the working class.In the hostile atmosphere of wartime, Tom Dafen Williams, James Griffiths and others endeavoured to maintain their pacifist beliefs and their principles in support of peace, social justice, human rights and a world free from war and conflict.[10] The situation was transformed in 1916 when the White House socialists expressed their opposition to military conscription during its passage through parliament. Military conscription was a difficult subject for the Labour Party which, at a conference in Bristol during the last week of January 1916, expressed hostility to conscription in any form. The Women's Labour League and the National Union of Railwaymen moved and seconded a resolution that declared 'its opposition to the Military Service (No2) Bill [the Conscription Bill] and, in the event of it becoming law, decides to agitate for its repeal'. The resolution was, however, neutered by Will Thorne, a pioneer socialist from London who in the 1890s came to Llanelli to organise the workers in the new gasworks into the union he had established. His successful amendment deleted the second half of the resolution, resulting in the party agreeing to accept the Bill if it became an Act. The Labour Party were in increasingly dire straits and, as the months went by, they, under protest, accepted conscription for both single and married men. At the ILP conference in April 1916, a resolution called upon the party to 'reconsider its affiliation with the Labour Party', but this was heavily defeated. The remaining, committed, radical members of the ILP had taken the issue as far as they could and W. J. Edwards from the Cynon Valley, whose autobiography *From the Valley I Came,* reminds us of their dedication:

*It was a crusade demanding all the devotion of a religion. It was less a political philosophy than a deeply spiritual cult. I had seen men and women gladly giving up their hours of leisure to further the cause. Some of the men, far gone with consumption, with death not far around the corner, would stand in the snow and rain giving out leaflets and then hastening an end which, indeed, they met without complaint. Others, because of their work in the ILP branch, lost their job.*[10]

Dr. Alfred Salter, a leading ILP pacifist from London, urged socialists of all nations to refuse support to every war entered into by any government, whatever the ostensible object of the war. There were rebels even within the Liberal fold, including William Llewelyn Williams, MP for Llanelli Boroughs since 1906.[11] He voted against the Conscription Bill and condemned forcefully the actions of his leader, David Lloyd George, who favoured military conscription. To him, Lloyd George had gone much too far.[12]

The monthly journal of the Welsh pacifists, *Y Deyrnas* [The Kingdom], was read in the White House library from the end of 1916 when it was first published, with editorials prepared by Thomas Rees, the Principal of Coleg Bala-Bangor, the Welsh Independent's theological college.[13] He was the most courageous nonconformist of his generation, and supporter of the Labour movement, who commented: 'Political nonconformity is shipwrecked – scattered by its own officers'.

That winter, under the auspices of the Central Labour College, more adult classes were held under the tutorship of D. R. Owen in the Amman Valley, the impact and influence of which incurred the wrath of the newly-launched monthly magazine *Welsh Outlook*. Two thousand young miners became 'out and out enemies of capitalism', claimed the magazine, as a result of the 'propaganda' of tutors like D. R. Owen and Noah Ablett, and ILP evangelists such as T. E. Nicholas.[14] James Griffiths was one of these campaigning miners who, in January 1916, voted in favour of a miners' strike if military conscription became the law of the land.[15] When it did, the British Miners' Federation told the revolutionary-minded miners of south Wales not to strike, but this did not silence the militancy of the coalminers who fought their battle for socialism every inch of the way. Those miners' leaders in the Marxist camp, such as Noah Ablett, A. J. Cook, Arthur Horner and S. O. Davies, would not remain silent, and were delighted, in March 1917, when the dramatic news came of the Bolshevik Revolution in Russia. The miners of Betws and Ammanford sang in celebration:

> *'Workers of the Vale of Amman*
> *Echo Russia's mighty thrust.'*

All over Britain, socialists welcomed the news of the revolution, with one newspaper claiming that it had 'created more joy in Merthyr Tydfil than anywhere else outside Russia.'

On 20 July 1917, 'the Fed' even tried to contact the Labour movement in Germany to create unity amongst workers, as many of the miners felt the need to establish a network of workers' councils on the pattern of the soviets in Russia. On 29 July, Griffiths and Tom Dafen Williams, with two hundred other delegates from the coalfield, travelled to a conference at the Unitarian Chapel in Swansea.[16] Dismayed at the militancy of the south Wales miners who, with constant strike action and industrial unrest, were more militant than workers in any other industry, the Government intervened to ensure that the conference attracted very little publicity. Lloyd George then set up a commission to investigate the origins of the industrial conflict which was causing a great deal of concern in capitalist circles. The report from the two commissioners from Wales, E. L. Chappel and D. Lleufer Thomas (who had strong empathy for the Labour movement), correctly emphasised that 'enmity to Capitalism was part of the philosophy of the majority of miners.'

The report also commented that 'the Labour movement in its entirety was being undermined by the propaganda of a small group of determined men.' While some in Ammanford believed that such a generalisation was true, Griffiths, a Christian socialist, was certainly not on the same wavelength as Noah Ablett, the Rhondda Marxist. Indeed, Griffiths was a reconciler and had friends and contacts in both camps.

The disagreements of 1914 had been serious but, by 1917, there was a completely different atmosphere and many strong-willed leaders in the anthracite coalfield were to be found within 'the Fed'. It was in 1910 that James Griffiths, as a delegate from Gwaith Ucha'r colliery in Betws, had attended, for the first time, the anthracite miners' conference – in the vestry of the Unitarian chapel in Swansea – which represented 60 mines ranging from Rock colliery in the Neath Valley to Hook colliery near Saundersfoot in Pembrokeshire. On the platform were the miners' leaders: Tom Morris, the chairman, from Celliceidrim colliery, Glanaman, who was flanked by the miners' agents, John D. Morgan from Ystalfera, and Dafydd Morgan from Rhos colliery in Tŷ Croes near Ammanford. Also on the platform was John D. Morgan of Cwmgors, the treasurer.

In the front row, next to the platform, sat a row of Lib-Lab stalwarts: Willie Owen from Blaenywaun colliery, Brynaman; William Bevan from Caebryn colliery, Penygroes; Rees Morgan of Brynant colliery, Cwmaman; and Joseph Roberts of Pontyberem. All were loyal defenders of trade unionism and they all addressed the conference in Welsh, signifying that Welsh was the language of trade unionism within the anthracite coalfield.[17]

The conference addressed the miners' main concerns of: the price of the dynamite to destroy the rock face; miners losing five per cent of their pay due to the depressed market; and the seniority rule, in particular in the collieries belonging to Sir William Thomas Lewis (Lord Lewis of Merthyr), yet within the leaders' strategy of 'evolution not revolution' could be summed up in the popular Welsh phrase 'Gan bwyll, mae mynd yn bell' [By taking it slowly, you can go far].

James Griffiths' attitude towards Sir William, however, was clear in the words of a couplet he liked to recite:

> Pan aiff Syr Wil i'r bedd          When Sir Will goes to his grave
> Yr hen golier – ddaw i'w hedd      The old collier will come to his peace

The delegate who always had plenty to say about the price of dynamite was Wil Jones, a miner from Pump Heol, near Llanelli. By 1917, in the heart of the Amman Valley where the pacifists had their stronghold, a trades council – consisting of 10 mine lodges and the local branches of several trade unions – had been formed, despite criticism from the local papers, to look after the interests of trade unionism and Labour.[18] Soon to be known as the Trades and Labour Council of Ammanford and Llandybïe, Tom Dafen Williams was elected as chairman and Griffiths elected as secretary. The treasurer was Evan Bevan, an official at Rhos colliery, who was from a remarkable family of trade unionists from the village of Saron near Ammanford, and of whom Griffiths once commented: 'I have complete faith in him.' The public meetings of the Trades and Labour Council – held on Sundays after the chapels' evening services – in the Palace Theatre, Ammanford, began with a programme prepared at the White House which regularly included guest speakers, and quickly became an important event in the social and political life of the Amman Valley. One of the most popular speakers invited to the Palace Theatre was George Lansbury, a Christian socialist in the tradition of Keir Hardie, who was the MP for the London constituency of Poplar and was a convinced pacifist.

During his speech at Ammanford, Lansbury emphasised that Christian socialists a should acknowledge that every war was a civil war: a war between brothers and sisters. Philip Snowden and his wife Ethel also came to address at least one of these meetings, as did Margaret Bondfield, one of the earliest women to be invited to be a member of the cabinet in the Labour government at the end of the 1920s.

The meetings were organised in the religious tradition of the valleys, opening and closing with uplifting hymns, and were accompanied with a bilingual pamphlet with the words so all those in attendance could sing along. Another item of interest, which pleased the large gatherings, were the solos sung by Gwilym Jones, a miner from Ystradgynlais. He was a first class baritone and Griffiths was always thrilled by his renditions of the spiritual *Go Down Moses – Let My People Go*. The socialist miners and working-class audience were enthralled every Sunday night by these semi-religious, political meetings that inspired them emotionally and intellectually.

In 1917, boundary changes to the East Carmarthenshire constituency gave hope to the ILP in Ammanford, which sensed they were on the threshold of a bright new era. The boundary commissioners suggested the disappearance of the Carmarthen Borough constituency, meaning the Liberal MP, W. Llewelyn Williams, a barrister and author, would lose his seat. Williams decided to stand for the Liberal nomination in the new constituency of Llanelli, against the Reverend Josiah Towyn Jones, but lost the selection contest.[19]

James Griffiths heard that Williams would be willing to contest the new seat in the name of the Labour Party, but nothing, however, came of this idea as Dr. J.H. Williams, who had stood for Labour in 1910, was enthusiastic to stand again. In Llanelli, when the Conservatives heard that Towyn Jones had won the nomination, they decided not to stand a candidate and potentially split the anti Labour vote, so the renowned Welsh nonconformist preacher had another four to five years to enjoy his tenure in the House of Commons.

However, when Arthur Henderson, who had followed Keir Hardie as leader of the Labour Party and who had played an important role in the war cabinet of Lloyd George, decided to leave the Lloyd George coalition and return to his post as general secretary of the Labour Party, the activists were encouraged in their endeavours to find a suitable candidate. Griffiths admitted years later:

> *I regard Arthur Henderson as the saviour of the party not only because he left the coalition but also because he changed the structure and the organisation of the party in 1917-18 and also opened the party to individual members, both men and women.*[20]

The Liberals, in order to keep their grip on the new constituency of Llanelli as they had done in East Carmarthenshire, were very content to receive the support of the Conservatives, their old enemy.[21] This angered the fast-growing socialist support in the constituency who believed the Liberals, like so many of their compatriots in the chapels, had betrayed the long and noble campaigning of the nonconformist radicals, such as one of James Griffiths' heroes, the courageous David Rees, the Welsh Independent minister of Capel Als in Llanelli who had stood up to the Tory establishment in the Victorian era.

When the election was held on 14 December 1918, 34 days after the Armistice, the working men who had survived the war, and now armed with a vote after the extension of the franchise to all men aged over 21, were disappointed to see Lloyd George ignoring them and, in his quest for power, agreeing a coalition with the Conservatives. As a result, the election saw a rift between nonconformity and the Liberal Party, with many of the disillusioned Liberals soon finding a new home in the Labour Party. The campaigning was unavoidably rushed, but it was an election that returned Lloyd George's coalition government with a huge majority.

In Wales, he won 25 seats,[22] and although there had been an extension in the franchise, it was generally a disappointing election for Labour, who were unable to win seats in coalfield seats such as Merthyr, Pontypridd and Llanelli, which all returned a Liberal MP.[23] The result in Llanelli, however, had a silver lining for the Labour Party:

| | |
|---|---|
| Reverend Josiah Towyn Jones (Coalition) | 16,344 |
| Dr. J.H. Williams (Labour) | 14,409 |
| Majority | 1,935 |

The election saw the Labour Party finish a little stronger than in 1910, when it had numbered only 42 MPs, as it now had 60, including one Co-operative MP and two 'unendorsed' Labour MPs. Of the 60, no fewer than 25 were candidates supported and endorsed by the Miners' Federation, and another 24 represented other trade unions. Of the 50 candidates put forward by the ILP, however, only three secured election, and local Labour parties had very disappointing results with only seven of their 140 nominees being successful. Griffiths came to the conclusion that his future was no longer within the ILP but rather in the vanguard of the Labour Party, which, after all, was through and through a party of the trade unions. More importantly, considering his industrial background, half of the trade union representation was drawn from a single union, the one which represented the mining communities of Scotland, England and Wales.

A major development had also occurred in Griffiths' personal life when, a month before the 1918 election, he had married Winifred Rutley.[24] This happy event had been precipitated thanks to an introduction from one of his great friends from Ammanford, Edgar Bassett, who worked for the Co-operative, and had just been transferred to their offices in Basingstoke. Bassett had written to Griffiths a few weeks after starting his new job asking, on behalf of a young girl called Winifred, what books he could recommend that had a socialist message.

During 1915-16, Edgar, James and two other friends, Tommy Thomas and Luther Isaac, had discovered *Germinal*, the novel of the French writer and social reformer, Émile Édouard Charles Antoine Zola, that had been published in 1885. The four Welshmen were immediately enthralled by Zola and eagerly sought out other authors to inspire them.[25] This quest led them to discover other writers of distinction, who had socialism as a living creed, especially H.G. Wells and George Bernard Shaw. Griffiths regarded books and reading as the world of magic, saying: 'I count myself fortunate to have been nurtured in a home which had its own world of books.'[26]

Following the voyage of literary discovery, which also included Antole France, Henri Barbussa, Jack London, James Griffiths wrote, in response to his friend's request, to the Hampshire lass with the greeting, 'Dear Comrade', before signing off with, 'Yours Fraternally'. The letter writing continued and, within a few months, Winifred visited him at Betws. His mother had her concerns, especially when it was clear that her son was serious about this young woman from England, as Winifred had no command of Welsh. After their first meeting, however, she gave him her blessing: '*Mae hi yn dda iawn – o gysidro*' ('She is very good – considering').[27]

Winifred's father, William George Rutley, worked in Potals Mill in Haverstoke, and her mother Rose Rutley (*née* Treacher) was the daughter of a carpenter. They were a family of devout Primitive Methodists, with her father a recognised lay preacher and Winifred playing the organ in the chapel services at Overton in Hampshire. The Methodists and the Congregationalists in Overton had a number of members who were supportive of the Labour Party, and a smaller number who had strong pacifist convictions similar to those of James Griffiths. The two young lovers quickly discovered they had a great deal in common, in particular a strong commitment to the Labour Party and, on 20 October 1918, they were married in the Congregationalist Chapel, Overton, after which they spent their brief honeymoon in Reading.

In the December 1918 election, during which James Griffiths was the agent for the Amman Valley, the Labour Party gained about 2,250,000 votes across the UK, out of the nearly 11,000,000 votes cast. He realised that Labour had a long way to go before it could have the privilege of governing the country, but he also believed that Labour would soon be the alternative opposition to the Tories due to the Liberals sacrificing, for the sake of power, their political principles and burdening their party with a serious problem through the clash of the personalities between H. H. Asquith and Lloyd George. This meant that they were bitterly divided in parliament, as well as in the country. Lloyd George had 127 Coalition Liberals while the other wing, the Asquithite Liberals, had just 34 MPs.

Clearly, the Liberals were in terminal crisis. They had declined from 272 MPs in December 1910, to 161 in 1918, and the vast majority of these were loyal to Lloyd George. Griffiths and his new bride, whom he called Winnie, realised at the beginning of their married life that their shared political journey, with their comrades, promised a new dawn to British politics. It meant the emergence of the Labour Party determined to improve the standard of living for the working class. James Griffiths hoped a new and a better world awaited him.

**Notes and References**

1.  For accounts of the Welsh pacifists in the First World War, see Dewi Eurig Davies, *Byddin y Brenin: Cymru a'i Chrefydd yn y Rhyfel Mawr* (Swansea, 1985); Aled Eurig Davies, 'Agweddau ar y Gwrthwynebiad i'r Rhyfel Byd Cyntaf yng Nghymru', *Llafur*, Vol. 4, No. 4, 1987, pp. 58-68. In the 1930s James Griffiths wrote on the coming of the First World War in August 1914: *'War came like a thief in the night. Our whole life was suddenly undermined, our dreams were shattered, our hopes were destroyed, – and the world has never been quite the same. Half my generation gave its life in the war, and the half that survived lost its confidence'.* James Griffiths, 'Whither Mankind', *South Wales Voice*, 1937, p.4.

2.  The Report of the Welsh Independent Conference at Rhyl (1913), p. 636. By the 1914 conference, held in Merthyr, there was a change of emphasis and opinion among the delegates. They compromised. See *Adroddiad Undeb Merthyr* (1915), pp. 1036.

3.  Thomas Jones, *Lloyd George* (London, 1951), pp. 46-8.

4.  William Evans, 'William Griffiths y Gof', *Amman Valley Chronicle*, 16 February 1928, p. 2.

5.  Kenneth O. Morgan, *Keir Hardie: Radical and Socialist* (London, 1975), pps.263-275, namely chapter 13, 'At Gethsemane' (1914-15).

6.  *James Griffiths, Pages from Memory*, p. 21.

7.  D. Ben Rees, 'David Thomas', in *Dictionary of Labour Biography* Vol.XIII, David Howell and Keith Gildart (eds.) (Basingstoke, 2011), p. 230.

8.  Edgar Bassett fought as a soldier in the Somme and was an opponent of the chapel and its activities. See Huw Walters, *Cynnwrf Canrif*, p.340. Amanwy mentions his memorial service in 1949. 'A rather strange meeting to most of us in Ammanford was held on Sunday night, a memorial to Edgar Bassett, organiser of the Ammanford Co-operative Society. It was organised by the Council of the Labour Party, and there was no reference to religion from beginning to end. The two speakers, great friends of the deceased were Jim Griffiths and Arthur Horner'. Amanwy, 'O Gwm i Gwm', *Y Cymro*, 8 April 1949.

9.  NLW, James Griffiths Papers, A3/1. Tom Dafen Williams was the president of the Ammanford and Llandeilo Trade and Labour Council in 1918. James Griffiths was the secretary.

10. W.J. Edwards, *From the Valley I Came* (London, 1956), pp. 103-4.

11. James Griffiths, *Pages from Memory*, p. 22.

12. Christian socialists, in north as well as south Wales, rebelled against Lloyd George, and became heavily involved in addressing meetings to urge fellow nonconformists to accept pacifism. The layman among them, who was later ordained, was a product of the Liverpool Welsh community, George M. Ll. Davies. The ministers included three ministers of religion Rev. J. H. Howard, Colwyn Bay; Rev. John Morgan Jones, Merthyr Tydfil; and the Baptist, Cernyw Williams, Corwen.

13. W. J. Gruffydd, poet and scholar, a member of the British Navy during the First World War, paid Principal Thomas Rees of Bangor a fitting tribute: 'I learnt to love him before I ever saw him, when I received *Y Deyrnas* when I was in a foreign land during the war; I believe till today that *Y Deyrnas* was one of the most important reasons that Wales did not lose its soul in the days of great insanity'. See W. Eifion Powell, 'Thomas Rees (1869-1926)' in *Dal i Herio'r Byd*, ibid., pps.25-31. Both Thomas Rees and his fellow professor, John Morgan Jones from Bala-Bangor Theological College, joined the Labour Party. See R. Tudur Jones, *Congregationalism in Wales* (ed. Robert Pope) (Cardiff, 2004), p. 227.

14. In an article, T.E. Nicholas said, 'While the war lasts I am going to preach every Sunday against it'. He did so, extremely conscientiously. See Islwyn Pritchard, 'Thomas Evan Nicholas (1879-1971)' in *Herio'r Byd*, ibid., pp. 16-22.

15. NLW, James Griffiths Papers, A3/2. A letter of G. H. Atkinson, 24 Albert Bridge, Battersea, to James Griffiths, dated 16 September 1921. He had been a student of James Griffiths in the National College Labour Class in Battersea. He states: 'For instance, if we'd had 300 men like you in Parliament in 1914, there would have been no war, no DARA, no Emergency Act and no unemployment'.

16. Ibid., A/4, 29-33 Miners Union.

17. Hugh Bevan, *Morwr Cefn Gwlad* (Llandybïe, 1971), p. 44.

18. The *Amman Valley Chronicle* stated on 3 February 1917: 'the workers are at least as patriotic as any other section of the community except, perhaps, those who are imbued with the principles or want of the principles, cf the ILP'. Even *Llais Llafur* was critical of socialists who were pacifists such as Keir Hardie, Philip Snowden and Ramsay Macdonald.

19. R. T. Jenkins, 'William Llewelyn Williams (1867-1922)', *Bywgraffiadur Cymreig hyd 1940* (London, 1953), p.1020, and the obituaries to him by J. Arthur Price in *Cymru*, XXXII, pp. 209-22, and *Welsh Outlook*, 1922, pp. 134-5.

20. James Griffiths, 'Welsh Politics in My Lifetime', in *James Griffiths and His Times* (Ferndale, 1977), p.20.

21. Deian Hopkin, 'The Rise of Labour: Llanelli 1890-1922' in *Politics and Society in Wales 18401922: Essays in Honour of Ieuan Gwynedd Jones* (eds. Geraint H. Jenkins and J. Beverley Smith) (Cardiff, pp. 161-182).

22. For the 1918 general election there is a page which summaries the results in Wales in, Arnold J. James and John E. Thomas, *Wales at Westminster: A History of the Parliamentary Representation of Wales 1960-1979* (Llandysul, 1980), p. 110.

23. NLW, James Griffiths Papers D 3/2 for the results in Llanelli, see also James Griffiths, *Pages from Memory*, p. 22.

24. Ibid., p. 23. James and Winifred agreed on socialism and pacifism. 'Jim wrote to me regularly and I answered every letter. We poured our protests about the war, and the condition of the world around us and about the way people were oppressed.' Winifred Griffiths, *One Woman's Story*, p.68. Winifred was born on 21 May 1895, the second of four children. She died in 1982 and left an estate valued at £61,647. See Carol Jenkins, 'Griffiths, Winifred (1895-1982)', *Oxford Dictionary of National Biography* (Oxford, 2004).

25. James Griffiths, *Pages from Memory*, p. 23. Many of the letters were to do with the War. See Winifred Griffiths, *One Woman's Story*, p. 68.

26. James Griffiths, *Pages from Memory*, p.11.

27. Ibid., p. 21

28. Winifred Griffiths, *One Woman's Story*, p.72.

David Rees Griffiths ( Amanwy), brother of Jim

Jim with his sisters and brother outside the home in Betws

Jim with his ILP comrades. From left to right (back row) Tommy Thomas, Gwilym Jones, Dai Price, J.Ll.E. and (sitting) Jim and Arthur Davies.

Jim after having been appointed a Miner's Agent

A.J.Cook the famous miner's leader

Jim and his wife Winnie and two of their children, Jeannie and Harold.

# 6

# College Days

To James Griffiths' working class generation, formal schooling usually finished in the primary school, with very few furthering their education or training at Grammar School.[1] The usual scenario for working class boys was to leave school at 11 or 12 as did his brother Gwilym Griffiths, or at 13 as did Griffiths himself, although, as the youngest son of the family, he was allowed to continue at school as long as it was possible. By the time Griffiths had started work in the colliery, a new emphasis on adult education was being propounded by serious-minded educational practitioners such as Albert Mansbridge, who established the Workers' Educational Association (WEA) in 1905 with the purpose of teaching the British working-class the key tenets of democracy and citizenship.[2]Mansbridge believed in the values of intellectual reasoning and culture, and his supporters were inspired by the same idealism. One of his foremost followers was William Temple, who became the Archbishop of Canterbury during the Second World War.

Tutorial classes under the auspices of the WEA were set up in the Welsh coalfield between the 1904-5 Religious Revival and the First World War, along with other courses organised by a number of industrial sectors. Classes entitled 'Science and Art of Mining' were held in the evenings to teach the basics of the coalmining industry and were intended to educate and train young men of ability to fill important administrative posts in the collieries. Griffiths joined one of these classes immediately after he began his working life, and he soon became popular with his tutor because of his ability in reading and writing: he was not so talented, however, in the arithmetic and statistical tasks known then as 'reckoning'. It was claimed then that a boy who could not 'reckon' would never become a colliery manager, however, in 1910, James Griffiths met a remarkable young educationalist, Henry F. Northcote, who made a huge impression on the students and subsequently visited Ammanford, annually, for the following nine years. Griffiths found him an inspirational teacher and later praised him in a tribute in the *Amman Valley Chronicle*:

> *He opened our eyes to the wonders of science, he attuned our minds to the philosophies of the sages. In the lecture room he was wonderful. With his fine voice and choice vocabulary, he could at the same time instruct and inspire. Few of us who were privileged to sit at his feet will ever forget those remarkable series of lectures. And our rambles, to Glynhir or Carregcennen. Yes, truly he was one of the deep formative influences in our life.*[3]

Northcote was a role model to Griffiths and his comrades. He had fought against poverty in his early life, as well as deprivation and disease, but due to his socialist convictions he had overcome it all, and finally entered the University of London to study science, where he became a scholar of some repute. Northcote made his last visit to Ammanford in September 1919, before having to undergo two operations in a Manchester hospital that winter.[4] He came through the first operation but the second was too much for his frail body, and he died at Salford Hospital, aged only 37, on 14 April 1920. James Griffiths was devastated and wrote a tribute to Northcote for the local paper, while studying in London.

Griffiths, who had joined the ILP as an 18-year-old, was fascinated with industrial history and economics, and when the WEA organised a class on politics and economics led by one of their talented tutors, William King – using the textbook *Economics for the General Reader* by Henry Clay –Griffiths was enthralled. The students in Ammanford were set the task of writing an essay each month and King was so impressed with Griffiths he encouraged him to enrol on a correspondence course provided by Ruskin College, Oxford.[5] This occurred during the period of conflict at the college between the staff and students, resulting in the establishment of the Central Labour College in London, and the emergence of a new movement called the 'Plebs League' which had its own magazine called *Plebs*.

When the Central Labour College reopened after the First World War, the South Wales Miners' Union offered a number of scholarships for promising working class leaders for a two-year residential college. The Lodge of Ammanford No 1 colliery, known in Welsh as Gwaith Ucha'r Betws, agreed to encourage Griffiths to sit an entrance examination – held in Swansea[6] – which, if successful, would provide him with a scholarship. As he was a married man, Griffiths was extremely fortunate in the support and indeed the encouragement that Winnie, his young wife, gave him. She was determined that he should sit the examination and, if he gained the scholarship, she would go with him to London to provide moral and financial support. Griffiths won the scholarship and had no need to feel lonely for half the students came from the mining valleys of south Wales with much the same background as himself. The College was situated in a large house in Earl's Court and his wife found lodgings in the same area, and landed a job with a firm of cleaners in Bayswater. On his first day at the Central Labour College, in September 1919, there were 40 students, of which 29 were freshers – every one of them in his 20s and early 30s – and everyone having been employed either in collieries, steelworks, or the railways in the industrial heartlands of Britain, such as Wales and County Durham.[7]

The students were to be introduced to the world of socialist ideology, in particular the books of Karl Marx as well as the work of Engels, Kautsky, Bukharin, and Trotsky.[8] They attended formal lectures, were encouraged to read Marxist literature, to participate in discussion groups and lived together as a student body.[9] Thomas Louth, the college secretary, expected all the students to obey the strict rules governing the institution: students were to be called by the morning delegate at 7 am daily – except Saturday when they were called at 6 am. Breakfast was served at 8 am; dinner at 12.30 pm; tea at 4.30 pm; supper between 9.30 pm and 10.15 pm, while on Sundays, breakfast was at 8.45 am and dinner at 12.45 pm. Students were not allowed to drink on the premises or play loud music, and to be in their rooms by 11 pm, although extensions to midnight could be obtained or refused on application to the principal. Every Saturday morning between the hours of of 6 am and 7.30 am, all students were required to clean their rooms, ready for inspection. A senior delegate made a daily tour of inspection between 9 am and 10 am and would report to the principal.

Among the students were a number of very able young men. One of the most charismatic of them all was Aneurin Bevan from Tredegar, the son of David Bevan, a miner and a Baptist, and an avid reader of books who had had a great influence on his sixth child. Apart from the local Sunday School, Aneurin Bevan had only ever attended Sirhowy Primary School where he abhorred the snobbishness of the headmaster, particularly when he humiliated a boy who had been absent from school because he had to share his shoes with his brother. Enraged by the injustice he was witnessing, Bevan picked up an inkwell and threw it with all his might at the headmaster. His biographer Michael Foot claims Bevan was absolutely delighted when the news arrived at his home in Tredegar that he could attend the Central Labour College. He felt that he had won a fortune. Foot adds:

> *The Labour College was then the Mecca of British revolutionaries. Bevan clutched the opportunity. He would go to London to learn – and to teach.*[10]

Disillusionment, however, soon set in:

> *Oddly, his two years at the Labour College left little mark, apart from a rooted distaste bordering on repulsion for London and all its works. He disliked the college routine of early rising, miserable meals and long lectures of which he scamped. The talk into the night was better; "why should I spend precious days at the lectures," he would taunt his more studious fellow students by saying, "when I can find out what you fellows have learnt all the week in a couple of hours".*[11]

In his memoirs, Griffiths is much more appreciative, gracious and grateful than Bevan, and he enjoyed every aspect of college life. In those days he was much more a conformist than Bevan, who regularly clashed with Thomas Louth, the college secretary and a former sergeant major in the First World War. After a few sharp clashes, Bevan conceded to Louth, that he had 'a sea of human kindness flowing invisibly beneath a rugged exterior'.

Another socialist from south Wales who had won a scholarship at the same time was Ness Edwards, later the MP for Caerphilly from 1945 to 1966. Edwards was born in Abertillery in 1897, the son of a miner and, like Bevan and Griffiths, he had been educated as a child in the nonconformist Sunday School, and left primary school at the age of 13 to work down the mine – in his case, at the famous Six Bells colliery. Like James Griffiths, Edwards had also contemplated becoming a nonconformist minister.

At the outbreak of war, he proclaimed himself as a pacifist and later joined the No Conscription Fellowship, an anti-conscription organisation founded by Fenner Brockway. In 1917 he was imprisoned as a conscientious objector and was forced to spend periods at Dartmoor and then at Wormwood Scrubs prisons. In 1919, Ness Edwards won a Miners' Union Scholarship to the Central Labour College, and made the most of his opportunities there. He may have had no time for devolution and rejected the notion of Wales as a nation, but he was supportive of calls for independence from British colonies and sought socialism on a global scale. This dichotomy, in many ways, represented the British Left's brand of international socialism that was a feature of the Central Labour College, and which remains to this day. In his personal papers, as well as in his memoirs *Pages from Memory*, Griffiths acknowledges the kindness of the founder of the college, principal Dennis Hird, the former principal of Ruskin College, who suffered bouts of ill-health and depended on one of his former students, W.W. Craik, to run the college in his absence.[12] Craik naturally became Hird's successor as principal.

Craik's economics tutor had been W.H. Mainwaring, later to become the MP for Rhondda East from 1933 to 1959. A Welsh speaker, Mainwaring introduced his students to syndicalism, something he had plenty of experience of when a member of the Rhondda group – Noah Ablett, Noah Rees, A.J. Cook, and Will Hay – which met before the First World War to discuss the needs of the mining industry. Mainwaring was also responsible for large parts of the syndicalist manifesto, *The Miners' Next Step*, published in Tonypandy in 1912.

The students at the Central Labour College were expected to prepare four essays (from 3,000 to 5,000 words in length) every month, encouraged to go to extramural activities such as open air meetings in parks and street corners, and conduct evening classes under the auspices of the college. First-year students were also required to attend all the lectures held at the college. As is almost always the case in a college of an ideological character, Griffiths also learned a tremendous amount from his fellow students.[13] In his second year, Griffiths was invited to be tutor in charge of three National Council for Labour Colleges (NCLC) classes: one was held in Battersea, the other in Mitcham, and the third in Luton. This meant a long train journey from King's Cross to Luton every week during the length of the course.[14]

Griffiths thoroughly enjoyed his stay in the college, in particular the opportunity to read books on industrial history, sociology, economics, trade union law and practice, as well as attend a course in philosophy, as set out in the *Positive Outline of Philosophy* by the German Marxist, Joseph Dietzgen, which he thoroughly enjoyed.[15] The students learned that the workers in Germany were not completely disillusioned and demoralised with their defeat in the First World War, and that there were progressive politicians like Friedrich Ebert and Philipp Scheidermann who had called for the establishment of a socialist state.
The students met well-known socialists both within the college building and across London, and were given every encouragement to visit the House of Commons to listen to politicians debating and discussing the questions of the day.

It was a privilege for the students to listen to some of the visiting tutors, such as H.N. Brailsford and J.R. Horrabin, who earned his living by drawing maps for the *Daily News*. The students were also well entertained by J.T. Walton Newbold who became in 1922 -3, the MP for Motherwell in the name of the Communist Party, and Clara Dunn who tutored the students once a week in the art of public speaking. As Griffiths noted:

> *She deserves a niche in the story of those days – because she helped Nye Bevan to overcome his stutter and so gave us one of the great orators of our age.*[16]

Griffiths enjoyed the social life of London. With Winifred, he went to political meetings, concerts at the Albert Hall, and theatre productions the Lyric Hammersmith.[17] He also noted going with Frank Horrabin, whom he greatly admired, to see Sybil Thondike acting in the play *The Trojan Woman*. He would regularly go to Marble Arch and Hyde Park Corner to listen to the soap box orators and the hymn singing of the Welsh exiles, which reminded him of Ammanford. Occasionally he would attend King's Cross Welsh Independent chapel to hear the poet-preacher H. Elvet (Elfed) Lewis or go to King's House Congregationalist chapel to hear the accomplished minister, Dr. Orchard.

One of Griffiths' most loyal college friends was Arthur Bryn Roberts from Abertillery, who had won a scholarship to the Central Labour College in 1919 and, as they were next to each other in the study-bedrooms, they were always enjoying each other's company. Like Griffiths, Bryn Roberts had begun work in the colliery aged 13, and after their college days they both returned to the coalfields. Roberts became a miner's agent in the Rhymney Valley in the 1920s before becoming the general secretary of the National Union of Public Employees from 1934 to 1962 (when he had to retire due to ill-health). James Griffiths never forgot the privileges he had enjoyed at the Central Labour College and in London during those two years. In his own style he mentioned his experience:

> *Two years away from the 'hooter', free from hard toil, surrounded by books, engrossed in argument – and sharing of life in the big city.*[18]

While a student in London, Griffiths witnessed one of the most distressing scenes he'd ever seen when he watched the funeral cortège and procession, starting from Southwark Roman Catholic Church, of the Irish Sinn Féin politician Terence Joseph MacSwiney (1879-1920) who had died in Brixton prison on 25 October following a 74-day hunger strike.[19] Griffiths greatly admired the Irish Republican, who had been elected Mayor of Cork whilst on hunger strike, for his bravery and wrote of his experience to his friends in Wales:

> *But even London paused for one brief hour while the slow funeral procession of a fanatic winded through its streets. They might have laughed at MacSwiney hunger-striking: MacSwiney dead silenced them.*[20]

Griffiths strongly believed that the people of England, and therefore its political institutions, never understood the Irish, and the ignorance of the Irish situation also extended to other parts of Britain.

> *The Irish are, to the average Englishman – and, I am afraid, to the average Welshmen – but fanatics. It seems to pass his comprehension why they should want a Republic. He hardly realises that the Irish have a language of their own, he was not told in school nor in the press of the long story of Irish oppression, of the long fight for freedom that still goes on and that MacSwiney gave his life for.*[21]

His distress at the passing of a teacher, poet, dramatist and scholar, in October 1920 was shared by at least one other individual in London that day, a young Vietnamese dishwasher in the Carlton Hotel who broke down and cried when he heard the news, saying: 'A nation which has such citizens will never surrender'. The young dishwasher's name was Nguyen Ai Quoc. In 1941 he adopted the name of Ho Chi Minh and took the liberation struggle to his own country, Vietnam.

Griffiths' letter goes on to compare and contrast Ireland and Wales, both Celtic nations, stating that one still retained, in spite of persecution and largely because of it, its intense national spirit. The other had lost it, except as a political cry for hack politicians[21] such as his own MP for Llanelli, the Reverend Josiah Towyn Jones and, to a lesser extent, the prime minister of the day, another Welshman and a Liberal politician, David Lloyd George. As a young lad of 13, he heard both of them addressing thousands from a platform placed on the cricket field of his home town. They were both fiery demagogues but what had they achieved for the Welsh nation? He heard Lloyd George tell the Welsh people at Ammanford:

> *Wales was to be free; it was to have Home Rule, its language must be preserved; its religion kept pure and made free. I heard of the wonderful contributions of small nations to human thought and culture, and "Gwlad Beirdd a Chantorion" had its own special contribution to make, and must needs be freed to express its soul. Ammanford – yes, Wales – was astir in those days with this gospel.*[22]

Griffiths believed Lloyd George had forgotten that message, yet dedicated himself to a new cause which he believed was greater than the boundaries of any country, a movement that encompassed the whole of humanity, but that did not mean forgetting his Welsh roots:

> *Yet we are not anti-national, yet we love our mother's language and our folk songs, and can honestly raise our hats and bare our heads to Terence MacSwiney, who died for the land of his Mother Machree.*[23]

That MacSwiney was imprisoned in Brixton, and allowed to die as a martyr in his struggle for a 'small nation', by the government of the very politician who had, in full oratorical flow, extolled Wales to work for self-government, made no sense to Griffiths. He also supported the Scottish socialist leader, John MacLean, who had been jailed several times for his opposition to the First World War. MacLean regarded the Irish struggle for independence as part of the struggle for world socialism, as Karl Marx had done 50 years before. In the Central Labour College library, Griffiths had read MacLean's pamphlet *All Hail, the Scottish Worker's Republic* in which he asked:

> *Are we Scots to be used as the bloody tools of the English against our brother Celts of Erin?*[24]

Griffiths read MacLean's call for Welsh workers (as well as their compatriots in England and Scotland) to organise a general strike for the withdrawal of troops from Ireland, and his fury towards his own people for allowing Scottish regiments to be stationed in Ireland to keep the Irish under the authority of Lloyd George and the British State.[25] While Griffiths was not a Marxist, and thus did not totally concur with MacLean, he certainly sympathised with the Scottish leader. Griffiths also showed a great appreciation of the Welsh social and political thinker and pioneer of the co-operative movement, Robert Owen, who first used the term socialism. The combination of left-wing ideology and an affinity with of the political and cultural aspirations of the Irish and Scottish people was very evident in Griffiths' essays and articles, especially when he returned home to the anthracite coalfield.

This Celtic radicalism led to clashes with Fred Thomas, the editor of the weekly *Amman Valley Chronicle*, and their fierce correspondence brought him friends as well as alienating others. In a letter to the editor on 23 March 1922, Griffiths condemned British Imperialism and its symbol, the Union Jack, via a basic question:

> *What does the "Union Jack" symbolise today? Exploitation of the poor at home, and even more ruthless exploitation of the poor in the Colonies. Ask Ireland, Egypt, India, and the Rand what the Union Jack stands for, and you'll get your answer: Black and Tans, Dyerism and "Nigger" driving.*[26]

His political education at the Central Labour College had certainly given him confidence and certainty when identifying injustice. It had also now given him a vision. The Welsh historian Dr J. Beverley Smith notes Griffiths' new, more strident outlook:

> *These writings suggest that it was the Labour College rather than the White House which made the more significant breach from earlier attitudes and which, for a while, served to bring within his own experience, and that of his immediate kindred, something of the tensions to which many of his contemporaries could bear testimony.*[26]

The Marxist influence of the Central Labour College was undoubtedly very strong, but Griffiths remained true to the Christian socialist upbringing of the Amman Valley: the theology of Reverend R.J. Campbell, the ethics of Jesus and his Kingdom, and the basic socialism propounded by Keir Hardie. In the Central Labour College he was also introduced to the poetry of William Morris and the writings of Edward Carpenter, and one can discern Griffiths' passionate socialism in an address he gave, as a student, to the Young People's Society of Christian Temple Chapel in Ammanford. He was first and foremost a Christian socialist, a combination of the passion of Keir Hardie and the moderate approach of trade unionists from the Welsh nonconformist background.

His brother Amanwy gives us a glimpse of the atmosphere of those days in his Welsh prose when writing about the Sunday School classes in Christian Temple chapel between 1905 and 1912. Many of the young men who attended the Sunday afternoon class were quite orthodox in their beliefs while the others were much more radical, claiming that Jesus was a social pioneer. 'Give the people bread' was the attitude of half the class, while the others prayed for a vision of the Cross of Calvary. Amanwy adds:

> *Dyddiau bendigedig oedd y rheini. Dyddiadau'r oriau byw mewn byd a bywyd. [Those were wonderful days. They were days when we lived in the world and in life.]*[27]

His younger brother James would agree that 'those were wonderful days', and the two years in the Central Labour College with its academic, Labour orientated left-wing syllabus taught him a great deal, as did the rich, varied social life and extra-curricular activities it encouraged.

The college made Griffiths very ambitious for change and his role in achieving it. He even stood as a miners' agent in the anthracite coalfield whilst a student in London, but was well beaten in the second ballot. [28] This clearly indicated that he was ready to leave his job as a miner and seek a role in the trade union. His apprenticeship at Christian Temple, the White House and the Central Labour College in London was over and he faced the future equipped to be an effective leader of men.

## Notes and References

1. NLW, James Griffiths Papers DE 4/3. This is what Griffiths himself said in a reference to the Gwynfryn Academy and why he never went there as his father and himself thought he would: 'That was the plan and while the first stage began to emerge, the wind of change which blew through the valley in a few years' time carried me away from the road which was to lead to the pulpit'. He acknowledged before the annual conference of the National Union of Mineworkers' in 1951 that religious nonconformity had been responsible for the rise and the strengthening of the union. See J. Griffiths MP, *The Labour Government: A record of achievement* (London, 1951), p. 7. He also hoped that the delegates to the union still treasured the Bible and reminded them of the Scriptures: 'I hope you are still a Bible-reading conference', p. 3.
2. C. R. Williams, *The South Wales District of the Workers Educational Association 1907-1957* (Cardiff, 1957), pps.1-24. According to the bibliophile Bob Owen, Albert Mansbridge, the founder of the WEA, was one of the 'most endearing men that I ever met'. See Bob Owen, 'Albert Mansbridge', *Lleufer*, Winter 1952, Vol. 8, No. 4, p. 181. One has to admit, though, that the WEA had not been as efficient or successful in Wales from 1906 to 1914 as it was in England. See Richard Lewis, *Leaders and Teachers*, p. 14, and see the *The Annual Report of the WEA for Wales*, the fifth report, 1911-1912.
3. J. Griffiths, 'The Late Henry F. Northcote', *Amman Valley Chronicle*, 13 May, 1920.
4. Ibid.
5. James Griffiths, *Pages from Memory*, p.24
6. NLW, James Griffiths Papers A1/8. The examiner was W. W. Craik. The successful applicants from the anthracite coalfield were James Griffiths from the Gwaith Ucha'r Betws colliery; John Llew Evans from Wernos colliery, Thomas Evans from the Tareni colliery and R. Glyndwr Thomas from the Gelliceidrim colliery. James Griffiths has no reference in his autobiography to the other three who entered the Central Labour College at the same time as him.
7. The history of the College is to be found in W.W. Craik, *The Central Labour College 1909-29: a chapter in the history of adult working-class education* (London, 1964).
8. NLW, James Griffiths Papers A1/15, a volume with the words *The Labour College, 1922* on its spine.
9. Ibid.
10. Michael Foot, *Aneurin Bevan: A Biography, Volume One 1897-1945* (London, 1967), p. 37.
11. Ibid., pp. 37-8. For the Louth confrontation with Bevan, see NLW John Lloyd Williams Papers (MP for Kelvingrove 1945-50), a fellow student at the college with Bevan and Griffiths. See Box 1/4.
12. James Griffiths, *Pages from Memory*, p. 25.
13. George Phippen, a fellow student from south Wales, acted as secretary for the Welsh students in their contact with the South Wales Miners' Federation.

14. Ibid., p. 25. See also, Tessa Blackstone, 'The Boy Who Threw an Inkwell: Bevan and Education', *The State of the Nation: The Political Legacy of Aneurin Bevan*, Geoffrey Goodman (ed.) (London, 1977), pp. 156-178.

15. Ibid.

16. James Griffiths, *Pages from Memory*, p. 25. J. T. Walton Newbold rejoined the Labour Party in 1924 and was their unsuccessful candidate against Winston Churchill at the Epping Constituency in the 1929 General Election.

17. Winifred Griffiths, *One Woman's Story*, p. 88.

18. *Amman Valley Chronicle*, 22 April 1920.

19. Jim Griffiths, 'Terence MacSwiney and Wales', *Amman Valley Chronicle*, 11 November 1920.

20. Ibid.

21. Ibid.

22. Ibid.

23. Ibid.

24. Ibid.

25. John Maclean, *All Hail, the Scottish Workers Republic* (Glasgow, 1920), p. 36.

26. James Griffiths, 'Union Jack', *Amman Valley Chronicle*, 23 March 1922.

27. NLW Amanwy Papers, *Dyddiau yr Ysgol Sul* [The Sunday School Days]. Professor J. Beverley Smith calls attention to the influence of the Labour College in London on his articles to the local paper, *Amman Valley Chronicle*. See J. Beverley Smith, 'James Griffiths: An Appreciation', *James Griffiths and his Times* (Ferndale, 1978), p.75. By then Griffiths was regarded as a leading left winger within the Labour Party in Ammanford and the anthracite coalfield. The influence of Marxism, an integral part of the Labour College, was very evident, but as Dr K. O. Morgan maintains, he never lost his love for his Welsh roots and the values of the Betws community. 'New left-wing leaders like James Griffiths were as staunch in their commitment to the traditional Welsh culture and the values of community and kith-and-kin relationship as ever the pre-war Liberals had been.' See Kenneth O. Morgan, 'Welsh Politics 1918-1939' [in] Trevor Herbert and Gareth Elwyn Jones (eds), *Wales between the Wars* (Cardiff, 1985), p.108.

28. In the first ballot, Jack Thomas had 3,028 votes, Rees Morgan 1,904, with James Griffiths coming in third with 1,169 votes. On the second ballot, Jack Thomas had 6,715, (40%), James Griffiths was second with 4,311 (25.7%) and William Jones 3,108 (18.5%). See Ioan Aled Matthews, *The World of the Anthracite Miner*, op. cit., p.318.

Aneurin Bevan addressing a meeting at Deeside in support of Eirene White

# 7

# Labour Party Agent

James Griffiths graduated from the Central Labour College in 1921, returned to Wales and both he and his wife found a home from home with Edgar and Dolly Bassett in Heol Las, Ammanford.[1] By this time Edgar was among the large number of socialists who had left the chapel. In his case it meant leaving an institution where his father and his brother had dedicated their lives as ministers of religion.[2] Griffiths was soon elected Chairman of the Lodge at *Gwaith Ucha'r Betws* (Ammanford colliery No.1), which meant at least an extra hour every day to deal with complaints and matters that concerned the miners.[3] He also took on the role of teaching during the evenings. At the end of the afternoon shift he would return to Heol Las to wash himself in a tub by the fire and enjoy a meal with his young wife before going out to teach an evening class. He had four evening classes every week: one in Ammanford, the second in Llandybïe, the third in Blaenau and the fourth in Tŷ Croes – all within reasonable walking distance of his temporary home.[4] In addition to his union and teaching duties he was also busy with Labour Party administration within the new constituency.

On 24 March, the Local Decontrol Bill became an Act with the practice ceasing on 1 April 1921. This left the Miners' Federation under its President, Robert Smillie, in a crisis. Both the Federation and the owners were at a complete deadlock with the miners having been without pay for three months. The owners had a definite programme, of extending working hours, cutting wages and reducing the retail price of coal, in order to win back the domestic as well as the export market.

The Miners' Federation asked for the help of the Triple Industrial Alliance, and on 8 April, the Railwaymen and Transport Workers voted in favour of combined strike action in support of the miners.[5] Frank Hodges, the Secretary of the Miners' Federation, was placed in an impossible position when he addressed a meeting of his fellow MPs, and Lloyd George seized on what Hodges had said as an offer to negotiate, inviting the Miners' Executive to discuss the whole affair with him. The Miners' Executive, however, disagreed with Frank Hodges as well as with Lloyd George and their stance brought on a crisis, when the Railwaymen and Transport Workers asked the miners to modify their attitude.

On 15 April 1921 – 'Black Friday' – the Miners' Executive pursued their hardline approach, and the triple alliance was split apart. 'Black Friday' signified the defeat of industrial left-wing and was to have serious consequences. A sense of anger and disillusionment set in among the moderate miners and left Griffiths and his colleagues feeling angered and frustrated by the betrayal of their trade union comrades.

He also saw clearly the potential consequences of mechanisation within the anthracite coalfield. Before the First World War, the use of coal-cutting machinery was minimal, but colliery owners knew that the miners, whatever their strength and work ethic, could not compete against the new machinery. The increasing use of electricity was another great improvement, but the most revolutionary technical changes occurred in the handling of coal at the pit – head.  South Wales had not been innovative enough compared with coalfields in Germany, France and other European countries.  Things changed with the introduction of washeries, new machinery which meant the need for less miners. Griffiths decided to leave the mining industry when he saw new opportunities within the Labour Party particularly the opportunity to serve the Llanelli constituency in 1922. The Llanelli Divisional Labour Party decided to appoint a full-time agent. Griffiths applied and was surprised that so many men of his calibre wanted the job.[6] He was appointed from a strong field and began his job in September 1922. Offices were provided for him above the shoe shop in the main thoroughfare of Llanelli, though he had to provide most of the furniture himself, including a writing desk. He knew that a political victory for Labour could be achieved and the opportunity came suddenly for him. Lloyd George had become unpopular because of his arrogant attitude to the selling of honours. His Conservative partners felt that they had no option but to force him to resign on 19 October 1922, and the following day Bonar Law became Prime Minister. The Labour Party had been on the alert, though James Griffiths had very little time to get ready. Dr J. H. Williams was again ready to be a candidate and was very enthusiastic to stand at the General Election.[7] He had stood in four elections and he was admired for his tenacity, though he was not at all popular with most of the miners and with a section of the Labour activists.

Griffiths realised that as a Labour agent he had to do three things for the forthcoming parliamentary election.[8] Firstly, he had to produce posters to be handed out throughout the constituency; secondly he had to inspire enough volunteers to canvas on behalf of the candidate especially for the vote of the miners and their families; and, thirdly, he had to arrange as many public meetings as possible. Among those who volunteered was a young woman who was pregnant. She was his own wife, Winifred Griffiths.[9] His brother Amanwy also volunteered and was asked to prepare an appropriate message in Welsh to place on the posters. He came up with the slogan:

*Mae'r Doctor sy'n gwella clwyfau dyn yn abl i wella clwyfau'r byd*

[The Doctor who heals the wounds of man is able to heal the wounds of the world.][10]

The Liberal MP, the Reverend Josiah Towyn Jones, decided to retire after ten years as a House of Commons politician and his successor as a parliamentary candidate came from a well-known Liberal family in Llanelli. George Clark Williams, a barrister who later became a High Court judge, was a strong candidate and was expected to retain the seat for the Liberals.[11]

In 1922 the Labour Party fought over two-thirds of all the seats in Great Britain, that is 414, as against 361 in 1918. At the dissolution of Parliament, the Labour Party held 75 seats; it lost 19 of them, but gained 86 other constituencies, including Llanelli.[12] The result, announced on the balcony of the Town Hall, was as follows:

Dr J. H. Williams (Labour)   22,213
G. Clark Williams (Liberal) 15,947

Majority                               6,266

The Labour MPs numbered 142, almost doubling in numbers since 1918. Griffiths was delighted with the result and also intrigued that one of his former tutors, J. T. Walton Newbold from the Central Labour College, had won Motherwell for the Communist Party in a four-cornered contest.In the new House of Commons, the miners had increased their representation to 42, and the number of trade union nominees had risen to 85 while the ILP had won 32 seats. The anti-war leaders against the First World War who had been defeated in 1918 regained seats in the new House, and the Labour Party made its greatest gains in Scotland, where the ILP was exceedingly active and popular. There were also large gains in Yorkshire as well as in south Wales, two other areas where the ILP were in the vanguard of the political struggle.

The task of the Labour agent was to look after the interests of the Labour Party branches and the individual members, as well as keeping in close contact with the different societies and communities that made up the constituency.

Griffiths's wife was as enthusiastic for the Labour Party as her husband. It was an ideal partnership. They moved from Ammanford to live in Llanelli and later in Burry Port. It was in Llanelli that their first child was born on 19 February 1923, a daughter named Jeanne Margaret who passed to glory in 1997. Their life had completely changed.[13]

James Griffiths saw the need for a regular newsletter, as a means of information and propaganda for the mining communities. This is how the Llanelli Labour News came into existence. It was to be a four-page newspaper, prepared centrally by the Labour Party.[14] Fifty per cent of the paper was to be devoted to the Labour Party and another fifty per cent kept for local news. In the constituency, Griffiths was the editor and the circulation manager as well as the distributor. He was able to get a number of young socialists to be members of the editorial board and also to act on the executive committee of the Llanelli Labour News. For a brief period, the paper proved a great success. The circulation rose to 10,000 copies a week and like many other similar ventures it survived only while its editor was heavily involved. But it worked well while Griffiths was the Labour agent in the Llanelli constituency, and when he left in 1925, it ceased publication.

Fighting General Elections was Griffiths's main contribution for the next three years.[15] The 1922 Government did not survive long, though the Tories had a majority of seventy-seven in the House of Commons. But Griffiths was glad of the development of the Labour Women's Section within the Labour Party. By the end of 1922 there were more than 1,000 Women's Sections in Britain with a membership of over 120,000. The growth of the organisation was an asset, and Griffiths knew that the women in his constituency were the backbone of the

Labour Party, especially in the town of Llanelli.[16]He also interested himself in the organisation of the young socialists and got them involved in a useful manner in the furtherance of the Llanelli Labour News. The work of the Youth Sections within the local branches was to be 'mainly recreational and educational' and they were encouraged by Griffiths. They gave him their full support during the 1922 election campaign.

Another General Election was held in 1923, only a year after the last one, and the dissolution of Parliament by Stanley Baldwin caught the Labour Party off guard in most constituencies where there were no full time agents.[17] The election took place on December 6 and the Liberals had an excellent candidate in R. T. Evans, and Major Beaumont Thomas, a high ranking officer in the First World War, stood for the Conservatives. In 1923 the Labour Party did well for the second year in succession in Llanelli:

Dr J. H. Williams (Labour)          21,063

R. T. Evans (Liberals)          11,765

Major Beaumont Thomas (Conservative) 5,442

Majority   9,928

Labour gained 63 new seats, raising the strength of the party to 191 while the Conservatives secured 258 seats and the Liberals polled nearly as many votes as Labour, but secured only 158 seats. Therefore, the Conservatives were the largest party, but they were outnumbered by the Labour and Liberal parties combined. The Liberals, through H. H. Asquith, decided to offer Labour, as the second largest party in Parliament, the chance of forming a minority government.

The Labour Party, under Ramsay MacDonald, decided to accept office.[18] Asquith had given Labour their big chance and Ramsay MacDonald, who had won the Welsh seat of Aberavon, was regarded in Labour Party circles as the Messiah mainly for his oratory and charisma. An illegitimate child from a Scottish background, he was the symbol of success, how the poverty of the working class could be overcome by determination and ability. And in the short period they were in power, the Labour Government tackled some difficult problems. Housing was a huge problem, and the successful enactment of John Wheatley's Housing Act gave additional subsidies to local authorities who were prepared to build houses to let at controlled rents. It made a very important contribution towards the solution of the housing problem in the cities which took up the scheme, in particular Birmingham, London and Liverpool. The Government did well in the educational world with Charles Trevelyan at the Board of Education. It was less successful on behalf of agricultural workers because of Liberal opposition. Ramsay MacDonald, acting as both Prime Minister and Foreign Secretary, had his successes but also his failures, in particular his handling of Indian and Egyptian affairs. Lloyd George was the chief architect of the collapse of the Labour Government, which lost a confidence vote in the House of Commons after just nine months in office. Dr J. H. Williams and his agent knew that the October 1924 election was going to be a difficult one. Griffiths arranged sixty-one public meetings for Dr Williams in the constituency in the space of just eight days. The topics emphasised in Llanelli were peace, unemployment, the need for housing and the value of brotherhood within the working class.

During the election campaign MacDonald was involved in what became known as the Zinoviev Letter affair. [19] The letter was said to have been written by Zinoviev, head of the Comintern, to the Central Committee of the British Communist Party, urging the adoption of subversive action as far as the armed forces were concerned. It also advocated military insurrection in the working class areas of Britain. MacDonald was in Manchester the day the Foreign Office received the letter and he agreed to sign a letter of protest to the Russian Ambassador in London. But the whole affair was badly handled by the Foreign Office, as well as by the Labour Party leader. The letter was published by the Daily Mail as if it were authentic on Saturday October 25, the very day Ramsay MacDonald was visiting Llanelli on his campaign trail. Many London-based journalists came to the town as they expected MacDonald to make a statement on the so-called Zinoviev Letter. Griffiths was pestered by these journalists in his office on the Saturday afternoon and had some respite when he promised them an opportunity that evening to question MacDonald before the public meeting. The whole affair was a plot between the Daily Mail, the Tories, and officials within the Foreign Office to make it impossible for the Labour Party to gain an electoral advantage.

In reality, this was an impossible situation. MacDonald had been asked to address half a dozen meetings in the constituency. Some of the journalists decided to go and get hold of him before the final meeting. When it came time to attend the last meeting of the campaign in Llanelli, the Market Hall was packed.[20] Hundreds of people were unable to get in. When MacDonald arrived, the large gathering broke out to sing the optimistic Welsh hymn of Watcyn Wyn, 'Rwy'n gweld o bell y dydd yn dod' [I see from afar the day coming.] The large gathering had been inspired by his oratory and after the Prime Minister had left the town, the Labourites of Llanelli still carried on singing the hymns of faith until the early hours of Sunday morning.

Griffiths called once more at his office after the Market Hall meeting. Within a few minutes, he heard a knock on the door and a young journalist walked in and told the agent: I belong to the Party and I came here feeling sure that Ramsay would announce that he had suspended the Foreign Office official, a man named Gregory, who had issued the 'Red letter' to the press and denounce the letter as a forgery. It's too late now, he added, he's let us down![21]

The journalist left the room without disclosing his identity to Griffiths. The publication of the Foreign Office note placed the Labour candidate in Llanelli and elsewhere in a difficult position. The most extraordinary thing of all is that MacDonald on that Saturday in Llanelli did not explain himself or point out that the letter was a forgery, and for the next two days, he kept quiet. This made the whole sordid affair ten times worse. On the Sunday he was still not communicating with Fleet Street. On the Monday, two days before the polling, he left the whole affair hanging in mid-air, and ignored the important point, which was simply the question of whether he endorsed the content of the statement from the Foreign Office or not.

The letter, and in particular the note, gave the Conservatives a trump card in the final days of the election. Every Labour candidate felt badly let down and made to look as if they were fellow travellers. James Griffiths never forgot the incident. J. H. Williams, especially as he had only won the selection by a whisker, could have lost his seat. His majority decreased. But he had enough loyal supporters for him to hold on to his seat. The result was as follows:

Dr J. H. Williams (Labour) 20,516

R. T. Evans (Liberal)        18,257

Majority    2,259

MacDonald had behaved dismally. Griffiths had great empathy with those socialists who argued loudly that MacDonald's action showed a clear lack of respect for the Labour candidates. The betrayal of the Labour movement and the sadness remained with him, and was aggravated further by the fact that MacDonald shielded the official in the Foreign Office, a Mr Gregory. To MacDonald, this officer had acted in the best interest of the party, believing implicitly that the letter could not be allowed to be published without a Government note to offset it. The officials had acted in an underhand way, but MacDonald did not condemn or reprimand them. Nor did he admit to anyone, including himself, that he had showed a total lack of judgement. There is no doubt that the Zinoviev Letter, MacDonald's antics and the behaviour of some Foreign Office bureaucrats as well as the proprietor, editor and journalists of the Daily Mail did tremendous harm to Labour. The enemies of Labour in the Tory supporting press had made sure that the publication of the letter was a lastminute election scoop.

It was difficult to understand the situation, but in Llanelli, Labour activists were stunned. Dr J. H. Williams kept his seat through the organisational skill of James Griffiths, but many outstanding Members of Parliament lost their seats, including Margaret Bondfield, Frank Hodges, Emanuel Shinwell, and Herbert Morrison. Every one of these Labour politicians except Bondfield were the victims of Liberal-Tory pacts in constituencies where there were three-cornered fights at the previous election. They tried this trick in Llanelli but it did not succeed due to effective work by Griffiths and his canvassers. The election result – which was rather dismal for Labour, to say the least, meant that the constituency could not afford to keep a full-time agent for much longer.[21]

Griffiths realised that he had to look for another job. The opportunity came to him to return to his first love, to serve the miners and their families. The coal industry had done extremely well while he had been a political agent but the competition from Europe was posing problems. Poland had not been able to dig coal in the manner it had done before the war, while German coal production had come to a halt during the French occupation of the Ruhr. In May 1924 British miners secured a better wage agreement, partly due to the sympathetic support of the Labour government.

In 1925 Griffiths saw an advertisement for a miners' agent under the auspices of the Anthracite Miners' Association, and he applied immediately to be once more among men for whom he had the greatest admiration. To James Griffiths, they were the heroes of the coalfield. He would have agreed with Colin Cross, the biographer of Philip Snowden, who wrote of the miners in this period:

Undertaking the most dangerous form of industrial work, with accident and disease constant companions, the miners had yet built up communities of culture, enlightenment and generosity. Their employers for generations had stood as the exemplars of the worst aspects of capitalism, and yet the miners had avoided violence in their policies and built up an idealistic political movement based on values of peace and compassion.[22]

But they were on the verge of a crisis. There was a hard struggle on the horizon. The Polish and German coal industries had made a comeback and the British coalfields were running at a loss. But the new miners' agent - like his heroes at the collieries – was never afraid of a struggle.

## Notes and References

1. Mrs James Griffiths, *One Woman's Story*, p. 91.
2. See, Amanwy 'O Gwm i Gwm', *Y Cymro*, 8 April 1949.
3. James Griffiths, *Pages from Memory*, p. 45. 'The ten years I spent in the service of the Welsh miners were some of the happiest of my life. For me the coalminers are the salt of the earth'. James Griffiths kept in his archives an important booklet. See NLW, James Griffiths Papers, LA 4/2, that is John Thomas, *The Miners' Conflict with the Mineowners* (London, 1921), pp. 1-70. The preface was written by George Baker, MP.
4. Mrs James Griffiths, ibid, p. 92.
5. Robert Taylor, The TUC: From the General Strike to New Unionism (Basingstoke, 2000), pp. 6-7
6. A full list of those who applied for the post of Agent is found in the NLW James Griffiths Papers A3/3. The name of Emrys Hughes, Abercynon, is to be found. He stood as a Labour Parliamentary candidate in Bosworth in 1923 and was elected as MP for South Ayrshire between 1946-69.
7. Dr J. H. Williams was not the preferred choice of the miners or the union as he was considered too old and not suitable. It was James Griffiths who saved him from being deselected, as Dr Deian Hopkin reminds us: 'Dr Williams survived as candidate largely because of the appointment by the constituency Labour Association of an able new organiser, James Griffiths, chosen out of a field of over 140 applicants from all over Britain. He brought vigour and political flair to the organisation but above all, he helped to mollify some of the internal critics. In his days as Secretary of Ammanford Trades Council, he was noted for his fiery left-wing views, and these gave him some cachet with the hard left. On the other hand, he was also emerging as a supreme pragmatist, highly acceptable to the trade unions, in whose ranks he would shortly rise high. For the moment, his contribution to the progress of the Labour Party was to shore up support for J. H. Williams, thereby imposing some kind of order on the movement. James Griffiths's appointment did not come too soon'. See Deian Hopkin, *The Rise of Labour: Llanelli 1890-1922*, p.179.
8. Arnold J. James and James Thomas, Wales at Westminster, ibid., p. 112 and p. 132. A great change happened to the Labour Party in 1918 as the party accepted for the first time individual members. See A. J. P. Taylor, English History 1914-1945 (Harmondsworth, 1970), pp. 334-5. 'Before 1918

the affiliated societies, political as well as industrial, could take their own line over policy without fear of embarrassing a future Labour government. The ILP for example could oppose the War, the miners could demand nationalisation of the mines. Now the Labour government wanted loyal followers and a free hand for themselves'.

9. Mrs James Griffiths, *One Woman's Story*, p. 95.

10. James Griffiths, *Pages from Memory*, p. 49.

11. Dewi Watkin Powell, George Clark Williams, Y Bywgraffiadur Cymreig 1951-1970 (London, 1997). His hope of keeping the seat for the Liberals was in doubt for the General Election of 1922. See A. J. P. Taylor, ibid., p. 254, 'The General Election of 1918 had been a plebiscite in favour of Lloyd George. The General Election of 1922 was a plebiscite against him.'

12. James Griffiths, *Pages from Memory*, p. 49.

13. Mrs James Griffiths, ibid., p. 96.

14. NLW, James Griffiths Papers A3/6, there are copies of the newletter, Llanelli Labour News, in his archives.

15. David Butler and Anne Sloman, British Political Facts, 1900-1975, (London and Basingstoke, 1975), p. 183.

16. It was not easy to win seats on local councils in the colours of the Labour Party. James Griffiths failed in Ammanford as his wife did in Burry Port. Mrs James Griffiths, ibid., p.99. NLW, James Griffiths Papers. Copy of Y Cymro, 8 November 1924. There was financial loss as a result of the 1922 General Election. See A 3/4 in the Griffiths papers. The Labour Party was extremely poor in the Llanelli constituency, they could not even buy the necessary furniture for the new Agent's office. James Griffiths himself had to bring his own desk to the office. See Mrs James Griffiths, *One Woman's Story*, p. 94.

17. James Griffiths does not refer at all to George Maitland Lloyd Davies who won the University of Wales constituency at the 1923-4 General Election and allied himself with the Labour Party. He was a pacifist of great renown in Wales and one would expect a fellow pacifist to refer to his victory. Deian Hopkin, The Rise of Labour: Llanelly, 1890-1922, p.181. 'More important, at the 1923 General Election, James Griffiths, the Labour agent, spent only half as much money as in 1922 and yet managed to hold up the Labour vote, with the Conservatives belatedly putting up a candidate, Labour secured a majority of nearly 10,000 over the Liberals'. As James Griffiths was a full time Labour agent, he was able to gather a great deal of authority into his hands. See Christopher Howard, 'Local Labour Party expansion in the 1920s', ibid., p. 78. 'As many parties realised without a secretary there was no effective organisation, and trade union officials were often the only people available for party work during the day'. Howard names James Griffiths as an example to prove his point as to the efficient organisation. See John Davies, *Hanes Cymru*, p. 525 for the 1924 General Election.

18. Ramsay MacDonald was regarded as one of the charismatic socialists. He was looked upon as one of the 'gods'. See Christopher Howard, 'Expectations born to death: local Labour Party expansion in the 1920s' in Jay Winter (ed.), *The Working Class in Modern British History: Essays in Honour of Henry Pelling* (Cambridge, 1983), p.73 and p.273. That was the opinion of another Labour activist who assisted MacDonald in Aberavon, Llewellyn Heycock. See the entry on him that I prepared for NLW Biography on-line. The historian A. J. P. Taylor has rescued MacDonald from being condemned without hope. To him he was unique: 'With all his faults, he was the greatest leader Labour has had, and his name would stand high if he had not outlived his abilities'. See A. J. P. Taylor, *English History 1914-1945*, p. 261.

19. James Griffiths, *Pages from Memory*, p. 52. For the background, see R. D. Worth, 'The Mystery of the Zinoviev letter', *South Atlantic Quarterly*, October 1950, 49/4, pp. 441-53.

20. NLW, James Griffiths Papers A 3/6. Llanelly Labour News. A concert was arranged at the Market Hall, Llanelli, with the Unemployed Miners Choir of Blaina, Monmouthshire being invited to the final meeting of the Election campaign. The sum of £2-11-8 was collected for their fund. The Liberal Party spent the sum of £336-4-0 in the Election campaign of 1924. The expenses of the Liberal Agent came to £75 while James Griffiths's expanses as the Labour Party agent came to £20. See A 3/9.

21. James Griffiths, *Pages from Memory*, p. 52.

22. Colin Cross, Philip Snowden (London, 1966), p. 218.

# 8

# Miners' Agent and Leader

In the National Library of Wales among the James Griffiths papers there is a letter from one of the miners of the Gwendraeth Valley.[1] He called himself 'Jack' and he wrote on 14 October 1925. It is a letter of support to Griffiths, who was applying for the post of miners' agent to the Anthracite Miners' Association. Jack felt very confident that Griffiths would succeed in his application, and even reminded him that he would get the support of at least 65% to 75% of the Gwendraeth Valley miners. The only miner who could win the day against him would be S. O. Davies, the miners' agent for the Dowlais colliers, near Merthyr Tydfil, who had been elected in 1918. Davies represented some 5,000 miners who worked in the collieries of Fochriw (which had the delightful Welsh names of Ras Las and Pwll Mawr), the two collieries in Bedlinog (Number 1 and 2), South Tunnel colliery as well as Nantwen colliery. 'S.O.', as he was known, had moved from the Mynydd Mawr colliery in Tumble, and on the wall of his office in Gwent House, Dowlais, could be seen a testimonial to his work as a checkweigher and his contribution to the mining community of Gwendraeth Valley during the First World War. S. O. Davies was in constant demand as a speaker for ILP political meetings. He shared platforms with outstanding speakers of the ILP, such as Ramsay MacDonald, Noah Ablett (miners' agent in Merthyr) and James Winstone. Within the South Wales Miners' Federation, 'S. O.' was well known. He, and Noah Ablett and A. J. Cook were the leading left-wingers who spearheaded the campaigns against the cautious policies of many of the Labour leaders within the Union in their struggle with the coalowners. To the owners the remedy was lower wages and longer hours, a blueprint for a bitter conflict. Without doubt, if James Griffiths won against S. O. Davies for the post of miners' agent it would be an outstanding victory. S. O. Davies, however, decided not to apply for this new post in the anthracite coalfield. Naturally, Jack Evans had decided to do his upmost to win supporters to Griffiths in the Mynydd Mawr colliery. The Mining Agents' District, which was looking for an agent, extended from the outskirts of Llanelli in Carmarthenshire to the Dulais Valley in west Glamorganshire. There were 73 collieries within this District.[2] Griffiths received his strongest support in the Gwendraeth Valley. For example, 500 miners voted for him at Mynydd Mawr, 457 miners in Pentremawr Colliery, and he received 306 votes from the Trimsaran colliery, a few miles outside Llanelli. His support dwindled in the Tawe and Dulais Valleys. Only six voted for him at Onllwyn colliery where Dai Francis (a communist leader of the miners in the post Second World War period) had his base and he gained a dismal four votes from the miners of Blaendulais (Seven Sisters) colliery. At the colliery in Ystalfera no one supported him. But he eventually gained a substantial majority, and was appointed as an agent.[3] Griffiths received 4,578 votes, while Gibbon Davies (brother of S. O. Davies) from Ammanford had 2,893 and J. D. Brazell from Ystalfera received 1,373 votes.[4] It is obvious that the miners of Ystalfera and Tawe Valley had supported Brazell rather than Griffiths. It was refreshing for Griffiths to receive from J. D. Brazell a sincere letter congratulating him on his victory.[5]

Griffiths received a number of other congratulatory letters. The Labour women's organizer, Elizabeth Andrews from the Rhondda Valley, was one of the dynamic figures within the Welsh Labour Party who contacted him. She had established a series of women's advisory committees as well as a regional federation for women, so they had a voice in the running of the growing Labour Party. She grieved that they were losing his input for a while, and expressed her appreciation for his 'kind support and his sympathy' on the political scene in Llanelli.[6] She knew of his dependable support as well as his wife's involvement in Labour Party affairs. She added her best wishes to Winifred and her daughter, Jeanne.

A letter arrived from a Welshman who was the secretary and Labour Party agent in Nuneaton in the West Midlands. William Lewis wrote: 'I have an idea that you will welcome the change in your life.'[7] Lewis noted the difficult task facing a political agent compared with the support given to a miners' agent from officers in every lodge.

The National Council of Labour Colleges (NCLC) movement remembered an ex-student of their college in London, and W. J. Owen, the organiser of Area No 4, from Cwm-Celyn, Blaina in Monmouthshire sent a letter to congratulate Griffiths and express his best wishes to him in his new position.[8] But the best advice he received was from his friend John James, who asked him to call at his home in Cwmgors where he had his office as a miners' agent. John James told him to remember that the miners: '…will come to you when they are in trouble. They will need your help and it will be your privilege to help them if you can. Remember always that what they will want most of all will be to share their trouble with you – so listen to their story patiently to the end; this will be the greatest service you can render them.'[9]

Griffiths never forgot his pastoral role and the wise words of one of the leaders in the anthracite coalfield. John James was a leader that James Griffiths admired immensely.[10] Griffiths was the representative of the Miners' Union covering all the mines from Trimsaran to Onllwyn. As he admitted:

> *Each day would bring its varied tasks: the settlement of piece-work rates for each seam of coal; the handling of disputes over allowances for 'abnormal conditions', seeking the reinstatement of a man who was sacked; and ensuring that those maimed or bereaved by accident or disease received the meagre compensation t which the law entitled them. The word 'compo' is written in blood in the annals of the miner.*[11]

It is incredible to us today, in an entirely different age, that in the 1920s there was not even a meagre 'compo' for the dreaded silicosis or the equally drastic pneumoconiosis. The miner would breathe polluted air as he worked underground, a combination of coal and rock-dust as well as the fumes of the explosives used to blast the coal and rock. When it was agreed in 1928 that silicosis was an industrial disease, the authorities made sure that a miner's compensation was as little as possible. He could never get compensation if the miners' agent could not prove that the miner was in charge of the machine that dug into the rock which contained 50% of the free silica. When a claim was disputed, Griffiths had to visit the colliery, 'accompanied by the pit leader, in search of silica rock.'[12] It was a difficult task and often he was expected to visit more than one colliery, especially if the miner who had silicosis had been employed there at some stage or other. One has to remember that of all the coalfields, there were more industrial disputes in south Wales than elsewhere in Britain. By the summer of 1925, nearly every region within the British coalfield was losing money and all the miners were on the minimum wage.[13] A rumour of a slump would spread like wildfire through the coalfields. The owners were keen on paying the miners less wages, and keen also to forget altogether the seven-hour day to which they had agreed six years earlier.

After the First World War, most of the collieries of the anthracite coalfield became the possession of two powerful companies, United Anthracite and Amalgamated Anthracite. The owners and directors of these companies had overspent their capital and the directors were determined to have their own way so as to recoup the money that had been lost. But the leaders as well as the lodge officials of the union were completely united in the anthracite coalfield. The majority of the miners were Welsh speakers, proud of their roots in their communities and their male voice choirs and their distinctive culture. A high percentage of those in charge of local colliery lodges were men of strong convictions; many of these men were Elders and Deacons in Welsh nonconformist chapels, and proud of their commitment to Christian socialism. These were people exactly of the same background, attitude and values as James Griffiths himself.

In the anthracite coalfield a number of unique practices developed over the generations. One of them was to do with the Priority Rule, which simply stated that the last person to be employed within the colliery was the first to be made redundant if the situation arose.[14] This was the spark that turned into a fierce fire that spread through the anthracite coalfield in the summer of 1925.[15] The conflict in Glyn-neath and in Ammanford itself was regarded as extremely serious. The Deputy Chief Constable of Carmarthenshire was beaten up by a gang of unruly miners. They could easily have killed him. The inhabitants of Ammanford witnessed strife and conflict.

The manager of No 1 colliery in Ammanford, where Griffiths had been a lodge official, had, unfortunately, not been consistent in applying the Priority Rule. The strike lasted from the beginning of July until 24 August 1925 and Griffiths supported the striking miners as he agreed with the Priority Rule and he wanted to see it implemented in a fair manner.[16] The possibility of the conflict spreading throughout the rest of the British coalfield was evident to the union leaders as well as to the government.

On 3 July, the Prime Minister, Stanley Baldwin, suggested a way out of the crisis. He was to set up an inquiry into the coal industry under the chairmanship of Sir Herbert Samuel, a former Liberal Minister, with three members: a banker, an economist and an industrialist. It spent the winter holding meetings, hearing witnesses and preparing a report of some 300 pages. They were given nine months to complete the task but in the meantime financial help was given to the industry to safeguard the wages of the miners and to ensure that they were being paid what was termed a 'living wage'. Leading Tory politicians felt that the government should prepare for a conflict with the British workers, in particular the miners. The Home Secretary, William Joynson-Hicks, saw Communism as the biggest threat and he managed to see members of the Communist Party under every bed. Under his jurisdiction, twelve leading communists were prosecuted that autumn under the Incitement to Mutiny Act of 1797. All twelve were found guilty and sentenced to prison.[17]

The report of the Samuel Commission was published on 6 March 1926. The Commission had done as had been expected and delivered a thorough inquiry but it was not a report that brought any satisfaction to the miners or their leaders.[18] The miners were not ready to compromise and they still remembered bitterly how they had been betrayed in 1919 when the Sankey Commission recommended nationalising the coal industry. Nothing had happened. James Griffiths knew first-hand of the strong feelings within the executive of the South Wales Miners' Federation.[19] As a miners' agent he was a member of that executive.

At their first meeting he contended that a serious crisis loomed on the horizon. Every miners' agent shared the same concerns.[20] After all, they also had worked for years at the coalface. They knew better than the Trade Union Congress that the miners in every part of the coalfield were in a bitter mood. As a miners' agent, Griffiths knew of the standpoint of A. J. Cook, who since 1924 had become Secretary of the Miners' Federation of Great Britain Their President, Herbert Smith, replied to all attempts at compromise with his famous phraseology: 'Nowt doing'. Cook too did not believe for one moment in compromise. He had prepared a slogan – 'Not a penny off the pay, not a minute on the day'. Cook, born in the West Country but brought up in the Rhondda, was regarded by the miners all over Britain as a hero.[21] They assembled in their thousands in the open air to listen to his passionate oratory. He stood with his sleeves rolled up and challenged the whole structure of government in the name of justice for miners. Cook was regarded by most leaders of the Labour Party as an extremist, but to James Griffiths and the miners in his community, his oratory was like inspiring. Sir Herbert Samuel and his team realised that both sides were immovable. The owners were not listening at all under the leadership of a Welshman from Pontarddulais, Evan Williams, the President of the Mining Association of Great Britain. He had a powerful position, though he owned only one colliery near Llangennech. The leaders of the miners also were immovable. The Commissioners could not agree on the urgency of nationalisation or whether to give support to the industry, and the capitalist class seemed to believe that the only answer in the short term was to reduce the wages of the miners.

The miners stood their ground but the government began to renew the Special Powers Act, and the owners were contemplating an increase in working hours at the coalface.[22] In the spring of 1925, the miners pressed the Government to accept an amended Coal Mines Minimum Wage Bill incorporating 12s 0d as the national minimum, and they also renewed their demand for a system of national pooling designed to enable the weaker districts to meet the cost. However, they soon came to the conclusion that the Stanley Baldwin government was hand in glove with the owners. Griffiths was in the middle of this biter industrial dispute, 'a grim baptism for a beginner' as he admitted, for he attended executive meetings in Cardiff as well as embarking on the longer journey to London for the Miners' National Conference.

The 1926 General Strike gave a tremendous boost to the militant spirit in the British coalfield. The serious poverty on the streets of the mining villages and towns, as well as within the homes of mining families, was apparent to any visiting journalist. The falling standards of living for the miners has been well documented. They were not given employment assistance or help from the Board of Guardians when the colliery was not working.[23] Guardians who were sympathetic could assist the mothers and their children by a payment of 12 shillings a week for the woman and 4 shillings for the upkeep of a child. The Local Education Authority could give free school meals to the children, but the LEA could also opt out of this assistance: there was no compulsion. The situation was made ever more bizarre by the actions of the Minister of Health, Neville Chamberlain. It is no wonder that he became a figure of hate in the mining valleys. The situation of the unmarried miner was a complete disgrace to a civilised society. He did not receive any financial support from any public authority.

There was no way out for him without the assistance of the union. The South Wales Miners' Fed contributed the vast sum of £330,000 towards the upkeep of the striking miners. To the delight of members of the Communist Party, established in 1920, generous donations were sent by miners and workers from the coalfields of the Soviet Union. Miners in south Wales praised their fellow miners in the Soviet coalfield. One of these was a miner from Abertridwr near Caerphilly, John Roberts, a disciple of the Welsh language revolutionary poet T. E. Nicholas ('Niclas y Glais') of Aberystwyth. He spoke so forcefully on every occasion he could: in the chapel, on the street corners in Abertridwr and in the Miners' Lodge, that the people of Senghennydd and of Abertridwr came to call him 'Jack Russia'.[24]  That nickname stuck to him for the rest of his life, and he kept to his Christian-communist beliefs until his dying day. [25]

Every community in the south Wales valleys became involved, and Griffiths took the initiative in his District, setting up soup kitchens in the miners' halls. He spent the union's money so as to ensure at least one good meal a day for the miners and their wives. Dr Marion Phillips, a socialist pioneer, organized women's committees all over Britain to collect for the miners' cause, and Welsh male voice choirs toured the English towns and cities to collect for their kith and kin back home in the mining communities. Griffiths was proud of their achievement, as he recalled in his memoirs:

The kitchens stayed open through the long months of struggle and there was not one day without a meal at the miners' hall. If, to the miner in the valleys, the world seemed to be against him, the weather was on his side through those glorious days of sunshine and luminous evenings of the summer of 1926.[26]

All kinds of initiatives were taken to bring comfort and hope to mining communities. Carnival bands were formed in the villages, arrayed in all the colours of the rainbow. They became part and parcel of the recreational activities of all sections of the community. These communities began to arrange home-made social events, such as an annual carnival, which became an event to cherish for decades to come.

By the beginning of winter 1926, every family in the Welsh coalfield had debts, and large numbers of children were to be seen without shoes. Some were carried to school on the back of their fathers, and the mothers were often denying themselves food so as to help their families. The struggle lasted seven months and as Griffiths admitted: 'Their loyalty had been magnificent. They had answered every call. They had endured months of privation… It was a terrible price to pay.' He, himself, had shared with the men the difficulties, the deprivations, and the debts:

> *Like theirs, my savings were exhausted and the future mortgaged. My wife had joined the womenfolk of the valley in their part in the struggle. Our home had become a 'surgery' where the maimed and afflicted came for help and sympathy. The miners looked to me for guidance and leadership, and I was resolved to give of my best in their service.*[27]

Griffiths, as a Labour Party politician in waiting, was concerned that the membership of the Communist Party had doubled in 1926.[28] The establishment and the development of the Miners' Minority Movement, an unofficial organisation, was an opportunity for a number of Welsh miners to have a platform for their syndicalist ideology. Two of the leading members, Will Paynter and Arthur Horner, both prominent communists, became miners' leaders within the British context, concentrating on union activities more than party political affairs. At the end of his life, Griffiths expressed his great admiration for the ability and determination of Arthur Horner who had been a 'thorn in the flesh' in his period as a miners' leader.

One wonders what might have happened if Horner had used his influence and devoted his gifts and talents mainly to the organisation of the Communist Party. It might have presented a major challenge to the Labour Party in south Wales. The communists were the main challengers to the Labour Party, on the political front, after Labour had gained the upper hand over the Liberals. After the strike had ended, Griffiths admitted that 'there must be a better way than this, I was sure, to win for these brave men the security and living standards their toil and sacrifice deserved.'[29] The whole community suffered, and there was a huge decline in the membership of the Miners' Union.[30]

The membership of 'the Fed' in south Wales declined from 124,000 in 1924 to 73,000 in 1927. This meant that the salaries of the officers suffered, the newsletter of 'the Fed' ceased to be published, and the matter that upset Griffiths most was the inevitable decision to cease their financial support for the Central Labour College in London which had been an important influence on his outlook and this commitment to the Labour movement. The establishing of a breakaway Miners' Union in Nottinghamshire, which came to be called the 'Spencer Union' was a serious setback, as was, in particular, the formation of an Industrial Union of South Wales Miners at Merthyr Vale colliery near Aber-fan in the Taff Valley in 1926. He also heard with a great deal of dismay that at least one colliery in the anthracite coalfield had been re-opened with blackleg labour.[31]

Griffiths had moved with his family from Burry Port to Ystradgynlais so as to be at the heart of the anthracite coalfield, in a central position for his work as a miners' agent.[32] It was at Burry Port that the second child Harold Morris was born in 1926. Ystradgynlais a Welsh speaking mining village is the birthplace of the last two children of Winifred and James Griffiths. Sheila Rose was born in1928, and William Arthur in 1931. The family loved the environment of Ystradgynlais and the freedom of the upper reaches of the Swansea Valley, with beautiful scenery within a few miles north of them at Abercrave, Cwmgiedd and Crai.

His wife became a Labour councillor and a fervent worker for the miners as well as the Labour Movement.

Griffiths came to respect the miner's leaders of the south Wales coalfield, and he singled out in particular the role of Vernon Hartshorn, a miners' leader about whom he had his doubts in the First World War because of his pro-war stance. He said of him: 'He had a clearer view and sounder assessment of the problems confronting the coal-mining industry than any of the other leaders.'[33] Hartshorn could see that the demand for coal would decline. Oil was becoming a competitor to coal.[34] Markets had been lost because of the 1914-18 war, but the new countries which had come into existence as a result of the Versailles Treaty were ready to subsidise the mining industry. The answer to this situation in the reasoning of the miners' leaders was to nationalise the industry, but they knew that the Samuel Commission had thrown cold water over such a proposition. The only remedy from the coalowners was to pay the miners less in their pay packets as well as to expect them to work longer hours and to sell the coal cheaper at home and in Europe than they had done before the costly strike.

When, in the early months of 1927 the Miners' National Conference was held, delegates from all over Britain secourted the same sad experiences. Collieries were closing, thousands of miners were without work, the owners were triumphant and determined to punish the union men who had stood their ground. Many of these leaders were victimized and the membership numbers fell. A message was sent to every miner and to the country at large which was still defiant:

> *The fight is not over. The conditions imposed by the owners cannot bring goodwill or the spirit of conciliation. Longer hours and lower wages cannot bring peace to the coalfields; nor will district agreements be allowed to shatter our strength and unity. Our organization is still intact and we are determined to recover the ground that has been lost.* [35]

As he returned to Wales after the Conference, Griffiths pondered what the words 'recover the ground that has been lost' really meant. He believed that they needed as trade unions to be loyal to each other, a unity that had been largely lost due to the bitter strike of 1926. One of the leaders who had the determination to heal the wounds of 1926 was the General Secretary of the South Wales Miners' Federation, Tom Richards, who had been elected on behalf of the miners to the Trade Union Congress (TUC) General Council.[36]

It was he who called Griffiths to his office in Cardiff in the early 1930s to discuss the relationship of the miners with the Trade Union Congress and to suggest that he (Griffiths) should apply for the post of Deputy Secretary of the TUC.[37] He received his application from the TUC General Secretary, Walter Citrine, in August 1931.[38] Griffiths requested a letter of support from A. J. Cook, General Secretary of the Miners, and in writing to Cook gave his reasons for his application. The reasons were simply this: his wife Winifred was keen to live nearer her beloved Hampshire, especially as 1931 was the year that she lost her father and she wanted to live nearer to her mother in her widowhood. London would be much more convenient than Ystradgynlais. In his letter, Griffiths mentioned how proud he was of the leadership of A. J. Cook.[39] He knew that Cook was suffering terrible physical pain, a culmination of his life as a miner in the Rhondda Valley and an accident at the coalface, and his health had declined following a brutal attack on him during the 1926 General Strike. His leg had to be amputated. Griffiths added: 'Carry on with your protest – you are saving the soul of the movement.'[40] But there were many trade unionists who would disagree vehemently with Griffiths. The politician who had become parliamentary sketch writer of The Times, Colin Coote, said: 'Cook was more like Hitler than any other Englishman in my lifetime. A reckless ranter, a ruthless revolutionary, if the industry had not been bankrupt he would have made it so to further his political beliefs.'[41]

Cook would have appreciated then that supportive sentence from the pen of a miners' agent, especially in the last months of his short and tempestuous life. Even Oswald Mosley at the height of his popularity within the Labour Party needed the support of A. J. Cook as well as his fellow MPs (seventeen of them) to issue the Mosley-Cook Manifesto. Cook died in November 1931, two months after he had received the appreciation of James Griffiths from the anthracite coalfield.

Griffiths was invited to London to see Dr M. I. Cinncane for a medical examination on Tuesday 29 September. The following morning he appeared before the Appointment Board as one of six on the short list. It is obvious that he had spoilt his chance of getting the post by asking Cook to supply the testimonial. To TUC leaders like Ernest Bevin and Walter Citrine, this was beyond the pale. If he had asked Tom Richards or some other moderate union leader his prospects would have been better. That same day Walter Citrine sent him a letter to explain that the TUC had appointed H. Vincent Tewson to the post, an individual who became a stalwart of the trade union movement. In the opinion of Tom Richards, the Trade Union Congress had not chosen the best candidate, but when he returned to Wales, Griffiths had more success within his own union despite the fact that Bevin and Citrine certainly did not want an admirer of A. J. Cook in the administrative office of the TUC. However Griffiths felt that his future was tied to the Miners' Union. When the General Secretaryship became vacant he threw his hat into the ring against S. O. Davies, Noah Ablett and Oliver Harris. He was badly beaten by Harris but he did not have to wait long for another opportunity.[42]

Griffiths was asked by a number of lodges to consider standing as a Vice-President of 'the Fed', and during their Annual Conference in November 1932 he was chosen for the role at the age of forty-two. He was one of the youngest to have been appointed. [43] All the pioneers who had established 'the Fed' in 1896 had retired or had died. One of the last was the President, Enoch Morrell. It was a privilege for James Griffiths to work under Morrell for two years before Morrell decided to retire. There were more miners in Wales than anywhere else in Britain, which meant 'the Fed' became powerful in the inter-war years. There were still 140,399 miners in south Wales and 11,066 in north Wales. Yorkshire had nearly as many miners: there were 97,598 in south Yorkshire and 45,071 in west Yorkshire; and in the Durham coalfield there were 109,110 miners with a further 83,933 in Scotland. To be President of the South Wales Miners' Federation was a very important position. The General Secretary of 'the Fed', Oliver Harris, wrote to Griffiths in March 1934 to inform him that 68 lodges had nominated him as President and a further 18 had nominated him as Vice-President.

In the Annual Conference on 13-14 April 1934 he was chosen without a contest as President. His first task was to pay a generous tribute to Enoch Morrel for his ten years' service as President. He emphasised that Morrell was of a 'pleasant disposition', with the result that he 'was a close friend to all those who worked with him'. Two hundred and forty-five delegates came to the Conference to discuss matters of importance to the future of 'the Fed', to welcome the new President, and to vote for the vacant post of Vice-President. Two well-known miners' leaders became the front runners for the post, pitting their talents against each other, namely Alderman Arthur Jenkins of Abersychan (the father of the politician Roy Jenkins) and the communist activist and inspirational leader, Arthur Horner, as well as another thirteen candidates. In the final vote Arthur Jenkins gained the support of 42,000 miners while Arthur Horner had 40,100 votes.

In his first address as President, Griffiths mentioned that the industry was losing miners due to pit closures. These pits were regarded, by their owners, as not being profitable. Furthermore, mechanisation meant the loss of men at the coalface. He referred to the fact that there were 10,000 miners over sixty years of age in the south Wales coalfield. He believed that these miners should be allowed to retire, allowing men who were out of work and young men in the prime of life to have an opportunity of entering into the mining industry.

The leaders of his chapel in Ammanford, Christian Temple Welsh Independent Chapel, under the chairmanship of Rhys Thomas, who had briefly taught him at Betws Board School, decided to hold a concert in honour of James Griffiths as the new President of the South Wales Miners' Federation on 2 May, 1934.[44] Thomas refered to the unique situation in the Griffiths household, with both James and Winifred serving the community of Ystradgynlais as magistrates. But now James Griffiths was the Miners' President and Thomas asked a rhetorical question: What were the influences that brought him such an honour? He answered it in three ways. First of all, the Betws Board School where he had been taught by the Headmaster John Lewis who, in his own opinion, had left an 'indelible mark on him.' Secondly, his home in Betws. Griffiths had been raised in a home where reading books and journals were a priority. To him a reader became a thinker and in Griffiths's case it had brought him to the stage of south Wales as a 'convincing speaker.' Thirdly, the chapel where he had learnt the worth of sacrifice, service and serenity and absorbed the moral standards that had been an important influence. Rhys Thomas added: 'When he, as assistant master, helped Mr Lewis, his predecessor in the Betws School, to draw up a list of boys and girls who were expected to make good, Jim Griffiths's name always occupied a prominent place.' To Councillor T. J. Parry Jones, Griffiths was a product of Welsh culture at its best. He added: 'Such a culture was unquestionably due to the Bethels in Carmarthenshire.' Councillor Abel Morgan spoke of his reputation in his early days as a 'revolutionary' – indeed a Bolshevik. But those days were over, and Griffiths was now a great moderate leader. Those were also the sentiments of the cultured miner Irlwyn who presented him with a walking stick. John Harries (Irlwyn) praised him for his astounding capacity as a debater on behalf of the miners, his knowledge of current affairs, and his learning, all on the altar of service to the working class.

During his short term of office as President, Griffiths had to face a large number of conflicts as well as the tragedy in the mining industry at Gresford colliery near Wrexham. On Saturday 22 September 1934, 261 miners were killed as well as three members of the rescue team, and one worker at the pit head, leaving 164 women as widows, 242 children without fathers, and at least 17,000 men unemployed as a result of the mining accident. Griffiths visited the Gresford colliery and met an old miner who told him that the miners who had lost their lives had received their wages of £2 on that very same morning before they descended to the bottom of the pit. An inquiry lasted thirty-eight days, at which the Miners' Union was represented by a well-known barrister and Labour intellectual, Stafford Cripps, as well as by D. R. Grenfell, an ex-miner and the Labour MP for the Gower constituency.

Griffiths was also concerned about the membership of the Spencer Union in the Taff Merthyr Colliery at Merthyr Vale.[45] His first plan was to persuade the miners of Taff Merthyr to join 'the Fed', and then he would inform the administrators at the colliery not to deduct from their wages any contributions to the Spencer Union. If miners were dismissed by colliery officials, the Miners' Union would defend them. The owners of Taff Merthyr Colliery decided to hold a ballot to give the choice to the miners between the two unions. Griffiths knew that the majority of the miners would not vote for the Spencer Union. The conflict came to a climax in October on a Saturday at Nine Mile Point colliery in Cwmfelin-fach near Blackwood in Gwent. On 12 October 1934 the miners who supported the Spencer Union came back to the surface first, so as not to meet the miners loyal to 'the Fed'. But these men decided to follow the example of Romanian miners: when they were annoyed with their employers they would stay down at the bottom of the pit till the matter had been resolved. This confronted Griffiths, and the Union Executive Committee, with a huge problem. It was a breach of the Coal Mines Act to stay down the mine beyond the permitted hours. These seventy-eight miners became heroes overnight as the news spread through the mining valleys of west Monmouthshire and Glamorganshire. By Sunday morning a large crowd had congregated at the top of the colliery.[46] The local brass band played and the wives of the striking miners brought sandwiches for their loved ones. The local chapels and churches remembered them in their prayers. The strike at Cwmfelin-fach inspired similar strikes in other areas of the Gwent coalfield, in particular in the Risca Colliery.

The Nine Mile Point colliery had been taken over by the Ocean Colliery Company, one of the sponsors of the Spencer Union. The general manager of the Ocean Colliery Company was one of the leading Welsh Baptists of Glamorganshire, W. P. Thomas, a Deacon in the Welsh Baptist chapel of Noddfa, Treorchy.[47] He had very little sympathy with the Labour movement. He was a Liberal of the old nonconformist type who always allied himself with the Conservative establishment.

Griffiths and his deputy, Arthur Jenkins, spent the whole week at Cwmfelinfach, acting as mediators between the Ocean Colliery Company and the sitdown miners. It took all the negotiating skills of Griffiths and Jenkins and after 176 hours underground, the miners decided to allow their leaders to come down and meet them. This was not a problem for the President nor the Vice-President as both were familiar with the task and life of a miner. Griffiths descended to the bottom of the colliery with the consent of the owners, and he never forgot the experience. It remained with him for the rest of his days. In Pages from Memory he wrote an outstanding piece:

> *The nine days below had left their mark; the elderly looked weary – the young had grown beards. I was greeted by the 'patriarch' who had opened and closed each day with prayer, and in between had transformed the staydown strikers into a choir. The leader escorted me to the platform – an upturned tub – and called for order. They listened to me intently as I explained the terms of the settlement, and plied me with questions. Then the leader announced that a vote would be taken for or against the acceptance of 'our president's recommendation'.*

> *'Down with your lamps!' he cried. 'And now all in favour, lift your lamp up; hold it while I count.' It was one of the proudest moments of my life when every lamp was raised. We sang 'Bread of Heaven'. This was the bread they could not deny us. Then, in good order, the older men first, they ascended the shaft to the sunshine and home.*[48]

The terms were simple. Not one of the striking miners was to lose his job, and 'the Fed' was the only Union to operate within the colliery in its relationship with the Ocean Coal Company. Another similar protest took place, on the threshold of W. P. Thomas's abode, at the Park and Dare Colliery in Treorchy. They stayed underground longer than the miners of Cwmfelin-fach. They came up on 23 October, after spending over one hundred hours at the bottom of the pit, and they were welcomed by Griffiths, fellow miners, and their supporters, including the Dare Colliery Male Voice Choir.

Another responsibility that came to Griffiths as President of 'the Fed' was to be involved in the Executive Committee of the British Miners' Union and to cooperate with the President, Joseph Jones, from the Yorkshire coalfield, and Ebby Edwards, who had been a leader in the Northumberland coalfield. The union decided to launch a campaign to increase the wages of the miners, emphasising that an extra two shillings a day should be paid to them. The leaders felt that to discuss this with the owners, or with the government, was a waste of time. The British people had been reminded of the sacrifice involved in the mining industry by the explosion at Gresford colliery in north-east Wales. The campaign was well received by the British public but not by the government, nor the coalowners. After a great deal of discussion behind the scenes, the Baldwin administration persuaded the coalowners to meet the miners' leaders. As a result wages were increased. The miners within the south Wales coalfield were now paid 8 shillings and 1 penny a day, the highest payment since 1924. Back home at Ystradgynlais, Griffiths felt that he had achieved two important victories in his first eighteen months as President. Nearly every miner who worked in the collieries of south Wales was a member of 'the Fed'; and now they were paid better wages than they had in the last ten years. The Spencer Union had been totally defeated.

As one old miner told Griffiths in Cwmfelin-fach: 'I was sure from the start that there was no abiding city for "them" in Wales.'[49] Griffiths, along with others, had won a moral victory. However, although this was an improving situation, in December 1934 the Conservative government decided to institute the 'household means test', which brought more conflict to the mining valleys. For every two men who had laboured in the colliery, one was unemployed.

James Griffiths spelt out in detail what it meant in the context of south Wales. Take a miner coming home to Betws at the end of the week with £2. 4s as his wage, while his son, who was unemployed, was receiving public assistance of 17s 0d per week. Under the new regulations the miner's wage of 44 shillings a week was regarded by the Government as a 'sufficient income for the family' and the son's assistance was cut off altogether.[50] There were many families where the situation had been reversed, with the son being the main breadwinner and the father being on the assistance.[51] This meant the father and the mother depended fully for every penny on the son. Of the 160,000 unemployed in south Wales in the middle of the 1930s, 100,000 of them had no way of surviving and therefore were at the mercy of the 'inquisition and indignity of the household means test'.

The union, on the President's suggestion, decided to take the initiative in opposing the household means test. A conference was arranged in Cardiff. It became more of a religious meeting in the style of a Revival than a meeting under the auspices of a trade union.[52] The hymns of Zion were sung with emotion and Griffiths knew of the thousands who had marched through the mining valleys to protest. In the Rhondda on 3 February 1935, at least 70,000 people had marched to De Winton Park in Tonypandy, while 20,000 heard Ernest Bevin in Pontypool and a similar number had heard Aneurin Bevan in Blackwood with all his oratorical skills at work, denouncing the stupidity of the Baldwin administration. Griffiths was asked to lead a deputation which included an ILP pioneer from Aberdare, Rose Davies, who had been a political colleague of Keir Hardie.[53] She was the first woman elected to the Aberdare Urban District Council, and the first woman to preside over the Aberdare Trade and Labour Council. A remarkable socialist, she was well loved in Glamorganshire.
The deputation went to see the Minister of Labour, Oliver Stanley, where Griffiths presented the case clearly, in a well-prepared brief. Stanley was impressed, thanked him for the presentation, and stated that he would consider the matter with his civil servants in more detail.

This was the last campaign in which Griffiths was involved as President of 'the Fed', and he was proud that the Miners' Union had spoken and acted in a positive manner for the working classes. Like his predecessors - Mabon, William Brace, James Winstone, Vernon Hartshorn, Enoch Morrell - Griffiths had been a miner himself, then a Chairman of the Lodge, a miners' agent, VicePresident and then President of the union. Like his predecessors he combined the Presidency of 'the Fed' with the work of a miners' agent, doing two jobs for one salary, plus an honorarium of £50 a year. He had thoroughly enjoyed his time, as he admits in his book Pages from Memory: 'The ten years I spent in the service of the Welsh miners were some of the happiest of my life. For me, the coal miners are the salt of the earth.'[54]

But ever since he had joined the ILP, he had been inspired by an ambition to represent the Labour Party in Parliament. He had promised his friends in Carmarthenshire, when he had been given his post as agent to the Llanelli constituency Labour Party, that he would come back to be considered as the successor to their MP. When Dr J. H. Williams died in 1936, Griffiths responded as his friends expected he would, hoping then that he could combine his role as President of the Union with that of an MP. However, the union felt that the key position of President of 'the Fed' could not be compromised in this way, and Griffiths accepted their recommendation with grace. Generous tributes were paid to for having given the Miners' Union such caring leadership. In a crisis in the history of 'the Fed', Griffiths he had revitalised its structure, its campaigning, and its outlook. As he admits, it was a difficult decision to make, leaving his life as a trade unionist for the life of a full-time politician:

> *If it had been any other constituency than Llanelli my decision would have been different. The decision was all the more difficult because my wife was anxious for me to stay on in my work for the union…. I made up my mind to say 'yes' to Llanelli and at the same time offer to continue in my post as President.*[55]

**Notes and References**

1. NLW, James Griffiths Papers A 4/3. The letter from Jack is dated 14 October 1925. I suggest that Jack is John Evans, one of the most enthusiastic members of the Labour Party in Penygroes and in the Carmarthenshire constituency. The only identifying elements on the letter are 'Jack, Gwendraeth Colliery'.
2. Ibid., A 3/4. The minutes of the Labour Party Constituency Meeting 1 April, 1923 – 31 March, 1924. These mining lodges were affiliated to the Labour Party: New Dynant, Pontyberem, Ponthenry, Llangennech, Gwendraeth, Trimsaran, Burry Port, Western Cawdor, No. 1 Colliery, Ammanford, and Acorn. James Griffiths had been in constant contact with them during his term as political agent.
3. There were 22 applicants for the post.
4. NLW, James Griffiths Papers A 4/4. Results of the first ballot.
5. Ibid., A 4/5. Miners Agent for the Anthracite District. A letter to James Griffiths from J. D. Brazell, Ystalyfera dated 8 December 1925.
6. NLW, James Griffiths Papers A 4/7. Letter from Elizabeth Andrews, Tonpentre, Rhondda to James Griffiths dated 8 December 1925.
7. Ibid., A 4/8. Letter of Walter Lewis, Secretary and Agent of the Labour Party in the Nuneaton Constituency to James Griffiths, dated 9 December 1925.
8. Ibid., A 3/7. Note-book, *Leader of the Miners, 1925-1936*. It is of interest that the Welsh weekly newspaper, *Y Cymro*, praises James Griffiths. His popularity was being recognised. See 'Nodion Y Cymro, Jim Griffiths, y Miners Agent', *Y Cymro*, December 12, 1925, p.4.  9. James Griffiths translated the advice he received from John James into English for *Pages from Memory*, p. 28. The *Llanelly Labour News* paid a tribute to John James, JP in its issue of 17 October 1925. 'He has been of service to the Labour Party throughout south Wales, to hear him and Keir Hardie in their flight of oratory to large crowds were an inspiration'.

10. Ioan Matthews, 'Hen Arwr Maes Glo Carreg: John James (1869-1942) in Hywel Teifi Edwards (ed), *Cwm Aman* (Llandysul,1996), pp. 320-49.

11. James Griffiths, *Pages from Memory*, p. 28.

12. ibid.

13. Robert Skidelsky, *Politicians and the Slump: The Labour Government of 1929-1931* (London, 1967), p. 13.

14. These are the words of Dai Dan Davies on the priority system in the anthracite coalfield: 'The difference between the leader and the ordinary rank and filer in the anthracite area is much less than in the steam coal. In the anthracite area, if you wanted to dismiss a man who was a bit of a "trouble-maker", they would have to take possibly a hundred men out before him (because of the seniority rule). [Consequently] you see you had lambs roaring like lions in the anthracite, and they had to be a lion to bloody well roar like a lion in the steam coalfield'. See Hywel Francis and David Smith, *The Fed,* ibid., p. 108.

15. This was part of the rule book of the anthracite district coalfield as Hugh Bevan explains in his autobiography, Morwr Cefn Gwlad, p. 51.

16. NLW, James Griffiths Papers D3/7. Details on the Ammanford and District Miners Committee. It is revealing that the Treasurer is Reverend W. Nantlais Williams, a local Presbyterian minister in Ammanford and Eddie Morgan acts as the Secretary. For the unpleasant disturbances and the 1925 strike in Ammanford, see Hywel Francis, 'The Anthracite Strike and Disturbances of 1925', *Liafur*, 1 (May 1973), pp. 15-28.

17. NLW, James Griffiths Papers D 3/7. Note-book, *Leader of the Miners, 1925-1936*.

18. John Davies, *Hanes Cymru* (London, 1990), p. 530.

19. Ibid. John Davies states that the majority of the miners of the anthracite coalfield were Welsh speakers loyal to the chapels. They were fewer in number than the miners in the steam coal areas but the 1925 Strike made them much more militant. One of the Nonconformist ministers who was a hero to the miners of Tumble and Amman Valley was the Revd. Tom Nefyn Williams of Tumble. Hugh Bevan, as a young man in the Ammanford area, saw T. Nefyn Williams attracting huge congregations to listen to his lectures, in different chapels, on his experiences in the First World War. See Hugh Bevan*, Morwr Cefn Gwlad*, p.29.

20. NLW, James Griffiths Papers D 3/7, Notebook, *Leader of the Miners, 1925-1936*.

21. John Davies, *Hanes Cymru*, p.531. James Griffiths in his Notebook, *Leader of the Miners*, gives an account of an interesting night he had in the company of Arthur James Cook in Larne, Northern Ireland, during the Annual Conference of the British Trade Unions which was held in 1925 in Belfast. Cook called all the Welsh delegates together so he could create a male voice choir. They sang the old favourites, from the Welsh hymn *Calon Lân* (Pure Heart) to The Red Flag, and when the Ulster Police came to seek so called 'terrorists' belonging to Sinn Fêin, Cook shouted, 'Come on lads, show them that we are Welsh miners. All together now – Calon Lân'. James Griffiths constantly rejoiced in his mining background, and the fact that Cook had come under the influence of the 1904-5 Religious Revival. He admired his early evangelical zeal as a boy-preacher, which was so pronounced during his life in the pulpit, on the miners platforms, in the open air, and his perorations at the conferences against the so called 'Satan', namely the owners of the collieries, and the worst of them all, to Cook, was the Welshman, Evan Williams. James Griffiths quotes in his notes the words of Philip Snowden about A. J. Cook: 'He did not know what he was going to say when he began to speak and did not know what he had said when had finished speaking'.

22. The Strike Committee were in complete charge of the mining communities as James Griffiths testified to Margaret Morris: 'We ran the country really – who should work and who shouldn't, whether this shop or that shop should be open, whether people who owned cars could

use them. We even gave permits to go and steal coal. In the anthracite, you don't have to dig far down into the mountain to find coal, so they'd come to us and say, "Can I have a permit because if I'm caught with a bag of coal, I'll be called a blackleg. So we gave them." See Margaret Morris, *The General Strike* (Harmondsworth, 1976), p. 60.

23. According to James Griffiths the 'communal soup kitchen' was what kept the miners and their families together. An interview with Dr Hywel Francis, 16 February 1970. See Hywel Francis and Dai Smith, The Fed, pps.56-7.

24. D. Ben Rees, 'John Roberts (Jack Rwsia, 1889-1979)', Biography on line, NLW.

25. John Davies, *Hanes Cymru*, p.535. Money came from the Soviet Union to assist the miners and their families. One should pay heed to the insight of John McIlroy: 'Wales was a stronghold of communism in this sense: individual communists were influential in the community, workplace and union. However, Welsh communism was never as powerful as a party, it was never as strong as a directive brain or strategic centre organising significant number of activities. The activists were more at the heart of things than the party'. See John McIlroy, 'Glowyr Cymru ym Mosgo: Welsh communists at the Lenin School between the wars', Llafur, Volume 8, No. 4, (2003), p. 74.

26. James Griffiths, *Pages from Memory*, p. 31.

27. ibid., p.32

28. James Griffiths, 'Welsh Politics in my lifetime' in *James Griffiths and His Times* (Ferndale, no date), p.32

29. James Griffiths, *Pages from Memory*, p. 32.

30. The Strike was catastrophic in its consequences, Dr Gwyn A. Williams claimed: 'The Fed went into the strike an army and came out as a rabble. Over 70,000 deserted. The combines moved in, practised wholesale and sustained discrimination, ruthlessly exploited the unemployed, set community against community. A south Wales industrial union was created under their auspices, William Gregory at its head, specifically directed against the "political SWMF"; it made gains in Western Monmouthshire and Eastern Glamorgan. By the end of the 1920s the Fed was fighting for its life.' See Gwyn A Williams, When Was Wales? p. 268. In an interview on 20 November 1972 to the South Wales Miners' Union situated at the University of Wales Swansea, James Griffiths said: 'After 1926, I think the miners made up their minds that we cannot solve our problems by industrial action and looked afterwards to a Labour Government to do it. So after 1926 you see the big growth of the Labour Party in south Wales in the coalfields generally and thereafter looking for a political solution and not for an industrial solution.' See Kenneth O Morgan, 'Welsh Politics 1918-1939', in Trevor Herbert and Gareth Elwyn Jones (editors), Wales Between the Wars (Cardiff, 1985), p.116.

31. Alun Burge, 'In search of Harry Blount: Scabbing between the Wars in one South Wales community', Llafur, Volume 6, no. 3, 1999, pp. 60-65, for the Spencer Union, see Hywel Francis and David Smith, *The Fed*, Chapter 4, pp. 113-144.

32. Mrs James Griffiths, *One Woman's Story*, p. 10.

33. James Griffiths, *Pages from Memory*, pp. 32, Margaret Morris The General Strike, pp. 276-7. James Griffiths explains to Margaret Morris his standpoint in much greater detail than he does in *Pages from Memory*, pp. 32-3.

34. Tom Richards, 'Vernon Hartshorn (1872-1931)', *Bywgraffiadur Cymreig hyd 1940* (London, 1953), p. 323; Peter Stead, 'Vernon Hartshorn: miners and Cabinet Minister' [in] Stewart William (ed.) *Glamorgan Historian*, Vol. VI (Cowbridge, 1969), pps. 83-94.

35. Ibid., p. 323. He was called in Dr Stead's article as the 'most influential man in Maesteg', ibid., p.83. The message is found in *Pages from Memory*, p. 33.

36. The MP for Montgomeryshire David Davies, the third generation of the Llandinam family who were involved as coalowners in the Rhondda Valley, regarded the strike as a tragedy to the coal industry, not only in Britain, but throughout the continent of Europe. Thus he wrote: 'The coal experts who met at Geneva early in January (1929) under the auspices of the League of Nations, were in agreement that the British coal strike of 1926 was not only a calamity for Great Britain, but it was disastrous also for other coal-producing countries in that it had caused an excessive production in those countries to offset which, with the re-entry of British coal into the world market, there was no equivalent growth in consumption'. See David Davies, MP, 'The Coal Position in South Wales', *Welsh Outlook*, Volume 16, no. 2, February 1929, p. 39.

37. James Griffiths, *Pages from Memory*, p. 34. It was Tom Richards who encouraged him to consider applying for a key trade union position. 'And, to my surprise he told me that he believed I could help and urged me to apply for the post then vacant of assistant secretary to Congress. I accepted his advice and in due time was notified that I was one of six on the short list, to be interviewed by the General Council.' Another person who supported him to the hilt was his wife, though she was by then a Labour Councillor for the Ynysgedwyn Ward, Ystradgynlais, a magistrate and member of the Board of Guardians. See H. C. G. Matthew and Brian Harrison (editors), *Oxford Dictionary of National Biography*, Volume 23 (Oxford, 2004), p. 1003.

38. NLW, James Griffiths Papers A 4/10. Letter of Walter Citrine to James Griffiths dated 25 August 1931.

39. Ibid., A 4/3. Letter of James Griffiths to A. J. Cook dated 29 August 1931.

40. Ibid.

41. Colin Coote, *A Companion of Honour: The Story of Walter Elliot* (London, 1965), p. 37. NLW, James Griffiths Papers A 4/17. Letter of Walter Citrine to James Griffiths dated 23 September 1931. See Robert Taylor *The TUC: From the General Strike to New Unionism* (Basingstoke, 2000), p. 50. Walter Citrine had no patience with left wing movements, who were heavily under the influence of communists, such as the Minority Movement and National Unemployed Workers' Movement.

42. Ibid., A 4/21. The results of the election for a General Secretary to the Fed. These were the results of the first ballot: S. O. Davies, 13,823, Oliver Harris, 11,082, James Griffiths, 6,392, Evan Williams 5,109, Arthur Jenkins, 4, 634, Noah Ablett 3,315. A total of 63,265 voted. In the second ballot Oliver Harris had 25,958 votes, S. O. Davies 24,064, James Griffiths 11,299 and Evan Williams 8,657. A total of 69,978 voted and 251 votes were spoilt making a total of 70,229. James Griffiths does not mention that he applied for the post in his autobiography for one of the key positions in 'the Fed'.

43. James Griffiths, *Pages from Memory*, p. 34.

44. Concert for James Griffiths, *Amman Valley Chronicle*, May 2, 1934.

45. James Griffiths, Pages from Memory, p. 35.

46. Ibid., pp. 37-8.

47. Ibid., p. 37.

48. Ibid., p.38.

49. Ibid.

50. Ibid., p.42

51. Ibid., p.43

52. Ibid.

53. Ibid.

54. Ibid, p.45.

55. Ibid.

# 9

## The new MP for Llanelli (1936-39)

James Griffiths knew that he had an excellent opportunity to follow Dr J. H. Williams as Member of Parliament for the Llanelli constituency. He had been extremely loyal and hard-working within the Miners  Union, a pioneer of the ILP and then the Labour Party. He had been a good friend and supporter of Dr Williams for twenty-six years, having supported him since his first election as a parliamentary candidate in 1910 and also when he became an MP in 1922. He had canvassed for him faithfully also in the 1918, 1923, 1924, 1929, and 1935 General Elections. Dr Williams died at his home Snowdon House, Burry Port, on 9 February 1936 at the age of sixty seven.[1] He had served the ILP and the Labour Party since its inception, and had received much better educational opportunities than James Griffiths. After all, a native of the Liverpool Welsh  he had been a medical student who graduated at the University College of South Wales and Monmouthshire in Cardiff, and he had then studied at the University of Oxford and finally at the London Hospital before becoming a General Medical Practitioner at Pwll, near Llanelli. [2] Two of his sons, Dr W. D. Williams and Dr Leslie Williams, followed in his footsteps as medical practitioners.[3] The South Wales Miners' Federation regarded the seat as one that they should support, and it was obvious to them that their President should become the next Labour MP. He was the ideal candidate as he had already close connections with the miners within the constituency.

A few regarded Dr T. Hughes Griffiths, a lecturer in the Extra Mural Department of the University College of Wales, Aberystwyth, and a cousin of James Griffiths, as a strong contender. After all he had been born in Caerbryn, Llandybïe, and worked in his early days as a miner before he embarked on the scholastic path and gained qualifications, including his doctorate, to assist him as a University Extra Mural lecturer in Adult Education. He soon gained a nomination from the colliery where he had worked, Emlyn Colliery in Penygroes, but that was the only support he received. The first Conference to choose a Labour candidate was held on 22 February 1936 in Ammanford, under the chairmanship of Councillor R.O. Rees from Garnant.[4] He was a schoolmaster who had done research on the Amman Valley Welsh dialect for his MA thesis, and he was also a Deacon and Treasurer of Bryn Seion Welsh Independent Chapel, Glanaman. R. O. Rees proved a dependable friend to James Griffiths. In this Conference, Griffiths received 28 votes, the Marxist tutor D. R. Owen from Garnant received 6, Dan Griffiths from Llanelli, a schoolmaster, received 2 votes and Dr T. Hughes Griffiths, 1 vote. The final selection Conference was held on 3 March when the trade unions, the Labour Party branches, socialist and allied societies would send their delegates to the Welfare Hall, Ammanford .[5] There were three on the shortlist: James Griffiths, Frederick Elwyn-Jones, a young barrister and a native of Llanelli, who later became an MP and Lord Chancellor, and Dan Griffiths, who had been a great supporter of the Labour movement in Llanelli and Ammanford, and had taught Elwyn Jones as a pupil in the primary school.[6]

James Griffiths gained the nomination without any difficulty. He had 158 votes, Dan Griffiths received 57 but Elwyn Jones had only 3 nominations. He had to depend in the end, in 1945, on the East End of London rather than his beloved Wales for his political career within the Labour Party. In the meantime the Liberals had chosen W. A. Jenkins, who had been MP for Breconshire and Radnorshire as their candidate.[7] James Griffiths knew that he could depend on the miners. But he also knew that with all the accidents in the coal mines, he was inevitably to lose many a staunch supporter and canvasser. This happened early in 1936. On 8 January in East Pit colliery in Gwaun Cae Gurwen a young miner, John Jenkins, aged forty-four, was killed. He and his son William worked together as miners. The son escaped from the fall of coal.

John Jenkins was a faithful member of the Miners' Union.[8] A few days after the nomination, Griffiths lost another supporter with the death of David Enoch Isaac from Brynaman, at the age of fifty eight. He died on 8 March 1936, after years of active service within the local branch of 'the Fed'. Griffiths fought the election as a mining representative. He emphasised everywhere in the campaign the failure of the Coalition Government to support the mining industry and in particular the standard of living of the miners. Gelliceidrim colliery in the constituency had been at a standstill for three weeks during the by-election campaign. A by-election is regarded by the activist as a golden opportunity to attract well-known figures to address meetings. Griffiths was glad to welcome George Lansbury.[9] He had recently resigned as leader of the Labour Party as he could not compromise on his pacifism. Ernest Bevin had delivered a violent personal attack on him because of his pacifist principles at the 1935 Labour Conference in Brighton. He accused Lansbury of 'taking his conscience round from body to body asking to be told what he ought to do with it.' Lansbury maintained his stand on his Christian pacifist conviction, and he gave a moving speech, but he could not agree with the Executive Committee's resolution on the Abyssinian affair, so he had no option but to resign as the Labour leader. Stafford Cripps was the other distinguished politician who came to speak on behalf of Griffiths in the by-election.[10] Cripps, like Lansbury, was reluctant to agree to a re-armament policy which they felt sure would be used not to support the League of Nations but to betray it once and for all.[11]  Cripps resigned from the Executive on the eve of the Labour Party's Conference in 1935 and Lansbury resigned as leader of the party. Clement Attlee took his place. Both Lansbury and Cripps came to support Griffiths because they knew of his leftwing views as a miners' leader as well as his pacifist convictions during the First World War. However, the invasion of Abyssinia by the dictator Mussolini and the Italian Army was the event that began to undermine Griffiths' long held pacifism. Lansbury argued in the by-election for the right of Britain to campaign for peace on the continent of Europe and hundreds of people in the constituency attended his meetings. He also mentioned that he and Dr Alfred Salter, Labour MP for Bermondsey, were intending to visit the USA on a peace campaign. Dr Salter was one of the few` Socialists who argued at the Brighton Conference for the absolute pacifist position. Other notable pacifists, such as Rhys J. Davies, were unable to identify themselves with him or with Lansbury.

Besides the visits of Cripps and Lansbury, the by-election was conducted in a low key manner. The result was more or less certain. The voting took place on 26 March 1936 and hundreds assembled in pouring rain, in the square outside the Town Hall in Llanelli, to hear the result:

> James Griffiths (Labour) 32,188 66.8%
> William A. Jenkins (National-Liberal) 15,967 32.2%
> Majority 16,221 33.6%

In his acceptance speech, Griffiths emphasised: (a) his opposition to the rearmament policy of the Government; (b) his opposition to the economic policies from the huge combines; (c) his gratitude to the mining communities for their solid support to the Labour Party and to himself as their candidate.[12]

There were celebrations in every part of the constituency, as 'our Jim' had won with a sizeable majority. This augured well for the future. His brother, Amanwy, gave a full description in the Amman Valley Chronicle of his brother's first day in the House of Commons. On 1 April six members of the family and supporters travelled by train from Llanelli and Neath to London.[13]  Among the six there was James and his wife Winifred, the new agent for the constituency, Douglas Hughes from Llanelli, Bill Jenkins and Amanwy. In Newport they were joined by Arthur Jenkins, Labour MP for Pontypool. After arriving in the House of Commons, they were welcomed by six MPs, all associated with mining, namely Sir Charles Edwards, MP for Bedwellty and a Labour whip; D. R. Grenfell, MP for Gower, Rhys John Davies, a native of Llangennech and MP for Westhoughton since 1921, Edward John Williams, MP for Ogmore since 1931, George Dagger, MP for Abertilery, and S. O. Davies, MP for Merthyr. All were ex-miners and proud of their association with Jim and the mining industry.[14]

In the afternoon James Griffiths was presented to the House and they all enjoyed hearing Prime Minister Stanley Baldwin, J. H. Thomas, Walter Eliot and Nancy Astor taking part in the debate. Winifred Griffiths and her brother in law, Amanwy, took the other three guests for a meal, then to the cinema, and then returned to Parliament to hear Ellen Wilkinson at her best. She wanted to see women who were employed in government being given the same pay as men. This was a sterling performance lasting 45 minutes.[15]

Amanwy and James went to their lodgings extremely tired. The following morning they had a full programme before them. Amanwy decided to see the play Night Shall Fall written by Emlyn Williams. After this, Amanwy went to the House of Commons to look for his brother and Ted Williams. When he arrived he was told that the Welsh poet and bohemian D. Emrys James, known as Dewi Emrys, had arrived. Dewi Emrys had come to the House of Commons with D. R. Grenfell, to welcome the new MP for Llanelli. Amanwy saw him in the gallery. He had long hair flowing over his shoulders and looked distinguished. He was invited to have tea on the terrace by Rhys J. Davies, who had known him before he left the Christian ministry for the life of a wandering minstrel. Three hours were spent in the company of Dewi Emrys, the poet who had composed Rhymes of the Road, which was published in 1928, and had mesmerised everyone with his flamboyant style.[16]  James Griffiths, Amanwy, Rhys J. Davies and Arthur Jenkins enjoyed his company and his contribution. James Griffiths and Arthur

Jenkins had never met the poet before that day, and they felt enriched as they listened to his 'scintillating speech'.

Before returning to Ammanford, Amanwy made his way to Charing Cross Road and the bookshops, where he met a number of Welsh people from the Swansea Valley, a sizeable number from Ystradgynlais and all glad that his brother had been elected as an MP. He completed his column by giving a sincere 'thank you' to the inhabitants of the Amman Valley:

> To finish, let me thank you on behalf of my family for being so kind and supportive to Jim during the by-election. We hope that not one of you will be disappointed in him at any time.[17]

His words were not in vain. His brother did much for the people he had known in his childhood and youth, and he found himself at home among most of his fellow Labour MPs. As a backbencher he came to know men who had been pioneers of the movement since the days of Keir Hardie. One of them was Will Thorne, MP for Plaistow. When he retired in 1945 at the age of eighty-eight he was followed by an admirer of James Griffiths, Frederick Elwyn-Jones. Will Thorne began his working life in a barber's shop, when he was only six years of age, but by the age of thirty he had established the Municipal and General Workers trade union. 1936 he had completed almost 20 years as the representative of the Plaistow constituency in the East End of London.[18] Another similar politician was Jack Jones of Silverton, an excellent defender of the dockers of London.[19] Around Griffiths were men like himself who had come to Parliament after years of experience in the mining industry, some representing constituencies in England, such as Gordon Macdonald, later Baron Macdonald of Waunysgor. Macdonald had been brought up in a Welshspeaking home in the mining town of Ashton-in-Makerfield in the Lancashire coalfield.[20] In 1924, he became a miners' agent in Lancashire. He remained in that post until he was elected Labour MP for Ince in 1929. Macdonald became a Labour whip in 1935 and took a prominent part in debates on the mining industry and on social questions. He and Griffiths became close friends as they had so much in common as socialists and as nonconformists. It was pure joy for Griffiths to be with his colleagues from the mining communities of south Wales, in particular Arthur Jenkins, W. H. Mainwaring and Aneurin Bevan. He felt satisfaction as he saw on the front bench of the Opposition, his neighbour D. R. Grenfell and also George Henry Hall, the MP for the Aberdare constituency, who years later became a member of the House of Lords. In the 1922 election Hall had been elected MP, defeating one of the most bitter and hard-hearted politicians of his time, C. B. Stanton, who had been so unkind to the Reverend T. E. Nicholas in the Khaki election of 1918. George Hall was an excellent platform speaker, an expert on the mining world, and Griffiths admired him for campaigning against the means test in 1934-5.

Griffiths new life as a backbencher gave him a great deal of satisfaction, but at times he felt dissatisfied. As a miners' agent and President of the Union he knew what was expected of him and at the end of his activities for the day in the coal mining valleys he would return home to his wife and children. But this was not possible in his life in Westminster as a politician. His working life began when he caught the train at Neath on Monday morning, leaving his wife in Ystradgynlais to discharge all the responsibilities for the children and carry out the needs of the home until he returned on Friday afternoon from Paddington.

His salary as an MP in 1936 was £400 a year, and he received an additional £100 from his union towards his expenses.[21] But £500 was not enough to sustain two homes (like many MPs, Griffiths had to find a place to stay in London). He knew that he could not afford to stay in a luxury hotel or one of the private clubs. He was fortunate to have a helping hand from the Labour MP for the Rother Valley, Edward Dunn, who had also been a miner.[22] They knew each other through their union involvement. Dunn had been elected MP in 1935. He stayed in a house in Bloomsbury, and James Griffiths could share a living room with him for five shillings a night, with breakfast included. He soon became aware of the difficult world of an ordinary MP, but at least he was within walking distance of Westminster. When the weather was pleasant, both men would walk to the House of Commons, but on rainy days they took a tram ride at the cost of two pence.[23]

After arriving at the House of Commons, his first task was to call for his correspondence. A new Member was allocated a locker about two feet by one in which to store his papers. Over the years this locker would have all kinds of material inside it. Jim had within seven years an overflowing locker, he and his friend Nye Bevan. Then he would enter the Library and if he could find a seat which he did more often than not then he could read and write letters to his constituents.[24] He could not afford a secretary to type his replies, and so he had no choice but to answer the letters in his own handwriting. He did this for many years. From the beginning he decided to answer every letter immediately. After completing this task he would spend the rest of the morning researching facts and figures to prepare his parliamentary and constituency speeches. He would spend the time from Tuesday morning to Friday morning dealing with his correspondence with his constituents and then studying books, papers and pamphlets that might be useful.

Jim used to enjoy the Library and in particular the Map Room which had been reserved by custom for the trade union members, among whom the miners' MPs were predominant. It was presided over unofficially when Jim arrived there  by George Dagger, the Labour Member for Abertillery, who had been a miners' agent like Jim and S.O.Davies. Dagger stood out among his comrades as he was always dressed  in wing collar and spotted bow tie. Jim enjoyed his company but often disagreed with his criticism of the Attlee Government industrial and social programme.

Another problem for him was the cost of his daily sustenance. He could not afford to eat in the House of Commons restaurant and so he used what was called Annie's Bar for snacks, in the Members' Lobby, and other meals in the tea room. It was a red letter day for him when the House of Commons Kitchen Committee provided low-cost high tea in the Members' Dining Room at six o'clock. The sittings in the House of Commons started at 2.45 p.m., and he never missed the prayers expressed by the Commons Chaplain, Canon Don.[25] He had a deep rich voice and it was a pleasure for the nonconformist Griffiths to hear him read the prayers. From his first day in the House of Commons, question time fascinated him, and it continued to do so right up to his retirement. He soon joined those keen politicians who asked the questions and in his second year as an MP he was runner-up in the number of questions asked. But he could not compete with Colonel Harry Day, Labour MP for Southwark Central, who was a great friend of Harry Houdini, the escapologist.[26]

The first question Griffiths asked was directed to the Lord President of the Council. He called for the establishment of a Medical Research Council investigation into silicosis. The Lord President was none other than Ramsay MacDonald who had upset Griffiths with his blunders over the Red Letter and by his tremendous personal ambition, which to many, became a betrayal of the Labour Party in 1931. He abandoned the Labour Party for which he had done so much for in its early years so that he could remain as Prime Minister of a National Government. To the jubilant Tories in 1931, with their 471 seats helped by the Labour defectors, MacDonald, J. H. Thomas and Philip Snowden, it seemed, as Francis Williams said, 'as though the Labour Party had been irretrievably destroyed and turned overnight into a mere rump of a party without possibility of recovery.'[27] But this never happened. Instead, Griffiths was invited by the very politician of whom he was wary, to come and see him. Macdonald welcomed him cordially and listened carefully as he explained the 'ravages of silicosis' on the life of miners in the south Wales coalfield.[28] After this meeting, Griffiths was assured that the government would act. In due course, a team of experts headed by Dr D'Arcy Hall visited the Welsh valleys. Their final report resulted, as Griffiths explained, in the scheduling of pneumoconiosis as an industrial disease.

Griffiths had to prepare his maiden parliamentary speech. He received advice from a number of supportive colleagues, and he decided to make the speech sooner rather than later. The occasion came in the debate when Neville Chamberlain had introduced his fifth budget. Chamberlain referred to the fact that he was going to spend £1 million to establish new industries in the so-called 'Special Areas'. These areas would receive financial support so as to establish factories and thus strengthen the local economy. Griffiths seized this opportunity. Of course, he was on familiar territory, for he could refer to the coal and tinplate industries which were struggling in south Wales. He spoke well, and the Chancellor praised him in winding up the debate.

The Chancellor's words were hollow; the truth was that Chamberlain did not hear Griffiths' speech. But the press reported his inspiring contribution. As a result of the press reports, he received a large number of invitations to address meetings in Labour constituencies. Immediately he became an evangelist for Labour in the Special Areas after the scheme was launched in January 1937.[28] A Programme of Action was implemented within five regions and at the Labour Party Conference of 1937 Griffiths gave an inspiring speech. Elizabeth Durbin wrote years later:

> Jim Griffiths, Ellen Wilkinson and others from the various areas spoke eloquently on their plight and praised the work of the commission, particular the attention it had brought them from Tory politicians and government officials.[29]

For the rest of his political life, Griffiths was always travelling. He was always on the road by car or travelling by train on his way to address meetings of Labour Party branches or constituencies. He also became popular with the producers of BBC radio programmes. Griffiths mastered the new medium, preparing talks in Welsh as well as English for radio.[30]

Within two years of being elected an MP, he was chosen as one of the official spokesmen for the Opposition.[31] His fellow Labour MPs had already shown faith in him. The Leader, Clement Attlee, felt that at least twelve backbenchers should have some experience as frontbenchers. The press called them Labour's Second Team or in rugby terms, 'Labour's Second Eleven'. The News Chronicle, which enjoyed substantial readership within Wales, praised the Labour member for Llanelli:

> *Labour's front bench has notably gained by the inclusion of Mr James Griffiths, a Welshman who had already made his mark on the backbenches as a thoughtful and fluent speaker. Mr Griffiths' promotion is rapid, he has been in the House for only two years.*[32]

If his maiden speech asked for the gift of presentation, he was now in an unique position. He was expected to sum up a debate before the vote was taken. Griffiths rapidly mastered this role, and was fortunate in the opportunities given to him to become involved in matters in which he was well versed, in particular unemployment and poverty in distressed areas. Griffiths received every assistance from his fellow MPs and his work on the front bench was highly regarded by the Labour leaders. For twenty-five years, he was a regular spokesman for the Labour Party in opposition as well as in government.

But Griffiths knew that the Welsh-speaking communities in the industrial areas of Carmarthenshire were suffering needlessly in the 1930s. The poverty and the suffering was devastating to the community that had moulded him. He knew that half the chapels in the coalfield belonging to his own denomination, the Welsh Independents, had a lack of ministers in charge of them, even though those ministers who had stayed had agreed to a substantial reduction in their salaries.[33] Yet the chapels within his constituency were in a much better situation than similar Welsh nonconformist chapels in the Rhondda and Cynon Valleys. This situation, and its repercussions, was a constant source of worry for him, the Welsh language was being neglected though the choral and musical tradition was bringing the songsters together. Griffiths felt that there was some hope in the Special Area Amendment Act, and he took part in the debate in 1937, an important measure to assist companies moving in to these distressed communities.[34] He identified with the sufferings of his constituents and on 29 March 1939 he opened the debate on the Report prepared by the Clement Davies Committee on the plight of those suffering from TB.[35] The mining and rural communities of Wales were the worst affected areas in Britain. His speech in Parliament on this occasion had a huge impact and the Labour Party published it in a pamphlet under the title, The Price Wales Pays for Poverty. The pamphlet sold out rapidly.

As an internationalist, Griffiths was concerned, like his hero George Lansbury, with the rise of Fascism and the deteriorating international situation. Lansbury admired the MP for

Llanelli. He was one of the first to welcome Griffiths to Parliament, and was always willing to give attention to the struggles of the south Wales miners on the pages of the Daily Herald. As a pacifist, Lansbury travelled throughout Europe in his crusade for peace. He, Percy Bartlett, and Corder Catchpole of the Fellowship of the Reconciliation, visited the dictator Hitler.[36] The Führer could not for a minute appreciate the standpoint of the three pacifists. They talked for two hours, to no avail. But, like David Lloyd George, Lansbury was mesmerised by the personality of Adolf Hitler. He realised on the one hand that he was a fanatic, but on the other that he was one of the great politicians of the continent. Lansbury also visited Mussolini. He saw him as a combination of Stanley Baldwin, Lloyd George and Winston Churchill: he was as courteous as Baldwin, an orator in the style of Lloyd George and as unsentimental as Churchill.[37]

After returning from Berlin and Rome, Lansbury decided to relate his experiences to a small group of his supporters, including Griffiths, in a room at Westminster.[38] In his first year as an MP, Griffiths visited Prague, attending an international conference of miners in August 1936. There he met a number of miners from Sudeten. He heard their first-hand experiences of how the Nazis in the Sudeten coalfield were pillaging and inflicting violence; and to them, their only hope was the working classes of the United Kingdom. Griffiths returned from Prague with the sentence uttered by the miners echoing in his memory: 'Our only hope is in you, the British working class. We depend on you.[39]

Later that month he was asked by Stafford Cripps and Ellen Wilkinson to consider visiting Danzig in the company of his friend and former colleague in 'the Fed', Arthur Jenkins.[40] Danzig had been established at the end of the First World War by the League of Nations. That February the Nazis won a majority in their Parliament, the Volkstadt. The two Welsh politicians were welcomed by the leaders of the trade unions, by the British Ambassador, and the Commissioner from the League of Nations, Sean Lester, an Irishman. He warned them of the situation, and that spies would be following them everywhere. The Commissioner told them to accept every invitation but to be on their guard against the spies. They did so, and on the last day but one, they were taken up the river Vistula. They spent the whole day on the river believing, in their innocence, that there were no spies on the boat, and that they could be free to express themselves. When the time came to leave Danzig, James Griffiths heard the same as he had heard in Prague: 'We depend on you and your country.' Later they learnt the sad truth that one of the men who had accompanied them and steered the boat up the Vistula was himself a spy.

After they returned from Danzig, Wales heard of an important symbolic gesture undertaken by three leaders of the Welsh Nationalist Party in the Llyn peninsula. In the early hours of 8 September 1936 at Penyberth, near Penrhos, on the outskirts of Pwllheli, there was an explosion. The three men decided to destroy some property belonging to the government in Penrhos, which was to be the site of a new airfield to train RAF pilots. This was the reason it was called a 'bombing school'. The three who took the blame were the dramatist and lecturer J. Saunders Lewis (born in Wallasey and educated at the University of Liverpool), the second intellectual was a schoolteacher from Fishguard who had been a Labour Party member, D. J. Williams, a miner at one time in Betws, and the Reverend Lewis Valentine, minister with the

Welsh Baptists in Llandudno was the third protestor. After setting the buildings on fire, the three went to the police station in Pwllheli to admit their crime and to pass on a letter of explanation to the Chief Constable of the county of Caernarfonshire.[41]

Griffiths did not disclose his feelings about the actions of the three 'heroes' as they were called in the Welsh language press, but his brother Amanwy, in his weekly column, had no hesitation in commending the actions of the three nationalists. The reasons why he did so were quite obvious. D. J.Williams had been a miner at Betws and a friend of the brothers. On that score one can suggest that his younger brother would also be supportive. It is certain that the friendship of D. J. Williams and the Griffiths family would override any other consideration. One has to remember that this was a period in Welsh life when socialists and nationalists in the colleges of Wales were very supportive of the action taken at Penrhos RAF site.

In the University College of North Wales, Bangor, a movement called Gwerin brought together budding nationalists and socialists. One of the socialists, Goronwy O. Roberts from Bethesda, wrote a Welsh song to praise Saunders Lewis, D. J. Williams and Lewis Valentine, who had performed an act of heroism in Welsh nationalist mythology. However, the vision of Gwerin was completely rejected by the Welsh nationalist hierarchy as well as by the leaders of the Labour Party in Wales.

In November 1936 an unemployed miner from the Rhondda Valley landed in Spain, and he is regarded as the first Welsh volunteer to serve the International Brigade against the armed forces of the dictator Franco, who was another leader of Fascism in Europe. Spain was in crisis and in a short period of time, the conflict became a devastating civil war. However, it inspired a huge number of miners and Socialists from Wales to travel to Spain. By the end of 1936 a volunteer from the Llanelli constituency, W. J. Davies of Ammanford, had arrived in Spain. Committees were established in south Wales to collect food and money in support of the International Brigades and the working classes in Spain. Griffiths involved himself, and in January 1938 he was invited to be a member of a Parliamentary deputation to Spain.[42] He travelled as one of seven MPs. The others were William Dobbie, who had been President of the National Union of Railwaymen, Major Milner, R. F. Fletcher, W. Whiteley, J. J. Davidson, and J. Henderson. The deputation was led by Bill Dobbie.

They travelled by train from Paris to Perpignan, and then in cars over the Pyrenees to the Spanish frontier where they were met by representatives of the Republican Government. From the frontier Griffiths travelled with Jock Davidson in a car driven by a Catalonian metal worker. Griffiths wrote a number of letters on his visit to Spain, to his wife and family, letters that were never referred to in his autobiography. In these letters, he referred to the crisis, and that it was not safe to travel at night, and that it was going to be difficult to fulfil all the deputation's engagements within a week. Griffiths praised the city of Barcelona whose citizens were welcoming to the visiting British MPs.

By Sunday night, 16 January, he was writing a letter from the Victoria Hotel in Valencia, a city 200 miles from Barcelona. He describes the scenery in detail, the mountains, vineyards, orange trees and the orchards. He wrote: 'An orchard of orange trees is the most beautiful sight I have ever seen.'[43] Had he forgotten the beauty around Betws? They were welcomed as visitors to stay near the orchard and fill a bag of oranges.

Griffiths thoroughly enjoyed the high temperatures, and especially the variety he saw in rural Spain: 'It was really indescribable in its beauty.' He does not mention in his correspondence if he had seen a bullfight, but knowing him, and his strong humanitarian convictions on cruelty, it is most certain that he did not. When he heard that the young people of Spain were becoming more interested in playing football than considering the life of a matador, he added the comment: 'Better by far to kick a ball – than torture a bull.'[44] The use of the word 'torture' says it all. [43]

Griffiths called in at a home for wounded soldiers and met young British socialists who had been injured in the conflict. Most of them were from families in Glasgow and Liverpool. He saw refugees from Germany and Italy, some of whom had escaped from the Fascists. They were also let into the hidden shelters that had been prepared for families who were exposed to the constant bombing. The British politicians experienced the atrocious conditions. Bombs fell near their vehicles. Indeed after arriving in Madrid the deputation was informed that the news was broadcast first of all by Franco's radio, and taken up by the BBC. It referred to the 'bombing of the British politicians in Spain as a warning to them to go home.' The British politicians telephoned the offices of the Labour orientated newspaper, The Daily Herald, to inform the Editor that every one of the seven MPs was safe and sound. Griffiths sent, in addition, a telegram to his wife, who had by now moved from Ystradgynlais to 32 Tanycoed, Burry Port. It said succinctly, 'all Labour MPs in Spain safe and sound.'[44]

The same night he wrote a letter to Winnie and his children. He referred to the journey of seven hours and of the glory of the capital city, Madrid. But what had moved him more than anything else was the horrific destruction of the Civil War. He said:

> I have seen war nearly at first hand, and it is terrible and yet the marvellous thing is life goes on. Here in this city [Madrid] the front line is only a mile away and yet life goes on.[45]

The next day, the deputation spent some hours in the company of General José Miaja. He was a colourful personality, well loved by the soldiers and citizens who opposed General Franco. At the end of the Civil War he escaped with the help of the British Fleet, to North Africa. Later the General emigrated to Mexico, where he spent twenty years in exile.

On his way home to Wales, Griffiths visited members of the International Brigade who had survived the ferocious fighting experienced in the battle of Teruel. At Tarragona he attended the funeral of five British sailors who had been killed when their boat had been bombed. They laid wreaths on their graves, and Bill Dobbie and Griffiths paid sincere tribute to their sacrifice.

After he arrived back in Burry Port, he became very busy in activities to support the Welsh volunteers in the International Brigades.[46] At least 177 Welshmen had volunteered, and of these 122 were miners from the south and north east Wales coalfield. Out of the 133, thirty three of them died in battle, and some were taken as prisoners by the Spanish Fascists.

One of the most remarkable miners and Welsh enthusiasts taken captive was Tom Jones of Rhosllanerchrugog, a mining village some three miles from Wrexham. He became known for the rest of his life within Welsh Labour circles as 'Twm Sbaen' (Tom Spain). Tom Jones was the last of the prisoners to return from Spain. Taken prisoner in September 1938, for months he was living under a death sentence. The Spanish government announced that he had been killed in the battle of Ebro, but through the efforts of his Member of Parliament Roberts Richard, James Griffiths, Will John and other MPs, his family came to know that he was a prisoner in Bargers prison. The Fascist authorities informed the government of Britain that they had to hand over £2 million before he could be released. At the beginning of April 1940 Tom Jones was able to return to his family at Rhosllanerchrugog mainly through the effective action of the MP mentioned.

The Left Book Club devised by the left-wing publisher Victor Gollancz had a branch in Ammanford with the socialist Edgar Bassett heavily involved. It gave tremendous support to the young men from the valleys who had gone to Spain to fight Fascism. Flag days were held in different towns in the coalfield on 19 and 20 February 1938 to raise money for the Welshmen out in Spain. The miners were willing to contribute six pence a week each towards their financial needs. Many a Welsh nonconformist chapel in the Llanelli constituency also responded. The Spanish cause needed not only money but also food and medical care, and the Women's Society of the Labour Party in Ammanford was involved on that front. For eighteen months, local socialists played a vital role in supporting James Griffiths in his campaign against Fascism in Spain.

In February 1937, Griffiths lost a close friend in Lewis Rees from Garnswllt. He came from the same background as Griffiths and was a reliable leader for the miners at Pantyffynnon colliery. It was always a treat to hear him presiding at the Lodge meeting of the miners. He would speak in Welsh with his fellow miners, the result of years attending the adult Sunday School and the weekly prayer meetings. Rees was a Deacon at the Welsh Baptist chapel of Noddfa in Garnswllt. Amanwy emphasised in his tribute to him that his socialism was based on the brotherhood of man as spelt out in the New Testament. He could not support a reactionary nationalism. Amanwy states that:

> Christ was an internationalist, and it is sad to see young Welsh people losing sight of this vision by flirting with insecure political movements, some of whom will inevitably disappear.[48]

This was also the standpoint of his young brother.

Later that year Amanwy and his brother paid tribute to another miner from the Pantyffynnon colliery, another example of a cultured collier. His name was William Lewis from Ammanford, and he worked underground every week, though he had reached his 80th birthday. A native of Cwrtnewydd in Cardiganshire, William Lewis moved with his family when he was a small child to the Amman Valley. He began working in the colliery when he was only seven years of age. Like Griffiths, he came from a large family, (eight children), but through the fellowship of the chapel and the Miners' Union, he had received a cultured upbringing which helped him in his hard and heavy daily work. He had worked in a number of collieries, and had been at Pantyffynnon colliery for thirty-four years. The Labour Party stalwart, John Harries (Irlwyn), wrote a poem in Welsh, describing his life as a conscientious head of the family and a hard-working miner. Lewis was highly thought of and was a Deacon in the Welsh Baptist chapel of Ebenezer in Ammanford. His son, the Reverend L. G. Lewis, ministered in the same denomination at Holyhead in Anglesey.

Another personal satisfaction to Griffiths was the success of his unofficial lieutenant, Frank Davies, who gained a seat on Carmarthenshire County Council on 4 March 1937. Davies gained 708 votes in the name of the Labour Party while David Jones, the Independent candidate, only gained 487 votes.

Griffiths took part in a House of Commons debate on foreign affairs on 24 March 1938 and emphasised the huge danger to the peace of the world from Fascism, which he himself had seen in Europe, at Prague, Danzig and in Spain. He criticised Prime Minister Neville Chamberlain for being weak, and he uttered two sentences which are most relevant: 'Democracy and freedom have no frontiers. Wherever the fight for them takes place, that is also our struggle.'[49]

The Fascists were active within Britain, and they organised, under the leadership of Sir Oswald Mosley, big marches in London with the deliberate object of upsetting Labourites in working-class districts. From the later months of 1937, there began to appear a growing demand for the widest possible coalition of working-class unity in the hope that Chamberlain would resign and be replaced by a government that would stand up to Hitler, Mussolini, Franco and all similar-minded dictators.

Griffiths, who had been a convinced pacifist all his life, was in a dilemma. His fellow socialist Stafford Cripps asked him, as well as Bill Dobbie and Ben Smith, to meet him. This was June 1939, when Germany's Finance Minister Colonel Count Johann Schwerin von Lutz Graf was in London. Stafford Cripps was most anxious that before Count Graf returned to Germany, influential Trade Union Labour MP's in Westminster should meet him as he was after all a member of the inner circle of Hitler. The five of them met in a private house in Mayfair and they heard his propaganda. Griffiths had heard it all before in Prague and Danzig, and mentioned to him his visits to Eastern Europe. Each one spoke on the same theme, reminding Graf that the Labour movement would be one hundred per cent behind the British government in its struggle for freedom against Fascism and Nazism.[50]

James Griffiths also met Edgar Ansel Mowrer, author of Germany Puts the Clock Back, published in 1933. In 1939 he came to address the Labour MPs and it was at this meeting that Griffiths the pacifist was convinced that he no longer had any choice but to stand up against Hitler and Mussolini. As Griffiths admits in Pages from Memory, it was at this meeting that he came to a definite decision. It was an important landmark in his political pilgrimage. He says that Mowrer described Mussolini as 'an unscrupulous adventurer with whom France and

Britain could make a bargain, if they were prepared to pay the price, but that Hitler was an insane fanatic with whom no bargain was worthwhile – we either had to crush him or be crushed by him.' Griffiths was not the only politician who had come to that decision: there were millions of ordinary people of every age who felt the same as he did.

He received a letter from a Spanish intellectual in France, Alfredo Matilla Jimeno, who had had enough of Franco and his violent ways.[51] Griffiths and Jimeno had earlier met in Spain, and Jimeno and his wife desired, above everything else, to emigrate to Mexico so that he could escape from the clutches of Franco. Matilla wrote from the Hotel du Portugal, Vernet-les-Bains in France to Griffiths: 'When you were in Teruel with me, you said that you would never forget us. And now, I remember your words.' Matilla had met both J. J. Davidson and Griffiths. Both of them helped Matilla on his way to freedom and a better way of life. The Spanish Civil War ended in March 1939 with the surrender of Madrid. By the time the 1939 Labour Conference met in Southport, Fascism had gained a great deal of ground in Europe. But Griffiths was quite content that he had resolved his 'pacifist dilemma' as he called it, and believed in the necessity of re-armament, even under a government of whose philosophy and policy he thoroughly disapproved.

**Notes and References**

1. Mrs James Griffiths, *One Woman's Story*, p.118. 'Early in 1936 Dr J. H. Williams, the MP for Llanelly, died, and at once letters began to reach Jim from friends in the constituency saying how much they hoped he would accept nomination for the by election'. He did not preserve these letters in the Archives he deposited at the NLW. Dr J. H. Williams nearly lost the nomination at the Selection Conference before the 1935 General Election. He gained the nomination by only one vote. See Tom Stannage, *Baldwin thwarts the opposition: the British General Election of 1935* (London, 1980), p. 219.

2. The information for Dr J. H. Williams comes from *The Amman Valley Chronicle and East Carmarthen News*, 13 February 1936, p.2. There is no photograph of him with the obituary. John Henry Williams, Snowden House, Burry Port left the sum of £33615-12-0.

3. Ibid.

4. Ibid., 27 February 1936, p. 5.

5. Ibid., 5 March 1936, p. 1.

6. Ibid., 12 March 1936, p. 3.

7. Ibid., 19 March 1936, p. 5.

8. Ibid., 16 January, 1936, p .5. D. R. Grenfell, MP delivered a lecture in Welsh on the 'Condition of Europe Today' at Glanaman.

9. James Griffiths, *Pages from Memory*, pp. 53-4. 10. 'Stafford Cripps at Ammanford', *Amman Valley Chronicle*, 9 April 1936, p. 6.

11. Ibid.

12. 'Cerddetwr', Colofn Cymry'r Dyffryn, *Amman Valley Chronicle*, 9 April, 1936, p. 2. James Griffiths wrote a manuscript called 'Voice of Wales' where he mentions the fact that he and other miners from south Wales who were given the honour of being MPs had trodden a difficult road to Westminster. 'We had all reached Westminster having travelled these same hard road – work in the mine service, in the union, and so on to Parliament carrying the 'blue scars' with us. For all of

us, coming to Parliament had been the beginning of a second career, and for most of us it had meant learning a new job in middle age'. See NLW, James Griffiths Papers, 'The Voice of Wales'.

13. 'Cerddetwr, Colofn Cymry'r Dyffryn', *Amman Valley Chronicle*, April 9, 1936, p. 2.
14. Ibid.
15. Ibid.
16. Ibid. James Griffiths was extremely proud of those MPs who like himself had been nutured in Nonconformity and knew the mining industry in all its aspects. In his manuscript 'Voice of Wales' he said: 'the old guard – William Jenkins, Charlie Edwards and Will John – men who so worthily represented the old tradition of the Sunday School and the "Big Seat" at the Chapel – men of character and integrity who served the constituencies and country with devotion'. NLW James Griffiths Papers.
17. Ibid. Rhys Hopkin Morris emphasised the 'persistence of the old Nonconformist attitude in the Labour Party in Wales. Like the Liberal representative of the earlier period, the Labour representatives of today have for the greater part been nurtured in this tradition'. See Rhys Hopkin Morris, *Welsh Politics* (Wrexham,1927), p. 15.
18. James Griffiths, Pages *from* Memory, p. 54.
19. Ibid.
20. Ibid.
21. NLW, James Griffiths Papers, D 3/12. Member for Llanelli.
22. Ibid.
23. Ibid.
24. James Griffiths, *Pages from Memory*, p.55.
25. Ibid.
26. Ibid.
27. Francis Williams, *Fifty Years' March: The Rise of the Labour Party* (London, 1949), p.45.
28. James Griffiths, Pages from Memory, p. 55.
29. Ibid., p. 56; Elizabeth Durbin, *New Jerusalems: The Labour Party and the Economics of Democratic Socialism* (London, Boston, Melbourne and Henley, 1985), p. 250.
30. NLW, Eirene White Papers. A draft copy by the father of Eirene White, Thomas Jones. James Griffiths was invited to prepare and present a talk on BBC Radio Wales on 15 February 1937 on the topic of Trysorfa Welfare y Glowyr. He explained how, following the Sankey Commission reports Parliament had passed a B. 11 imposing a tax of a penny on every ton of coal that was produced in Britain to be used for the miners and their families. This was the basis of what he called on the radio in Welsh *Y Geiniog Gyfareddol*. The proceeds had succeeded by 1937 in creating 31 new pithead baths in the south Wales coalfield, then had built numerous halls, and arranged playing fields as well as the Talygarn Rehabilitation Centre for miners with its beautiful gardens. See Centre for Written Archives of the BBC in Wales, NLW, Talks 1937, P-T.
31. NLW, Eirene White Papers. Thomas Jones, CH, 'Minister of National Insurance and Social Security'.
32. NLW, James Griffiths Papers, D 3/12.
33. In the 1930s there were a number of outstanding nonconformist preachers who ministered within the constituency, such as D. J. Lewis, Tumble; Robert Ellis, Tŷ Croes; D. J. Davies, Capel Als, Llanelli; Jubilee Young, Seion Chapel Llanelli and Dr D. Tegfan Davies, Christian Temple, Ammanford.
34. See Steven Thompson, Unemployed Poverty and Health in Interwar South Wales (Cardiff, 2006). Thompson maintains on pages 22-3 'Not only did south Wales experience higher levels of

unemployment than other areas of Britain, but the unemployed in south Wales were out of work for longer periods of time'.

35. *Hansard*, Vol. 345, 22 March 1939, col. 1331; it was republished as a pamphlet *The Price that Wales Pays for Poverty*. The background and the arguments are to be found in 'Wales and Health' in *Transactions of the Honourable Society of Cymmrodorion 1939*, pp. 55-100, that is the papers which were delivered by Clement Davies, William Jones, Dr D. Rocyn Jones, Sir Percy Watkins, James Griffiths and Sir Robert Armstrong-Jones in a seminar held by the Cymmrodorion in London on 31 March 1939.

36. Vera Brittain, *The Rebel Passion: A short history of some Pioneer Peace-Makers* (London, 1964), p. 52. She has a portrait on Percy W. Bartlett, pp. 86-95 and T.C. Catchpool, pp. 52, 60 and 94.

37. On Lansbury's peace missions in 1937, see D. Lukowitz, 'George Lansbury's Peace Mission to Hitler and Mussolini in 1937', *Canadian Journal of History*, 15 (1980), pp. 67-82; 'Visit of Mr George Lansbury, MP to Berlin', 20 April 1937, TRA, 37/207/45/35228. On Lansbury as a pacifist, see D. Ben Rees, 'George Lansbury' in *Heddychwyr Mawr y Byd* (ed. D. Ben Rees) (Liverpool and Llanddewi Brefi, 1982) pp. 7-75.

38. James Griffiths, *Pages from Memory*, pp. 60-1.

39. Ibid., p. 61.

40. Ibid., p. 62. 41. Kenneth O. Morgan, 'Welsh Politics 1918-1939' in *Wales Between the Wars*, pp. 106-8.

42. James Griffiths, *Pages from Memory*, pp. 64-66.

43. NLW, James Griffiths Papers, B 1/31. A letter written on Sunday night, 16 January 1938 from Victoria Hotel, Valencia to his wife W. Griffiths.

44. Ibid., B 1/34. Letter of James Griffiths to his wife from Madrid dated 19 January, 1938.

45. Ibid.

46. Ben Pimlott, *Labour and the Left in the 1930s* (Cambridge, 1977), pp. 86-92.

47. NLW, James Griffiths Papers, B 61/36. A concert in the Public Hall of Felinfoel on Thursday, 14 March 1938.

48. NLW Amanwy Papers. A copy of his Welsh article on Lewis Lewis in the Amman Valley Chronicle.

49. James Griffiths, Pages from Memory, p. 66.

50. Ibid., p. 67.

51. NLW, James Griffiths Papers, B 1/37. Letter of Alfredo Matilla, Hotel du Portugal, Vernet-lesBains to James Griffiths, no date.

Jim in Oxford in 1938

Jim with his niece May Harris (1905-76) from Ammanford.

# 10

## An MP in the Perilous Second World War

By 1939 James Griffiths was regarded within the Labour Party as a safe pair of hands. He was highly respected and regarded himself as the representative of the Welsh working class and welcomed letters from every part of Wales. The Secretary of the North Wales Quarrymen Union wrote regularly to him on the needs of his members in the slate-quarrying centres of Bethesda, Nantlle Valley and Blaenau Ffestiniog.[1] At the 1939 Annual Conference at Southport, the Labour Party discussed the activities of three rebels: Aneurin Bevan, Stafford Cripps and George Strauss, and considered expelling them from the Parliamentary Party. Griffiths was unhappy about this proposal; he was, at heart, a reconciler and his task was to keep good relationships between the left wingers and the right wingers. He sympathised with the clear call of Bevan, Cripps and Strauss to work with the communists in the Popular Front against Fascism.[2]

Griffiths was completely dissatisfied with the government of the day, which was trying to appease Hitler. At this stage it was more afraid of Bolshevism than Nazism. When a peace treaty was signed between the Soviet Union and Germany in August 1939, the left wingers felt they had been betrayed. Ten days after signing the Nazi-Soviet pact was signed, German soldiers were marching through Poland. The following Sunday, 3 September 1939, Prime Minister Chamberlain announced that Britain was at war with Germany. As all of his generation felt, Griffiths knew that they were fighting without the resources needed to win. Within a week, the cargo boat Winkleigh from Cardiff had been torpedoed by German U-Boats in the North Sea.

As a Welsh speaker, Griffiths raised an important question in Parliament in October 1939. He asked the government for its position with regard to Welshspeaking conscientious objectors who would have to appear before tribunals. He was given an answer on 26 October by the Minister of Labour, Ernest Brown, a staunch member of the Baptist Church. Brown spelled out the policy which was much more enlightened than a great number of pacifists had ever envisaged. Griffiths was told that every conscientious objector would be given the right in the tribunal to express himself in his native language. All the tribunals in north Wales would have these facilities, and conscientious objectors from south Wales who opted to speak in their mother tongue would be allowed to appear before one of these Welsh language tribunals.

One of the notable chairman of these tribunals was Sir Thomas Artemus Jones, an advocate for the legal status of the Welsh language. But he did not accept the argument that a conscientious objector could be released from his obligation to serve his country during the war merely on Welsh nationalistic grounds. To him the only argument that stood scrutiny was the religious standpoint. He was criticised for this view by staunch nationalists but he did not change his opinion. In a note in his archives, Griffiths mentions that 2,920 conscientious objectors had been given the opportunity of arguing their case in Wales before the tribunals, and most of them had based their objections on religious grounds.[3] The government was willing to respect their conscience. Not one Welsh Christian was imprisoned for his religious motivation.

But this did not mean that they did not suffer by being harassed in their communities, dismissed by unsympathetic employers, and often embarrassed publicly because of their pacifist convictions. A classic example was the poet and scholar, Dr Iorwerth Cyfeiliog Peate, founder of the Welsh Folk Museum at St Fagans, near Cardiff. Griffiths sent him an important letter on 18 October 1939 outlining why he himself could not anymore accept the pacifist standpoint that had meant so much to him for decades. He opened his heart to Peate in his letter written in Welsh:

> *I was convinced that we had to stop those who were threatening Europe and the world since 1935 – when the countries of Europe failed to stand against the actions of Mussolini on Abyssinia. This was the result of our failure to build a new Europe at the end of the 1914-18 War and our failure to make the League of Nations a vehicle to assist the needy and to achieve justice. Yes, if Germany had stayed in the League, and argued its case in Geneva – but knowing of these problems we would be on the way to a settlement without war. It could be done by reason and fairness. But the foundation of every effort to have peace is for every nation to be faithful to its vows and to honour its agreements.*[4]

Griffiths felt that Hitler had betrayed the world and that there was no choice left but to stand up to him. He enlarges on this in his Welsh language letter to Dr Peate which I have translated:

That is the big problem today. Hitler has broken every agreement so that we have no faith left in him. I had hoped that his speech the other week would have given a new opportunity. But his terms are based on him conquering the east. We would have to accept his terms with regard to the nations that will be conquered, they will have no rights whatsoever. The next step is for this country to spell out its terms in a reasonable manner. I have told my Party to make this clear and without any hesitation to him, and I hope that an outline of such a policy will be spelt out in Mr Attlee's speech today. It is difficult to underline the need for justice in a letter. I would very much like to have a conversation with you on this complex subject.[5]

Griffiths, however, could not agree with some of Welsh authorities, especially in the cities of Cardiff and Swansea, who demanded that those individuals who worked for them sign a declaration that they were in favour of the war. He was perplexed at the action of the National Museum of Wales in dismissing Peate from his employment because he had appeared before a Conscientious Objector Tribunal. Griffiths was deluged by letters sent to him protesting at the actions of the Museum authorities. He took a prominent part in the campaign to reinstate Dr Peate. At the Annual General Meeting of the Court of Governors of the Museum, on 24 October 1941, he led the attack against monstrous decisions of the Executive Officers.[6] On the platform that day, seated behind the desk, one could see the President of the Museum, the Earl of Plymouth, the Director, Dr Cyril Fox and the Secretary, Archie Lee. During the whole debate, they were severely rebukerd by four strong minded

MPs' The authorities were fiercely criticised by Aneurin Bevan, James Griffiths, Ronw Moelwyn-Hughes, representing Labour, and D. O. Evans for the Liberals. In the words of the academic  Sir Thomas Parry, these speakers nearly 'roasted them', and the meeting voted with a huge majority to reinstate Dr Iorwerth Peate immediately. The conviction politicians had won the day. Griffiths had strong views with regard to the thrust of a coalition government.[7] The Labour Party was to him an amalgam of collectivism and individualists [8] Collectivism was welcomed by him in nationalization but not in conscription.

Like Keir Hardie, he had no time for coalition government. When Neville Chamberlain invited Clement Attlee at the beginning of the war to join the National Government, he refused the invitation. The situation was different by May 1940 when the Labour Party Conference was held in Bournemouth. Ever since the Southport Conference in 1939, Griffiths had been a member of the National Executive Committee (NEC). When the NEC met on the eve of the Conference, the thorny subject of a possible coalition was discussed once more. Chamberlain had again approached Attlee. This time Attlee was ready to consider the proposal and so were the Labour Party delegates. But Labour could never accept the 'Man of Munich', as Neville Chamberlain was called, or indeed his possible successor, Lord Halifax, as prime minister. The only statesman that Labour would accept was Winston Churchill. Without this hardline approach of the Labour leaders, Churchill would never have become prime minister. At the age of sixty-five, Winston Churchill became Prime Minister. His words echoed to Transport House: 'I felt as if I were walking with destiny, and that all my past life had been but a preparation for this hour and for this trial'.[9] It was a wise move for the sake of Britain, but not an easy one for Labour politicians. They were expected to support their leaders as ministers of the crown as well as to keep the unity of the party. When the Parliamentary Labour Party met, they agreed on two matters. Firstly, to agree that Labour MPs not in government should be allowed to sit on the opposition benches, and secondly, to select by a vote, a small group of MPs to sit on the opposition frontbench. Griffiths was nominated and elected as one of this group under the guidance of Hastings Lee-Smith and Frederick PethickLawrence. The ILP stalwart, James Maxton, protested at this structure, arguing that the ILP rather than the Labour Party should be the official opposition.[10] They had four MPs and as they were utterly opposed to the war, they surely should have been entitled to act as the official Opposition, he argued.[11] The parliamentary authorities were placed in a difficult position. The Speaker consulted the writings of Erskine May, the Victorian expert on constitutional issues, and was able to convince Maxton that the official opposition should be the largest grouping, which after all was the Labour Party.
The system worked well. The small committee of Labour MPs kept in touch with Attlee and his few fellow Labour ministers who were members of the coalition government. Griffiths was very concerned about the neutrality of Eire, and wrote to Attlee on 28 June 1940 at the possible danger that Northern Ireland, as well as Wales, could be exposed to attacks from German aircraft. He wrote:

> *I have what the Americans call a 'hunch' that Hitler's attack will come upon us through Ireland. I have called the attention of the War Office to some places in West Wales where an attempt might be made – either from Ireland, or now, from the west coast of France. One, in particular, Pendine sands – a stretch of sands about seven*

*miles long – and a mile deep at low tide. It is like concrete and literally hundreds of planes could be landed there. Last week, I met in the House a large number of New Zealand soldiers. I found in conversation that many of them were of Irish extraction – and they talked of their visit to the old country – Ireland. Is it not possible to get Eire to accept Dominion soldiers to help in the defence of Ireland? It should be possible to attack by Germany.*[12]

Griffiths raised the same matter when he spoke at the Rotary Club in Llanelli at the beginning of July, a few days after writing to Attlee. In his speech he emphasised how his fellow Welsh MPs wanted adequate provision to safeguard Wales. His ideas of a German invasion via Pendine and getting a united Ireland to accept Dominion soldiers were difficult to comprehend as Eire had declined to belong to the Commonwealth, and had declared itself neutral in the conflict. But he received a typical Attlee communiqué: 'We are fully seized with the Irish position. You can, I am sure, imagine all the difficulties. We are doing all that is possible.'[13]

But this was small comfort to an MP who had witnessed the damage a German bomb had done to the road near the Royal Ordnance Centre in Burry Port near his home. He wrote to Sir Gerald Bruce, the Commissioner for the Welsh region, about the bombing that had taken place affecting two farms and an Anglican Church in his constituency.[14]

In the spring of 1941 Griffiths, a proud son of Welsh nonconformist parents, got involved in a debate on the possibility of opening theatres on a Sunday. Griffiths, like J. B. Priestley's father, was a devoted lover of the Sabbath. Unlike Jonathan Priestley, he never refused to listen to reason and he never tried to win the argument with an explosion of temper. But he was convinced, like the Liberal MP D. O. Evans in Cardiganshire, that the Welsh Sunday was a blessing to be cherished. It was a day of worship for Christians and, for those who did not attend chapels or churches, it could be a day of relaxation and rest. Griffiths received a great deal of correspondence on the matter, and he believed that Whitehall and Downing Street should treat Wales as a country which had a different language and a different tradition with regard to Sunday observance. He clashed with Lady Nancy Astor on this issue, and told her in no uncertain terms:

> *I would far rather we should go back to the nonconformist conscience than to a world without conscience. I believe it is in the best interests of the nation and of the work people of this nation to keep Sunday a day of rest, a day of reflection, and to refuse to commercialise it, and that is why I shall go into the lobby for the prayer.*[15]

Griffiths enjoyed a huge following among Welsh nonconformists in his constituency. There were a number of Ministers of Religion who identified with his outlook, and he was delighted to welcome the Reverend O. R. Davies as a Welsh Independent minister to Bethel, Garnant, at the beginning of July 1940. Davies remained in Garnant over the years and involved himself in Labour Party affairs.

Within his constituency, Griffiths was highly popular because of his personal approachability and his sincerity. This can be discerned in a column in the Amman Valley Chronicle at the beginning of May 1941, written under the name of 'Watchman'. It asks the question: Who, today, is Wales's leading figure in the House of Commons? We would single out Mr James Griffiths for the honour. Not only does he contribute to the most important debates in the House, but he also finds time to actively interest himself in affairs appertaining to the well being and progress of his native valley. Why, it has become a general thing to write to Mr Griffiths about it, and his unfailing courtesy and promptitude in dealing with the correspondence sent to him has won the admiration of all.[16]

This is a tribute that any politician would be very glad to receive, and a month later in the same paper the Executive Committee of the constituency Labour Party included a further tribute, underlining the tremendous respect that the Prime Minister, Winston Churchill, had for their MP.[17] Griffiths defended Wales, and in his constituency he was hard working. He became literally the MP for Wales in the war years, and he was highly thought of for his command of politics, economics, current affairs, and in particular his interest in foreign affairs. Among the large circle of journalists who had a high regard for him was Hanen Swaffer of the The Daily Herald. His message in 1940 to the Labour movement was simply: 'Make use of Mr James Griffiths MP – the Miners' Leader. The country needs men with a clarity of vision similar to him for the defence and preservation of our great democracy.'[18] Many of his fellow Labourites in the constituency felt that his parliamentary speeches should be gathered together and published in book form. Most probably that would have happened but for the war years and the rationing of paper. There seemed to be no end to his constituency involvement during the war. On 23 May 1941 he shared a platform in Garnant with the Conservative politician and future prime minister, Harold Macmillan, author of the important volume The Middle Way.[19] A week later Griffiths spoke in Ammanford, sharing a platform with Labour MP for the Aberdare Valley, George Hall. He received a standing ovation when he spoke on Irish neutrality in the war, sincerely hoping that the Dail would allow British ships to use the harbours and ports of Eire.[20]

On St David's Day 1942, Griffiths delivered a radio talk in English praising the contribution of the Welsh League of Youth in defending the language and its culture. In a typical paragraph, Griffiths said: 'For one of our most virile movements in Wales today is "Yr Urdd" – the Welsh League of Youth. And it is significant that the name given by the Welsh League of Youth to its clubs is Aelwydydd – Hearths. There is no Welsh equivalent to the English word "clubs".' He also spoke of his love for the Welsh language, adding, 'a love of our language that does not deny an appreciation of others.'[21]

The Labour Party heeded the words of Swaffer and Griffiths was given a great deal of responsibility when he was asked to address some of the Reconstruction Conferences organised by the Labour Party.[22] He spoke at ten of the fifty Conferences that were held. From his notes it is clear where these conferences were held – the conference held at Kettering represented the Midlands, Wimbledon was the venue for the industrial belt south of London, Exeter served the West Country, the heart of rural England, and the Conference in Norwich was held in the week of Hitler's brutal reprisal raid. Griffiths added: 'Hitler's spite gave that Conference an intensity of purpose that made it memorable. One could feel the resolve and determination of the people deepened by their tragedy.'[23]

Two of the conferences were held in Cardiff, when a total of 893 delegates, representing the Labour movement, attended. These conferences gave the Labour Party hierarchy and all those who attended a great deal of confidence. By 1942, a large part of the movement felt that the British armed forces as well as the Red Army were slowly getting the upper hand over the Germans and their allies. Griffiths emphasised that they did not want to return to the 1930s. Unemployment, industrial strife, the rampage of TB in Wales, and the failure of appeasement were distressing to politicians of the sensitivity of James Griffiths.

The Reconstruction Conferences emphasised four principles:

(i)     Full employment for everyone. This was a priority for Griffiths: 'The men in the forces, and the men and women serving the War effort- will come back permanently one day to their communities. When they do, they must come back to a job. There must be a a colliery, a firm and a factory for them to earn a decent wage. And that place must guarantee them a secure livelihood.'[24] Griffiths felt that Britain must plan its economic life so that each individual had a secure place. This seemed to be the constant cry of the delegates.

(ii)     Then the Labour Party must rebuild a Britain that will be worthy of those that have preserved it. This meant not only building houses, shops, public buildings but also communities, as well as planning the location of industry. Griffiths added: 'And this must be done by the creation of a National Authority – with powers to do the re-building and with regional authorities to carry out these plans in all the regions of Britain. We must build a home for our people. That is the dominant note.'[25]

(iii)     To prepare an adequate and comprehensive system of social services. Great efforts had been made in the past but it was not enough. To Griffiths: 'We must weave all our various social services into one complete service. It must bring everyone within its fold. It must cover all those eventualities that destroy the livelihood of an individual or a family, sickness, accident, old age-all must be provided for. The Community must provide a secure and adequate livelihood for all those who meet with misfortune. And such a scheme must provide for the endowment of children by a State system of family allowances.'[26]

(iv)     To care for children and young people by preparing a democratic system of education. Griffiths admitted; 'At all the Conferences I attended, the view was urged that provision should be made for all the young men whose careers have been interrupted by the calls of the Nation should be enabled to complete their careers as the guest of the State. And there is also the resolve that our educational system must do more to train youth for their individual careers. It must fit them for their tasks as citizens. They are citizens of a democratic system. They are all members of the community. They will have to play their part in the rebuilding of our country and of the world. And they must be provided with the training for citizenship that is essential for that task. They should be taught with two principles at stake, firstly to assist them to seek a career and employment, and second to be worthwhile citizens.'[27]

They all felt that victory was within their grasp.[28] For these men and women had suffered and sacrificed for their future. They were determined, as Griffiths realised, to 'secure the fruits of victory'.[29]

In addition to his involvement with the Reconstruction Conferences, Griffiths was very well loved within the Fabian Society during the war years. The politician Eirene Lloyd Jones (later Eirene White, MP for East Flintshire) paid him this tribute: 'He is one of the most popular chairmen at Fabian Summer Schools, bringing to that inhibited, middle-class audience the directness and warmth of his own simpler, working-class outlook. His personal kindness and consideration for young candidates and party members are unfailing.'[30]

Griffiths's wife mentions in her memoirs how he addressed a Fabian Summer School in Dartington Hall in south west England. Winifred decided to drive him to the Summer School, and they thoroughly enjoyed the journey from Burry Port, visiting Gloucester, Bath and Wells on their way to Devon.[31] They also enjoyed the friendship of the leading Fabians and the discussions as well as the lectures.

Griffiths was invited to be a member of a powerful sub-committee on International Affairs, under the chairmanship of the publisher and political theoretician, Leonard Sidney Woolf.[32] Griffiths came to know through this committee the leading intellectuals of the Labour Party, in particular Harold Laski, Richard Henry Tawney, Barbara Wotton, Margaret Cole and her husband, the Oxford don, G. D. H. Cole.[33] Griffiths was the only MP on the committee besides John Parker, MP for Dagenham, and General Secretary of the Fabian Society.

Within the fraternity of Labour MPs from mining constituencies, and also those who had been miners themselves, he was regarded as loyal and dependable. The Labour Party invited him to prepare a booklet on the history and future of the coal industry. This booklet was entitled *Between Two Wars: Coal* and had a preface by Sir William Lawther, a miners' leader. The booklet created quite a stir and the Coal Mining Association produced and published in 1942 a reply under the title *Coal in Peace and War: A Reply to James Griffiths*, MP.

Griffiths was asked to address a public meeting on Sunday night 20 June 1942 in Gwaun Cae Gurwen on the report by Dr D'Arcy Hall on silicosis. After all, the miners in the anthracite coalfield suffered much more from the disease than miners in any other British coalfield. Griffiths felt that the coal owners and the miners' leaders had been at loggerheads for much too long, with the result that they had wasted much valuable time. He considered this to be a tragedy of the first order.

On 19 June 1942 he was delighted to be invited to the opening of a canteen at his old colliery in Betws. The canteen could cater for at least 100 miners at one sitting. His wife, Winifred, spoke at the opening with a message to the wives of the miners to encourage them to use the new facilities which had taken so long to become a reality. However, Griffiths was not completely satisfied with the promises made by his colleague D. R. Grenfell to the miners of south Wales.[34] David Rees Grenfell was a member of the government, and he was very severely rebuked by Amanwy in his weekly column in the Amman Chronicle.[35] Amanwy said Grenfell had worked for years underground and it was unbelievable that he still had not given a more supportive hand to his comrades in the mining industry. It would have been better if Grenfell had resigned from the government rather than giving such weak promises to the south Wales miners, he said. These promises, Amanwy reflected badly on the minister and ill served on the miners who had helped him to become an MP and later a member of the Government. It is obvious that Amanwy would not have written such a strong attack Grenfell without the knowledge of his brother, and it easy to suppose that one can hear the voice of James Griffiths in this severe criticism.Griffiths was very concerned that so many miners were leaving their collieries for the armed forces, with the result that there was a shortage of men to work in the coalfield. To overcome the crisis, young men were conscripted during the Second World War to work in Britain's coal mines under the Emergency Powers (Defence) Act of 1940. In 1943 Ernest Bevin, Minister of Labour and National Service, directed that one in ten men called up between the ages of 18 and 25 should go down the mines, and the scheme continued for a while after the end of the war. These were the 'Bevin boys', but Griffiths, with all his admiration for Ernest Bevin, the trade unionist par excellence, was not content with the scheme. He felt was a short-term answer to the serious problem of recruiting men to work in the collieries.

Griffiths welcomed the move in 1942 to put the coal industry under the jurisdiction of the Ministry of Power, a department headed by Gwilym Lloyd George, MP for Pembrokeshire. There was no hesitation in the minds of the anthracite coal miners that this was the way ahead toward nationalisation.[36] Indeed, public opinion largely agreed that this was the only means of achieving satisfaction for the miners. This move was part of the reconstruction that was so important to Griffiths. To him the goal was to create a just, neighbourly community after the horrors of the war and he describes his hopes in *Pages from Memory*. The publication of Sir William Beveridge's report at the end of 1942, Social Insurance and Allied Service, was well received.[37] The National Government printed 635,000 copies and all were sold out within a few days. The Trade Union Congress, the Co-operative movement and the Labour Party expressed their support for this important document and called for its speedy implementation at the end of the war. The establishment of the Welfare State was the inevitable outcome, and three days were allocated in February 1943 for the House of Commons to discuss the Beveridge Plan. Griffiths moved Labour's motion urging the Churchill coalition Government to accept the proposals of the Beveridge Report.

The Prime Minister had convened a group of ministers to discuss the Report and the chairman of this cabinet committee, Sir John Anderson, MP for the Universities of Scotland, opened the debate on behalf of the Coalition. Anderson (later Lord Waverley) had been one of the most able civil servants of his generation. For a period he had been Governor of Bengal in India, and on his retirement in 1937 he was persuaded to stand for parliament. He did so in a by-election in 1938. Within a year of his victory he joined Neville Chamberlain's cabinet. Churchill failed dismally in his judgement by giving Anderson the task of opening the debate.[38] In his presentation he expressed his doubts about the Beveridge plan, creating dismay among the most progressive members of the Coalition, but giving the Labour Party the initiative. In addition, a similar response came from another ex-civil servant who had become a politician, Sir James Grigg, Secretary of State in the War Office. He refused to allow a concise summary of the Beveridge Plan to be circulated to the men and women in the Armed Forces, because he did not want to give the impression 'that the scheme was settled Government policy, whereas in fact no decision of any kind had been taken'.[39] The Anderson speech, Grigg's veto, and the general lack of leadership on the recommendations of the report by Churchill gave Griffiths and his colleagues in the Labour Party the distinct impression that the Beveridge Report was to be shelved if the Conservatives were returned to power at the end of the war.[40]

In a meeting of Labour MPs during the second day of the debate it was decided to table a motion expressing complete dissatisfaction with the government's attitude to the Beveridge Plan and calling `for its early implementation. It was also resolved to carry the motion to a vote in the House of Commons. Griffiths who was given the task of moving Labour's amendment and on 18 February 1943 he did so brilliantly. According to contemporary accounts it was a 'rousing speech, frequently cheered by the Labour Party.' Griffiths underlined the merits of the plan:

> *The plan has, among others, these three great merits: first, it is comprehensive. It brings within the range of social insurance practically every citizen in this country. It brings them all in instead of dividing the country into sections and saying that one section shall be brought in and another left out. The second great merit is that it provides security from want in adversity by warranting a minimum subsistence income, whatever the cause and however long the period. Lest there be here or in the country any idea that Sir William Beveridge is proposing that people shall be given such a standard of life that they will be tempted to become malingerers, I would point out that what he proposes is a subsistence income related to need and based upon standards which he outlines in his report. He ends the anomalies by which the benefit which people get in adversity depends not, as now, upon the need the adversity creates, but upon how the adversity arose. The plan proposes that a minimum subsistence income shall be provided for people in adversity, whatever may be the cause and however long the period. The third great merit of the plan is that it consolidates our social insurance and allied services into a single scheme under the direction of a single ministry and with unified administration.[41]*

Griffiths added:

> *I suggest that the question which we ought to ask ourselves is not whether we can afford the plan, but whether we can afford to face the post-war period without it… We have called our youths to the Services… we have called for sacrifices, and… I hope we shall remember that we owe these people a debt that we must honour and that we shall begin to honour that debt today.[42]*

This was a critical debate. Griffiths's motion was supported by 119 MPs, including David Lloyd George, who cast his last vote in the Commons, and Arthur Greenwood, who had, while serving in cabinet, originally commissioned the Beveridge Report. Herbert Morrison was not well pleased, and made a plea for the Labour MPs to support the Coalition

Government. This was a considerable Parliamentary revolt against the Coalition and Griffiths's robust presentation was praised at the Labour Party's annual conference in London during June 1943. The left-wing MP for Nelson and Colne, Sydney Silverman, moved an amendment criticising the Coalition Government's 'timidity'. Griffiths had given hope to the Labour movement's progressives throughout the British Isles. At the end of the division, Griffiths turned to Sir William Beveridge and said: 'This debate, and the division, makes the return of a Labour Government to power at the next election a certainty'.[43]

As a result of the debate and his clear leadership, Griffiths was called upon to address meetings on the future of Britain after the war. The Fabian Society honoured him by inviting him to deliver the October Lecture in 1943 and again in 1944.[44] Griffiths was one of a small circle given this honour: the others were Harold Laski, R .H. Tawney, G. D. H. Cole, Sir William Beveridge and Aneurin Bevan. Griffiths and Bevan were the only two MPs among the distinguished Fabian lecturers and both came from the mining background of south Wales.

In his Fabian lecture under the title 'Industry – Servant of the People', Griffiths argued in favour of nationalisation, and the need to ensure that the work carried out in these nationalised industries should be fulfilling. He enlarged on this lecture when he was invited to address the Annual Conference of the British miners in 1943 by calling for the development of democracy within the industry, and the need for every section, the miner, the engineer and the administration, to co-operate.

At this time Griffiths received an invitation from Brendan Bracken, a Minister of Information, and a politician close to Churchill, to undertake a long lecture tour of the USA.[45] This would entail being away for four months, visiting twenty-eight states, and addressing meetings in every town and city in which he stayed. Bracken expected him to represent the British parliament as an ambassador and send a clear message to the political establishment in the United States. A highlight of his visit was to meet the Welsh American miners' leader, John L. Lewis. He saw Lewis at his office in Washington, and Lewis asked him to visit his mother when he passed through the town of Springfield in Illinois, and to speak to her in Welsh. Lewis never forgot the fact that Griffiths did exactly as he had asked.[47]Throughout the four months, he kept his family informed of his movements and the welcome he received from the east to the west coast of America. His visit was exciting to him and well received. A local American paper published a letter from one of his admirers which stated: 'It is a pity that we do not have more people to represent the working class like Jim Griffiths. Good luck, Jim; it is a long time since we had a Welsh-born Prime Minister.'[48]

He mentioned often in his speeches and lecturers two of his fellow Welshmen: Robert Owen, born in Newtown, and David Lloyd George, brought up in Llanystumdwy. Griffiths argued that Robert Owen had not received the accolade that he deserved from the Welsh nation. To him, Owen had been more influential on the life of the world than any of the Welsh heroes, Owen Glendower, John Penry and Henry Richard. After all Owen was the Apostle of Co-operation, not only in Wales and Britain, but throughout the world. Griffiths often mentioned in his radio talks and his addresses interesting information with regard to Lloyd George.[49] He returned from the USA on board the Queen Elizabeth, and later wrote an account of his American odyssey in his Pages from Memory.[50]

In 1944, Griffiths was invited to be a member of the committee that the Labour Party established to prepare for the general election at the end of the war, under the chairmanship of Herbert Morrison. This was the committee that prepared the manifesto, under the title, Let us face the future. To Griffiths, the workers and their families deserved to be among the priorities of any Labour government. In March 1945, the British miners, in no uncertain terms, criticised Lord Porter's report published at the end of January. The report did suggest better pay for the miners but not in line with their expectations.

The Porter Report did not support the traditional rights of miners to have extra payments for extracting coal from difficult seams or the right to have coal at a lower price delivered to their homes.[51] On 6 March 10,000 miners came out on strike in the Monmouthshire coalfield, and the action spread to the collieries in the Llanelli constituency. By 11 March most of the collieries in south Wales were idle, and five days later the miners of Yorkshire and Scotland joined the Welsh miners. Griffiths intervened to persuade the miners to discuss the matter with the coal companies, and he succeeded in achieving a compromise. On 12 March, 38.5% of the Welsh miners returned to work, though there were a number of lodges still dissatisfied. These were difficult days for the miners. Between September 1939 and October 1944, as Griffiths reminds us, there were 514 stoppages in the south Wales coalfield. It was a time of change. On 1 January 1934 'the Fed' became a region within the British Union of Miners. To Griffiths, the best hope of the miners was the return of a Labour government the next general election.

There were a number of Labour intellectuals who had a very high regard for Griffiths at the end of the Second World War. Among them one would cite Douglas Jay, a civil servant since 1941, who stayed with James and Winifred Griffiths and the family at their home in Burry Port in July 1944 and realised immediately the knowledge his host had of Welsh economics, politics society. This is what he wrote in his autobiography years later:

> *Jim Griffiths was almost unique in possessing all the Celtic oratorical gifts at their best and in full measure, and a high degree of practical common sense at the same time. He also represented admirably the old nonconformist conscience of the Labour movement, which was still strong in 1944.*[52]

This is a fine tribute by a keen observer, who had been brought up in the lap of luxury, and had never known the harsh, hard tasks of a coalface miner, as Griffiths had.

The death of David Lloyd George on 26 March 1945 brought to an end an important chapter in Welsh political history.[53] Griffiths had mentioned Lloyd George in the war years in radio talks, and in his addresses in the USA in particular to the Welsh societies.

James Griffiths was to play an important part in the development of the Welfare State. The best-selling author Sue Townsend expressed the mood of Britain at the end of the war, when she wrote:

> *By the time the war ended, the people were more than ready for the Welfare State. They were sick of eating the crumbs off the table – they wanted to pull up the chair and join the feast. The Beveridge Report gave them hope; it recommended the setting up the Welfare State.*[54]

The vision Griffiths had had since the 1920s was finally being implemented when the Welfare State became a reality between 1945 and 1950.

**Notes and References**

1. NLW, James Griffiths Papers A4/72. Letter of R. W. Williams to James Griffiths dated 20 June 1939.
2. Mark M. Krug, *Aneurin Bevan: Cautious Rebel* (New York and London, 1961), p. 55. Cripps and Bevan shared a platform on a number of occasions with the two communist leaders, Harry Pollitt and William Gallacher. The slogan of these meetings was 'United Front of the Workers. Class to fight Fascism and War'.
3. NLW, Iorwerth Cyfeiliog Peate Papers A1/5. Letter of James Griffiths to Iorwerth C Peate.
4. Ibid.
5. Ibid. The cause of Iorwerth C. Peate A 1983/127, A 1985/109, A 1988/121. James Griffiths stated that he received more letters in his post bag on the manner in which the Welsh National Museum treated Iorwerth C. Peate than any other issue. See *Cymro*, November 1, 1941, pps.1 and 12. Dr I. C. Peate received strong support, when his pacifism came before the Museum Council on 24 October 1941 in Cardiff, from these Welsh politicians, Sir William Jenkins, D. O. Evans, R Moelwyn Hughes, Evan Evans, S. O. Davies, Aneurin Bevan, James Griffiths, Will John and Robert Richards.
6. Thomas Parry, *Amryw Bethau* (Denbigh, 1996), pp. 321-4.
7. Keith Laybourn, *The Rise of Socialism in Britain c.1881-1951* (Stroud, 1997), p. 136.
8. Stephen Brookes, *Labour at War The Labour Party during the Second World War* (Oxford, 1977), p. 146.
9. David Cannadine, *In Churchill's Shadow* (London, 2002), p. 105.
10. A. Marwick, 'James Maxton and his place in Scottish Labour History', *Scottish Historical Review*, April 1964, 43 (135), pp. 25-43.
11. NLW, James Griffiths Papers B3/13. Letter of James Griffiths to Clement Attlee dated 28 June 1940. See also B 3/10, a letter dated 19 March 1942.
12. Ibid. Letter of Clement Attlee to James Griffiths dated 1 July, 1940.
13. Ibid. Letter of James Griffiths to Sir Gerald Bruce.
14. Ibid. The account of the MP for Llanelli.
15. Watchman, 'James Griffiths', *Amman Valley Chronicle and East Carmarthen News*, 8 May 1941, p. 4.
16. 'Gwladgarwr', Tributes to James Griffiths, MP, *Amman Valley Chronicle and East Carmarthen News,* June 12, 1941, p.4. 'His outstanding resistance to the Means Test has been very successful

and his enthusiastic campaign in supporting the War Weapons Week in the Amman Valley and other districts has been highly approved and commended'.

17. Ibid., 23 May 1941, p. 4., Amman Valley and District War Weapons Week.

18. Ibid., 30 May 1941, p. 2.

19. Ibid.

20. NLW, James Griffiths Papers, 'The War Years'. 21. Ibid., B3/1. 'Labour Looks Ahead. Impression of the Reconstruction Conferences'. A Conference was held in Norwich during the bombing on the city.

22. Ibid.

23. Ibid.

24. Ibid.

25. Ibid.

26. Ibid.

27. Ibid.

28. Ibid.

29. Ibid.

30. NLW, Eirene White Papers, 'A Portrait of James Griffiths'.

31. Mrs James Griffiths, *One Woman's Story*, p. 123.

32. The life and work of Leonard Woolf is to be found in three volumes; *Beginning again: an autobiography of the years 1911-18* (London, 1964), 260 pp; *Downhill all the way: an autobiography of the years* 1919-39 (London, 1967), 259 pp; *The Journey not the arrival matters: an autobiography of the years 1939-69* (London, 1969), 217 pp.

33. For Laski, see H. W. Deane, *The Political Ideas of Harold J. Laski* (New York, 1955), 383 pp. For Tawney, see T. S. Ashton, 'Richard Henry Tawney (1880-1962)', *British Academy Proceedings* 1962, XLVIII, pps.461-82. For Barbara Wooton, see her volume, *In a World never made: autobiographical reflections* (London, 1967), 283 pp. For Margaret Isabel Cole, see *Growing up into a revolution* (London, 1949), 252 pp.

34. It is possible that we find the feelings of James Griffiths in the criticism of his brother Amanwy on D. R. Grenfell. See NLW, Amanwy Papers, for a copy of the article in Welsh.

35. NLW Amanwy Papers.

36. The successor of James Griffiths in 'the Fed' believed that 'nationalisation was not socialism' but it was an 'important step in the right direction'. See Arthur Horner, 'Nationalisation of the Coal Industry', *The Labour Monthly*, Vol. 28, no. 2, 1946, pp. 45-6.

37. James Griffiths, *Pages from Memory*, p. 71. 38. Ibid., 'It turned out to be one of Churchill's errors of judgement'.

39. Ibid.

40. Ibid.

41. Hansard, 18 February 1943.

42. Hansard, 18 February 1943.

43. Ibid.

44. James Griffiths, *Pages from Memory*, p. 72.

45. Ibid.

46. Ibid.

47. NLW, James Griffiths Papers, B 2/19. A letter from Reverend Daniel Hughes, Detroit, September 20, 1943 after hearing he intended to visit the USA, and pleading on him to call on the Welsh Society of Detroit. The Christian socialist minister says: 'Don't forget Detroit, please. *Bob llwydd*

*ar ei daith yno* (Best wishes on your journey here).' The Secretary of the Chapel where Daniel Hughes ministered was Walter Perrott, a native of Llanelli.

48. James Griffiths, *Pages from Memory*, p.74-5; Amanwy, 'Wil y Painter', *Amman Valley Chronicle*, 7 July 1949 (another article that I received from Dr Huw Walters).

49. NLW, James Griffiths Papers B2/6 *Travelling to the United States of America*.

50. NLW BBC Written Archives, James Griffiths 'O'r Senedd', April 18, 1940.

51. Ibid., B 2/21. Alex Shennan, Chicago, sends a letter dated 9 October 1943 to thank JG for his talk to the first Rotary Club in the world, the club that Paul Harris brought into existence in 1905 and which is known as Rotary No. 1 Chicago, and also his contribution to the Illinois St Andrews Society where he spoke.

52. 'The Porter Award aggravated rather than soothed the discontent in the coalfields. In the poorer paid districts, such as South Wales, the minimum rates were raised to a level which upset the lower wage rates actually being paid. Men whose roles had previously been different found themselves receiving the same rates.' See, J. E. Williams, *The Derbyshire Miners: A Study in Industrial and Social History* (London, 1962), p. 858.

53. Douglas Jay, *Change and Record: A Political Record* (London, 1980), p. 190.

54. Donald McCormick, The Mask of the Merlin: A Critical Study of David Lloyd George (London, 1963), p.301.Years after his passing James Griffiths would still remind his audiences on the radio and public meetings of the charisma of Lloyd George: 'He had spent an unforgetable hour in his company'. 'See NLW BBC Written Archives Centre, Talks BBC 0-Z, James Griffiths,' Mis yn y Senedd' (Month in Parliament), delivered on 31 July 1953 in Welsh on Radio Cymru.

55. Sue Towsend, *Mr Bevan's Dream: Why Britain needs its Welfare State* (London, 1989), p. 3.

# 11

## Labour's Success in Wales

 James Griffiths took advantage of every opportunity that came his way to present the William Beveridge Plan. In his press statements, in his speeches, including his tour of the USA, he often mentioned the 'new world' that would come into being when victory had become a certainty. He did so in the name of freedom and social justice. He worked closely with Herbert Morrison, who was convinced that Labour would win by a combination of the working class and the middle class working together for the good of Britain.

Griffiths felt that Wales was ready for a breakthrough and he was always ready to remind the Labour hierarchy of his optimism. He read the published work of his famous rival, Aneurin Bevan, Why Not Trust The Tories (1944), written under the pseudonym Celticus. Bevan argued, with conviction, that one had to win the argument over the Conservatives, and that they were unbelievably uncaring.  That is why he did not want Labour to be too coalition-minded and too wedded to the wartime consensus. He loved to use the word 'socialism' in his writings and in his speeches. Griffiths agreed with him. Indeed, in his address to his electorate in Ebbw Vale, Bevan said: 'The Labour Party is a socialist party; and I am proud of this.' Bevan did not agree on the needs of Wales in terms of devolution as Griffiths did. Griffiths had heard Keir Hardie often, a dedicated Home Ruler, who included this commitment in every election address he prepared from 1888 to 1910.[1] The clearest commitment was prepared in 1918 by the General Secretary of the Labour Party at the time, Arthur Henderson. He outlined the reasons for Labour's commitment to Home Rule for Wales:

> It is hardly possible to conceive an area in which a scheme of Parliamentary self-government could be established with better chance of success than Wales. All the problems that embarrass statesmen and challenge the imagination of reformers are to be seen in Wales, reduced to manageable proportions. Given self-government, Wales might establish itself as a modern utopia and develop its own institutions, its own culture, its own ideal of democracy in politics, industry and social life, as an example and an inspiration to the rest of the world.[2]

This commitment remained with the Labour Party in the inter-war years, though it had been more or less abandoned by 1931. In the General Election of 1931 the Labour Party in England suffered an electoral defeat on a huge scale. In Wales it was an entirely different story. Wales had become a Labour stronghold in the mining valleys, and Bevan realised that the British Labour Party needed Welsh support if it was to win power and govern in the future.

James Griffiths, on the other hand, had grasped the implications of what Henderson had argued for in the 1918 manifesto. During his term of office as Secretary of the Welsh Parliamentary Party, a unique institution at Westminster as it brought together all the political parties to co-operate for the sake of Wales, he was given the opportunity to consider devolution. All Welsh MPs were invited to be part of the organisation and in the 1930s all parties were represented within the WPP as the Welsh Parliamentary Party was known. During the period that he acted as Secretary – 1938 to 1945 – the party representation was made up of 18 Labour MPs, 6 Liberal and 11 Conservative MPs. Griffiths was a member of a deputation of Welsh MPs under the leadership of Morgan Jones, MP for Caerphilly, who went to see the Prime Minister, Neville Chamberlain on 30 June 1938.[3] They had two important matters to discuss: the need to establish a Welsh Office and also to establish the office of a Secretary of State for Wales. In his letter, dated 29 July 1938 to Morgan Jones, the Prime Minister indicated his sympathy and acknowledged the devolution argument but argued that Wales was already treated fairly. He states in his letter: '...Wales is receiving the special treatment which was one of the objects of the deputation. I am satisfied of the efficiency of these arrangements, and I do not consider that Wales would receive any practical advantage from co-ordination of the various activities in a single department'.[4] He felt that it would be a costly business to establish a new Welsh Office, and that one could not expect Parliament to vote for such a drastic measure. In addition, the comparison with Scotland, which had its own legal system as well as administrative functions, was crucial. His views were clearly expressed in his long letter.

On the other hand, since Henry VII's Act of 1535, Wales had been closely incorporated with England and there had not been, and there is not now, any distinct law or administrative system calling for the attention of a separate minister. This was followed by the ultimate rejection: 'In these circumstances, while I fully appreciate the motive which led the members of the deputation to approach me, I fear that I must ask you to inform them that I do not feel able to comply with the request which they made when we met.'[5]

Aneurin Bevan had to admit that he agreed with the argument as for him, at that time, Wales did not have its own distinctive problems.[6] The problems of steel workers in Ebbw Vales were the same as those in Scunthorpe, and this was true of all trades and occupations. Yet James Griffiths retained a vision of a Secretary of State for Wales. He did a great deal of work for Wales in this period, and one could argue that it was his efforts in this period which eventually proved to the Labour Party and Harold Wilson that he should be the first choice for the position of Secretary of Wales in 1964 when the Welsh Office was established. He sent, in his capacity of Secretary of the Welsh Parliamentary Party, a letter to the Prime Minister, Winston Churchill, dated 7 July 1943 on the same lines as the one sent to Chamberlain five years earlier.[7] The Chairman of the Welsh Parliamentary Party was Arthur Evans, Tory MP for Cardiff South. Lady Megan Lloyd George and Aneurin Bevan were the Vice-Chairs, while D. O. Evans acted as Treasurer. Griffiths was the Secretary. In a letter of 13 August 1943 from Arthur Evans to Griffiths, he was asked to form a sub-committee to discuss the question of a Secretary of State for Wales.

The actual memorandum was prepared by Clement Davies, Liberal MP for Montgomeryshire in collaboration with Ronw Moelwyn-Hughes, Labour MP for Carmarthenshire. Arthur Evans advised his colleague, Griffiths, to send, without delay, a message to the Prime Minister before he (Griffiths) embarked` on his long tour of the USA. Though Arthur Evans's seat was marginal (he had a majority of only 541 votes in 1935), he had a fervent Welsh spirit. This was his promise to Griffiths: 'You can rely on me to keep the flag flying.'[8] Griffiths had been present at the important meeting held at the National Eisteddfod of Wales in Cardiff in 1938 under the chairmanship of Dr William George, the brother of David Lloyd George. It was a meeting to discuss the possibility of removing the bar against the use of the Welsh language in the courts in Wales. Shortly after the establishment of Churchill's Coalition Government in 1940, the Welsh Parliamentary Party received letters from different organisations stimulated by the Eisteddfod meeting in Cardiff. They went into action and took the matter up with the Home Secretary at the time, Herbert Morrison. The result was the Welsh Courts Act of 1942. Griffiths underlined the importance of this campaigns:

> *The importance of the Act was that this was the first time that the 'Tudor Ban' on the use of Welsh in the courts was removed. Although the provisions of the Act have been criticised and later modified by another measure with which, as Secretary of State for Wales, I was concerned, that Act of 1942 has its place in Welsh history.*

Then he mentioned how he welcomed the Act for Welsh was not a 'museum language' but a living language. He felt that the Bill which became the Act is 'a recognition of a nation, because to recognise a nation is to recognise its language'[9]

The Welsh MPs felt that they had achieved a great deal when the Welsh Courts Act of 1942 became a reality, and this could have inspired them to call again for the government in Westminster to consider the establishment of a Secretary of State for Wales. But they had to be patient. Winston Churchill was in no hurry: he had enough on his plate as a war leader. But there is a letter that he wrote to Lady Megan Lloyd George, dated 2 January 1945.[10] It is obvious that she had written to Churchill and included the argument of the Welsh Parliamentary Party on the possibility of having a Secretary of State for Wales. Churchill mentions that these recommendations were receiving consideration but it was obvious that there was not a hope that a Conservative Government would implement such a proposal. This is clearly stated in this paragraph:

> *The difficulty is that a proposal of this nature has such far-reaching implications in the administrative sphere that detailed consideration has to be given to it by the many authorities concerned. These authorities are of course heavily burdened with war tasks.*[11]

The war was enough of a reason for Churchill to bury the proposal completely. Churchill had very little sympathy with the hopes of patriotic Welshmen on devolution.[12] Throughout the war, both he and Attlee were reluctant to give Wales any special treatment.[13] They, as we have mentioned, agreed to the passing of the Welsh Courts Act of 1942, and then the introduction of the Welsh Day Debate in Parliament, implemented on 17 October 1944, the first ever in the history of the Westminster Parliament, but nothing else.

On the eve of Labour's Annual Conference in Blackpool in May 1945, until the defeat of Japan. Labour's leaders were split on the proposal. Bevin, Dalton and Attlee were sympathetic but Manny Shinwell, Aneurin Bevan, James Griffiths and the Chief Whip, Will

Whiteley, were now convinced that Labour should go for an early general election. The Labour Conference agreed with them, and before the end of the conference, Churchill had called a general election. Parliament would be dissolved on 15 June. Polling day would be 5 July. Griffiths was invited on behalf of the Labour Party to deliver a party political address on radio on 18 June, and he did so, underlining the importance of the mining industry.[14] He believed in 1945 that the future of Britain depended on coal. If the industry succeeded, he said, on the basis of that success, a Labour government could build a prosperous Britain. Griffiths emphasised the profit made by the coalowners between 1939 and 1944, which was in excess of £90 million.[15.]

*The British Coalfield*

| Year | Production | No of Coalminers | Personal production per man |
|------|-----------|-----------------|---------------------------|
| 1939 | 231,337,900 | 766,300 | 301: 9 |
| 1940 | 224,298,800 | 748,200 | 299: 4 |
| 1941 | 205,344,300 | 697,600 | 295:8 |
| 1942 | 203,633,400 | 709,300 | 287:1 |
| 1943 | 194,493,000 | 707,800 | 274: 8 |

In 1938, 48.5 million tons of coal were exported. The result of the war was to do away with the exporting of coal from Wales to European markets. Griffiths was solid in his support of the mining industry, but he was also conscious of the danger of putting too much emphasis on the industry as had been done in the past.[16] This was why he supported the idea of the new light industries that came into his constituency. He believed that these new industries were important for retaining the Welsh people in their communities, for he knew that the younger generation was willing to opt out from the old tradition of the son following the father to the coal mine. He was not too pleased with the situation, and in many ways he was omitting to remember the dangers and the harshness of the industry.

Furthermore, there was a world of difference between the time that he had left the coal mine as a miner in 1922 and the situation in 1945, in the mining industry as well as in society as a whole. He noted in his radio broadcast that the fundamental choice was to do with public ownership or private ownership:

> *The real choice in between Public Ownership – in the interest of the nation – and Monopoly Control, for the profit of the few. That is the choice we have to make on July 5th.*[17]

Griffiths emphasised the failure of the economic system in the inter-war years: 'It failed to provide work for more than a tenth of the nation's workers.' He went on to give examples of the sufferings endured in the Welsh mining communities as a result of the greed of the combined companies. Instead of organising industry to put idle hands to idle machines to feed hungry mouths, in reality, he argued, the combined companies created a scarcity. They dumped food into the sea to keep up prices and profits. They bought up shipyards – not to work them, but to close them down.

These accusations were gaining support, especially among those from the working classes who listened to his broadcast. Then he referred to his own experience, and he mentions the ordinary people of the valleys as his 'own people', meaning the miners:

> *I have seen people – and what it has meant to my people – and what it had made of my industry, coal, and to my old workmates in the pit. I have seen fine men thrown on the scrap- heap, eking out their lives in enforced idleness. And splendid women were wearing away their lives in worrying where their next meal was to come from. And the young turned sour and embittered by frustrated hopes to be born, to grow up, and to grow old, and to die on the dole.*[18]

He appealed at the end of his presentation for the opening of a new chapter in the history of the mining industry and the life of the miners. This broadcast inspired the Welsh miners who were campaigning hard for the return of a Labour government and the nationalisation of the mines. No organisation in Wales did more towards this goal than did the Welsh miners. As Abe Moffat said of the Scottish miners of the period:

> *They gave more money then any other trade union, and in the mining constituencies they gave financial assistance to ensure the return of a Labour Government. In addition, every year the Scottish Miners' Union gives financial assistance for the organising of mining constituencies over and above their political levy and affiliation fees.*[19]

This was the same in Wales as far as the miners were concerned. Griffiths's hope was that the miners would have, at last, a better deal, and that new hope would dawn over the mining valleys, and a more prosperous period for the working class in Britain.

Griffiths knew very well what suffering meant. The minutes of the Labour Party and trade unions in Llanelli lists, consistently, the matters he had to deal with as MP. When the local Labour councillors and trade unionists discussed the intention of the government to establish a system to hand out coupons for clothes, this particular minute said it all: 'That we [shall] ask James Griffiths, MP to support any measure that will aid the working class.'[20]

Griffiths's leisure time was non-existent. A deputation came to see him on the situation with regard to the steel industry in 1941: Wales was one of the centres for steel production. A report prepared by Stanley Davies to the Executive Committee of the Labour Party and the trade unions on the situation was discussed. Griffiths promised to discuss the whole situation with two fellow MPs who had shown support to the steel industry, D. L. Mort, MP for Swansea East, and Sir William Jenkins, MP for Neath. D. L. Mort had worked in the industry before been elected an MP in a by-election in 1940, while Sir Williams Jenkins, like Griffiths, had been a miner and miners' agent. In his address at the Llanelli Constituency Labour Party on 21 July 1941, Griffiths spoke the heavy industries which were finding it difficult to survive, and the need to expand the economic base of south Wales, the purpose being to bring new industries into the constituency.[21]

He said he was using his influence with the government to utilise empty factories in Llanelli for producing war equipment. His executive committee in the Llanelli constituency were extremely impressed with his determination. Without doubt, Griffiths was the most influential member on the Welsh Advisory Council. He never forgot his priorities — to care for the miners and their communities; to support devolution for Wales — and it was no wonder that he was known throughout the coalfield as 'our Jim'.

Griffiths realised that the most important element in Wales since the First World War had been to safeguard its land and people. The culture of industrial south Wales and its social life, as well as its industries, were closely inter-linked and needed to be safeguarded. The War Office had its eye on Welsh land. At the beginning of the war the Epynt Mountain was taken over and the Welsh communities in that part of Breconshire uprooted. This brought the closure of the Babell Welsh Calvinistic Methodist chapel forever. The polymath, T. I. Ellis, mentions how three Welsh MPs had given support to the campaign of *Undeb Cymru Fydd* to safeguard the land of Wales.[22] The first two were Labour MPs, Robert Richards of Wrexham and James Griffiths. The third MP was the Liberal, Clement Davies. The farmers who had lost their land received better terms because of the efforts of these three MPs. No part of Wales was safe from the War Office plans: from the Preseli Mountains in Pembrokeshire to the hills above Tregaron in Cardiganshire; from the rich lands in the Vale of Clwyd to the area around the village of Trawsfynydd in Merionethshire.[23] Trade unions were an essential part in the Labour Party's campaign for the 1945 General Election. Llanelli was fortunate in that it had a full-time political agent in the person of W. Douglas Hughes, appointed in 1935. He was an excellent administrator, very much like the Secretary of the Labour Party in Wales, Cliff Prothero, who had come to the job in 1944 following the tragic death of George Morris in the wartime blitz on Cardiff.[24] Both Prothero and Hughes, were hardliners with regard to any meaningful co-operation with the two parties that challenged Labour in south Wales, the Communists and Plaid Cymru.

The 1945 general election took place after a war which had touched the lives of every person in Britain in some way or other. This was an old-fashioned campaign: by the 1950s, television was beginning to play a more prominent part in the campaigning. In 1945 the parliamentary candidate was expected to work hard, to visit homes, factories, collieries and to address four or five public meetings every night. Then, at the end of the campaign, a large eve of poll meeting would be held. This was the general pattern as it happened throughout Wales up to 1974.

However, three weeks were needed after the voting for the task of collecting and counting all the votes of soldiers and others from the Armed Forces overseas. Business people usually had two votes and so did university graduates. This unfair selection system was removed for the 1950 general election. The votes of members of the Armed Forces in the 1945 Election were extremely important to the success of Labour in England, and to a lesser extent in Wales and Scotland. Former service people were grateful for the leadership of Winston Churchill during the war, but were not so certain he would ensure a better world for them after all the suffering and destruction. Joseph Stalin was amazed when he heard that Churchill had lost the election and Attlee had won. He would never have allowed Russia to remove a prime minister so that his former Deputy, a much less charismatic figure, could lead them in government.

Attlee was stunned with the amazing result – 393 Labour MPs, as well as 6 other socialists, were elected against 213 Conservatives and 12 Liberals. In Wales the work of Griffiths and Bevan, in particular, had borne great fruit and the results were dramatic. By 1945 Wales was, without doubt, a 'Red Wales'. Labour had seven new seats, three seats in Cardiff, one in Newport, another in Swansea West, Llandaff and Barry, as well as the constituency of Caernarfonshire. Altogether Labour had won 25 seats in Wales. Some of the south Wales mining seats returned majorities of over 20,000, particularly Caerphilly, Neath, Ogmore, Pontypridd, Aberdare, Abertilery, Bedwellty and Ebbw Vale. But it was Llanelli where Labour had its best result in Wales.

These are the final results for Llanelli. There were 73,785 voters in the constituency, and 74.8% of them turned out to vote. Griffiths's chief opponent was G. O. George for the Conservatives. He received 10,397 votes, 18.9% of the poll, while J Griffiths gained 44,514 votes, 81.1% of the votes cast. The majority of 34,117 was an incredible result. This was the second best result for Labour in the whole of the UK.

Labour had made a great impact in Wales. It gained more support there than in any other part of Britain. Some 58.5% of the voters of Wales had opted for Labour candidates, while only 48% had done so in the whole of the United Kingdom. The MPs from mining backgrounds enjoyed tremendous support. They included the two most notable mining MPs in the Britain, Griffiths and Aneurin Bevan. But there were other remarkable Labour MPs from Wales with mining backgrounds returned to Parliament: in particular George H. Hall in Aberdare, the controversial Stephen Owen Davies in Merthyr, (the left-winger universally known as 'S. O.'), William H. Mainwaring, who had a difficult task in defeating the communist, Harry Pollit in the Rhondda East constituency. Other ex-miners who were returned to Parliament included Ness Edwards in Caerphilly, D. R. Grenfell in Gower, D. J. Williams in Neath, George Dagger in Abertilery, Arthur Jenkins in Pontypool, Tudor Watkins in Brecon and Radnor, and William G. Cove in Aberavon as well as Will John, who was returned unopposed for Rhondda West due to the high regard in which he was held by the miners as well as by Welsh nonconformists. This was the last time this happened in Wales in an election for a Westminster seat.[25]

But the Labour Party in Wales also did well in rural seats in the 1945 general election. Caernarfonshire was gained by Goronwy Roberts while Anglesey, Merionethshire and Pembrokeshire were nearly won from the Liberal MPs. All three became marginal seats. However, Ronw Moelwyn Hughes, a distinguished barrister, was defeated in Carmarthenshire.[26] For the first time in its history, Cardiff became a stronghold for the Labour Party. The city had gained three notable MPs in the person of Hilary Marquand, a university professor (who was elected for Cardiff East), George Thomas, a son of the Rhondda but a teacher in Cardiff (who was elected for Cardiff West), while James Callaghan, a native of Portsmouth and a great admirer of James Griffiths, gained Cardiff South from the Conservatives.

The Welsh Labour MPs were all men. The only woman who stood for the Labour Party in Wales was Eirene L. Jones in Flintshire East. She came close to winning the seat from the Conservative Nigel Birch, but failed.[27] Of the Welsh Labour MPs elected in 1945, all of them except two were from Wales or Welsh descent. Ten of them were fluent Welsh speakers.

Some had experienced a great deal of poverty in their early lives, having had to start work as miners when they were just thirteen or fourteen years of age. Others had seen much sacrifice by their parents on their behalf. George Thomas mentioned often, and with conviction, his mother's sacrifice when his father deserted them as a family during the First World War. Some had seen the capitalist system at its worst. A few, like James Griffiths and Ness Edwards, had been conscientious objectors during the First World War, while others had given years of service within a number of trade unions and the trade union movement. Furthermore, every one of the twenty-five new Labour MPs was a product of chapels, Sunday Schools or churches. Two of them had been ostracised from their chapels: Aneurin Bevan and W. H. Mainwaring. S. O. Davies had been expelled from his Welsh Independent theological college at Brecon for his 'heretical' views, while Will John was honoured by being chosen as President of the Welsh Baptist Union. George Thomas became a Methodist lay-preacher and later Vice President of the Methodist Conference; Tudor Watkins was a Deacon with the Welsh Baptist chapel in Brecon. Robert Richards had taught an adult Sunday School class in a Welsh Wesleyan Methodist chapel in north Montgomeryshire, while James Callaghan was always grateful for his upbringing in the Baptist chapel in the south of England and its Sunday School. D. R. Grenfell had been a personal friend of the Revivalist Evan Roberts, and he was closely associated with the Welsh Independent chapel in Gorseinon. Griffiths was not as faithful to the chapel as those whom we have mentioned but he always referred to his own chapel upbringing in Ammanford and how he had received inspiration from its Band of Hope and Sunday School which had stood the test of time.

It had been a long hard struggle from 1906 to 1945 for many of them, including Griffiths. But he was completely satisfied with the 1945 General Election.
There were new opportunities and responsibilities awaiting him and his fellow Labour MPs. At one of his meetings in the Llanelli constituency, a young comrade stood up and sang a popular song with these prophetic words:

> *Oh what a beautiful morning,*
> *Oh what a beautiful day,*
> *I've got a beautiful feeling*
> *Everything's going my way.*[28]

One could not have asked for more. Griffiths and Manny Shinwell were virtually alone among Labour's leading figures in having predicted victory, but neither of these optimists could realistically have predicted such a stunning victory.[29] It was the most pleasant shock that James Griffiths had ever experienced.

**Notes and References**

1. James Griffiths, *Pages from Memory*, p. 158.
2. John Davies, *Hanes Cymru*, p. 521.
3. The letter of Neville Chamberlain is found on pages 158-9 of *Pages from Memory*.
4. Ibid., p. 159.
5. Ibid.
6. 'He failed (Aneurin Bevan) to see the differences between English sheep and Welsh sheep', Carwyn Jones, *The Future of Welsh Labour* (Cardiff, 2004), p. 8.
7. The letter has been reproduced on p 160 of *Pages from Memory*.
8. NLW, James Griffiths Papers B3/13. Letter from Arthur Evans to James Griffiths dated 13 August 1943.
9. James Griffiths 'Welsh Politics in my lifetime,' in *James Griffiths and His Times*, p. 37, also 'Welsh in Courts', *Amman Valley Chronicle*, 22 October 1942.
10. The letter is reproduced in *Pages from Memory* on p. 161.
11. James Griffiths, *Pages from Memory*, p. 161.
12. See *Y Cymro*, June 26, 1943 on the front page where there is an open letter probably written by Judge Artemus Jones to the Prime Minister, Winston Churchill. It is a hard hitting polemic: 'How can Mr Attlee be so blind to public opinion as to try and damp the desire of the Welsh Members for a Welsh Secretary of State?' The letter attacks the standpoint of the Welsh nationalists: 'Not the least serious disservice which the political extremists who call themselves nationalists have rendered to Wales on these days is the bad impression their nonsense about the War has left upon the British public. If the so-called "leader" of the group had his way, he would see Wales a second Ireland, with himself in the role of de Valera and Swansea and Cardiff filled with the ambassadors of Germany and Italy as the Irish parts are today. The group of separatists represent nobody except a handful of illbalanced cranks and immature teachers and students – the workers of Wales are behind you in your valid efforts to beat the Nazis and Fascists and to secure the triumph of freedom and the Christian way of life. That is why we urge you to do your best to undo the mischief done by Mr Attlee's unhappy blunder. A Welsh Secretary of State can be appointed by a stroke of the pen and matters of education, local government and trade pertaining to Wales can be assigned to a Welsh Office on the model of the precedent established in Scotland half a century ago.'
13. John Pennant, 'Attlee's No to Wales will be remembered', *Western Mail*, June 26, 1943, p. 2.
14. NLW, James Griffiths Papers, B 3/13.
15. Ibid.
16. Kenneth O. Morgan, 'Leaders and Led in the Labour Movement.' 'The Welsh Experience', *Llafur* 6(3) 1994, p. 112; James Griffiths, *Glo*, p. 26. A miner from Resolven, Bert Lewis Coombes, had portrayed the life of the miners in his volumes, These Poor Hands: the autobiography of a miner working in south Wales (1939), These Clouded Hills (1944) and the documentary, Miners' Day (1945). It was interesting to receive a letter from John Peter Jones, organist of Bethel Welsh Independent chapel, Caerphilly, on 5 October 2012, praising the miners that he remembered in his childhood in the 1940s, who served as lay preachers in Glamorganshire and Gwent: 'I well recall the miners who preached at Bethania CM Chapel (Ystrad Mynach), who spent all their spare time in the local Institute libraries. What outstanding men they were.'
17. NLW, James Griffiths Papers, B3/13.
18. Ibid.
19. Abe Moffat, *My Life with the Miners* (London, 1965), p. 83.

20. NLW, Deian Hopkin Papers. *The minutes of the Labour Party and the Trade Unions Llanelli,* 1941.

21. Ibid.

22. T. I. Ellis, *Undeb Cymru Fydd 1939-1960* (Aberystwyth, 1960), p. 3. Saunders Lewis praised the movement in his weekly article in the *Faner*. See 'Cwrs y Byd', *Baner ac Amserau Cymru*, May 26, 1943, p.11.

23. T. I. Ellis, ibid.

24. NLW, Cliff Protheroe Papers and his autobiography Recount (Ormskirk, 1982), p.44.

25. A short entry on William John MP is to be found in Welsh Hustings 1855-2004, p.152.

26. For Ronw Moelwyn Hughes, see *Welsh Hustings 1855-2004*, p.139 and 213.

27. Eirene White nearly gained a Conservatives safe seat for the Labour Party in 1945 against Nigel Birch. See David Lewis Jones 'White, Eirene Lloyd, Baroness White', NLW Biography on-line.

28. A personal conversation with James Griffiths during the National Eisteddfod of Wales in Llanelli, August 1962.

29. Arnold J. James and John E. Thomas, *Wales at Westminster*, p. 152 and p. 236.

# 12

# One of the Architects of the Welfare State

Wales was very proud of the Welfare State, one of the biggest achievements of the reforming Labour government of 1945 to 1951.[1] Ever since the efforts of David Lloyd George before the First World War, a number of measures had been introduced by successive governments to assist those in distressing circumstances whether through disability, illness, unemployment or old age. There is no doubt that the Beveridge Plan, announced during the Second World

War, had given the impetus towards the achievement of a Welfare State. Two Welsh MPs from the same mining background and contemporaries at the Central Labour College, Aneurin Bevan and James Griffiths, were key figures in the welfare provision of the Attlee administration. Soon after the 1945 election results, Griffiths received a message from London at his home in Burry Port, for him to be ready to travel to see the new Prime Minister, Clement Attlee. This meant one thing and one thing only: that he would be offered a post in the new administration. A number of influential Labour leaders, including Hugh Dalton, Ernest Bevin and Herbert Morrison, thought highly of James Griffiths. The contributions of Griffiths in debates in the House of Commons since 1936 and his loyalty to the party had endeared him to Attlee. After arriving at 10 Downing Street, Griffiths was taken to the Cabinet room. There, waiting for him, was Attlee, sitting in the Prime Minister's chair, and by his side William Whiteley, the Chief Whip and a politician who had been in his young days a miner in the Durham coalfield.[2]

Attlee greeted Griffiths kindly and then offered him a post in the new government as Minister of State for the Colonies. When he noticed that Griffiths didn't say 'Yes' or 'No', he then asked if he desired another position. Griffiths answered him immediately: 'I would. I would like to be the Minister of National Insurance.' The Prime Minister responded: 'That is a good idea. The matter is settled. Good day and good luck.' Griffiths returned to Burry Port with the job that he had hoped for. He realised that his decision for the post of Minister of Pensions meant that he would not become a member of the Labour Cabinet. If he had accepted the post of Secretary of State for the Colonies he would have been in the Cabinet.[3]

When he arrived back in Burry Port he was welcomed by a group of journalists and photographers including many from London newspapers. Some of them could not believe that a new Minister of State lived in an ordinary house and that his wife looked after the home and family without any female assistance. Even more than that, at the time, Winifred Griffiths, was under great strain, caring for her mother who was deteriorating in physical health. By the end of August 1945 it was obvious that she was desperately ill, and on the first Monday in September she passed away, and was laid to rest at the Anglican church in Pembrey.[4]

James Griffiths soon realised that his new commitments were very difficult without a permanent base in London. He was paid a salary of only £5,000 a year. This was at least three times more than he had received as an MP. But the fundamental question he had to face was how he could sustain a house in Wales and a flat in London at the same time.[5]

After a long discussion they decided as a family to move to live in London. By Easter 1946 they had found a large flat in Putney Heath to rent. For the first nine months he travelled weekly from Burry Port to his office at 6 Carlton House Terrace and then to Westminster. On his first day at this office, on 7 July 1945, he wrote to his agent, Douglas Hughes, as excited as a young child: 'It is very interesting and exciting and there will be a lot to do. I will be sworn in tomorrow morning.'[6]   He expressed his gratitude to his political agent in Llanelli, as well as sending greetings to his wife, and their daughters, Glenys, Llewela and Elen.

In the new department he was fortunate in the support of his two parliamentary secretaries, both unpaid: George Lindgren, MP for Wellingborough, and Tom Steele, MP for Lanark. They were both staunch trade unionists within the railway industry.[7]   Another unpaid post, but extremely useful for the minister, was his private parliamentary secretary, Bernard Taylor, who had started work as a miner in the Nottinghamshire coalfield as a lad of fourteen. He became a close friend and retained a high regard for Griffiths for the rest of his life.[8]

Griffiths was also fortunate in his Permanent Secretary, Sir Thomas Williams Phillips, a Welshman from Cemaes Road in the Machynlleth area, and a fluent Welsh speaker. As n influential   civil servant he had the gift of drafting minutes clearly and concisely, and had drafted answers to parliamentary questions on issues which Griffiths had often not foreseen.[9]One of the first decisions the minister took was to implement the Family Allowance Act which was already on the statute book and ready to be implemented as soon as possible. The vision behind this came from Eleanor Rathbone, a member of a radical Liverpool merchant family, who had been elected in 1929 as an Independent for the Combined University seat.[10] She had been involved with the campaign for Family Allowance since the First World War, and had gained supporters from every political party. Griffiths had a great regard for her. Beveridge had recommended that every child, except the first, should receive five shillings a week towards his or her care. Griffiths decided to implement family allowances immediately.

The first task was to find the money, for Britain was virtually bankrupt. The cost of fighting the Second World War had been tremendous. Its debt to other countries had grown from £76 million to £355 million. Griffiths's implementation of the Family Allowance Bill was most impressive. One has to remember this financial crisis and marvel at how much the Labour government was to achieve between 1945 and 1950. Britain was helped by the USA's Marshall Plan.[11] The title given by historians for the years 1945-51, the 'Age of Austerity', is a graphic description. Those of us who remember those days will not forget the restrictions that were imposed on the whole population including bread rationing in 1946, as well as potato rationing and clothing restrictions in 1947.

Griffiths had many discussions with his friend the Chancellor of the Exchequer, Hugh Dalton, and he was extremely successful in his negotiations over family allowance. The first family allowance to be paid on 6 August, 1946. Initially it was paid out to two and a half million families. Griffiths, accompanied by his wife Winnie, visited Stepney Post Office at 8.30 a.m. to pay the first allowance. The mother who came first to the counter was Mrs Mary Ann Hall, thirty-five years of age, the wife of a dock labourer. A mother of children she received the sum of fifteen shillings from Mrs Griffiths. Mrs Hall's children were among the 7,000,000 who received the first allowances.[12]

Griffiths would on some occasions take Arthur Greenwood, who was in charge of a sub-committee on Pensions and National Insurance, to see Dalton. After one of these visits, Dalton wrote in his diary on the National Insurance provision:

> *The cost is formidable, but we can manage it. I had a bit of a fight to insist on the principle of retirement pensions but they finally agreed to 26s a week for a single person, as against only 10s now – so I have more that doubled this – and 42s for a married couple, to be increased by 2s a week for a single person and 4s a week for a married couple for every year of continued work, before retirement from 65 to 70 for men and from 60 to 65 for women. Of course, the Old Age Pensioners' Association will try to auction this up. But I have insisted, both to Greenwood and Griffiths, that we must stand firm on this, and I think there is a good chance that we shall, since the rates of 26s and 42s run right through the Bill, for sickness and unemployment benefit, as well as for pensions.*[13]

It was on 1 August 1946 that the National Insurance became a reality, to the delight of the minister who had steered it through to the House of Commons. He managed to carry the Opposition with him. At least eighty-three Parliamentary measures went through the House of Commons in the first year of the Labour government, and, according to some MPs, the atmosphere was electrifying, similar to a religious Revivalist meeting. These were the words of the young Labour MP, George Thomas:

> *Each night as we trooped through the division lobbies someone would call out, 'Come on, George, strike up' and I would start to sing 'Guide me, O thou great Jehovah.' Instantly, there would be a mighty choir singing its way through the lobby.*[14]

George Thomas was one of a large number of new MPs most impressed with James Griffiths. One of the most significant battles of the 1945 Parliament was over the repeal of the 1927 Trades Disputes Act, which was long overdue.[15] It was an Act which had been introduced by politicians such as Winston Churchill in the wake of the 1926 General Strike to undermine the political levy and restrict trade unions. The repeal brought joy to the Labour ranks.

Griffiths did receive a great deal of criticism from the weekly Welsh language paper, Y Faner (Banner), and its columnist Saunders Lewis. To supporters of the Labour Party who were readers of Y Faner, it was disappointing to read the comments on the National Insurance Act. Saunders Lewis did not agree with anything that the government had done in a period of austerity. On 17 April 1946 in his weekly column he wrote that it 'was better to be lost with Owen Glendower than to sit with James Griffiths in Whitehall and Westminster.'[16]

But to those on the Labour benches in Parliament, Griffiths was the person to undertake the task of piloting the Bill through the different stages until it was safely on the statute book. His experience in the coalfield stood him in good stead, particularly with his first legislation, namely the Industrial Injuries Act 1946 which effectively nationalised routine compensation, taking it away from the employers and private insurance companies. Griffiths had his own traumatic experience from the Welsh Valleys of '' the compo mman ''- the servants of private insurers who would regularly persuade the victims of mining and industrial injuries to settle for unworthy settlement rather that defying them and taking them to court. It was such a difficult task to tackle the torturous  law which surrounded, workmen's compensation. James Griffiths was proud of the new legislation with weekly benefits and disablement pensions paid to those who deserved assistance and the formation of tribunals rather than costly litigation that was used used to settle cases.  He travelled throughout Britain to remind Labour Party activists of the social revolution that was being implemented through   the Industrial Injuries Act. The Picture Post in the 16 March 1946 edition devoted a number of pages to describing his trip to Ferryhill, a mining village six miles from Durham. It was a village of 11,000 inhabitants, and 5,700 of the men worked in three coal mines situated on the outskirts of the village. The visit was recorded by a sympathetic journalist, Sydney Jacobson.[17]

He informs us in his account that the minister was glad to be in Ferryhill even though there was a great deal of snow in Durham that weekend. A large meeting was held in the Miners' Hall, where he had the opportunity of explaining to the miners and their wives the plan that was to be implemented for them. He talked about the vision which had inspired those gathered to vote for the Labour Government, namely that a sick person would never have to depend anymore on a provision that reflected the Poor Law and the Means Tests of the 1930s. Griffiths mentioned the place of the mother and how a grant during the birth of her child, that is 36 shillings allowance for thirteen weeks as well as a grant of £4, would greatly help her. He explained in detail the new Old Age Pension scheme, and how it was going to be paid for, and all the provisions for the individual when ill. This was a comprehensive package.[18] He finished his address by identifying himself with the miners and their families. He left Ferryhill after having had his photograph taken with Wilfred Tuck, who had been a miner in the collieries of the village for forty years.[19] The next port of call was West Hartlepool. There he would be addressing another large audience of trade unionists and members of the Labour Party, before catching an overnight train back to London. In the final sentence of the article, Jacobson stated: 'He's got a big job on hand; there are Ferryhills all over Britain waiting for him to carry it though.'[20]

The minister realised his responsibilities to his own electorate, and he was highly admired for combining both roles so well. Llanelli Town Council presented him with the Freedom of the Town in October 1945. He encouraged businesses to move to the area. He mentioned to his agent a company called Metal Springs Ltd which wanted to build a new factory, and how he and others were advising the company to consider building it in Llanelli. He suggested to Douglas Hughes that they should ask the mayor of Llanelli to give a welcome to the directors of the company and prepare some refreshment as a token of his hospitality, and the agent agreed with his guidance.[21]

Griffiths maintained on 27 March 1946 that life was particularly hectic for him and one can discern this in his correspondence, in particular to his agent. On 15 April he mentions: 'I get no end of letters from the division and outside, asking for jobs and all of course voters for me.'[22]

A month later he was on his way to the constituency, staying with Mr and Mrs Reg Rees of Denton Avenue, Llanelli. They had been neighbours in Ystradgynlais and close friends. Griffiths's daughter Sheila was also staying there as she was on school practice at the primary school of Maider Street, Llanelli. By June 1946 Griffiths and his family had settled at 17 Wildcroft Manor, Putney Heath, London. Later that month he travelled to the Labour Party conference at Bournemouth. At the end of the conference, Hugh Dalton spoke with passion on the prospects for Britain as a result of ministers of the calibre of James Griffiths.[23] It was all as a result of what he called the 'Jim Griffiths Act.'

An event of significance at the conference was the voting for candidates the National Executive Council (NEC). In Bournemouth the seven on the NEC were re-elected, but there was a change in the order. As Aneurin Bevan was ill, he missed the conference, but that did not deny him the first place in the popularity stakes. Second came the intellectual Harold Laski; in third place, James Griffiths; and in fourth place, Hugh Dalton. There were only 4,000 votes between the three, each of them Labour Party heavyweights. Then came Herbert Morrison, some 30,000 behind Dalton, followed by Philip Noel-Baker, with Emanuel Shinwell bringing up the rear. The year before, Laski and Shinwell had both been bracketed as one and two in the list. Shinwell was a colourful character and he mentions how he delved into the archives of the Ministry of Fuel and Energy to look for some relevant material on the nationalisation of the coal industry. He had a surprise to see that the only literature available in the department was a volume written by James Griffiths in Welsh, published in 1945 under the title *Glo* (Coal).

In 1946 Griffiths was among three Welsh MPs who were honoured by the University of Wales, Aneurin Bevan, and George Hall being the other two. These two were cabine ministers while Griffiths was not in the cabinet. All three had begun their working lives as boy miners. They were all presented for the Honorary degree of Doctorate in Law by Principal Ivor L. Evans, Aberystwyth and welcomed by the historian Sir James Frederick Rees, Principal of the then University College of South Wales, Cardiff (now Cardiff University) and a well-known Fabian in his younger days. They were honoured in the company of Welsh poets of distinction and others who had been involved in the early days of the Labour movement.[24]

In the period 1946-1947 Griffiths was pleased with the factories that were built within his constituency. In early 1947 he worked on the needs of the Pulman Springfield Factory. It had been located in Pantyffynnon, near Ammanford during the war, and through his efforts, it became one of the largest employers in the area, producing furniture and beds. It provided work for unemployed miners, for the disabled and for women. When in full production it had a work force of 1,100, and of these, 37% were disabled. The factory depended a great deal on contacts providerd by Griffiths's, in particular with regard to the supply of steel. In a period of shortages the government was responsible for distributing steel to companies, and Griffiths made sure that the Pullman Springfield had its fair share.

The efforts of the local District Council, the County Council, and, in particular, James Griffiths helped bring many companies to the Amman Valley, such as Cyc-Arc and Company Ltd, Teddington Control Ltd, Hardens Tool and Gauge Ltd, Southern Welding Ltd, Remploy, John White Ltd, Alan Raine Knitwear Ltd, Dalandin Ltd and Cwmgorse Press and Fabrication. Technological inventions were beginning to revolutionise the industries of the area.

The needs of individual men and women meant a great deal to Griffiths and he had a great concern for their welfare and livelihood. He never, if he could help it, missed a meeting within his constituency with local representatives. But sometimes he was unable to be present, and he was concerned in October 1946 when he could not welcome personally Alice Bacon, a loyal disciple of Herbert Morrison, when she visited the constituency. It was Griffiths who had invited her in the first place. He urged his agent to give her visit all the publicity that he could in the local press.

Though the constituency had become a very safe Labour seat, the party machine needed constant attention. On 3 January 1947 he sent a cheque for £25 to the local Constituency Labour Party, which considering that he was being paid £5,000 a year, was not too generous. His agent, W. Douglas Hughes, was rather concerned in particular with the attitudes of the Miners' Union officers in Cardiff towards the cost of maintaining a Labour office and agent in Llanelli.[25] Griffiths felt that the presence of Arthur Horner as general secretary of 'the Fed' was part of the problem, but he could not see any purpose in complaining to him. He concluded that their only option was to enlarge the membership of the Labour Party in the constituency. He had a strong case. He was very concerned with the contemporary employment situation and especially with how to keep the men in work. This was why he welcomed the nationalisation of the coal industry on 1 January 1947, and in May 1947, got involved in discussing the possibility of locating new steelworks within the Llanelli area.[26] A steelworks plant was planned from 1947 at Margam, near Port Talbot, and the setting up of a huge plant was also a possibility for Trostre near Llanelli to replace the obsolete tinplate industry there. The town clerk and mayor of Llanelli came to see him and Griffiths explained in detail all the deliberations in which he been already involved. He had in his possession the confidential reports that had been prepared. But he was very much on his own. The Steel Industry Board as well as the leader of the union, Lincoln Evans, seemed to be against the location of a steelworks in Llanelli. But in the meeting that had been arranged, James Griffiths made a strong case for the new mill to be located at Llanelli. The result of this was that the government asked the Steel Industry Board to reconsider fully the plans for the future of the industry in west Wales. The Board was asked to discuss the sociological implications of the plan, especially its impact on Llanelli and the area around it, before it came to a decision. On 6 June 1947 Griffiths maintained that the location at Llanelli had not been lost. He was very well aware of the need to have in their midst large corporations that could be held accountable. Griffiths felt that he had done his utmost as a lobbyist and he was still confident.

Griffiths also realised that if his pleadings and lobbying were successful then the neighbouring Labour MPs in the Swansea area would be unhappy, to say the least. After all, for three months in 1947 the Welsh Steel Company had been preparing for a possible site at Felindre, near Llangyfelach, on the outskirts of Swansea. He admitted to his agent: 'It's embarrassing for me as the charge will be made that I used my influence as minister to get the decision.'[27]

Griffiths felt deeply that he in particular should keep a low profile, and argued that Llanelli had been chosen as it was so dependable on the tinplate industry. Llanelli was still known as 'Tinopolis'. Without the new works within its boundaries, Carmarthenshire would disappear as a significant centre of the tinplate industry. He also believed that the Trostre works would assist the renewal of the industrial villages which had suffered greatly from serious unemployment. These towns and villages included Bynea, Llangennech, Hendy, Pontarddulais, Gorseinon and Gowerton. This would be a bonus to the Gower and Llanelli constituencies. To him it was essential to avoid any bitterness between Llanelli and Swansea on the proposed development. If another similar steel works was needed, it should be located on the outskirts of Llanelli. He told Douglas Hughes not to disclose too much information to the local and national press, in case they gave the impression that it had been his victory: 'If they do that I, as a minister, will be in a difficult position.'[28]

A day later Griffiths mentions that the Swansea MPs were being assisted publicly by James Callaghan who had raised vital questions concerning the steel industry, hoping soon for a parliamentary debate.[29] Even though Griffiths had been cautious, indeed the phrase he used was 'a stiff upper-lip', he could not avoid upsetting David R. Grenfell, who had been in the vanguard of the Llangyfelach-Felindre project. The decision to locate the works at Trostre was the result of a huge struggle, and it was Griffiths who won the day. We can agree with the local historian Byron Davies that the decision to locate the huge works at Trostre had created a chasm between the two Labour politicians, Griffiths and Grenfell, 'a permanent bitter resentment.'[30] In the 1950s Grenfell became very critical of his neighbour, and the argument always reverted to three disagreements: firstly on the coal industry, secondly on devolution and thirdly on what had happened in the Trostre v Felindre affair.

Wales and its destiny was an important concern for Griffiths. He found himself in a key position as a minister, able to use his influence to strengthen the ties that were so important and to consider, in his own time, constitutional matters. He had pleaded the case for a Secretary of State for Wales when it had been raised in 1946, when a deputation under D. R. Grenfell and W. H. Mainwaring went to see Attlee. But they were unable to convince Herbert Morrison, the Deputy Prime Minister, or Stafford Cripps, President of the Board of Trade, of the need to create this major new department to look after Welsh affairs.

On the other hand, it was impossible to silence the members of the Welsh Labour Party outside the ranks of the MPs who were in favour of devolution; men of substance, such as David Thomas of Bangor, Ifor Bowen Griffith of Caernarfon, Cyril O. Jones, a solicitor in Wrexham and Huw T. Edwards, the trade unionist. In September 1946, after receiving the negative response from Attlee, Morrison, and Cripps, the energetic Edwards prepared a memorandum under the title Problems of Wales. It was sent immediately to Morgan Phillips, a native of Bargoed and general secretary of the Labour Party. He, if anything, was even more of a unionist than Attlee or Morrison.[31] Huw T. Edwards, in contrast to James Griffiths, agreed with the decision of the Labour government to refuse at present the call for a Secretary of State for Wales. The Trade Unionist Edwards would have liked to see a Commissioner for Wales with an Advisory Committee to assist him. On the other hand, David Thomas, Cyril O. Jones, lwan Morgan, the Labour candidate in Cardiganshire, and I.B. Griffith called for a much more radical remedy: a Welsh Parliament.[32] James Griffiths had his hands tied as a minister, but he believed in campaigning for a Secretary of State for Wales. A White Paper was issued in 1947 entitled Welsh Affairs. The Welsh Labour Regional Council, established with Cliff Prothero as Secretary, became an influential body in Welsh politics. Over the years, Prothero has been criticised for being an anti-devolutionist but it is of interest that it was he who prepared a report based on the memorandum of Huw T. Edwards. Furthermore, James Griffiths always praised him highly. He said in 1973:

*I regard Cliff Prothero, the Secretary of the Council of Labour, as one who paved the way to the establishment, in 1964, of the Welsh Secretaryship and Office.*[33]

Prothero gave the report the title Democratic Devolution in Wales. This was sent to the prime minister and all the Welsh Labour MPs before the Welsh Day Debate in the House of Commons so that devolution could be on the agenda.[34] It was impossible to silence the voice of Labour devolutionists from Wales. Early in 1948 Griffiths contacted Goronwy Roberts, a politician elected MP in 1945, whom he respected for his strong convictions on Welsh affairs. Griffiths was determined to maintain the momentum for devolution within the Labour Party. He undertook the task of preparing a document to be presented to the prime minister on the value of an established Advisory Council or an Economic Council for Wales. The responsibility for preparing this document was given to Goronwy Roberts, and a copy is to be found among his papers at the National Library of Wales in Aberystwyth.[35]

It is of interest that this memorandum was probably initially prepared by Ifor Bowen Griffith, Caernarfon, for Goronwy Roberts. I. B. Griffith knew the cultured people of the slate quarrying areas of Caernarfonshire well, for he was one of them. In his covering letter he argued that a 'higher standard of living under a Labour government was mainly responsible for the call for selfgovernment.'[36] He does not give a reason for the statement, but many an individual has reasoned in similar manner: 'We do not need to campaign anymore for our standard of living. So we can afford the luxury of fighting for the rights of Welsh speakers of our ancient language.'[37] In another paragraph, I. B. Griffith argued in Welsh:

*So we are not only socialists but also Welsh and conscious that we belong to a special nation and we believe that we cannot give to the Welsh the blessings of socialism without giving it a measure of self-government. We believe that the fruits of the Welfare State will not be available to everyone without devolving a great deal of the Central Government in London. Part of that devolution will be to create a Parliament for Wales within the British Federal Union, and this should be done as soon as possible.* [38]

This memorandum was not released for publication but it assisted the small group, comprising three MPs, namely Robert Richards, Ungoed Thomas and Goronwy Roberts, to prepare a more detailed document. This was discussed in April and July 1948. By this time it was felt that there was a need for two bodies to cater for Welsh affairs, an Economic Council under the chairmanship of a cabinet minister such as Aneurin Bevan or James Griffiths, as well as an Advisory Council with its own chairman. The Advisory Council could concentrate on issues concerning the cultural and social life in Wales. A deputation of Welsh Labourites, including Cliff Prothero and Huw T. Edwards, travelled to London to discuss these options with Herbert Morrison, who had invited Griffiths, Aneurin Bevan and a number of other Labour MPs, to the meeting on 29 October 1948.

It was obvious that Morrison was ready at last to compromise a little. He accepted Huw T. Edwards's proposal for an Advisory Committee, but he did not agree that a cabinet minister should act as chairman, or indeed agree to the idea of having a Commissioner for Wales. [39] On 13 October 1948 he explained in a letter to James Griffiths why he was against the proposal: he was afraid of creating a 'Buffer Minister' which would create unnecessary problems. [40]

Towards the end of his life, in a letter to John Morris, then the Secretary of State for Wales, James Griffiths mentions his disappointment that Aneurin Bevan had supported Morrison, and as a consequence postponed for a decade the creation of a Secretary of State for Wales. [41] In the end, all that emerged from the documents, debates, and deputations was the Council for Wales and Monmouthshire, a non-elected body that would meet once a quarter to discuss the priorities and developments in the economic and cultural life of Wales. This Council would convey to central government the impact of its policies on the people of Wales and Monmouthshire. The members of the Council would be nominated, and its meetings would be held in private, without any members of the press or the public being present to listen to the discussions.

At the Welsh Labour Party conference in Swansea in 1948 the Council was welcomed: 'It is felt that this arrangement (a Council for Wales) would be far more satisfactory that the appointment of a Secretary of State.' But the Welsh Labour conference did not express the convictions of some of the Labour Party's campaigners for devolution. S. O. Davies of Merthyr saw the Council as completely worthless and scores of Labour councillors were also critical, including the most prominent of the early Labour Party pioneers, David Thomas of Bangor. Of the 182 local governments in Wales only 13 were supportive of the Advisory Council that had been brought into existence. At least 72 of them were apathetic, though they favoured the standpoint of James Griffiths of having a Secretary of State for Wales. At least 68 local authorities were against the idea of a Council, and 21 Councils never bothered to answer.

The Welsh Nationalist Party (Plaid Cymru) called the proposed Welsh Council in Welsh 'Cyngor Anobaith' ('Hopeless Council').[42] The president of Plaid Cymru, Gwynfor Evans, would argue at every opportunity that Labour leaders of the calibre of Griffiths had to submit their convictions to Herbert Morrison and Sir Stafford Cripps. The most irritating criticism coming from Gwynfor Evans was that the devolutionists within the Labour Party, especially Griffiths and Goronwy Roberts, had failed dismally in their campaign for a Secretary of State for Wales since 1946 when the prime minister turned down Griffiths's plea for the establishment of such a post. Clement Davies and the Liberals described the plan as Labour's effort to establish a 'Soviet Council' and they stated their own policy of a federal Parliament for Wales. To the surprise of Labour the Conservatives seized on the opportunity to put forward the promise of a Minister for Wales. They were implementing what the Conservative MP for Flint, Nigel Birch, had expressed in the House of Commons in 1946: 'I do not believe that Wales would have gone through what she has gone through if she had had a Minister in this House to speak for her.'[43]

There were a number of individuals who coveted the position of Chairman of the Council for Wales and Monmouthshire.[44] Cliff Prothero was one of the candidates, and so was the north Wales trade unionist Huw T. Edwards. Some of the names mentioned were identified with other political parties, including Sir Ifan ab Owen Edwards, founder of the League of Welsh Youth, prominent Liberal and the son of the Liberal MP and visionary for Wales, Sir Owen M. Edwards.

Griffiths believed that Huw T. Edwards, who could compose strict-metre poetry, was the ideal candidate. When he was asked for his opinion by Herbert Morrison, and more important still by Clement Attlee, he gave the same reply: 'Huw T. Edwards – he is the truly representative Welshman.' Edwards was selected. Griffiths maintained that the choice of the chairman was the main reason why the Council for Wales, a body of twenty-seven nominated members, succeeded so well between 1948 and 1958. Under the guidance of Huw T. Edwards, a number of important reports to do with the needs of Wales were published. One can agree that the most influential reports which the Council for Wales and Monmouthshire published were on the legal status of the Welsh language, and on Welsh devolution. It argued and presented detailed recommendations for a Secretary of State for Wales with a seat in the cabinet as for well as the establishment of a Welsh Office, and its report on devolution was highly valued by the leaders of the Labour Party in Wales and helped the political organisation in its understanding of the needs of the nation. It also prepared a valuable report on the needs of rural mid-Wales.

Griffiths became chairman of the Labour Party between 1948-49, and this brought more engagements and responsibilities. The Home Office invited him to address meetings all over the country from Blackpool to Norwich, from Lowestoft to Llangennech. On 28 September

1949 he mentions to Douglas Hughes that they should meet to prepare a strategy to confront the threat from the Welsh nationalists. 'I sense,' he said, 'that the nationalists are exceedingly busy.'[45]

There was a good reason for his concern: in particular the decision of Gwynfor Evans and his executive committee in Plaid Cymru to launch a campaign on the legal status of the Welsh language.[46] On St David's Day 1949, Evans challenged the Welsh societies, and especially the Welsh nonconformist chapels, to sign a petition calling for official status for the Welsh language. There were a large number of successful Welsh language chapels in the Llanelli constituency. Take as an example, the chapel where Griffiths himself had been nurtured, Christian Temple, in Ammanford. It was not a Welsh language chapel in decline. Indeed, it was gaining members. In 1913 it had 601 members, in 1931 784 members, while in 1955, its membership stood at 854.[47] There were similar chapels in the town of Llanelli and in the Gwendraeth Valley. Their voice and presence could not be ignored. Indeed, by the end of March 1949, at least six hundred Welsh societies and Welsh chapels had responded, so naturally Gwynfor Evans was content.

Griffiths was not pleased that the Labour government was not ready to discuss the petition. Gwynfor Evans was elected a councillor for Llangadog on Carmarthenshire county council. The Labour Party for the first time had won control of the council. 'We are the Masters now' were the famous words of Griffiths's agent, Douglas Hughes, who was leader of the council after the May elections. Jim had wonderful friends and supporters among these Labour councillors. He paid tribute to so many of them over the years such as Haydn Lewis which was one of his disciples.[48] From now on Griffiths could not be indifferent, if he ever was, to the utterances of his agent, or to Gwynfor Evans' unpopularity among many of the Welsh Labour MPs and the Labour councillors on the Carmarthenshire County Council.Gwynfor Evans decided to join the Independent Group on the county council, made up in the main of a coalition of Liberals and Conservatives. To the councillors from the Labour stronghold of the Llanelli constituency this meant only one thing: that the leader of Plaid Cymru was a pseudo-Tory. There was a very great chasm between the attitude, background, philosophy and experience of Gwynfor Evans and that of the Labour Party councillors. Douglas Hughes could not suffer Gwynfor Evans, especially when he remembered his own background as a steelworker in contrast to Dan Evans, the father of Gwynfor Evans, a successful shop owner in Barry.

Though Douglas Hughes was a chapel-goer and a Welsh speaker, he admitted that he could not agree with Evans's action in speaking in Welsh when addressing the county council. Gwynfor Evans's campaign on behalf of the language deserved to be supported by Labour councillors, but it was not to be. Carmarthenshire County Council witnessed a constant struggle between Gwynfor Evans and the Labour group as he argued for the overhaul of the council as far as the language was concerned, especially in the world of education. The standpoint of Gwynfor Evans on the county council in 1949 was extremely important, and the former leader of the Welsh nationalists, Saunders Lewis, saw him in an entirely different light. Indeed, in his weekly column in the Welsh language newspaper Baner ac Amserau Cymru, Lewis mentioned that the efforts of Gwynfor Evans on behalf of the language were a clear indication of 'the deadliness of the chapel-orientated Labour atmosphere'. To Saunders Lewis, the Labour Party was involved with 'materialistic socialism' while the spiritual values were being cherished by Gwynfor Evans and other leaders of Plaid Cymru.

Griffiths disagreed with Saunders Lewis. To Griffiths the Labour Party was not just a political party: it was a movement, a way of looking at life, with a tremendous loyalty to one's class and background. The Labour movement was above all to serve the ordinary people. To him the period from 1945 had been very successful.[49] Labour had been elected in 1945 on a manifesto that had promised huge changes. It had promised to establish a Welfare State by rearranging the social services, by remembering those who needed care, and Labour was determined to create a National Health Service which would bring comfort and hope to the sick and the disabled. The government had made a strenuous effort to implement this new programme. Above all, the new National Health Service was welcomed in Wales. It was a miracle in itself, revolutionary in its obligations. One could agree with the tribute of Amanwy in his weekly column concerning the architect of the National Health Service:

> *If Aneurin Bevan had done nothing but bring the Health Service into existence in the country, he would have succeeded in claiming the respect and the affection of millions of people who have been stricken on life's journey.[50] The same could be said of his own brothe in arms, James Griffiths, another architect of the Welfare State. In fact the historian Kenneth O. Morgan did pay him a similar compliment.[51]*

As a Cabinet minister, Griffiths was immensely competent. He made an excellent impression as Minister of Insurance in 1945-50 though he was, of course, on a pretty safe ticket in implementing the Beveridge proposals with measures for National Insurance, National Assistance and Industrial Injuries compensation. The National Insurance Act was was a needed measure which followed the Industrial Injuries Act. The National Insurance Act included state-run insurance, paid for by employers, employees and the general taxpayer, from cradle to grave. But the Act included unemployment and sickness benefits, maternity grants and allowances, allowances for dependants, retirement pensions and a small grant of twenty pounds death grant which was nearly enough to pay for a funeral in 1946. Griffiths was more generous than Beveridge had been, and  the new pensions were to be paid in full and began three months of the 1946 Act  becoming law. The final reform was brought together in the National Assistance Act. This Act was safely piloted through Parliament by Griffiths and Bevan and it declared the end of the existing poor law. Indeed Jim Griffiths's Bills went through the House of Commons with Conservative assent and barely a dissenting voice. Griffiths had found drafts of them on taking office, which hev expanded, modified and added too to produce measures which had full support of the parliamentarians. Griffiths had been one of the most important politicians for transforming Britain. This he did by his vision and by 5 July 1948 the country at large had been given a new lease of life. Bevan had achieved a miracle in the NHS and so had Griffiths in setting up with Eleanor Rathbone the family allowances and then his unique insurance cover for every adult in Britain. James Griffiths was responsible for creating a vast empire to handle the 25 million contribution records, plus the records of 6 million married women and the expected 300,000 references to them every day .Britain social security system created by Jim Griffiths was the envy of the civilised world. He and Bevan had achieved the impossible in three years by determination, faith and strong convictions.

It is most unusual for any political party to keep all its promises while it is the government of the day. In addition, the Labour government had the task of overcoming difficult hurdles in the lives of people who had been at war. Everywhere resources were scarce: food in the homes, and firewood for heating the houses. Then came the atrocious arctic winter of 1947, but despite all these hurdles, the Attlee administration did achieve its goals. It is easy for a historian to be too generous to the government on health and insurance and to forget their forgetfulness, especially on the matter of Welsh devolution and the promise of a Secretary of State for Wales. They also were to many within Wales apathetic with regard to the furtherance of the Welsh language and the provision of more financial support for Welsh culture. On these issues, Labour lacked political sensitivity.

But one has to remember that the strength of the Government was its loyalty to the original manifesto. To James Griffiths, one of the most important events took place on 1 January 1947, when the collieries of Britain came into public ownership. When they voted to nationalise the coal mines, Jim Griffiths led his fellow Labour MPs through the Division Lobby to a mighty chorus of the tune 'Cwm Rhondda'. This had been a long struggle and Griffiths had been involved in the coal industry since 1904. The National Coal Board (NCB) came into existence, and the militant miners were surprised that the majority of the new management appointed to the NCB were people who had never supported nationalisation in their lives and had never been involved in the Labour Party. These mining leaders felt that there should have been more representation from the trade union movement within the National Coal Board. But it was not to be But at least there were notice boards placed on top of every colliery bearing the words 'This colliery is now managed by by the National Coal Board on behalf of the people ' Manny Shinwell, the Minister of Fuel and Power, pleased Jim no end by bringing in immediately a five – day week for the miners. The coal industry was also being mechanised on a huge scale, and collieries were beginning to be closed even under the new sympathetic regime. At least thirty-four collieries were closed in Wales between 1947 and 1950, and these closures took place to the annoyance of Jim in the anthracite coalfield as well.

But the Labour government at least tried to build a new Jerusalem in Britain. The chief architects were Aneurin Bevan and James Griffiths. Once I believed that Griffiths was the second-in-command. But in 2020 I believe that both desrve to share the glory for their achievemnents, as architects of the Welfare State. They both owned a great deal to the Prime Minister Clement Attlee who allowed both of them a great deal of freedom in implementing their great innovations in health and social insurance. They owed a great deal too to the Chancellor Hugh Dalton. Both Bevan and Griffiths like Jack Lawson, Minister for War, George Isaacs, the Minister of Labour and George Tomlinson, Minister of Education had left school at eleven or twelve years of age to work in collieries, a printing works and a cotton mill. These five were self educated politicians and Attlee was proud of what each one of them did as Ministers in his Government .In the House of Commons at the end of the 1945-50 Labour government Bevan stated his objective: 'If I go down in history for nothing else, I will go down at least as a barrier between the beauty of Great Britain and the speculative builder who has done so much to destroy it.'

At the end of this period, Bevan had provided homes for two and a half million people, and was able to build, by 1951, a million new homes. His contribution was unique. So too were the efforts of James Griffiths, a politician who was popular with both the left and the right wings within the Labour Party, who had taken responsibility for implementing a great deal of Sir William Beveridge's Report of 1942. In his recollections, James Callaghan, a great admirer of Griffiths, emphasised the importance of that report:

> *All these new developments were no less than a charter of human rights. It meant that the quality of life in post-War Britain could, if they chose, be entirely different from that before the War. Bevan and Griffiths won our greater equality: it all meant that the worst evils of poverty and old age could be swept away. The aims were achievable and practicable. I bought my own personal copy of the Beveridge Report and carried it with me in my kit bag as a missionary would carry the gospel. The test of where a man stood on the Beveridge Report was the benchmark of whether he was a friend or a foe.[52]*

But Griffiths was not immune to criticism. Many of his Welsh critics had been unhappy that he had discarded his pacifism in the Second World War. Others felt that he should have done much more lobbying on the policy for a Secretary of State for Wales. To others, especially in his constituency, his obvious irritation with Ireland during the war was commendable. Some of the more militant nationalists and socialists felt that he was putting his ambition before his convictions. This came to a head in the attack on him by members of the new movement, the Welsh Republicans, called in Welsh '*Gwerinaethwyr*', who had broken away from Plaid Cymru after their annual conference in Ardudwy in August 1949. Most of the leaders were mature students from the University of Wales.[53] Gwilym Prys Davies was one of the most articulate of its members, and it was he who approached Gwynfor Evans with the suggestion of having a socialist front to bridge the gap between the political left and Plaid Cymru. Evans turned down this innovative suggestion. To him the communists were unbelievers and their allegiance was to Moscow rather than to Wales. Furthermore, Gwynfor Evans was determined to get his own way as far as Plaid Cymru was concerned. In April 1949, Plaid Cymru's Executive Committee under intense pressure from its President decided by twelve votes to three to ask those who supported the Republican cause to resign immediately from the Party, or to cease their activities. By the time of the annual conference it was obvious that all those who propounded the Republican cause would be asked to resign. At least fifty of them left to create a new political movement, and on 24 November 1949 two of them, Joyce Williams from Swansea and an exsoldier, Haydn Jones from Pontardawe who had married Mair Lewis the daughter of Saunders Lewis, were removed from the visitor's gallery of the House of Commons after shouting out the word 'Quisling' when Griffiths was addressing Parliament.

160

The protestors threw copies of their manifesto into the chamber, most of the leaflets falling on the opposition benches. Griffiths as well as Gwynfor Evans were continually criticised by these rebels.[54] Griffiths used the word 'fascists' to describe the Republicans. To use such an emotional, unfair word was uncharacteristic of Griffiths. At this time, Griffiths was preparing for a possible general election.[55] He and Herbert Morrison were given the task of drafting the Labour Party manifesto. It was finally published under the title Labour Believes in Britain. This document was accepted by the Labour Party conference in 1949, though Griffiths as well as Aneurin Bevan felt that there should have been more emphasis on nationalisation. Bevan proposed, seconded by Griffiths, that they should follow the nationalisation route, but Morrison and Attlee disagreed vehemently. The cabinet decided on 13 October that there was no immediate need to call a general election. Griffiths agreed with the decision, quite contrary to Bevan and Gaitskell. To Griffiths, the importance of the government of 1945 to 1950 had been its determination to implement the Beveridge plans and its emphasis on the universality of the benefits. To him there was always political embarrassment involved in applying the hated 'means test' of the 1930s and in administering anything other than a universal benefit. Though Eleanor Rathbone had agreed that the family allowance should be given to all the children in a family except the eldest, she and Griffiths realised that this was not the full system that they wanted, but in difficult times, they had no choice but to be selective.

Many a Welshman was proud of the achievements of the first Labour government. The father of the extraordinary Welsh librarian Alun R. Edwards was a staunch Labourite. He lived in rural Cardiganshire in Llanddewi Brefi but he had worked in the mining village of Maerdy (called Little Moscow in the 1920s) in the Rhondda Valley.[56] His world had changed dramatically with the coming of the Welfare State and in 1949 he was extremely grateful for the work of Nye Bevan and Jim Griffiths, two of the foremost reformers who had been involved day after day in drawing up the provisions of the Welfare State. As Dr Gwyn A. Williams reminds us:

> *Wales, of course, shared fully in the massive spiritual transformation effected by the coming of the Welfare State, the National Health Service, the restoration of dignity and honour to a degraded people.*[57]

**Notes and References**

1. Martin Pugh maintains 'For Attlee's administration soon came to be seen as the most successful of the entire post-war era'. See Martin Pugh, *Speak for Britain: A New History of the Labour Party* (London, 2011), p. 286.
2. James Griffiths, *Pages from Memory*, p. 77.
3. The biggest surprise was that 12 individuals from the working class were ministers of the Crown and 11 of them in the cabinet. See A. J. Davies, *To Build a New Jerusalem: The British Labour Party from Keir Hardie to Tony Blair* (London, 1996), p. 223.

4. By the end of August 1945 the mother of Winifred Griffiths was seriously ill. She died in September and the funeral of Mrs Rose Rutley was held in the parish church of Pembrey. See Mrs James Griffiths, *One Woman's Story*, pp. 125–9.

5. For a number of reasons, London was ideal for the family. Jeanne was contemplating applying for a post in a hospital in Middlesex, Harold was in the RAF. Sheila was accepted for training at the Rachel Macmillan Teacher Training College in Deptford. They had rented a large flat in Putney by Easter 1946.

6. NLW, Deian Hopkin Papers, Douglas Hughes Collection. 7 July 1945. He said 'It is very interesting and exciting and there will be a lot of work to do'.

7. Both were members of the Transport Salaried Staffs' Association, a trade union within the railway industry.

8. Lord Taylor, *Uphill All The Way: A Miner's Struggle* (London, 1972) p. 139. He says: 'On reflection, I have no doubt that my decision to accept the invitation was great. I have no regrets, and, during the five years I worked with Jim Griffiths, he afforded me every facility to participate in the work of the Department and I was privileged to be in at the discussions when the legislation was being prepared'.

9. James Griffiths, *Pages from Memory*, p. 80.

10. The father of Eleanor Rathbone (1872-1946), that is William Rathbone (1819-1902) was a Liberal MP for Caernarfonshire from 1880 to 1895 and was extremely generous to Welsh education. His daughter idolised him and wrote his biography, *A Memoir* (London, 1905). For Eleanor Rathbone, we have a study of her by Mary Stocks, Eleanor Rathbone: *A Biography* (London, 1950), and for her family's background, Lucie Nottingham, *Rathbone Brothers: From Merchant to Banker 1742-1992* (London, 1992), p. 118.

11. For the Marshall Plan, see Kenneth O. Morgan, *Labour in Power 1945-1951*, pp. 64, 239, 269-72, 336, 357, 366, 388, 411 and 495, and Chapter VIII, 'The American Loan' in Hugh Dalton, *Memoirs 1945-1960, High Tide and After* (London, 1962), pp. 68-89. Dalton says of the plan: 'Without it, trade, employment and living standards would have collapsed quite suddenly with severe hardships and sharp threats to social stability'.

12. The visit of James Griffiths and his wife was recorded in the *Evening News*, 6 August 1946, p. 1.

13. Hugh Dalton, *Memoirs 1945-1960*, pp. 65-66.

14. E. H. Robertson, George: *A Biography of Viscount Tonypandy* (London, 1992), p.88.

15. Martin Pugh, *Speak for Britain*, pp. 286-7, where he says: 'In 1945-6 alone, seventy-five pieces of legislation were enacted, the government brought a fifth of the economy under state control, introduced the welfare state, maintained full employment, kept inflation low and generated an exportled boom – all under the enormously difficult conditions inherited from wartime'.

16. Saunders Lewis, 'Cwrs y Byd', *Y Faner*, 17 April 1946.

17. Nicholas Timmins, *The Five Giants: A Biography of the Welfare State* (London, 1996), pp. 127-138; Sydney Jacobson, 'Security Comes to a Northern Village', *Picture Post*, Volume 30, No. 11, March 16, 1946, pp. 7-8.

18. Ibid.

19. Ibid.

20. Ibid.

21. NLW Deian Hopkin Papers, Douglas Hughes collection, 27 March 1946.

22. Ibid. Letter of James Griffiths to Douglas Hughes, 15 April 1946.

23. NLW, James Griffiths Papers. In his talk on *Radio Cymru* (BBC) under the title '*Y Mis yn y Senedd*' [A Month in Parliament] on 21 May 1946, the MP Will John mentions that James

Griffiths and Aneurin Bevan were the two politicians 'who are quickly climbing to prominence in the Parliament of Britain'. See NLW, Centre for Written Archives of the BBC in Wales, Talks, M-Z, p. 2.

24. Ibid. A talk in Welsh on Radio Cymru, 'A Month in Parliament' by Robert Richards, MP on 18 June 1946, pp. 1–2.

25. NLW, James Griffiths Papers. Douglas Hughes to James Griffiths. James Griffiths felt that the most practical option was to increase the membership of the Labour Party in the constituency so as to have a better financial footing.

26. Llanelli had suffered extensively between 1934 and 1945. A large number of chemical works were lost, as were Machynys Brick Works and the tinworks in Machynys in 1941 and 1942. See Robert Protheroe Jones, 'Vanished Industries of Machynys', *Amrywiaeth Llanelli*, no. 10, 1995 and 1996 (Llanelli, 1996), pp. 43-48.

27. NLW Deian Hopkin Papers, *Douglas Hughers Collection*, Nos. 31-128.

28. Ibid.

29. It was not at all easy to have the upper hand over the Labour Party structure in Swansea as Martin Pugh argues in Speak for Britain, p. 291. 'Labour's post-war story is even more eloquently told by Swansea, whose two constituencies were represented by union sponsored members each endowed with £300-£350 annually, and were run by Percy Morris who was both an alderman and MP for Swansea West'. See also, Dinah B. M. Evans, *The Dynamics of Labour Party Politics in Swansea*, PhD Thesis University of Bangor, 2008, pp. 51-67.

30. Byron Davies, 'The Construction of the Trostre Works', *Amrywiaeth Llanelli* (n.d.), pp. 68-72; NLW Labour Party Archives File 28. Letter of D. R. Grenfell to Cliff Prothero (no date, but sometime in 1953) He maintains: 'I do not feel called upon to spend any time discussing Home Rule in any form. I am a Socialist and not a Nationalist'. D. R. Grenfell was specific in a letter to Prothero on 2 October 1953: 'I do not want to speak of Home Rule, or of a Parliament for Wales'. There was no promise of a Secretary of State in the Labour Party manifesto of 1945. James Griffiths was not among the seven Parliamentary candidates for the Labour Party in 1945 who supported the idea of a Secretary of State for Wales. These seven were Cledwyn Hughes (Anglesey), Tudor Watkins (Brecon and Radnor), Huw Morris Jones (Meirionethshire), Goronwy Roberts (Caernarfon), R. Moelwyn Hughes (Carmarthen), W. Mars-Jones (Denbigh) and Arthur Pearson (Pontypridd). See Alan Butt Philip, *The Welsh Question: Nationalism in Welsh Politics 1945-1970* (Cardiff, 1975), p. 277.

31. A Welshman, Morgan Phillips, General Secretary of the British Labour Party, was opposed to the idea of a Secretary of State for Wales. He told the Labour candidate in Flintshire 'My own view, as a Welshman, is that to pretend that a Secretary of State is adequate to solve the problem of Wales is impracticable political thinking'. See the Archives of the Labour Party CS/WAL/4, Morgan Phillips to Eirene M Jones, 15 June 1945. Aneurin Bevan was also not convinced. See Lord Cledwyn, *The Referendum: the end of an era* (Cardiff, 1981), p. 10.

32. This was not a phenomenon belonging to the 1940s. The argument for devolution was heard among Welsh Socialists in the 1930s. Cyril O Jones, a solicitor in Wrexham, complained in 1930 at the negative attitude of the Labour government on devolution. Jones stood as a parliamentary Labour candidate on numerous occasions. See Archives of the University of Bangor, *The Bangor Manuscripts* 19205.

33. James Griffiths, *James Griffiths and his Times*, p. 42.

34. Gwyn Jenkins, *Cofiant Huw T. Edwards* (Talybont, 2007), p. 110.

35. NLW, Goronwy O Roberts Papers C1/6. Part of a memorandum from Ifor Bowen Griffiths, (Caernarfon, no date).

36. Ibid.

37. Ibid.

38. Ibid.

39. Gwyn Jenkins, ibid., p. 115.

40. NLW James Griffiths Papers C2/20. Letter of Herbert Morrison to James Griffiths dated 13 October 1948.

41. NLW, John Morris Papers A1/28. Letter from James Griffiths to John Morris, dated 29 January 1974.

42. Rhys Evans, *Rhag Pob Brad* (Talybont, 2005), p. 122. James Callaghan felt that he and James Griffiths deserved commendation for their contribution to the success of the docks of South Wales. See James Griffiths Papers, C 2/20. Letter from James Callaghan to James Griffiths dated 24 November 1948: 'South Wales Ports are doing very well indeed and I think we ought to take credit for our share in that. High level of dock charges are not due to government but to ship owners and the exporter and the importer. Commercial transactions 'and as such the minister's influence is limited'.

43. Hansard, 1946.

44. Gwyn Jenkins, ibid., p. 246.

45. NLW James Griffiths Papers. Letter of James Griffiths to Douglas Hughes, 28 September 1949.

46. NLW, Pennar Davies Collection. Letter from Gwynfor Evans to W. T. Pennar Davies, dated 25 May 1949.

47. The Christian Temple chapel in Ammanford increased immensely under the ministry of the Reverend Dr. D. Tegfan Davies.

48. Rhys Evans, ibid., p.125; James Griffiths paid a noble tribute to Councillor Haydn Lewis. See James Griffiths, 'My Last Talk with Haydn', *South Wales Guardian*, May 4, 1972 (this article came to me through the kindness of Dr Huw Walters).

49. One of the main promises of the Labour Party manifesto in 1945 was the nationalisation of key industries. See Norman Chester, *The Nationalisation of British Industry 1945-51* (London, 1975).

50. NLW Amanwy Papers, *Tribute to Aneurin Bevan*.

51. See Note 11.

52. James Callaghan, *Time and Chance* (London, 1987), p. 96.

53. Even with the formation of the welfare state, the leaders of the Labour Party had not prepared themselves adequately before the general election of 1950 according to Douglas Jay. He was one of four people who prepared the manifesto, Labour Believes in Britain. The other three were Herbert Morrison, and the two Welshmen, James Griffiths and Morgan Phillips. See Douglas Jay, *Change and Record: A Political Record* (London, 1980), p. 193.

54. Among the prominent Welsh Republicans there were Cliff Bere, author of the pamphlet, *The Welsh Republic* (Cardiff, 1947), Trefor Morgan a businessman who founded the insurance company, *Y Darian*, the librarian and poet, Harri Webb who edited the magazine, *The Welsh Republican* from 1950-1958, and Ithel Davies, the barrister who stood as a parliamentary candidate for the new party in Ogmore in the General Election of 1950. The group attacked James Griffiths, and two of them decided to enter the gallery of the House of Commons and throw a bundle of leaflets when the minister (JG) was addressing the House.

55. For their philosophy, see *The Welsh Republican (1950-58)*.

56. Personal knowledge.

57. Gwyn A. Williams, *When was Wales? A History of the Welsh* (London, 1985), p. 284.

Jim with Honourable H.S.Lee, CBE at a tea party in Ipoh on 30-5-1950

Jim presenting Hon. Mr Vasey with his award at the 21 Club in Nairobi, Kenya

Jim on his tour of India

Jim and Dr Edith Summerskill on their visit to Israel

# 13

# In Charge of the Colonial Office

By the end of 1949, James Griffiths was ready to pass on the responsibilities for the Ministry of Pensions to another politician.[1] He had seen the nationalisation of the coal industry, civil aviation, railways, electricity and gas, and road haulage without a great deal of disagreement. It was obvious that the days of the British Empire were coming to an end after the Attlee administration gave independence to the Indian sub-continent and Burma as well as Ceylon; and that Britain was ready to support the new international body established after the war, the United Nations.

Attlee called the general election of 1950 at the end of January. Polling day was 23 February. Most of the Labour leaders believed that the electorate would support them for another term in their 'socialistic efforts' which had worked so well. On the other hand, the Tories believed that they had a golden opportunity to upstage the Labour Party. The 1950 election was important as it did away with the business vote and the university seats; graduates of the University of Wales could no longer have two votes, one as a graduate and one as an elector in the constituency. Though the University of Wales seat disappeared, Wales still had the same number of constituencies because the county of Flintshire was divided into two. The Welsh people voted overwhelmingly for Labour. It amounted to a vote of 58% in support of Labour, nearly the same as in 1945.

The south Wales mining constituencies were solid for Labour and many of the MPs, who were themselves ex-miners, had over twenty thousand majorities. The most successful of them all was James Griffiths in Llanelli with a majority of 31,926 over the Tory candidate. For the first time Plaid Cymru had a candidate. He was a Welsh Baptist minister at Bancffosfelen, the Reverend D. Eirwyn Morgan. If every constituency was like Llanelli, Labour would not have had cause to worry, but across the country the Labour Government scraped in with a majority of only five. The Liberals were still holding on in Wales: five MPs were elected, though they had only nine MPs for the whole of Britain.

After the election Griffiths was invited to see the prime minister, and this time he hoped to be included in the cabinet, and to have responsibility in the Home Office. Attlee informed him that he deserved a new brief and he wanted him in the cabinet. Griffiths thanked him for his confidence, and then Attlee followed by inviting him to become the Minister for Colonial Affairs.[2] Griffiths was completely surprised for he had always admired those politicians who had concentrated their efforts on the colonies, such as Fenner Brockway and Arthur Creech Jones.[3] Both these men had been dedicated and knowledgeable politicians on colonial affairs. Arthur Creech Jones was one of the founders of the Fabian Colonial Bureau, and with Dr Rita Hinden he had brought a new dimension to the Labour Party. Griffiths, in his autobiography, pays Creech Jones a great tribute:

*The four years in which he served at the head of the Colonial Office gave him an opportunity of implementing some of the policies he had so tenaciously advocated over the years. He was a hard worker, an able administrator and utterly devoted to his work. He was one of the outstanding Colonial Secretaries of the twentieth century. I was greatly honoured in being asked to follow a Minister of his calibre and was under no illusion that this would be a test as well as an opportunity.*[4]

Griffiths in *Pages from Memory* gives the impression that he had not given all that much attention to foreign affairs. Attlee had another reason for choosing Jim Griffiths. The other front runner for the post was Aneurin Bevan. He would have immensely pleased to be given the opportunity for he knew so many of the politicians of the Commonwealth. Attlee preferred Griffiths for he was a safer pair of hands and that was the main reason why James Griffiths was invited to be the Minister for Colonial Affairs. He admitted to the Annual Miners' Conference of Great Britain in 1951 that the task he was given was not easy. 'It is a tough job', he told them. 'Yes, it is a hard job. What we are seeking to do is to build up new democracies in the world, and I want to ask your help, for in building up these new democracies, we want to do all the things that I have mentioned.'[5]

But we know that he had been involved for years. Because of his commitment to the the Fabian Society he had been discussing colonial affairs for over a decade. Some of the elder statesmen of the Society, such as George Bernard Shaw and in particular Beatrice Webb, had a very high regard for him because he had been involved in the war years in colonial affairs. After all, he was one of the few working-class MPs who had done so, and the only Welsh MP who had addressed so many conferences and summer schools under the Colonial Bureau of the Fabian Society. One finds an important essay by Grifiths in the volume The Way Forward, published by the Fabians in 1950.[6] Dr Rita Hinden states in the preface that it was originally an address given by Griffiths to the Colonial Bureau of the Fabian Society. She adds in her preface:

*Mr Griffiths' speech loses most in the printing. His brothers, miners of the Welsh coalfield and Labour Party members throughout the country have long known the Secretary of State as an orator of the first order. It is no exaggeration to say that those who heard this speech delivered will never forget the experience.*[7]

The title of his essay was 'The Way Forward in the Colonies.' He gives his philosophy in this sentence: 'Democratic self government cannot be given to a people, it must be won by them. It means winning the battle against internal enemies – ignorance and poverty, disease and squalor.'[8] Griffiths goes on to argue that the Labour government of 1945-1950 had done more to improve the lives of the inhabitants of the colonies than the Conservatives had done in twenty years. There were no universities established in the colonies before 1947 except in Malta and Hong Kong. But the Labour government established institutions of higher education in Malaya, the Caribbean, the Gold Coast and in Nigeria. He made himself crystal clear on racism:

*Let me make one thing abundantly clear, that no doctrine of race superiority has any place in our colonial policy; and let me repeat it – it cannot be repeated too often – that the task of the greatest importance is the building up of confidence and goodwill.*[9]

The Second World War had been an eye opener to politicians in the colonies. They realised that the European imperialists were not as powerful as they had thought they were in the inter-war years. The fall of France in 1940 showed how frail was their supposed strength, and the Japanese had shown in south-east Asia how easily they could overrun Dutch and British colonies. The authority and status of the imperial countries were undermined and this gave the leaders of home rule and self-government a great deal of confidence. Many or most of the imperial countries, except Portugal, had lost the will to rule and to keep their colonial subjects under their control.

The Labour government was convinced that it should adapt the Fabian concept of Commonwealth. This would allow Britain, the mother country, to keep strong economic and social ties with the colonies. The invitation to join the Commonwealth was to be extended to every colony. The plan was unveiled to the leaders of the Commonwealth in a conference held in 1949, to discuss the future of the British Empire in the light of the independence of India and Pakistan.[10] From this conference sprung the Labour Party's approach during the ministry of James Griffiths. India was the model, with its prime minister and the whole structure of democratic government in existence. The political class, which had been led by Mohandas Gandhi in the inter-war years, had no problem in achieving for the teeming masses in India their own government in 1947. Gandhi, who rose from obscurity to become a world icon until an assassin's bullet brought his life to an end in 1947, had been an inspiration. By 1950, India was a force to be reckoned with, and the only contact between it and Britain was the king and the new organisation centred on the Commonwealth. The crown became the symbolic figure of the unity of the Commonwealth.

This was the background to the time that Griffiths spent as Colonial Secretary. It was a short period of nineteen months but it was to be the most exciting time in his life, full of endeavour and travel as well as adventure, encouraging the emerging trade unions everywhere he went, confronting the most reactionary white settlers, whom he met at the conferences. In 1950 Griffiths, with his skill as a reconciler, was responsible for fifty-three colonies on behalf of Britain. Every minister in the Department of Colonial Affairs had to spell out his mission. Griffiths announced that:

> *The central purpose of our colonial policy is to guide the people of the colonial territories to responsible self government within the Commonwealth, and in partnership with them to establish the conditions upon which self government can be firmly built.*[11]

Six months later, in a conference arranged by the Fabian Colonial Bureau, he expanded on the way forward to this objective. He explained in detail the situation in Malaya and asked the question: 'What, for example, would happen in Malaya if we got out today?' He gave the answer: 'It would not be independence; it would be the subjugation of Malayan people by a ruthless minority, and the subjugation of their country into a docile satellite.'[12]

It is easy to believe that the Colonial Office was a most interesting place for a politician in 1950. As Griffiths explained, the Colonial Office had not worked itself out of its job, as it had done by the 1960s. In 1950 it was a miniature Whitehall, with the Secretary of State holding all the portfolios. The Secretary of State had a permanent secretary and two deputies as well as the assistance of seven officers, of the rank of assistant under-secretaries. Each of these men had charge of a number of territories which had been placed into categories. These were: East and Central Africa, Eastern Asia, the Mediterranean, the West Indies, the Western Pacific, the Atlantic and Indian Ocean.[13]

The department also had a number of advisers to deal with agriculture, forestry, inland transport, fisheries, labour, and legal matters, including a chief officer of medicine, an inspector general of colonial police, and directors of geographic, topographic and geological surveys. From the very beginning, Griffiths's period as Colonial Secretary was a busy one. He was expected to reply to letters and questions and protests from members of the House of Commons on the matter of security in Malaya. Soldiers as well as policemen were sent out to Malaya at the end of 1949 and at the beginning of 1950 to keep law and order. The Government of Australia sent some soldiers there as well. Immediately after his appointment, Griffiths met the prime minister and the Minister of Defence, Emanuel Shinwell,[14] Lieutenant-General Sir Harold Briggs was invited to co-ordinate the whole operation. He had made a name for himself in the Burma campaign. His tactics became known as the 'Briggs plan', the implementation of which was a success, for it silenced the terror, and allowed Malaya to prepare itself for unity and subsequent independence.[15] But the Conservative backbenchers were rightly concerned – as were the Labour leftwingers – with the ruthless war that was taking place, and they were agreed that Griffiths, a man of peace, should visit Malayan Villages, the rubber planters and the British soldiers.

In May 1950, Griffiths undertook the journey, accompanied by John Strachey from the War Office.[16] It was to take a month and they were expected to discuss the situation of the colony with leaders of the different movements, and in particular representatives from the Chinese, Indian and Malayan communities. Griffiths wrote a letter on 2 June 1950 from the King's House, Kuala Lumpur, to Douglas Hughes in Llanelli.[7] He described the ten confrontational days which had been experienced, and all the manifold problems that had been discussed, dealing with economics, politics, sociology, but more than anything else, with racial hatred. He added that the journey and the discussions on Singapore and Malaya had been a wonderful experience, and he would not have missed it for the world. But he realised that there was no way he could restore law and order in Malaya.[18] In actual fact the violent conflict, the killing and the terror went on to be a fact of life for the next ten years.

Griffiths was severely rebuked for his colonial policy by a group of his supporters in the constituency at the beginning of 1951. A letter was sent, signed by John Rosser Davies and one hundred others, all of them socialists from the Amman Valley. This letter was published in the Welsh language weekly newspaper, *Y Cymro* (Welshman), on 9 February 1951.[19] What had upset John Rosser Davies and his fellow signatories was the policy of the Labour government towards Malaya, in particular remembering that a large number of Welsh soldiers were involved. The letter states:

> *The truth is that there are a large number of Welsh men that we admire, who are sweating and suffering in the unhealthy jungle. We are not proud of this, Jim, as the boys are not there to safeguard Britain or there to release Malaya from a terrible ordeal. But they are there to fight against the environment so as to ensure greater profit to the proprietors of the rubber plantations and the tin mines which flows to the pockets of capitalists in Britain.*[20]

John Rosser Davies could not be content seeing Welsh soldiers being killed and maimed in Malaya and he disagreed vehemently with the stewardship of Griffiths as minister. This is apparent in his last paragraph:

> *For the war in Malaya, and the exploitation of the miners of Nigeria and the working masses of the Gold Coast is in accordance with the policies of the Labour government. You should extend a helping hand to the developing nations so that they can rise and stand on their own two feet and determine their own fate. That has been the traditional policy of the Labour Party.*[21]

Some of the signatories to this letter had been socialist comrades with Griffiths at the White House in Ammanford during the First World War, but they were now at loggerheads with him. It is obvious that the left-wing socialists of those days had not changed markedly in their convictions with regard to pacifism and anti-imperialism. It is certain that the colonial minister was not, for one moment, an imperialist but it is true that his attitude to war and conflicts had changed significantly since the First World War.

The minister was keen to visit Africa, and to uphold the valuable work done by his predecessor, Arthur Creech Jones, who lost his seat in Shipley in 1951 by eighty-one votes. Through the efforts of Arthur Creech Jones and a commission under the chairmanship of Mr Justice J. H. Coussey, it was decided to proceed with a constitutional plan for the Gold Coast. This recommended that a new legislature should be set up consisting of eighty-four members almost wholly elected by a popular vote in a ballot conducted on an adult franchise.Griffiths knew one of the key politicians of the Gold Coast, Kwame Nkrumah. He had been a key figure in the political movement there, the United Gold Coast Convention, but after his disagreement with his fellow leaders, he had formed his own political party, the Convention People's Party (CPP). Like many African politicians he had spent a period in prison and he was in prison when the election was held from 5 to 10 February 1951.[22]

Naturally, the election had received a great deal of publicity as it was the first time a British colony on the African continent had arranged an election to choose senators – even more interesting still in a country where half of the population were illiterate.Griffiths recognized that this election would be of great significance but he had every confidence in the governor, Sir Charles Arden-Clarke.[23] He was to be the last British governor of the Gold Coast.

Arden-Clarke was a first-class administrator, a wise statesman who had served Britain and the Gold Coast well from 1949 to 1957. Observers came from all over the world to keep an eye on the election, so to avoid fraud and unfairness. The CPP won the day, though Kwame Nkrumah had been initially against the election. Griffiths consulted immediately with the governor, and suggested that Kwame Nkrumah and his fellow political prisoners should be allowed out of prison. He also invited Nkrumah to join the government with the title of 'Leader of Government Business'. Griffiths used all his charm to get the leaders of the CPP, including the most awkward of them all, Nkrumah, on board. It was a great moral victory for the Welshman to have been responsible for the first democratically-elected government in British West Africa.

When Nkrumah and his fellow leaders came to London to discuss with Griffiths and his civil servants the future of their new African country, they received a warm welcome. The minister had a high regard for Nkrumah. He admired his way of presenting his cause, his intellectual ability and his colleagues, Kojo Botsio and Komla Agbei Gbedemah.[24] However, Griffiths became disillusioned by the end of the decade by the foolish behaviour of Nkrumah, in particular his decision to appoint himself as King-President of his country which by then had been named Ghana, and his failure to keep his friends, Gbedemah and Botsio, working with him. Nkrumah also fell out with Joe Appiah, the son-in-law of Sir Stafford Cripps.[25] Griffiths, felt that Ghana had so much potential in 1951, but by 1960 the original promise and vision had been tarnished.

Griffiths retained a great deal of interest in the African continent, and in 1951 he had the opportunity to travel to East and Central Africa. He took advantage of the opportunity to travel over Whitsun and spent three weeks in Uganda and Kenya. His wife Winifred accompanied him, as well as Andrew Cohen, an adviser, and Angus Mackintosh, his private secretary.[26] Griffiths was amazed by the beauty of Uganda, the beautiful mountains such as Ruwenzori Mountains (often called the Mountains of the Moon), and the wild animals in the national parks. Griffiths flew from one part to another of this large country. He saw the results of the Cotton Growers' Co-operative at Namungalwe in the eastern part of Uganda. To him the vision of Robert Owen of Newtown and the Rochdale pioneers had worked effectively. Griffiths appreciated the opportunity to address the leaders of the co-operative movement in Namungalwe and he was given the honour of addressing the Lukiko, the 'parliament' of the Buganda State.[27]

The King of Buganda, Mutessa the Second, was away on an official visit to London. Griffiths realised that the tribes had their own plans for the future, especially when independence came. Some of the tribes, such as the Kabaka and Lukiko, were afraid that their ancient heritage would suffer when independence became a reality. In the University College of Makerere they had another concern: they were afraid that the government in Britain would not transfer power to the young, intellectually-able generation who had worked for independence. The minister realised that the big problem for Uganda was to reconcile the old and the new: that the tribes and ethnic groups within its borders were striving to make their country a united and dependable state.

Griffiths and colleagues then travelled to Kenya and his observations on that country were similar. He thought that nature had created a paradise but Man in his stupidity had spoiled the precious garden and turned it into a desert. When he was asked for his comments on Kenya, he described it as: 'God's own country with the devil's own problems.'[28] They travelled to every part of the country, in an aeroplane from Nairobi to Mombasa, and visited the villages of the African tribes, towns and farms where the Europeans were living, including Britons who had settled in the countryside.

They spent several days in Nairobi. There Griffiths realised that a huge task faced the civil servants and politicians: to prepare a constitution which would create an atmosphere of co-operation between the different tribes as well as the Indian community of Nairobi and other migrant communities. The Indians had been the real pioneers in Kenya and they had brought into existence a fine network of railways. By this time they were concentrating their efforts on the world of commerce. Griffiths felt that he had to remember the farmers who had migrated from Britain as well as South Africa, without ignoring the communities of Arabs who had settled in Mombasa and the area around the town. Griffiths had met deputations from each one of these communities at the beginning of his service as Colonial Secretary. This is what inspired him to prepare a document for the three new states of Uganda, Tanganyika and Kenya. The simple message of his statement in parliament in December 1950 was that the goal was 'home rule within the Commonwealth'. To him, self-government meant respect for all the communities that had settled in East Africa and he encouraged them to understand each other and work together. They could succeed and flourish by co-operation. Griffiths's task on this trip was to consult and discuss the changes that were to be implemented, and so again he met with representatives from each one of the ethnic groups as well as the native tribes. He met Elihud Mathu, from the Kikuyu tribe, a leader who had been educated at Oxford University before returning to serve his country. It was a special experience for Griffiths to meet Kamiti Watihuo, who was ninety, and the only one from the Kikuya tribe who remembered the white man moving in to farm on the land of his ancestors.[29] Jomo Kenyatta, idolized by the Africans in Griffiths experience, gave a half-hearted welcome to the presentation and the programme spelt out by Griffiths.

After he had left Jomo Kenyatta without receiving the moral support he had hoped for, Griffiths had another session that was much more positive in the company of A. B. Patel, the leader of the Indian community. But Patel was a politician who feared the future due to the squabbling among his own followers. From the moment he met him, Griffiths came to admire him immensely. Patel had come under the influence of Mahatma Gandhi, and he also had a high regard for Nehru.[30] He supported Griffiths's proposals, though soon afterwards he opted out of his role as leader. Patel eventually left Kenya, the country of his adoption, and returned to India utterly disillusioned.

After meeting A. B. Patel, Griffiths had an opportunity to discuss the detail with members of the European Legislative Council. After the retirement of Albert Keyser, a pioneer of the European Community, because of ill-health his place was taken by a member of the younger generation, Michael Blundell. A great deal on the visit of the Welsh politician is to be found in Blundell's book, *So Rough as Wind*, where he claims that Griffiths became highly emotional when a fellow European accused the British Labour government of preparing the way for self-government on the Gold Coast. Blundell claims: 'Griffiths reacted rather sharply, banged the table with his fist, and in his strong Welsh voice said: "And what was that alternative man? Bloody revolution, that's what it was".'[31]

I communicated with Blundell through his son after reading the above quotation as it is a most intriguing glimpse of James Griffiths. In the first place, James Griffiths quoted the exact words in Pages from Memory but does not make any comment to explain his emotional outburst. He does not give a reason for raising his voice and banging the table with his fist. Had the discussions with Kenyatta rattled him, or had the attitude of Blundell and the white settlers upset him? This is an example, in my opinion, of when Griffiths, a highly emotional individual, lost his cool temperament. Perhaps it was not the only example, but one of the few instances when the man of peace was ready to strike the table and use strong words. He had been deeply upset. But in spite of the outburst, Griffiths later that day had an invitation to the home of Blundell.

Michael Blundell's home was in Subokia, a beautiful district in the highlands of Kenya, and the purpose of this meeting was to give an opportunity for Griffiths to meet European farmers who had right-wing views.[32] Without fear or favour, the minister explained to them that the choice before them was either unity and co-operation or the spilling of blood in a painful conflict over self-government. On the last day of his visit to Kenya, on 28 May 1951, Griffiths invited the leaders of all the communities to come to Nairobi to meet the governor of the country, Sir Philip Mitchell, and he kept notes of the meeting. They came to an agreement on the goal of self-government of the three countries and the ways of achieving that goal.[33]

After a brief adjournment, everyone accepted all the proposals and the proceedings ended with a graceful tribute by Blundell to Griffiths, and a very charming reply was made by him in response. So it all was settled in an atmosphere of sober responsibility and goodwill, thanks to the personal influence of this remarkable man who had spread goodwill wherever he had been in Uganda and Kenya.Unfortunately, not all the leaders in Kenya appreciated the efforts of James Griffiths. Indeed, the sadness of 28 May 1951, despite the agreement among the leaders, was that a large number of people in every community and tribe disagreed vehemently with the principles of the British Labour government. Jomo Kenyatta had shown quite clearly where he stood, and he kept away from the final meeting in Nairobi, sending one of his colleagues to represent the Kikuyu people. Within eighteen months of this meeting in Nairobi, Kenya began to suffer severely from the Mau Mau uprising. Griffiths summed up fairly the situation when he wrote:

> *What I do know is that during my visit not a single person of all those I met –*
> *African, Indian, Arab, European – or any of the colonial officers, ever mentioned the*
> *Mau Mau to me. I believe that the truth of the matter is that each of the racial*
> *communities was so completely locked up within its own separate world that none of*
> *them knew what was happening in the closed world of its neighbour.*[34]

That was the tragedy of the situation in Kenya. Indeed, this tragedy was repeated in all the countries on the continent of Africa in the early 1950s. But the end result of the confrontation in Kenya was to be independence, and a word of commendation by Griffiths to Jomo Kenyatta when he called him one of the greatest African leaders as well as praising the wisdom of the white settlers such as Michael Blundell. Even with all his many gifts as a reconciler, not every leader in the colonies was complimentary about Griffiths. He was criticised for taking the lead himself and starting the discussion on the situation with regard to the countries of Southern Rhodesia, North Nigeria and Nyasaland, without the necessary consultation.

These discussions began on 8 November 1950 to create what came to be called the Federal State of Rhodesia and Nyasaland. The cabinet exerted pressure on Griffiths and Patrick Gordon-Walker (the Secretary of the Commonwealth who had specific responsibility for Southern Rhodesia) to give strong support to the three countries so as to strengthen the relationship between them.[35] There was a great deal of migration between 1945 and 1950 from Britain, as well as from the Afrikaans communities of South Africa, to Rhodesia, and in particular to Southern Rhodesia. It was soon realised that the Broederbond, a secret society among the Afrikaan nation, were extremely active in Southern Rhodesia where Sir Godfrey Martin Huggins, a proponent of white minority rule, had been politically active for a long period. In Southern Rhodesia the Democratic Party believed in the supremacy of the white race. In other words, they were supporting apartheid ideology as they had done in South Africa. In the face of such tensions, Griffiths felt that he had to be proactive and suggested a draft document for a federal model for what came to be called the Central African Federation.

He had no intention of merging the three countries, but rather giving an opportunity for political and social advisers to discuss a federal draft model. At all times Griffiths was ready to promote the rights of the native population, to improve the material life of the ordinary people, and then to define the relationship between the federal government and the regional governments. In the federal government there would be a Minister for African Affairs from each of the three countries. This official was to be appointed by the Minister for the Colonies in London. The recommendations were published and Griffiths and Gordon-Walker travelled to Africa to discuss the structure with the political leaders, and then hold a conference for the three countries neas Victoria Falls. Before this conference, Griffiths visited two countries, Northern Rhodesia and Nyasaland, while Gordon-Walker travelled to Southern Rhodesia. Clearly Griffiths was very busy. He attended one hundred meetings, most of them involving white miners. He had sessions among miners who had emigrated from British coalfields, and among them one miner from the Amman Valley. It was a distressing experience for him to find out that this Welsh miner looked upon the natives as a lower class. Griffiths also realised that many of the white miners employed black boys to work inside and outside their homes for a pittance. But he also met miners who, like him, refused every aspect of apartheid. A miner who had left Britain told him: 'This is like the old butty system, with its boss and hirelings which our forefathers fought against in the bad old days back home. We should be fighting it out here.'

This trip lasting three weeks was a wonderful opportunity for Griffiths to learn of the complex situation in Africa, before attending the Victoria Falls conference. The conference was most difficult, especially when Sir Godfrey Huggins suggested that the Africans from Nyasaland should leave immediately. Huggins argued that on principle they were opposed to the federal concept. James Griffiths refused this absurd suggestion by reminding them of their responsibilities. After all, they were there at his invitation as the responsible minister of the British government. If the chosen delegates from Nyasaland had to leave the conference, then he himself would leave without delay. Huggins was not at all pleased, and his comment later was that the minister had turned the conference into a 'natives' tea party'.

The conference was a great disappointment to the minister, but he realised that he could not do much more at that stage and that he would have to be cautious and review the whole proceedings: in particular, the arguments and the statements that had been pursued. There would be a need to safeguard the interests of Nyasaland and Northern Rhodesia, and to be alive to the threat from apartheid ideology, which could be transferred easily from Southern Rhodesia.

Griffiths and Gordon-Walker returned to Britain on the threshold of another general election. They could not carry on with their plans – indeed, the Federation came into existence on 1 August 1953 under a British Conservative government. Sir Roy Welensky became the prime minister of the Federation in 1956. His views on Griffiths are to be found in his book, 400 Days – The Life and Death of the Federation of Rhodesia and Nyasaland, published in 1960. But Griffiths had tried his best in countries that did not want to listen to a British government or British empire which they wanted to leave in order to seek independence. Griffiths had made a valuable contribution in a short period: so much so that he was almost chosen to be the foreign secretary.[36]

Because of ill health, Ernest Bevin resigned as foreign secretary on 10 March 1951 and there was a great deal of discussion behind the scenes before Herbert Morrison was chosen by Attlee. Bevin himself would have much preferred Griffiths as his successor. Other Labour leaders agreed, especially Hugh Dalton. This was his opinion of the Colonial Secretary: 'Griffiths was shaping well at the Colonial Office, where he had been Secretary of State for just over a year. He was showing considerable independence in mind and was not unduly influenced by official advice. This independence might have borne rich fruit in Africa.'[37]

Earlier Griffiths had been a conspicuous success as Minister of National Insurance. He had piloted a major part of social service legislation through parliament and into operation. Griffiths had shown himself an efficient and sensible administrator, as well as a man of deep and simple humanity. He was a most loyal and unselfish colleague, and a former miner, who had served both in the colliery and exerted moderate industrial leadership in the South Wales Miners' Union before he entered parliament. Following Arthur Henderson and Ernest Bevin, he would have continued the line of trade union Foreign Secretaries in Labour governments.

Hugh Dalton discussed possible candidates with the prime minister. He maintains: 'I was for Griffiths.'[38] Another politician who was mentioned was the well-known barrister, Sir Hartley Shawcross. In the end, Attlee chose Morrison. It was a huge blunder, to say the least, but the politician who had the biggest disappointment was Aneurin Bevan. Not one of those around Attlee was in favour of Bevan. Hugh Dalton, however, stated in 1962:

> *Looking back with the great advantage of hindsight, I think now that it would have been better if Bevan had become Foreign Secretary in March 1951. But I did not think so then, nor did Attlee, nor as far as I know, did any of those who advised him.*[39]

One could argue that to ignore Bevan for two important posts – Chancellor and Foreign Secretary within a short period of time – had railed the rebel greatly.

Griffiths was not upset. He had been greatly enriched in his role as Secretary of State of the Colonies.[40] He never nursed a disappointment, and saw the best in everyone. He wrote with wisdom about Sir Roy Welensky when he realised that there was no hope for the white man if he did not co-operate with the black leaders. But he did worry that Welensky had not identified himself with progressive Europeans such as Sir John Moffat (from the family of David Livingstone) in Northern Rhodesia, or with Garfield Todd, a prominent politician in Southern Rhodesia.[41] Todd had a great deal of charm and had extended a hand of friendship towards leaders such as Kenneth Kaunda. He was, as always, on good terms with his racist friends, who hindered him in the idea of the Federation but in the end prepared the way for a reactionary politician such as Ian Smith.

Clearly, for a short time in his life Griffiths was prominent on the world's stage. He was a servant to the changes that gained momentum and transformed the British Empire into a Commonwealth of independent nations. He prepared the ground for the independence of the following nations: Trinidad and Tobago, the Gold Coast, Sierra Leone, North Borneo, Nigeria, Dominica, Grenada, St Lucia, St Vincent, Singapore and Gambia. On the threshold of the 1951 general election Griffiths felt, with a great deal of justification, that he was satisfied with his efforts in the post of the Secretary of State for the Colonies and that he had succeeded in keeping in touch with many of the progressive African leaders. Griffiths was always supportive of the African leaders in their efforts to raise the standard of living of their people. He hardly ever criticised the failure of many of these newly-independent countries to function as they should, or the leaders who could not resist the temptation of corruption.
In August 1951 Griffiths spent a two-week holiday in Genoa in Italy. He felt the need for a complete rest. From Genoa, he wrote to wish his agent well on his wedding to the socialist schoolteacher, Loti Rees Hopkin [42] Both had experienced bereavements and were marrying for the second time. In his letter of 31 July 1951 to Douglas Hughes, Griffiths stressed the value of a home for a person in public life:

> *A man in the public life needs an anchor or his life will become unbearable. This is where a home is of value, the best place, indeed the safest anchor. May you two have long life, happiness in service and among friends.'*[43]

Loti and Douglas Hughes with many others worked effectively within the Llanelli constituency as they arranged their campaign in October 1951.[44] Once more James Griffiths had an excellent result in Llanelli:

| | | |
|---|---|---|
| James Griffiths (Labour) | 39,731 | 72.5% |
| Henry Gardner (Conservative) | 11,315 | 20.6% |
| Revd D. Eirwyn Morgan (Plaid Cymru) | 3,765 | 6.9% |
| Majority | 28,416 | 51.9% |

The result in Britain was disappointing for the Labour Party though they had the largest number of votes; 13,948,883 people voted Labour. This was the best result by any political party in the history of the British parliament. But because of the first-past-the-post voting system, the Conservatives, with the support of 13,718,199 of the electorate, formed the new government.

They won 321 constituencies compared with 295 for Labour. Because the Liberals decided to contest only 109 constituencies, the Conservatives were handed constituencies that could have gone to the Liberals. Though Clement Davies, the Liberal leader, had many positive attributes, it was obvious that he felt closer to the Conservatives than to Labour. Indeed, he had considered seriously the invitation given to him by Winston Churchill to join the new government as a minister.[45] The Liberals lost two seats to Labour in Wales: T. W. Jones from Ponciau, near Rhosllanerchrugog, won Merionethshire, while Cledwyn Hughes, a solicitor in Holyhead, won Anglesey from Megan Lloyd George.[46] This gave the Labour Party twenty-seven constituencies in Wales. Both T. W. Jones and Cledwyn Hughes became friends and admirers of Griffiths, identifying with the radical nonconformist background with a strong involvement in eisteddfodic Welsh culture. They were on the same wavelength as Griffiths. The election meant that the plans and policies Griffiths had prepared in his time at the Colonial Office could not be implemented. On the other hand, there was a positive effect from the result. It meant that Griffiths was now free to concentrate his talents and his experience in the service of his own country rather than nations of Africa and Asia.[47]

**Notes and References**

1.  J. Beverley Smith, 'James Griffiths: An Appreciation', in *James Griffiths and his Times*, p. 91. 'The Ministry of Labour was an office for which he seemed particularly well suited'.
2.  James Griffiths, *Pages from Memory*, p. 90. Among the letters congratulating him he was extremely grateful for the one he received from the Reverend Tom Nefyn Williams, whom he had known in the turbulent 1920s. This sincere greeting came in a letter written by the MP, Goronwy Roberts, a great friend of Tom Nefyn Williams. James Griffiths wrote to Goronwy Roberts in his

letter dated 19 April, 1950 'Thank you for the letter of 14 April and your conversation with T. Nefyn Williams. I take his comments seriously and thank him for his words of congratulation'. See NLW, Goronwy Roberts Papers, 0200302280 C1/2.

3.  James Griffiths, ibid., p. 90 'Clem Attlee seemed to sense my reluctance and told me that he was confident that my proven capacity as an administrator, and ability as a parliamentarian, would be equal to the challenge of the new office'.

4.  Ibid., p. 91

5.  NLW James Griffiths Papers. *Notes for the Miners' Conference.*

6.  NLW, James Griffiths Papers B 6/3. James Griffiths in the Summer School in the Colonies, September 1950. There were representatives from Sudan present. The School was held in Queen's College, Oxford under the chairmanship of Sir John Shaw. See James Griffiths, Arthur Creech Jones and Rita Hinden, *The Way Forward* (London, 1950), pp. 1-40. The preface was prepared by Rita Hinden and it was she who praises James Griffiths as a first-rate orator.

7.  Ibid.

8.  James Griffiths, *Pages from Memory*, p. 93.

9.  Ibid., pp. 108-9.

10. A. H. Hanson & Janet Douglas, *India's Democracy* (London, 1972), pp. 32-52.

11. James Griffiths, *Pages from Memory*, p. 93.

12. Ibid.

13. Ibid.

14. Ibid., p.94.

15. Ibid., pp 94-5.

16. Ibid, p. 95.

17. NLW Deian Hopkin Papers. Letter of James Griffiths to Douglas Hughes, 2 June 1950.

18. Griffiths, ibid., p. 94.

19. An Open Letter in the Welsh Language to James Griffiths on the front page of *Y Cymro*, 9 February 1951, p 1.

20. Ibid.

21. Ibid.

22. James Griffiths, *Pages from Memory*, p. 93.

23. Ibid., p. 103.

24. Ibid.

25. Ibid.

26. NLW, Deian Hopkins Papers. Letter of James Griffiths to Douglas Hughes, dated 2 June 1950. Mrs James Griffiths, *One Woman's Story*, p.144. 'He insisted that I should go with him. He said there might never be such a chance again – and there never has been. It cost us £330 for my air fare, but the experience was well worth the money'.

27. James Griffiths, *Pages from Memory*, pp. 103-121.

28. Ibid., p.112.

29. Ibid., p.109. See also James Griffiths Papers B6/5, Colonial Territories (1950-1).

30. Ibid., p.110.

31. Ibid.

32. Ibid., p.111.

33. Ibid.

34. Ibid.

35. Ibid., pp. 112-118. His successor as a Colonial Secretary from the Conservative Party, Oliver Lyttelton, said of him: 'Jim Griffiths, the outgoing Colonial Secretary came to see me. I had

always liked him in the old days, but his emotional approach to public affairs was to draw me first to boredom and finally to exasperation'.

36. Mrs James Griffiths, ibid., p. 143.

37. Hugh Dalton, *Memoirs 1945-1960: High Tide and After* (London, 1962), pp. 359-60. 38 Ibid., p. 360.

39 Ibid., p. 362.

40. James Griffiths, *Pages from Memory*, p. 119.

41. Ibid., p.118.

42. NLW, Deian Hopkin Papers. Letter of James Griffiths to Douglas Hughes dated 31 July 1951.

43. Arnold J. James and John E. Thomas, Wales at Westminster, p.154.

44. J. Graham Jones, 'Edward Clement Davies, 1884-1962' in *Dictionary of Liberal Biography* (editor Duncan Brack) (London, 1998), pp. 92-4.

45. Emyr Price, *Yr Arglwydd Cledwyn o Benrhos* (Pen-y-Groes, 1990), p.15 'Labour only won two new seats in 1951 throughout Britain and Anglesey was one of them'.

46. Just over a decade later one of the most outstanding civil servants, Sir Hilton Poynton, was concerned that the Colonial Office was on the verge of amalgamation. See D.J. Morgan (ed.), *The Official History of Colonial Development*, Volume 4 (London, 1980), p. 24.

# 14

## James Griffiths: The Reconciler and Socialist Revisionist

The 1950s were a difficult period for the Labour Party in view of the disagreements within the party on foreign affairs, and the fact that the Labour Party was divided into three camps, the moderates, the left wingers, and the right wingers. The supporters of Aneurin Bevan were the left-wingers, and his supporters became known as 'the Bevanites'.[1] The supporters of the Left as a whole disagreed with the foreign policies of Clement Attlee, Ernest Bevin and Herbert Morrison which, in the main, were anti-Soviet, in support of the United States' and in favour of the further stockpiling of armaments.Aneurin Bevan had his golden opportunity to rebel when the Chancellor, Hugh Gaitskell, insisted on charging for false teeth and spectacles under the National Health Service to help meet the costs of armaments. Bevan immediately objected but Gaitskell refused to budge. Griffiths agreed with Bevan but did not believe it was a resigning issue.[2]  But on 22 April 1951 that is what Bevan did, supported by Harold Wilson, President of the Board of Trade, and John Freeman, another  minister.

His most trenchant criticism was that the armament programme of Britain, in conjunction with that of the USA, was going to undermine the economy of Britain, creating unemployment and a fall in the standard of living of the working classes. Bevan also attacked the Chancellor on the grounds that he had more interest in rearming Britain than safeguarding the high standards of the National Health Service. Wilson and Bevan explained their views in a pamphlet published in the summer of 1951 under the title *One Way Only*. By the time the Labour Party conference was held in Scarborough in the first week of October 1951 Bevan had gained many more supporters.[4]

Though Bevan and his followers supported the Labour Party manifesto in 1951 this was not worth much as Labour lost the general election. Griffiths did not publicly criticise Bevin's behaviour he could not ignore the harsh words of Sir Norman Angell on the failure of Labour in the 1951 general election. It is no secret that a great many in the Labour Party, especially on the trade union side, regarded Mr Aneurin Bevan a far greater menace than Mr Churchill to the world of the British workers' desires.[5]

Angell's words suggests one reason for the failure of Labour to win the general election. It underlines the importance of the support of trade unions to the existence and the success of the Labour Party at General Elections. Ernest Bevin was a remarkable trade unionist, who managed to get all the union bosses on his side, in support of NATO and the anti-Soviet foreign policy at the height of the Cold War. The tendency of the trade union is to plead for the status quo with the exception of unions such as the Miners' when they were led by staunch members of the British Communist Party.

Arthur Deakin, who had close connections with Wales, could not agree at all with trade unionists who supported communism or even the left wing section.[6] As General Secretary of the Transport and General Workers Union from 1945, Deakin became one of the most important figures in the Labour movement of the 1950s. He could not identify himself with Bevan or with his supporters within his union, such as Huw T. Edwards.[7] There were other leading trade unionists who opposed Bevan. Sir William Lawther was one of them, a miners' leader, who said of him in 1952: 'that his feet were in Moscow and his eye on 10 Downing Street.'[8]

We need to remember that the attitude towards the Soviet Union was an important strand in the ideology of the right- wingers within the Labour Party. Another important aspect, which James Griffiths embodied and supported, was its loyalty to the Labour Party, and its leadership. Solidarity was the keyword in the world of trade unionism: there was nothing more destructive to Labour's chances of electoral victory than the lack of party solidarity. This was the besetting sin of Aneurin Bevan and his followers as far as Deakin and Griffiths was concerned.

The concern and the opposition to the party leaders is reflected in the trade union journals and newsletters. In November 1952 in an article in the journal of his union, Thomas Williamson, the leader of the National Union of General and Municipal Workers, said of the unofficial organisation called Bevanism:

> *This organisation has been at work for some two years or more. Its methods have been directed towards the undermining of the leadership, and its ultimate objective the usurpation of power... The trade union movement cannot stand aside and ignore what is taking place.*[9]

Another element in the Labour ideology of the period after the Second World War was the demand by the trade unions to adopt practical policies, which were regarded as moderate, evolutionary and which could improve the lives of the ordinary mass of people, so creating a better world. Griffiths acknowledges in his autobiography that he was regarded as one of the moderate people, though in his youth he had the image of a troublemaker. He maintains of the 1950s:

> *Throughout this period I was often described as a middle-of-the-road man. For myself I prefer to think of my role as a reconciler, ever seeking to promote unity, and to prevent rival factions and personal antagonisms from tearing the party to pieces.*[10]

This is an important paragraph, and an aspect of his life which has not been given much prominence by historians of the Labour Party, though he did include a chapter on himself as a reconciler in his book Pages from Memory.[11] As a reconciler his constant purpose was to support unity and cooperation and to ensure that his fellow leaders would not destroy the electoral chances of the Labour Party. He always saw the Labour Party as a movement that owed so much to the trade unions, to the working classes and to intellectuals and men and women of conscience from the middle classes.[12]

Griffiths mixed socially with those intellectual elements of the middle class through his involvement with the Fabian Society.[13]   We know that he gave a great deal of his energy and time to this socialist society. Griffiths lectured in the Fabian Easter School in London in 1952, when James Callaghan was its director. Five men were invited to deliver key lectures, namely Michael Young from Labour Party headquarters, Hugh Dalton, ex-Chancellor, Lord Hungarton, the politician Anthony Crosland and James Griffiths. He also addressed the Fabians at their meeting during the Labour Party conference on the Challenge of the African Continent.

The other speakers were fellow MPs John Dugdale and James Johnson, as well as Sir Richard Acland, founder member of the Commonwealth Party. In the chair was Eirene White who had won Flint East for Labour in 1950. In the Annual Fabian Dinner held at the House of Commons on 29 November 1952, Griffiths was invited as the guest speaker and this clearly indicates his standing and popularity within the Fabian Society. At least one hundred and forty intellectuals and members of the Society turned up to the Dinner, including the President of the Society, Professor G. D. H. Cole, who was largely responsible for recruiting in the 1930's Hugh Gaitskell and Douglas Jay as Oxford graduates into the Labour Party.G. D. H. Cole was the chief inspiration for the important volume New Fabian Essays, and nearly all the contributors were in his circle, including Ritchie Calder, Science Editor of The News Chronicle, Cole's wife Margaret, and James Griffiths with his concern and responsibility for the British Colonies.

The Labour Party conference in October 1952 was held in Morecambe. It turned out to be a quarrelsome affair.[14] The leaders of the unions were determined to keep Bevan and the Bevanites as quiet as was possible, and they succeeded in the Organisational Committee. Barbara Castle and Ian Mikardo were kept out of the debates, and the restrictions extended even to Bevan himself, who was allowed to take part in only one debate.[15]   Gaitskell and his followers had much more of an opportunity to partake in the conference proceedings. The climax of the conference was the election to the National Executive Committee (NEC), and from among these Clement Attlee, as leader of the Opposition had the opportunity to consider future spokesmen if he wished.

The Bevanites had worked hard in the different constituencies to gain support for politicians of the Left. The result was a stunning victory. Aneurin Bevan had more votes than anyone else, Barbara Castle came second with 200,000 votes, and Ian Mikardo and Tom Driberg gained their places in the popularity stakes, and, for the first time, Harold Wilson and Richard Crossman were elected to the NEC. Two of the old guard, Herbert Morrison and Hugh Dalton, lost their places on the NEC. The only politician outside the Bevanite organisation who retained his place was James Griffiths, no mean achievement. Lisa Martineau, the biographer of Barbara Castle, tries to denigrate his achievement by stating: 'The only non-Bevanite to survive was James Griffiths, a man in the unhappy position of being acceptable to all.'[16] In reality he was not in an 'unhappy position' at all from 1951 to 1955, as we shall see by analysing the support he received from his fellow Labour MPs for a place in the hierarchy of the Opposition.[17] The results of those elected to the Opposition Cabinet are shown below.

(The details of the election for 1951 have not been discussed, but those elected are marked by an asterisk*).

|  | 1951 | 1952 | 1953 | 1954 | 1955 |
|---|---|---|---|---|---|
| James Griffiths | * | 194 | 180 | 170 | 186 |
| Hugh Gaitskell | * | 179 | 176 | 170 | 184 |
| F. Soskice | * | 111 | 168 | 164 | |
| Hugh Dalton | * | 140 | 159 | 147 | |
| J. Ede | * | 189 | 134 | 125 | |
| Alf Robens | * | 148 | 133 | 140 | 148 |
| Dr Edith Sumerskill | * | 130 | 129 | 142 | 133 |
| Philip Noel-Baker | * | 121 | 118 | 125 | 100 |
| James Callaghan | * | 137 | 160 | 124 | 148 |
| G. Hale | * | 113 | 106 | 121 | |
| Aneurin Bevan | * | 108 | 126 | | |
| Harold Wilson | | | | 120 | 147 |
| E. S. Shinwell | * | 124 | 108 | 126 | |
| Arthur Greenwood | * | | | | 91 |
| R. Stokes | * | | | | 77 |
| George Brown | | | | | 101 |
| G. R. Michison | | | | | 76 |

The voting details show that Griffiths, the reconciler, was the first choice every year except 1954, when he shared the honour with Hugh Gaitskell.[18] One has to compare the support he received with the support given to his fellow MPs, in particular Hugh Dalton, Aneurin Bevan, James Callaghan and Emanuel Shinwell. Parliamentarians knew of the ability of Hugh Dalton, of the charisma and oratory of Aneurin Bevan, the confidence of James Callaghan and the debating skill of Shinwell, but none of them were near to achieving the popularity of James Griffiths in Parliament. The only politician who could compete with him in the Labour Party popularity stakes in the 1950s was a future leader of the party, Hugh Gaitskell. In 1952, Gaitskell was third on the list, but in 1954, as we have seen, he gained 170 votes, the same as Griffiths.[19]  On 14 December 1955, Hugh Gaitskell was elected leader. He won the day against Aneurin Bevan and Herbert Morrison. Gaitskell had 157 votes, Bevan was well behind with 70 and Morrison a poor third with 40.

The success of Gaitskell in 1955 was an opportunity to redefine socialism in the British context and, indeed, the whole ideology of the Labour Party.[20] Gaitskell, Crosland and a number of other leaders such as Griffiths belonged to the 'Socialist Revisionists'. This is the term that Bevan used for them in the volume *In Place of Fear* (1952), with regard to the future of socialism and the ideology of the Labour Party. He said:

*Perhaps a better term would be Socialist Revisionists. These are people who want to substitute novel remedies for the struggle for power in the State. They suggest that an extension of public ownership is an old fashioned and outmoded idea.*[21]

These were the new thinkers who were keen to adapt the ideology of Labour to a more prosperous, affluent generation.[22] These ideologues had a magazine called Socialist Commentary to discuss and present their opinions. The magazine came into existence through the efforts of refugees who had arrived in Britain from Germany in 1942. These socialists had come under the influence of a German philosopher, Leonard Nelson (1861-1927).23 The gist of their standpoint was the need for socialism to adapt a moral position, rather that a scientific base such as Marxism. The chief figure within the Socialist Commentary was Dr Rita Hinden, the editor, and James Griffiths came to admire her, as well as becoming a sympathetic supporter of the editorial board.[24] In 1952 they organised what came to be called the Socialist Union, and in 1953 in the House of Commons they founded the group, 'Friends of the Socialist Commentary'. Griffiths was one of the founder members. Hugh Gaitskell became the treasurer.[25]

The Socialist Commentary was ready to support the traditional viewpoint when it needed guidance. It devoted a great deal of consideration to the foreign affairs of the USA at a time when the Bevanites were anti-American.[26] Denis Healey was one of the experts within the Socialist Commentary on foreign affairs.[27] His articles in the Magazine from May 1951 until February 1954 bring together the standpoint of the Socialist Revisionists.[28] A number of articles on Industrial Assurance appeared in the Socialist Commentary with an introduction by James Griffiths in February 1950.[29] To Griffiths: 'The Labour Party must now become the guardian and the expression of the radical spirit'.[30] It was a scoop for the monthly journal to invite R. H. Tawney in 1952 to redefine socialism for a new age. He did so brilliantly in the Socialist Commentary by emphasising:
(a) that the initial emphasis behind the Labour movement, which was still relevant, was moral, rather than economic or scientific;
(b) that the State institutions, including the State itself, was to exist on behalf of the people and to serve it;
(c) that the Labour movement had always placed socialism within a democratic framework, with an emphasis on freedom of opinion in debate and in print, with freedom to worship and to meet in public; and finally
(d) an un-dogmatic approach to political problems.[31]

What was being achieved in Britain was a partnership between trade unionists, organisations such as the Fabians, and individuals of the calibre of H. G. Wells and Sidney and Beatrice Webb. Griffiths was the example of the Socialist Revisionist that R. H. Tawney had in mind in his article. From its beginning the Socialist Union emphasised that its purpose was 'to consider the obligations of socialism in [the] modern world' of the 1950s. The first pamphlet that they produced appeared under the title of *Socialist: A New Statement of Principles*, and this received a great deal of publicity as it was publicised as being anti-Marxist.[32]

The Labour movement was established on principles of freedom, equality and brotherhood, as well as on the political, economic and social networks which were needed to sustain democracy and to serve its citizens.[33] The pamphlet offered a philosophical basis which inspired individuals to work within the Labour movement. Support was given to the 'Revisionist Socialists' by James Griffiths when he wrote the introduction to the pamphlet, and this gave it credence for a large number of people within the Labour Party. Those involved in the Socialist Union were appreciative of his views as he, in his position as colonial spokesman for the Labour Party in parliament, brought others with him to launch the manifesto.

The pamphlet Socialism: A New Statement of Principles was presented in a press conference by Griffiths and his fellow Welshman, Morgan Phillips, General Secretary of the Labour Party.[34] Griffiths persuaded Clement Attlee to be the main speaker to present the pamphlet as well as its authors. Attlee said: 'I have read this with great enjoyment and admiration. It certainly expresses in far better language than I command the views which I hold and the faith I believe.'[35] The publication received a warm welcome by the English daily press, but it was ignored by the Welsh language and the Anglo-Welsh press. It was severely criticised by the weekly Tribune who called it 'Sunday School Socialism', a movement to which Griffiths was willing to pay tribute, for it had always been an important early experience at the chapel in Ammanford.[36] Griffiths knew that when it came to elections, and particularly local elections, the chapel vote was still important. In this period in south-west Wales, three-quarters of the 335 local councillors above parish council level were members of the Labour Party and approximately one-third of these were middle-class individuals deriving most of their support from their chapel connections. Of the total of councillors, 120 were trade union leaders, 130 were chapel leaders, and 80 held both type of office.

The Socialist Union published another pamphlet in May 1953 on foreign affairs, arguing that, in the contemporary world, life was too complex for old-fashioned socialism.[37] Three years later in 1956 another pamphlet was published under the title Twentieth Century Socialism, but it did not have the attention it deserved because it was overshadowed by an important volume published in the same year from the fertile mind of Tony Crosland entitled The Future of Socialism.[38] At the same time John Strachey had his Contemporary Socialism published. By this time Strachey, who knew Griffiths well, had been completely disillusioned by the Marxism that he had expressed in his volume The Nature of Capitalist Crisis published in 1935.[39]

During the period 1950 to 1956 the influence of Griffiths and those already mentioned within the Socialist Union, the Fabians and the Socialist Commentary, provided a turning point in the development of democratic socialism within the Labour Party. It is no wonder that R.H. Tawney paid a great compliment to Griffiths by emphasising that he had kept his reputation as 'the best evangelist in the Party'. The chief reason for this was that a great deal of the early ILP socialism of his younger years was still important to him, as well as the desire to adapt his beliefs to an age that was much more affluent than his early days in the anthracite coalfield. This is part of the Socialist Union manifesto:

*Every person, no matter what his origins or endorsements, wants to make the most of his life in his own way. His claim to do so… deserves the same respect as the next man's… It is an equality that rests simply and surely on their common humanity. Social privilege is the failure of society to accord this equality a respect to the claim of its members.*[40]

It is obvious that Griffiths played an important role in the process of revisionism in the history of the Labour Party. He and his wife were against elitism, welcoming egalitarianism and democracy in every aspect of life, and the result of this was their emphasis on the need for secondary education, in particular comprehensive schools. One has to give full credit to the efforts of Tony Crosland, James Griffiths and the Socialist Union on education.

In Wales in this period some of the nationalists and republicans called Griffiths a hypocrite because he supported independence for the British colonies, but opposed the campaign for a parliament for his own nation. At Llandrindod Wells on 1 July 1950 the campaign had began, at a conference held under the auspices of Undeb Cymru Fydd. Liberals and members of the Welsh Nationalist Party were in the forefront of this campaign. The exception was the rebel Labour MP, S. O. Davies, who represented Merthyr in Parliament.[41] He was the most well-known Labourite on the platform in Llandrindod, sharing the struggle with Gwynfor Evans, Megan Lloyd George, Ifan ab Owen Edwards, T. I. Ellis and a Liverpool Welsh Presbyterian, J. R. Jones. Cliff Prothero, Secretary of the Welsh Council of Labour, criticised the purpose of the conference.[42] The campaign started slowly. They had to wait until the National Eisteddfod of Wales meeting at Llanrwst in August 1951 to launch the petition. The hymn writer and eisteddfodwr Reverend  H. Elvet Lewis, usually known by the word Elfed  and in in his ninetieth year, was the first person  to sign the petition at Llanrwst. Indeed, there were some socialists within Plaid Cymru who had very little enthusiasm for this parliamentary petition: that was the attitude of D. J. Davies from Gilwern, who had worked with James Griffiths for the ILP in his younger days at Ammanford.[43] Both were  then miners and D. J. Davies was himself a pioneer of the Labour movement in the Amman valley .[44]

In many ways 1952 was a disastrous year for the campaign for a Welsh parliament.[45] On the other hand, Winston Churchill showed his political cleverness by appointing a minister for Welsh Affairs. His choice was inspirational: David Maxwell-Fyfe, a Liverpool-based politician. Within a short time, the new minister had decided that the Forestry Commission could not have more land in Carmarthenshire to plant trees, and by February 1952 the War Office had to abandon its plans to use eleven thousand acres of land in the heartland of Welsh life and culture, the  Lleyn peninsula, for army training. The new minister had enough political flair to demonstrate his empathy with the aspirations of Welsh people who were concerned for their way of life. Indeed, he did enough to persuade Sir Ifan ab Owen Edwards to write a letter to Gwynfor Evans to suggest that 'there was no need now for a movement to unite us on a nebulous matter which we call "Parliament for Wales".'[46] There were leaders within the Labour Party who shared his viewpoint.

Griffiths did not express his opinion on the campaign for a while, but he spoke clearly against it among his greatest supporters at the Welsh Miners' conferences. Throughout 1952 the campaign was virtually at a standstill, and the historian must wonder whether, had Griffiths been spearheading it, the outcome would have been different. Of course, there is no clear answer to this hypothetical question. But it is credible to suggest that the campaign would have only gathered momentum with the support of the majority of the Labour Party in Wales, but this would not have been possible without Griffiths supporting the campaign. A number of Welsh-speaking Labour MPs, Cledwyn Hughes, T. W. Jones, Goronwy Roberts, S. O. Davies and Tudor Watkins, did try and give leadership but two of them were elected to Parliament only in 1945 and the other two in 1951. But most of those heavily involved had very little knowledge, except for S. O. Davies and Tudor Watkins, of the industrial, cultural and social life of south Wales.

At least four of them were more in tune with Bevanism than Fabianism or the Socialist Union. They could be easily hurt. They were thin-skinned, particularly when they heard Gwynfor Evans, a fellow campaigner, scathing in his criticism of them, especially those who supported a Welsh parliament within the Labour Party. In October 1952, Cledwyn Hughes could not accept anymore the barbed criticisms and he expressed his disappointment in public, seeing 'so many members of the Welsh Nationalist Party criticising his party with such bitterness.'[47]

One can say that the campaigners for a parliament for Wales believed that they and they alone had the right to speak in the name of a Welsh Parliament. But the historical evidence indicates that such an attitude was completely unacceptable to Griffiths. This was enough of a reason for him not to identify with the campaign. There was a great deal of criticism of the strategy of Gwynfor Evans, who concentrated the resources of Plaid Cymru to fight parliamentary seats in 1950.[48] Then in 1951, with another General election imminent, it was decided to keep to the strategy of their president but to concentrate on a few constituencies, namely Aberdare, Rhondda West, Llanelli and Wrexham.[49]

What were the reasons for choosing Labour seats with huge majorities as the focus of their efforts? Why did they choose to put up a candidate in Llanelli rather than in Cardiganshire? Was not this the time for Plaid Cymru to show its readiness to co-operate with friends of Wales in every political party for the sake of the nation? But by deciding to concentrate Plaid Cymru's resources to fight for James Griffiths's seat in Llanelli, they indicated a glaring central strategic weakness.[50]

By November 1953 Herbert Morrison, an anti-devolutionist, decided that he could not, in view of the letters sent by Cliff Prothero and Morgan Phillips on the question of a Welsh parliament, be unconcerned with the campaign. Guidance was needed from the Labour Party hierarchy in Transport House. On 11 November the answer came. The British Labour Party announced, in line with the attitude of the Welsh Council of Labour, that they would not be supporting the campaign for a parliament for Wales. As a result five Labour MPs, S. O. Davies, T. W. Jones, Goronwy Roberts, Cledwyn Hughes and Tudor Watkins, were in trouble. Each were members of nonconformist denominations, namely the Presbyterian

Church of Wales, the Welsh Independents, the Welsh Baptists and the Scots Baptists, known in Welsh as Bedyddwyr Albanaidd. Indeed, T. W. Jones was a minister within Bedyddwyr Albanaidd. The only one of the five who would be tempted to rebel against the Labour Party's position was S. O. Davies, though the leaders of Plaid Cymru believed that a Welsh Labour Party could come into existence as a result of the Morrison dictat. It was extremely naïve to suggest this, however, and indeed, instead of giving support to the 'Gang of Five', they were unashamedly criticised by Plaid Cymru's members.

By March 1954, four months after the announcement of the British Labour Party, the Labour Party in Wales was opposing the petition, and this was confirmed by the Welsh Council of Labour and by their Annual Conference. Griffiths expressed his own viewpoint clearly in a letter to his friend, Iorwerth Cyfeiliog Peate, who was the director of the Welsh Folk Museum in St Fagans, near Cardiff.[51] In the letter, Griffiths raised a matter which had made him so uncomfortable for decades: the Plaid Cymru propaganda which had portrayed the Welsh Labour Party as an English party rather than the party of ordinary Welsh people. He said in Welsh of those Labour MPs who 'were not Welsh speaking': 'The English members from Wales believe that the narrow spirit comes in often in the speeches that are made by those who support the Parliament – by stating specifically at English Labour Party and English Government'.[52] He called the attention of Dr Peate, who was against bilingualism, to the reality that could not be ignored: 'We cannot avoid the fact that we are now a bilingual nation and that we cannot carry any policy for Wales without the co-operation of large number of people from the valleys who are Welsh in spirit but who have either lost their language or never had a command of it. Those are the facts – we cannot ignore or flee from them.'[53] Furthermore, he told Dr Peate that the policy which had been published on behalf of the Labour Party 'represents the agreement that is possible today', a wording which suggests that the door for further developments was ajar.[54]

In his regular column in the *Liverpool Daily Post*, Cledwyn Hughes expressed his disappointment that the wrangling of a political party was a constant stumbling block to the collaboration that should have taken place. He explained that the criticism of leaders such as James Griffiths had undermined the campaign for a parliament in Wales. Hughes referred to the sadness of the situation and to the opposition of Labour Party zealots: 'deep resentment throughout the rank and file of the Labour movement in Wales at the persistent and abusive attacks made by certain elements in the Principality on some of the most highly respected Welsh Labour leaders.'[55]

The miners, the loyal friends of James Griffiths, could not stand the constant sniping from the leaders of Plaid Cymru, and it is no surprise that the miners of south Wales voted against the campaign for a Welsh parliament in May 1954.[56] Earlier in the year, Griffiths protested against the behaviour of Huw T. Edwards, who appeared in the Welsh parliament campaign meetings in two towns in the constituency, namely Ammanford and Llanelli.[57] When Cliff Prothero heard of this, he was furious, and Griffiths felt that Edwards, whom he had helped in his career, had belittled him. Edwards defended himself in a letter to his MP, Eirene White, introducing himself as a socialist who was in favour of '… a Federal Parliament, but never, I hope forgets his socialism… I cannot see how sharing a platform with other supporters

189

weakens Labour's cause.'[58] Griffiths felt that the trade unionist Edwards, of all people, had forgotten the favours and the loyalty that was expected of him by his comrade.

In 1955, the campaign came to its climax when S. O. Davies had the opportunity of presenting a Private Members' Bill to the House of Commons. Griffiths did not support Davies. He saw the Bill as a means of destroying the economic unity of Britain, while to George Thomas, the measure verged on madness, and Thomas called on MPs in England to reject the bill on every count, so as 'to save the Welsh from themselves.' The campaign came to an end for the time being, but Griffiths knew that he had a responsibility to raise the need quite soon for a measure of devolution for Wales.

The period 1950-1954 was difficult for the Griffiths family. In 1950 he lost his brother, John Griffiths, at the age of sixty-four. He still lived at the old home in Bryn Villa, Betws. The funeral took place in the Calvinistic Methodist chapel in Betws and the family came together in their sorrow. At the end of 1953, on 27 December, his brother David Rees Griffiths (Amanwy) died at the Middlesex Hospital, leaving his close-knit family in sorrow: Mary Griffiths, his wife and the two daughters, Mena Griffiths and Mallt Davies, three sisters and, of course, James Griffiths himself. He always called his brother by the Welsh version of David, namely Dafydd. He regarded him as a character of the anthracite coalfield, steeped in literature and nonconformity. In a letter to the trade unionist Huw T. Edwards he confessed: *'Mae bwlch ar ei ol yn fy mywyd i a'r teulu'* ('There is a chasm after him in my life and the family'[59]

The funeral service was held on 31 December in Christian Temple, Ammanford, where Amanwy had been a deacon.[60] The service was conducted by his minister, the Reverend Dr D. Tegfan Davies, and eighteen non-conformists ministers attended, as well as one vicar. The service was for men only. This was the practice in many of the mining areas, with the women attending only the service at the home. They did not attend the chapel or church service, or the service in the cemetery or in the crematorium. Among the ministers present at the funeral of Amanwy were a number of poets, such as William Evans (Wil Ifan), as well as those who had come under his influence in the colliery or in his days as a school caretaker at the Amman Grammar School, such as the Reverends Gomer M. Roberts and D. Eirwyn Morgan. The mining community was represented by Sid Jones and Tom Morgan, secretary and chairman of the Pantyffynnon colliery Lodge where Amanwy had been employed for many years. In addition to his thirty-three years as a miner at Pantyffynnon, he had worked as a miner for a short period in Betws. Representing the Labour Party was the MP for Abertilery, the Reverend Llywelyn Williams, and Alderman Douglas Hughes. Aneirin Talfan Davies from the BBC in Cardiff was also present. He was the radio producer who had suggested that Amanwy should portray David, in Paul Dickinson's film, as the contribution of Wales to the Festival of Britain in 1951, a celebratory occasion after the hard years of the Second World War.

The BBC was again represented by Mansel Thomas, the world of Welsh drama by Dan Matthews from Pontarddulais, and journalism by Emlyn Aman. Among the large congregation of men, Plaid Cymru was represented by Gwynfor Evans, a politician about whom Amanwy had written a prasiseworthy article a few months earlier. He wrote it in Welsh: 'The boys of the Labour Party [in County Hall, Carmarthen] will not swallow his political medicine without the clashing of teeth sometimes, but they have not ceased to respect him. He is a gentleman of the first order, and well worthy of the Chair of the Union of Welsh Independents.'[61]

It was a great privilege for James Griffiths to be invited to address one of the meetings of the Union of Welsh Independents, during the chairmanship of Gwynfor Evans, held at Penygroes (in the Llanelli constituency), on 31 May – 3 June 1954. The title of his address was Gobaith y Byd (The Hope of the World).[62] He dealt with the huge changes that had taken place through science and technology and how these found their influence in every continent.

The sections on Africa and Asia reflected his understanding of the problems that had beset these two continents. He did not dismiss optimism – indeed, his speech contains a great deal of it, in particular towards the end of his address. The address was published in the Annual Report of the denominations affairs, but it is arguable that Griffiths did not do justice either to the title or to himself. He could have argued for the hope of establishing a welfare state in every country in the world, or he could have considered the contribution of Jesus Christ as the Hope of the World from the standpoint of a Christian socialist. It seems that he did not give to his listeners in Penygroes or to us, his readers, the address he had actually in mind when he titled his address *Hope of the World*.

In the by-election at Aberdare in the summer of 1954 Griffiths understood that the votes of the majority of the electorate which used to be given to the two main political parties were now beginning to be shared with other political parties. Labour choose a local politician, Arthur Probert, as the candidate, and he succeeded comfortably in keeping the seat which had been held by Emlyn Thomas, a Welsh-speaking ex-miner and secretary of a Welsh Independent chapel in Trecynon, near Aberdare. Probert had made himself clear long before the by-election that he had no intention of getting involved in the devolution issue. He wrote in 1953: 'A Parliament for Wales does not deeply move the masses of the people. Not many are convinced it is the best way of getting' "fair treatment" or "fair shares" for the people of Wales. It is hardly practical politics.' Probert naturally was not pleased that Gwynfor Evans as a Welsh nationalist succeeded in increasing the vote of Plaid Cymru against the socalled 'British parties' in this by-election.[63]

On 5 April 1955 Winston Churchill decided to retire and transfer his responsibilities as Prime Minister to the Foreign Secretary, Anthony Eden, who took over the following day. Eden had waited a long time for this political crown. The Budget was announced on 19 April and six pence was taken off income tax. The electorate felt much better because of that move, and in Anthony Eden the Conservatives had a man of experience in the Foreign Office. He also looked handsome on television. After all, the general election of 1955 was the first time television played a key role in the democratic process.[64] Eden outshone Attlee on the television screens. Griffiths presented a party political broadcast, mainly on the colonies, in which he emphasised that two-thirds of the world's population was living in poverty. The message was not popular or appealing to the vast majority of the electorate who felt that the burdens of the war and the restrictions that had been imposed afterwards were slowly disappearing, and a more affluent world was on the horizon, in which they deserved to share. The appeal to the purse rather than to their conscience was foremost on the lips of the Conservative politicians in 1955.

It was obvious that public meetings were becoming less essential than in earlier general elections. But Griffiths as a leading Labour orator was in great demand and he travelled extensively to address meetings in Gravesend and Lewisham, then to Wandsworth, then on to Stroud and Gloucester, before addressing public meetings all over Wales, from Flintshire to Anglesey in north Wales, to Cardiganshire, Pembrokeshire, Swansea and Cardiff before moving back to his own base in the Llanelli constituency.

On balance, he felt that there was a great deal of apathy among the voters, but he also admitted that the policies offered by Labour were not very exciting. In its manifesto the Labour Party called for the re-nationalisation of road transport and steel and offered a compulsory national service.

After all, a large number of Welsh soldiers had fought in the Korean War: 488 soldiers belonging to First Battalion of the Welsh Regiment had been sent to Korea in 1951, and they were there until November 1952. The decision of Megan Lloyd George in 1955 to leave the Liberal Party and join the Labour Party was an exceptional coup for Labour. Goronwy Roberts and in particular James Griffiths were instrumental in her conversion. Cledwyn Hughes expressed his pleasure that Megan Lloyd George was at last joining the Labour Party. He added: 'but it is high time for her to take a definite step. She would have had a good chance of winning Wrexham, if only she had come across at the Rhyl National Eisteddfod in August 1955,' as she had, in the opinion of the MP for Anglesey, 'originally intended.'[65]
At the constituency in Llanelli a problem arose on 16 May 1955, when the Plaid Cymru candidate, the Reverend D. Eirwyn Morgan, submitted his nomination papers with three Welsh words on them. Naturally, as a minister of religion at Bancffosfelen, this Welsh Baptist minister described himself as 'Gweinidog yr Efengyl'/Minister of the Gospel'. But this was not acceptable to the Returning Officer.[66]  Eirwyn Morgan had to resubmit his nomination papers in English before he was accepted as a parliamentary candidate in the general election. This proved, if it needed to be proved, that the status of the Welsh language within its own geographical territory needed drastically to be changed. Eirwyn Morgan protest, supported by Griffiths, was an important step in changing the climate of opinion.
At the election the Conservatives won easily. They had the support of 49.7% of the electorate, while Labour had 46.4%.[67] Yet in Wales, Labour was still the party of the people.[68]    In Llanelli the result was as follows:

| | |
|---|---|
| James Griffiths (Labour) | 34,021 |
| T.H. Skeet (Conservative) | 10,640 |
| Reverend D. Eirwyn Morgan (Plaid Cymru) | 6,398 |
| Majority | 23,381 |

Griffiths could face another period on the front bench of the opposition in Westminster with the confidence that 66.7% of the Llanelli electorate had voted for him as their MP.68

## Notes and References

1. Ralph Miliband, *Parliamentary Socialism* (London, 1960), p. 296, argues that this event was the beginning of a group of parliamentarians who accepted discipline. Before then they were a 'fairly loose group of MPs without any hard centre' under the banner of Keep Left.

2. 'But only two Ministers shared Bevan's views that charges breached the principles of a free service – Jim Griffiths and Harold Wilson; and of these, Griffiths, reluctantly accepted them'. See John Campbell, *Nye Bevan and the Mirage of British Socialism* (London, 1987), p. 233; Philip Williams, *Hugh Gaitskell: A Political Biography* (London, 1979), p. 250.

3. John Campbell, ibid., pp. 241-2. Bevan did not receive a great deal of sympathy for his stance, and so James Griffiths did the right move to most of the Labour MPs. Even Bevan's partner, Jennie Lee, felt that he had for once spoken without much spark on the question of charging for some items to do with the National Health Service. See Jennie Lee, *My Life with Nye* (London, 1981), p. 223.

4. Aneurin Bevan had his followers among the Welsh Labour MPs, such as George Thomas. He had the shock of his life when he asked Jennie Lee to dissuade Bevan from resigning. Her answer: 'You yellow-livered cur, you're just like the rest. You're another MacDonald or Snowden. Go away from me!' Thomas could not believe he heard such ferocity. See George Thomas, *Mr Speaker: The Memoirs of Viscount Tonypandy* (London, 1985), pp. 69-70.

5. Norman Angell, *After All: The Autobiography of Norman Angell* (New York, 1952), p. 168. For a study of Angell, see, Martin Ceadel, *Living the Great Illusion: Sir Norman Angell, 1872-1967* (Oxford, 2009).

6. See a study on him by a left wing historian, V. L. Allen, *Trade Union Leadership: based on a study of Arthur Deakin* (London, 1957), 339 pp. Deakin regarded Connah's Quay on Deeside as his home after he had moved to the TGWU headquarters in London, and he returned regularly to North East Wales. See Gwyn Jenkins, *Cofiant Huw T. Edwards*, p. 78.

7. Gwyn Jenkins, ibid., pps.77-8.

8. *The Times*, 8 October 1952, p.4.

9. T[homas] Williamson, 'Disloyalty within the Labour Party' in *NUCMW Journal*, volume 15, No. 11, (November, 1952), p. 336.

10. James Griffiths, *Pages from Memory*, p. 122.

11. Ibid., chapter 9, 'The Role of the Reconciler', pp. 122-139. Not every Labour politician praised him for taking 'the role of the reconciler'. The left wing politician, Ian Mikardo, had no time for him. He said that Griffiths placed 'both his hands on both his hearts'. See Ian Mikardo, *Backbencher* (London, 1988), p. 127.

12. James Griffiths, ibid., p.122. 'It is a role which suits my temperament, and which my experience in trade union work had moulded into a pattern of behaviour. If a man is to serve his cause he must be true to himself. When I joined the ILP I did not regard it as just another party thirsting for power, but as a cause akin to a religion'.

13. Ibid., p. 72.

14. Stephen Haseler, *The Gaitskellites* (London, 1969), pp. 62-3.

15. Lisa Martineau, *Politics and Power: Barbara Castle: A biography* (London, 2000), p. 117. Ralph Miliband calls Griffiths a member of the 'Old Guard'. See Ralph Miliband, *Parliamentary Socialism: A Study in the Politics of Labour* (London, 1979, second edition), p. 326.

16. Lisa Martineau, ibid., p. 118.

17. Ibid. Philip Williams, *Hugh Gaitskell*, expresses it much better than Martineau when he describes Griffiths as 'the one leader without enemies', p. 306.

18. Stephen Haseler, ibid., p.37 based on *The Times*, 14 November 1951, 20 November 1952; 6 November 1953, 19 November 1954 and the NEC Reports, 1951-5.

19. James Griffiths, ibid., p. 133. 'I was asked to stand for election by those who thought that it would be advantageous to choose a deputy who could bring a wider experience to the service of the new leader and who would co-operate loyally with him'. In other words, a reconciler.

20. Stephen Haseler, *The Gaitskellites*, p.41 'The New Leader' [Hugh Gaitskell] gave revisionism and the revisionists the important and decisive role which they had hitherto lacked'. Griffiths was a great admirer of Gaitskell and believed that the tactics of Nye Bevan of not standing if Gaitskell did the same had upset a number of his supporters. Griffiths makes the observation: 'It was altogether too Machiavellian and created cynicism, and finally decided many to turn and vote for Hugh Gaitskell, who won easily with 157 votes to Nye's 70 and Herbert's 40'. He felt disappointed that Morrison was at the bottom of the poll. See James Griffiths, ibid., p. 145.

21. Aneurin Bevan, 'The Futility of Coalition', *Tribune* (13-26 June 1952), p. 1.

22. Haseler, *The Gaitskellites*, p.68.

23. Mary Saran, 'Leonard Nelson (1881-1927)', *Socialist Commentary* (October 1947), p. 14.

24. James Griffiths, *Pages from Memory*, p. 91, where he mentions how Dr Hinden had supported Labour MPs to take an interest in issues to do with the colonies.

25. Haseler, ibid., p. 69.

26. One of the Welsh Labour MPs who was anti-American was S. O. Davies. He said in the House of Commons in 1950,
    'the hysteria which exists among American leaders, the deliberate, grotesque, persecution of outstanding Americans, their fantastic doings in the guise of uprooting un-American activities and the terribly dangerous megalomania of such people in whose possession are the most horribly destructive weapons which have ever cursed the world of ours', *Hansard*, 5 July 1950.

27. Bruce Reed and Geoffrey Williams, *Denis Healey and the Politics of Power* (London, 1971), p. 99. 'Bevin as Foreign Minister had built his policy on alliance with the United States and opposition to Soviet expansion. Healey, together with other intellectuals like Strachey, Younger, Mayhew and Prentice, provided the intellectual backing for such policies.'

28. Ibid., 'Healey's essays, and articles in the magazine, Socialist Commentary established him as the major intellectual force behind collective security'. For example in 1951, he prepared three articles for *Socialist Commentary*. See Haseler, *The Gaitskellites*, p.73.

29. Preface by James Griffiths, W. Ewart, P. W. Anton, A. A. Best, J. Thompson, 'Industrial Assurance', *Socialist Commentary* (February, 1950), pps.43-46.

30. James Griffiths, 'The Road Back', *Socialist Commentary* (December 1951), pps.272-3. To him the radical tradition was a valuable heritage 'The Labour Party' he said, 'must now become the guardian and the expression of the radical spirit'.

31. R. H. Tawney, 'British Socialism Today' in *Socialist Commentary* (June 1952), pp. 124-5. Tawney emphasised the standpoint of Griffiths within the history of the Labour Party; 'It developed as the product of a fusion between the experience of an already vigorous trade unionism and the work of organisations and individuals like the Fabians and the
    Webbs'. The quotation is found on p. 124.

32. *Socialism: A New Statement of Principles* (London, 1952), pp. 1-64.

33. Haseler, ibid., p. 89. Tony Crosland emphasised the need for equality as a basic concept within socialism. See Anthony Crosland, *The Future of Socialism*, p. 125.

34. Haseler, ibid., p. 75.

35. Ibid.

36. *Tribune* (11 July 1952), p. 3.

37. *Socialism and Foreign Policy* (London, 1953), pp. 1-78. 'Socialist principles cannot provide in advance the cut and dried solutions to detailed problems which some people may be looking for. But, as we have shown, they can provide what is of inestimable value – a set of values', p. 77.

38. Haseler, *The Gaitskellites*, p.79-80; *A. Crosland, The Future of Socialism* (London, 1956), 540 pp.

39. For a portrait in words of John Strachey, see J. K. Galbraith 'John Strachey', *Encounter*, September 1963, 21(3), pp. 534.

40. Haseler *The Gaitskellites*, p. 80

41. Robert Griffiths, *S. O. Davies: A Socialist Faith* (Llandysul, 1983), p. 170.

42. Ibid., pp.169-70. 'In a press statement issued on March 29 [1950] the [Welsh Regional] Council [of Labour] Secretary, Cliff Prothero dismissed what he called "the frivolous demand for home rule" claiming that it emanated from "a small number of people who represented no serious body of opinion in Wales".

43. D. J. Davies was one of the early pioneers of the Labour Party in Ammanford and Llandybïe. For D. J. Davies, see Ceinwen Thomas, 'D. J. Davies' in Derec Llwyd Morgan (ed.) *Adnabod Deg* (Denbigh, 1977), pp. 140-153.

44. Rhys Evans, *Gwynfor: Rhag Pob Brad*, pp. 145-6.

45. NLW, Gwynfor Evans Papers E/1983.

46. *Y Cymro*, 10 October 1952.

47. Alan Butt Philip, The Welsh Question – Nationalism in Welsh Politics 1945-1970, pp. 257-61.

48. Ibid.

49. The editor of the Welsh language periodical *Y Ddraig Goch* argued that the Welsh Nationalist Party was already within the House of Commons in the speeches of S. O. Davies on Parliament for Wales. See Robert Griffiths, ibid., p. 175.

50. Gwyn Jenkins regards James Griffiths as the most conscientious MP for devolution, who was been criticised by the radical nationalists for his pseudo-holiness and his uncertain stance on Wales. See Gwyn Jenkins, *Prif Weinidog Answyddogol Cymru*, p. 138.

51. NLW, The Papers of Iorwerth C. Peate A 1/5. The letter of James Griffiths to Iorwerth C. Peate dated 23 March 1954.

52. Ibid.

53. Ibid.

54. Ibid,

55. Liverpool Daily Post, 31 May 1954. The same criticism came from Dr Huw T. Edwards 'I charge the Welsh Nationalist Party with being the one barrier to Welsh unity'. See Huw T. Edwards, *They went to Llandrindod* (Cardiff, 1954), p.43.

56. Robert Griffiths, ibid., p.179. The Miners Conference was held in Porthcawl on 10 May 1954 'Welsh mining MPs, with the exception of S. O. hardened in their opposition to the campaign and successfully negotiated speaking-rights for Jim Griffiths and Dai Grenfell (MP for Gower) at the Conference. Unfortunately the anti-devolution camp's scaremongering could only have profited from the contradicting replies of Home Rule supporters'.

57. Gwyn Jenkins, ibid., p.138.

58. Ibid., p.139.

59. NLW Papers of Huw T. Edwards A1/177 A letter of James Griffiths to H.T. Edwards 19 January 1954. For the literary output of Amanwy see Huw Walters, 'Cerddetan: Golwg ar Rhyddiaith Amanwy' in *Cynnwrf Canrif*, pp. 318-71; idem., 'David Rees Griffiths ('Amanwy') 1882-1953', *The Carmarthenshire Antiquarian*, 35 (1999), pps.89-102.

60. NLW, Amanwy Papers. In these papers we have a large number of articles which is essential for our understanding of both brothers, James and David Griffiths.

61. NLW, Amanwy papers. An article in Welsh on the Amman Valley.

62. This is not the first time James Griffiths addressed the Annual Conference of the Welsh Independent denomination, *Yr Annibynwyr Cymraeg*, as they are known. He did so in 1936 when the conference was held in London. He spoke with passion and the by-product was a delegation from the nonconformist chapels of East Glamorganshire to see the Prime Minister on 22 July 1937. See, R. Tudur Jones, *Hanes Annibynwyr Cymru* (Swansea, 1966) p. 285. For the contribution of James Griffiths in 1954 see *Adroddiad Undeb yr Annibynwyr Cymraeg Penygroes a'r Cylch*, May 31, June 1-3, 1954, pp. 45-60 for James Griffiths's address on *Hope of the World* in Welsh.

63. By-election at Aberdare, 28 October 1954, Arthur Probert Lab 24,658 69.5%; Gwynfor Evans Plaid Cymru 5,671 16.0%; Michael Roberts Conservative 5,158 14.5%; Majority 18,897 53.5%. See Beti Jones, Etholiadau Seneddol yng Nghymru 1900-75, p.118; NLW Labour Party in Wales Papers, No 106 in the file on Devolution. Letter of Arthur Probert, 22 September 1953.

64. Griffiths felt that they were caught napping for the 1955 general election. James Griffiths, *Pages from Memory*, p. 141.

65. NLW Cledwyn Hughes Papers, A1-A18.

66. Beti Jones, Ibid., p.122. James Griffiths has no references in his autobiography to this incident. Indeed he does not mention the name of the Revd D. Eirwyn Morgan (a favourite of Amanwy since his school days in Ammanford) though he fought on four different occasions for Plaid Cymru in the Llanelli constituency against Jim. For D. Eirwyn Morgan, see Ivor Thomas Rees, *Welsh Hustings 1885-2004* (Llandybïe, 2005), pps.206-7.

67. NLW, 23091E, Letters of Graham F. Thomas. Letter of James Griffith to Graham F. Thomas dated 5 June 1955 where he reviews the election campaign, complaining of the bickering between the right wingers and the left wingers, the industrial problems and the fact that so many natural Labour supporters stayed home rather than voting. But he is content that Wales had been loyal with 27 constituencies supporting Labour out of 36 constituencies.

68. The trade unionist Huw T. Edwards felt that Wales as a country was so fortunate in the calibre of its MPs in this period, middle of the 1950s. See Huw T. Edwards, *They Went to Llandrindod*, p.43.

# 15

## Deputy Leader of the Labour Party

Immediately after the 1955 general election Griffiths considered in great seriousness the verdict of the electors. He realised that the Welsh nationalist condidate in Llanelli had saved his deposit and this meant as far as Griffiths was concerned a moral victory to them. In his archives he referred to the success of Plaid Cymru, in particular in identifying themselves with the younger generation. These young people had exercised their first ballot by opting for a Party which had a great deal of appeal for many of them who were products of the Welsh League of Youth and steeped in Welsh culture. It was these cultured nationalists who had voted for the Welsh Nationalist party rather than for him who embodied those 'values' as he saw it. His greatest disappointment however was to hear that the able politician Tony Crosland, after five years in Parliament, had lost his seat in South Gloucestershire. He was one of the most important ideologues of the Fabians and his magisterial volume The Future of Socialism had already exercised a great deal of influence. Griffiths hoped he would be returned to parliament soon in a by-election. In the meantime, Hugh Dalton sent a letter to Clement Attlee, dated 1 June 1955, which created quite a stir in the Westminster village. The thrust of the letter was to suggest that his generation should give way to the younger generation. This is one paragraph which created quite a headache for Griffiths:

> It is essential, in my view, that, from the start of the new Parliament there should be a much younger Shadow Cabinet. In the last Parliament this body, as I once said to you, was becoming more and more a shadow of the past and less and less a Cabinet of the Future.[1]

Then Dalton expanded:

> Of its fifteen members when Parliament was dissolved, no less than nine, of whom I am one, are over 65 this year and, of these nine, four are over 70. Five years hence, when the legal term of his Parliament ends, all nine of us will be over 70, and some nearing 80![2]

Griffiths was sixty-five years of age in 1955. Dalton wrote a second letter to Attlee with a number of suggestions with regard to the composition of the Opposition Bench in Parliament. With Griffiths, Dalton had a completely different approach, as he explained in his letter to Attlee. Jim Griffiths, in my view, should continue on the Parliamentary Committee. He has very special gifts and is the youngest of us nine veterans. But it is time to think of Ede, Shinwell, Willy Hall and Noel-Baker, as well as myself, to go. After all, it's quite a good life being a Privy Councillor in Parliament, even if you aren't on the Parliamentary Committee.[3]

Dalton was interfering in his usual manner, emphasising also that Attlee should carry on even though he had lost two general elections in 1951 and 1955, a disaster for any political leader. Dalton leaked his correspondence to the press, in particular the Daily Mirror, The Times, Manchester Guardian, Daily Express as well as the Daily Herald.[4] They gave publicity to his initial argument for young leaders within the Labour Party high command. Some of the old guard like Shinwell, Chuter Ede and Willy Whiteley attacked Dalton for allowing the press to be involved.[5]  In the first meeting of the shadow cabinet, Shinwell initiated a debate on the Dalton letters. Dr Edith Summerskill argued that the most important asset was experience, and believed that this was to be found in the political lives of Dalton, Ede and Shinwell.[6] Hugh Gaitskell spoke at the meeting referring to the noble contribution of Dalton to the Labour movement. Then Griffiths spoke in his own inimitable manner. He referred to the contribution of Hugh Dalton to the Labour Party and Dalton's support of younger politicians, such as Roy Jenkins and Tony Crosland.[7] Griffiths also mentioned how much Dalton had been involved on behalf of the government with the depressed areas in the post-war period of 1945-50. On 23 June voting took place for twelve candidates to the shadow cabinet. Fifty-four MPs stood as candidates and Griffiths once more came top of the poll. The backbench MPs in particular ignored Dalton's argument. In view of Griffiths's popularity among his fellow Labour MPs the press began to name him as a possible successor to Attlee. The Daily Express began the rumour, the Sunday Times repeated it, as did the articles of the Welshman Percy Cudlipp in the *News Chronicle*. To Cudlipp who later became the editor of the Daily Herald, Griffiths was the most acceptable politician within the parliamentary Labour Party, and he had exercised an important role as a reconciler between left- and right-wingers. An exception to the rule among journalists was Henry Fairlie, the Tory-minded columnist of the *Spectator*, who had very little regard for Griffiths as a man or as a politician.

Then on Wednesday morning 7 December 1955 Clement Attlee resigned after twenty years as the Labour Party leader. The Deputy Leader was Herbert Morrison, an ambitious politician, but who failed dismally, as did Aneurin Bevan, to wrestle the leadership from Attlee. Though Attlee wanted to give the job to a younger man it was incredible that a politician of so little charisma had kept it safe in his hands for two decades. It was Hugh Gaitskell who eventually won the contest; Griffiths decided not to stand for the party leadership.[8]

Herbert Morrison was hampered by the fact that he was declining physically, much more than any of his peers, including Attlee. Griffiths was in robust health. The south Wales politician, Ness Edwards, was in the forefront of the campaign to persuade his friend from college days to stand for the post of deputy leader. Edwards asked Jim to welcome a deputation to see him on the issue, under the eagle eye of Anthony Greenwood. Griffiths met them in Bournemouth on 8 June during the annual Labour Party conference. Six politicians came to see him that day: Tony Greenwood, Michael Stewart, Arthur Blenkinsop, Lena Jeger, George Wigg and Richard Plume. Another four staunch supporters were unable to join them on this occasion, namely Kenneth Younger, John Strachey, George Strauss and Fred Lee. The same day Dalton came over to see his old friend Jim to insist that he should stand for the important post. Attlee was of the same opinion. He felt that Griffiths should not say no without considering carefully the honour and the responsibility involved in the post of Deputy Leader. Before the end of the day, another four Labour MPs brought the same message as those who had come earlier in the day. These included two colleagues from the Welsh coalfield as well as two brothers, namely Ness Edwards, Harold Finch and   the Llanidloes born Bernard and Arthur Moyle.

Griffiths gave the same reply to each one of his supporters, that he would sleep on their kind words, and consider the options in the next few days. There was one politician for whom he had a great regard and whom he would prefer not to stand against him. This was none other than Aneurin Bevan, whom he had known since 1919.[9] He often felt great empathy with him, as both were ex-miners. He also felt that Bevan had done so much harm to his own political ambitions. Ever since his resignation from the government in 1951, Bevan had been a constant source of trouble to the leadership of the Labour Party as well as to some trade union leaders.

Sometimes, according to Griffiths, Bevan gave the idea that he would like to work for the good of the Labour Party, but then he saw himself as another David Lloyd George or a Winston Churchill who would come to the rescue in a crisis when Britain needed an inspiring leader. But on other occasions he was a natural rebel. Griffiths saw this on 13 April 1954 in the House of Commons when Bevan got up from the front bench as Attlee, who had addressed the House, sat down. Bevan   spoke passionately on the frontbench giving his own view on Foster Dulles' proposed creation of a South East Asia Nato.  His whole demeanour was so different to Attlee. It was as if he wanted to brush the leader aside as one of yesterday's politicians. Bevan's behaviour in that debate and his general stubbornness was enough of a reason for a number of key politicians on the National Executive to consider reprimanding him. Griffiths always battled hard against those who argued for Bevan's expulsion from the party. Griffiths was, after all, a reconciler and he argued sincerely for the important role Nye Bevan played in the life of the Labour Party. It was such a masterful performance that he won the support of Harold Wilson and Hugh Dalton as well as Clement Attlee. On the other side, ready to expel him were the loyalists Herbert Morrison, Hugh Gaitskell and Willie Whiteley. The NEC voted by 14 to 13 votes not to expel Aneurin Bevan. He was saved by another member who had been partly convinced by the contribution of Griffiths. She was Jean Mann, who was also a friend of Jennie Lee, Bevan's wife.[10] She had enjoyed the friendship over many years and honestly believed that such a friendship should come before any kind of regulations and political discipline. A subcommittee was established to consider the case of Bevan. The members of the sub-committee were Barbara Castle, Clement Attlee, Hugh Gaitskell, James Griffiths, three trade union leaders, and Edith Summerskill as chair. Griffiths was an important person in this sub-committee, as his priority was to safeguard the unity of the Labour Party, rather than teaching Bevan a lesson. Attlee was of the same opinion, for he had always been a stickler for the unity of the Labour Party. Barbara Castle admired the flair of Bevan. They had been friends for years in the Bevanite movement and both were prominent left-wingers.

These three in particular saved Bevan from being cast aside from a front bench position, or being denied the opportunity of standing for the post of Deputy Leader. Though Bevan was a strong contender for the post, Griffiths, in his heart of hearts, thought he could win in a contest with his fellow Welsh MP. But a good number of politicians argued that Hugh Gaitskell and Aneurin Bevan could never work together as leader and deputy leader, and so Griffiths was the ideal candidate who would in every way support Gaitskell.[11] Others felt that Bevan deserved to be deputy leader as he had failed in his quest to be leader. But Griffiths knew he had the upper hand because after all, he was acceptable to many on the left as well as all the right-wingers, and because of that he could even win against one of the most charismatic politicians in the history of the party. The contest was difficult. Eventually Griffiths was elected by 141 votes to 111, a majority of 30. Who would have thought in 1919 in the Central Labour College in London that two of the Welsh students who were there from the collieries, one from Betws near Ammanford the other from Tredegar, would thirty-four years later be competing for the post of deputy leader of the Labour Party?

Most of the Welsh Labour MPs, under the leadership of Ness Edwards and Harold Finch, as well as the intellectuals in the Labour Party such as Douglas Jay, voted for Griffiths. So did the younger MPs such as Roy Mason, the MP for Barnsley. To Griffiths this victory was the climax, up until then, of his political career. He mentions in his autobiography the important victory he had achieved: Following the excitement of the election for leader, that for the deputy leadership was conducted quietly and without personal bitterness. I was naturally pleased with the result, and felt deeply honoured by the trust reposed in me.[12]

In Griffiths's private papers in the National Library of Wales there is a document of forty-four pages in his own handwriting reviewing the year of 1955. It is a loss that he did not do the same for 1956 as that year was a difficult one for all the Welsh MPs. Tryweryn was the word which was carved into the history of the Welsh nation, with far-reaching consequences for years to come. Liverpool City Corporation was determined to build a new reservoir in Wales as they did in Llanwrin, Montgomeryshire in 1890. Dolanog, a small village and a valley in north Montgomeryshire was the first choice for building the reservoir, but in view of the connections of that area with the remarkable eighteenth-century Calvinistic Methodist hymn writer Ann Griffiths, Liverpool City politicians were advised by a few knowledgeable civil servants to reconsider the location. The next area that came up for scrutiny was the Tryweryn Valley in Merionethshire, and the Liverpool Corporation cleverly gave the impression that it was showing respect to the Welsh people by not proceeding with the plan to drown Dolanog. The controversial flooding of the Tryweryn valley cast a shadow over Welsh political life which has remained much longer than anyone had anticipated. It seems to us today that wellknown Welshmen within the Labour Party, such as James Griffiths or Aneurin Bevan, were afraid of giving the clear leadership that was needed in Wales. But Griffiths saw clearly, as did Goronwy Roberts, Tudor Watkins, Cledwyn Hughes, and T. W. Jones, as a result of the Tryweryn episode, that they had the task of strengthening the voice of the Welsh nation in Westminster. The yearly debate around St David's Day was rather a dismal affair. Though many had welcomed a Minister for Welsh Affairs from the hands of the Conservative government, one had to remember that he had very little authority in reality and neither did he have a separate office in Cardiff to sustain his status. The yearly White Paper was welcomed, but it did not contain enough to please the Welsh nationalistic element among the Labour MPs and especially as the Welsh Nationalist Party had no representative in Westminster at that time.

The decision of the Labour Party MPs in Wales to support Hugh Gaitskell and James Griffiths as leader and deputy was a positive step in the history of Welsh politics. Gaitskell was much readier to consider Wales and its needs than Clement Attlee had ever been and much more than Herbert Morrison who postponed a decision on the future of Wales as long as he could. As we have already seen, Attlee had a high regard for Griffiths. This can be seen in his handwritten letter wishing him and Gaitskell well as Labour leaders:

> *I am sure that with Hugh and yourself at the helm we shall shake up the Government. I shall always think with gratitude of your fine wonderful service through the years. Vi joins me in sending good wishes for 1956 to you and yours.* [13]

This was also the feeling of many who were concerned with the needs of Wales as a nation and country. The shame of Tryweryn and the constant demand in many a rural constituency for positive thinking on a campaign for a parliament for Wales brought Gaitskell and Griffiths to consider the implications for the Labour Party as far as the life of the Welsh people was concerned. After visiting a number of constituencies in Wales in 1956, Gaitskell sent a comprehensive message to Morgan Phillips calling for a discussion as well as a decision on devolution in the name of the Labour Party. He added:

> *This is perhaps of no great importance in the south but it should help to hold and possibly win seats in north and central Wales. If we have a policy statement it will have to take account of the difficult question of the constitutional issue. Jim and I are at any rate pledged to consider this further. We shall of course, have to consult the Regional Council as well as the Parliamentary Group.* [14]

The consequence of the letter from Gaitskell was action. In 1956 a committee was set up to represent the NEC, the Welsh group of the parliamentary Labour Party and the Welsh Regional Council to consider and to give leadership to the constitutional question. The responsibility for chairing this committee was given to Griffiths, and soon he repeated the call that he had made from the platform of the National Eisteddfod of Wales in Llandybïe in 1944: a Secretary of State for Wales. But there was no unity on this issue in 1944 or indeed in 1956; rather there was clear opposition from a number of his colleagues and some of his college friends, in particular Ness Edwards. The MP for Caerphilly, Edwards was supported by Iorwerth Thomas from the Rhondda, another bitter and staunch enemy of Welsh nonconformity. Both were afraid that the appointment of a Secretary of State for Wales would lead to independence and a parliament for Wales. The attitude of the Welsh Regional Council of the Labour Party was confused to say the least. This is why some Labour Party stalwarts were frustrated at the situation with regard to socialism and devolution. Cyril O. Jones, a Wrexham solicitor, expressed himself in no uncertain terms in a letter to Huw T. Edwards:

> *I am greatly disappointed by the readiness of the contemporary Labour Party to abandon socialism and to embrace insignificant matters. Devolution, for example, has been abandoned, and even men like James Griffiths are prepared to grant Home Rule to all the nations but his own. Most of the Labour MPs from Wales are opposed to Home Rule for Wales.* [15]

Griffiths had been unfairly criticised by Jones. Griffiths knew that at last he could count on the support of the leader of the party, and that there was some hope that he could even in the long run win over Aneurin Bevan to the cause of devolution. The optimist and reconciler was at work, and Griffiths maintained his position with conviction. Cliff Prothero notes that his contribution was essential. He could never understand why Scotland had a Secretary of State, but Wales had been denied the right to have one.

Griffiths used all his powers as a negotiator in an attempt to persuade other members of the committee of the justice of his case. The last two meetings of the committee were chaired by Gaitskell, and according to all the evidence, the Report of the Welsh Council became part of Labour Party policy. Two important politicians who sat on the committee changed their minds. The first and the most influential of them to do so was Aneurin Bevan. Prothero gives us an eye-witness account:

> *After several meetings of protracted and heated discussion and now what turned out to be the final meeting and right in the middle of a very heated debate to everyone's surprise Mr Aneurin Bevan proposed that we include in our policy statement that a Secretary of State for Wales will be appointed.*[16]

Bevan turned on the way out of the meeting and told some of his staunch allies such as Cledwyn Hughes, 'well now that you've got it, we must make the best use of it.' The other politician who changed his tune was James Callaghan. He changed his mind as he believed that priority had been given by the government of the day to the building of the Forth Bridge, rather than the Severn Bridge, because the Secretary of State for Scotland was in the cabinet. This was one of the most important victories for Griffiths on Welsh devolution in his tenure as deputy leader of the Labour Party.

In January 1957 the Welsh Council, under the chairmanship of the trade union leader Dr Huw T. Edwards, published its Third Memorandum recommending the establishment of a Secretary of State for Wales. It was one of the most important documents published by the Welsh Council. It recommended that the secretaryship should have sufficient powers and a department to sustain it. Griffiths believed that the Labour Party at long last was giving guidance to the Welsh nation. To make the situation complicated, on the same day that a debate took place in the House of Commons on the Third Memorandum, the City of Liverpool Council presented in the House of Lords a private parliamentary measure giving it the right to build a reservoir across the valley of Tryweryn, with dire consequences. It meant the drowning of the village of Capel Celyn, and obliterating a Welsh speaking community which had existed for centuries. Griffiths felt the need to send a letter to Goronwy Roberts to thank him most sincerely for the polished speech that he delivered to parliament on 4 July on the subject of the drowning of Tryweryn. Griffiths told him: 'The force of your advocacy was reflected in the vote (in the circumstances) was a splendid tribute to Tom and you.' Tom was T. W. Jones, the Labour MP for Merionethshire. The end product was the vote in the House of Commons a few months later, when the bill was passed. Not one MP from Wales voted in favour, but the Bill passed easily, with 175 votes for and 79 against. T. W. Jones and Goronwy Roberts worked diligently in the defence of Tryweryn, as did many others, in particular the leader of Plaid Cymru, Gwynfor Evans, as well as the local people in Capel Celyn and Bala under the guidance of Dafydd Roberts. A few days after this, on 8 July 1957, Goronwy Roberts was asked by Griffiths to find a capable person who could convey the policies of the Labour Party on education and the needs of the countryside in north Wales.

This person was expected to be well versed in management as well as a convinced Labourite. We are not told if Roberts fulfilled the role, for he was not always known as one who completed such tasks on every occasion, though he was an able speaker, thinker and author of countless articles in the Welsh language weekly, *Y Cymro* (The Welshman).

In February of that year a by-election was held in the Carmarthen constituency as a result of the death of the Liberal MP Sir Rhys Hopkin Morris. Two women stood out in this contest: Megan Lloyd George who had left the Liberal Party to wave the Labour Party flag; and Jennie Eirian Davies, the wife of a Presbyterian minister and product of the Carmarthenshire countryside, who had fought the 1955 general election and had made a huge impact as the Plaid Cymru candidate in that election as well as in the public meetings of the by-election. Griffiths was glad to see Megan Lloyd George winning the adjoining constituency as he, like his father Williams Griffiths, was a great admirer of her father, indeed of the whole Lloyd George family.

Even though Jennie Eirian Davies was an outstanding political candidate, she lost her deposit, something that did not happen to the Plaid candidate in the Llanelli constituency in the 1955 general election. Winning back Carmarthen for Labour and in particular having the input of Megan was a boost to Labour. There was a strong group of chapel-orientated socialists in Carmarthenshire. This was the background that Griffiths emphasised often in his speeches. He underlined that he was a Welshman proud of his country and of his language. These were the important words that he spoke after his revolutionary change of heart:

> *I am Welsh – we are all – proud of my country, proud of its language. I want to sustain it. One of the imponderables – the Minister will understand this, too – is the fear that in this modern age of television and all the rest, the language will die. I do not want it to die.*[17]

What did he have in mind? If he was a philosopher or a poet he might have expressed his concern even more fully. But Griffiths was underlining the fact that Wales was a nation, with its own language and culture, and there was a need to safeguard the heritage in the context of a mass culture which encompassed one nation after another. One has to ask the question: what was responsible for the change of attitude? Why had this rich Welsh vein not been emphasised earlier. We can only suggest that the death of his cultured brother Amanwy in 1953 had made him reconsider his Welsh commitments. David Rees Griffiths had strong convictions on Welshness as well as on socialism. His death helped awaken his brother to a huge task, reminding him that he was brought up in the Welshspeaking village of Betws and that he was above everything else a Welsh-speaking Welshman.

The action of Liverpool in drowning Tryweryn valley was an event which created a large number of passionate nationalists for Plaid Cymru. The action also influenced nationalist socialists such as Griffiths. Life is brief and there is no time to stand and stare and postpone your concerns. The key to understanding what brought about this change in Griffiths's approach and attitude lays somewhere between his bereavement at the loss of this brother in Ammanford and the sadness of a community drowned in Merionethshire, because those leaders called to safeguard Wales were not militant enough and were outvoted by English-minded MPs who were unable to understand the Welsh way of life, based on an ancient language and culture.

In April 1956 Griffiths had the opportunity of meeting Nikolai Bulganin and Nikita Khrushchev, an event which indicates the status Griffiths held within the Labour hierarchy and the respect shown to him within the British political establishment.[18] He sat next to Soviet leader Khrushchev at the dinner in Chequers which was arranged on Sunday night 22 April, and the conversation between turned to the coal mining industry as both were ex-miners. Khrushchev mentioned the huge development which was taking place in Siberia and the Urals where new coalfields had been opened. At their second meeting on 23 April, Khrushchev lost his temper after Gaitskell (whose wife was Jewish) raised the question of the situation of the Jewish people in eastern and central Europe. An emotional argument took place between Aneurin Bevan, supported by Sam Watson, and Khrushchev and Bulganin. Griffiths reminded Khrushchev of the support given by the British Labour Party to Russia in the 1920s. His feelings at the end of this meeting in the Harcourt Room at the House of Commons were:

> *It wasn't a happy evening. K. was tough and blunt, and at times arrogant. I left feeling disturbed and unhappy; I thought we were regarded as less amiable because Social Democracy is the real alternative to Communism – and we meddled about social democrats in prison. Co-existence seems the only chance: co-operation seems far away, real coperation and confidence far, far away!*[19]

Britain faced a great crisis in 1956 when the Suez Canal was nationalised by Egypt's President Nasser. Both Britain and France had huge financial interests in the Suez Canal Company. To complicate the situation, half the oil used in Britain, Scandinavia and Western Europe was shipped from the Middle East through the Suez Canal. Gaitskell and Griffiths supported Prime Minister Eden in Parliament but Labour could not support the use of force, or ignore the United Nations Charter, and public opinion in the United States and elsewhere. President US Eisenhower, could not see his way to supporting Britain or France. This was a dismal misunderstanding.

Without the necessary discussion, Eden prepared with France for Israel to occupy the Sinai desert and the plan was implemented on 29 October. Anglo-French aeroplanes destroyed the Egyptian air force on 31 October, and within 48 hours, Egyptian forces sank forty-seven ships in the Canal. Because of the stupidity of Eden and his cavalier attitude towards the United Nations, who called on him to cease fighting, the attitude of the Opposition suddenly changed. Aneurin Bevan took the initiative in the Suez crisis and addressed a crowd of 30,000 in Trafalgar Square on Sunday afternoon, 4 November, and then as the shadow Foreign Secretary he delivered in the House of Commons on 5 December one of the most impressive speeches in the history of Parliament. That was the verdict of Griffiths as well as Megan Lloyd George. Tony Benn wrote in his diary: 'it was cool, calm and deadly.' Though the government won the vote, Bevan's speech delivered a mortal blow. Eden was ill and realised that he could not remain as prime minister. He resigned on 9 January 1957, and Harold Macmillan became prime minister.

There were two matters that were of great concern to Labour MPs, as Griffiths testified. The first matter was the atomic and hydrogen bomb. Under Attlee Labour had approved the large-scale production of nuclear weapons. In March 1957 the Macmillan government announced that they were going to hold a number of atomic trials on Christmas Island in the Pacific. Gaitskell and Griffiths came to the conclusion that the trials should be postponed for the time being and called on other nations to follow suit. Gaitskell as well as Griffiths knew that this topic was complicated and difficult for party leaders. The words of Gaitskell to a friend summed up the attitude of both politicians:

> *The H Bomb is an almost impossible subject for us. It is impossible to reach a real logical conclusion without splitting the party. So I am afraid we just have to go on with compromises.*[20]

But the hopes of the Leader and his deputy were shattered by the time the Annual Conference was held in Brighton. The Transport and General Workers Union had a new general secretary. Arthur Deakin and his successor, Jock Tiffin, both died in 1956. This meant the election of Frank Cousins to the key post. Cousins was a committed unilateralist.

Griffiths was in a difficult position, as he admitted to his agent Douglas Hughes in a letter dated 4 April 1957.[21] These were days of strife, and he was afraid that the Labour Party would be split from top to bottom. He admitted: 'My endeavour has been to cement the Party'.[22] Then he goes on to discuss the debate on nuclear weapons, hoping that the Labour leadership had compromised so as to safeguard the unity of the party. He knew that Conservative politicians and the press would attack Labour for apparently being split on the issue of nuclear weapons, but to him the main concern was 'that we kept a unity.'[23] The creation of good relationships was important to Griffiths. He wanted to build bridges whenever there was a need to do so. In April 1957 he arranged with Jirí Hajek, the Czechoslovakian ambassador in London, that Llanelli's Hywel Girl's Choir would go on a tour of the eastern European country.[24] He wanted his agent Douglas Hughes and his wife, Mrs Loti Rees Hughes, to go with the choir on its journey to help create goodwill, with a country that had suffered so much destruction and pain.

At the Annual Labour Conference in 1957, an emotional battle on nuclear arms took place between the unilateralists and leaders of the calibre of Gaitskell and his deputy who wanted to preserve the status quo. Judith Hart, a left-wing MP representing a Scottish constituency, presented the case in a memorable speech to the conference:

> *I want to say… that if this party this morning does not renounce the hydrogen bomb we are being far more wicked than any member of the Tory Party, because there is not one of us in this Conference Hall, there is not one person on the platform or in the galleries who does not firmly believe that the hydrogen bomb is an evil thing.*[25]

Griffiths could not but agree, especially given his pacifist stance during the First World War. The leadership was spared embarrassment by a stirring speech from Aneurin Bevan who had visited Crimea in September 1957. There President Khrushchev told him that if Britain took a unilateral decision to get rid of the hydrogen bomb it would have no influence on the

Politburo. In his speech to the 1957 Conference, Bevan spoke these words which have been quoted often in history books:

> *But if you carry this resolution and follow out all its implications and do not run away from it you will send a British Foreign Secretary, whoever he may be, naked into the Conference Chamber. Able to preach sermons of course, he could make good sermons. But action of that sort is not necessarily the way in which you take the menace of the bomb from the world.*[26]

The Bevanities were disgusted with their hero. Two of them, Barbara Castle and Ian Mikardo, attacked him immediately. As his biographer John Campbell admits: 'Their own Nye had dismissed the righteous aspiration of the Left as so much hot air.'[27] His powerful contribution changed the whole debate. The leadership of the party easily gained the upper hand, with 5,836 votes to 781,000 for the unilateralists.

But the unilateral movement was not beaten. In February 1958 the Campaign for Nuclear Disarmament came into existence with the Anglican Canon John Collins from St Paul's Cathedral, the philosopher from Penrhyndeudraeth, Bertrand Russell, the historian A. J. P. Taylor and the socialist Michael Foot as the leading lights. A. J. P. Taylor described CND as 'a movement of eggheads for eggheads.' The movement spread to all parts of Britain and became an integral part of the life of idealists, young and old, within the Labour Party, Plaid Cymru and the Liberal Party. The movement received a great deal of publicity particularly around the time of its annual march from Aldermaston to Trafalgar Square with Canon Collins in his clerical garb leading the thousands in protest.

The second problem which faced the Labour Party in 1956-57 was the old chestnut that had existed since 1918: public ownership. To examine the matter fully, the annual conference of 1956 set up a committee under Griffiths.[28] One of the most important members of the committee besides the chairman was Harold Wilson. The committee's report was published under the title Industry in Society and its recommendations were accepted by the British Labour Party. It called for the renationalisation of the steel industry and the haulage industry and for the extension of public ownership to any industry or part of an industry, which was proved, after a detailed study, to have failed to serve the British people. Gaitskell, Griffiths and Aneurin Bevan gave their wholehearted support to Industry and Society. It reinforced the message that had been heard consistently from the lips of Labour leaders since the end of the First World War.

However, the Left felt uneasy, though others from the Right, such as Herbert Morrison, were also aggrieved as they felt that the document was critical of the efforts made by past Labour governments to nationalise certain industries. Barbara Castle and Ian Mikardo, two members of the NEC, felt betrayed by the leaders, in particular Gaitskell and Griffiths. Gaitskell expressed his frustration with Castle and Mikardo when he informed Richard Crossman: 'If they can't stand by a document which, like Industry and Society, they have helped to draft on the NEC, I wouldn't trust them in Cabinet.'[29]

At the Annual Labour Conference of 1957 Jim Campbell, from the National Union of Railwaymen (NUR), proposed that they should reject Industry and Society, and insert a list of the industries that a Labour government would nationalise when its opportunity came. Herbert Morrison spoke against the document, though he was not opposed in principle, but argued that they should reconsider the need for nationalisation.[30] In the meantime Aneurin Bevan persuaded Frank Cousins and his delegates from the TGWU to refuse support for the NUR proposal. Cousins spoke well and endorsed the report. The NUR failed dismally.[31]

Throughout 1958 the leaders of the Labour Party expected Harold Macmillan to call a general election, especially in the autumn. With Griffiths in a pivotal position, his leadership and his emphasis on the Welsh proverb 'Mewn Undeb Mae Nerth' (In Unity There Is Strength) gained a great deal of support in the Labour movement. By the time the annual conference met in Scarborough in September, it was obvious that there would be no general election before 1959. Griffiths was content: the conflict and disagreement within the party had died down. But in the 1950s it was impossible to be involved in the Labour Party without disagreement, mainly on the nuclear weapons issue. One matter raised its head at Scarborough which created a debate, this time on education as a result of the document prepared by the NEC called Learning to Live. Griffiths was given the task of presenting it to the delegates. It had seven educational, priorities for the next Labour government. These seven were to be implemented, according to Griffiths, within the next five years. They were:

(i)    classes of not more than 30 children
(ii)   closing schools in the poor, deprived areas of cities
(iii)  better provision for the disabled
(iv)   closing schools where young children of 5 years of age were co-existing with teenagers of 15 years of age
(v)    raising the school leaving age to 16
(vi)   11+ examination to be eliminated
(vii)  rearranging schools on the principle of the Comprehensive School.[32]

Griffiths's first sentence to the conference was: 'The most important single reform we could now make in our education system is to reduce the size of classes.'[33] He reminded the delegates that one third of primary school children were being educated in classes of more than 40. In the high schools the situation was not so critical; two-thirds of the children were in classes of less than 30. Then Griffiths dealt with the 11+ examination. To him this examination deserved to be scrapped. He dealt with the comprehensive schools. He admitted that there were fears; the fear of losing the grammar school standards and the fear that talented children would suffer. He believed that there was a need to keep the academic standards, and indeed to improve on them. The deputy leader expressed himself with confidence, emphasising the vision to his fellow Labour members:

> ...I believe we can maintain the traditions and improve the standards in the new system  which we propose to create and make those standards and traditions available to many    more than the tiny proportion of children who get them now.[34]

This was a vision that began in a conversation that took place between Patrick Gordon Walker and George Brown as far back as 1954. The vision was to improve substantially the education of grammar schools so that they achieved the standards of public schools. This was to be a silent revolution, achieved without expecting any parent to pay. But Learning to Live was afraid of tackling the public school, except for suggesting that a Royal Commission should be appointed to discuss their future. But the conference was in no mood to forget the hot potato, the question of the public schools, and an interesting contribution from Fred Peart, MP for Workington, and one of the disciples of R. H. Tawney. Peart reminded the conference of Tawney's philosophy: 'He wrote a book on equality. Professor Tawney said that no nation can call itself civilised unless its children attend the same schools…'[35] Peart failed with his amendment, though TGWU (the largest union) supported him. The vote went against him and the private schools were to be left alone. Griffiths had once more made his case well as one of the elder statesmen of the Labour Party.

Within a month of the conference Griffiths heard of the resignation of Huw T. Edwards as Chairman of the Welsh Council. The Chairman and the Council had received his wholehearted support over the years and he was grateful for their important reports on Welsh issues. Griffiths knew that the Welsh Council's report on the administration of local government published in 1957 was of the highest standard.[36] The Prime Minister refused its recommendation of transferring a number of administrative responsibilities to the care of the Secretary of State for Wales. Huw T. Edwards believed that the Conservative government was stubborn; indeed, he admitted that there was not a chance of Whitehall understanding the aspirations of the Welsh people while the Conservatives were in power. His resignation was received without regret from the Tory politicians: indeed, they were glad that Edwards was out of the limelight. But he proved a difficult person to silence, as David Maxwell Fyfe and Henry Brooke admitted on a number of occasions.

Another important development in the 1950s was the attempt of Ness Edwards, MP for Caerphilly, to establish in parliament a Grand Committee for Wales.[37] Edwards was a complex personality, controversial and yet a clever politician and a dependable supporter of Griffiths from their college days in London. It is obvious that he had discussed with the deputy leader the memorandum which he had prepared for the Order of Procedure Committee of the House of Commons to discuss administrative matters pertaining to Wales. Earlier in the century they had established a Permanent Committee to consider Bills which were only relevant to Wales, a measure that meant a great deal to Lloyd George in 1907. Due to the fact that Welsh matters did not come before the House often, the facility of this committee was not implemented. The memorandum prepared by Ness Edwards was discussed by the Committee and then, in July 1959, a debate took place in the House of Commons. The government refused to establish a Grand Committee at once but R. A. Butler promised to consider the whole matter in due course.

He did so and recommended the setting up of a Grand Committee. It came into existence on 5 April 1960. Cledwyn Hughes admitted:

*It was in my opinion, a valuable development as it provided an opportunity for Welsh members to discuss matters of importance to Wales while Ministers were present to give answers.*[38]

Another great concern of Griffiths and the whole Labour Party was the colonies and the movement for colonial freedom on the African continent. To many a member of the Labour Party this was what made them so different from members of the Conservative Party. From February 1958 onwards, Barbara Castle had been sending reports of the atrocities which took place in the camps which housed the members of the Mau Mau rebellion. The Minister for the Colonies, Alan Lennox-Boyd, could not escape her proddings.

He testified in the House that her concerns were 'misleading and incorrect'. A year later Labour called for an independent inquiry, but this was turned down by the government. In May 1958 the news came that eleven individuals who had been imprisoned in the Hola camp had been killed with incredible violence. The government refused to discuss the atrocity for two months, but in the end a debate was allowed on 27 July before the summer recess. Griffiths was extremely knowledgeable of the situation in Kenya, and his opinion was greatly esteemed by the new African leaders who were appearing on the world scene.

By Easter 1959 Griffiths recognised the need to strengthen the electoral machine on the threshold of an election. The agent Douglas Hughes arranged a conference in May where the delegates from the branches came together to discuss the network. Griffiths explained in a letter to his agent, dated 30 May, that there was a real need to strengthen the effort of Douglas Hughes to increase Labour membership, in particular in the Gwendraeth Valley.[39] He mentioned the townships of Tumble and Cross Hands as two centres where they needed to canvass every house. He mentioned that Morgan Phillips, who was not in good health, had informed him that he believed that the general election would be on either 21 or 28 October. He suggested that they should hire the Market Hall in Llanelli for the 20th and the 24th of October so that they could hold their eve-of-poll meeting.

Then in the letter he offered some advice to Hughes's wife Loti Rees Hughes, the Labour candidate in Cardiganshire. This is of interest to this author who gave her his commitment and spoke on her platform throughout the constituency for a period of three weeks. Elfed Williams from Aberystwyth and I would precede her from one village hall to another. The advice of Griffiths to Loti Rees Hughes was for her to refrain from attacking the popular MP for the county, Roderick Bowen, in her speeches. That was the mistake Iwan Morgan made in 1945, 1950 and 1951 when he was the Labour candidate.

The Reverend D. Jones-Davies did better in the 1955 General Election by concentrating on the manifesto rather than personal attacks on the Liberal MP. Griffiths believed, as the main architect of the Welsh manifesto, that the Labour Party had a comprehensive programme to offer the electorate. Indeed the NEC decided to establish a sub-committee, under his chairmanship, to prepare a Labour Party manifesto for Wales. Hugh Gaitskell had a meeting with Griffiths and agreed that the manifesto would include the promise of a Secretary of State for Wales as well as creating a Welsh Office without setting out in detail the powers that would be transferred.[40] Griffiths admits in his autobiography:

*To my intense satisfaction they unanimously agreed and for the first time the Labour Party pledged itself to include a Secretary of State for Wales in the next Labour government.*[41]

The manifesto was reinforced when Gaitskell came to the Welsh Labour Party Conference to pledge his commitment as leader.[42] His promise was received enthusiastically. The manifesto was announced in September 1959, and though Griffiths was nearing seventy years of age he worked like a Trojan. He emphasised the needs of the countryside as well as a stronger voice for Wales in the cabinet. It was a great disappointment for him to hear that Huw T. Edwards was leaving the Labour Party after a lifetime of service to join Plaid Cymru. The Welsh language press mentioned the possibility of others following him, in particular the pioneer of the ILP in Gwynedd, David Thomas, Mrs Mary Silyn Roberts, another WEA stalwart, and Professor Huw Morris-Jones, all three residents of Bangor. But none of the three left the Labour Party for Plaid Cymru. The nationalists did not gain more significant support through the action of Huw T. Edwards. If anything they declined in most of the constituencies, even those where they had some hope such as Carmarthenshire. Even with all his efforts on behalf of Tryweryn, Gwynfor Evans had fewer votes in Merionethshire in the 1959 general election than he had had in 1955. Labour held its own in Wales. Morgan Phillips expressed the feelings of all the leaders of Labour when he said that Griffiths had done 'excellent work' during the general election campaign. Though the Labour Party had a more efficient organisation than it did in 1955, the results were still disappointing in thre rest of Britain England was a conservative country, even labour supporters in the urban areas of England were afraid of too much radicalism.

Labour did badly among young people; people aged between eighteen and twenty-four were very reluctant to vote Labour. Only 10 per cent of the middle class supported Labour. In Scotland and industrial areas of Lancashire the party increased its vote, but the biggest shock of all was to realise that around 30 per cent of the working class had voted for the Conservative Party. In Wales, Labour had done well in every constituency where they had an MP except for Cardiff South East. James Callaghan came close to losing the seat to the Conservative candidate, Michael H. Roberts. He had a majority of 868 this time, down from the 3,240 majority that he had in 1955. Loti Rees Hughes failed to oust Roderick Bowen in Cardiganshire. In Llanelli Griffiths had a majority of 24, 49743 one of the best results for Labour in Wales.[44]   Aberdare was as strong for Labour as was Llanelli: Arthur R. Probert, a local trade unionist, had a majority of 24,305. The exact figures for Llanelli were as follows:

| | | |
|---|---|---|
| James Griffiths  (Labour) | 34,625 | 66.7% |
| H. Gardner     (Conservative) | 10,128 | 19-5 |
| Rev. D. Eirwyn Morgan (Plaid Cymru) | 7,176 | 13.8% |
| Majority | 24,497 | |

By then, Griffiths was in the happy situation of knowing that he was personally well placed to implement full-blooded Welsh policies, such as establishing a Secretary of State of Wales role, when Labour won a general election: he had held high office and he was well liked by left and Right within the party as well as in constituencies where Labour had a strong base throughout Britain.[45] He was on good terms with Gaitskell, and in view of their close collaboration, they would persuade the Labour Party in Wales that the time had come to change its negative attitude towards the Welsh language and the culture associated with the language. Griffiths could be criticised for being lukewarm for some years on the principle of devolution but he succeeded brilliantly in the end. He seemed to have come of age and he was able to give leadership on the issue of a parliament for Wales, as well as on on the role of the Welsh nation within the context of the United Kingdom . He could have done more on the Tryweryn issue, rather than leaving the parliamentary campaigning to T. W. Jones, Tudor Watkins and Goronwy Roberts, but with hindsight he could be content that the huge task of gaining the support of the Labour Party for devolution for Wales was fought by him and won.[46] Though there were a large number of difficulties on the way before the dream became a reality, and in 1959 opponents to face of whom he knew nothing about, he became to many the symbol of a new Wales on the horizon.

## Notes and References

1. Hugh Dalton, *Memoirs 1945-1960: High Tide and After* (London, 1962), p. 413.
2. Ibid.
3. Ibid., p. 414. 4. Ibid., p. 416. 5. Ibid., p. 417. 6. Ibid., p. 418.
7. Ibid., p. 419.
8. Philip Williams, *Hugh Gaitskell: A Political Biography*, p. 297.
9. Michael Foot, *Aneurin Bevan*, Volume 2 (London, 1973), pp. 554-5.
10. Greg Rosen, *Old Labour to New: The Dreams that Inspired, the Battles that Divided* (London, 2005) p. 192.
11. James Griffiths, *Pages from Memory*, p. 133.
12. Ibid., p.134-5.
13. NLW James Griffiths Papers B3/22. Letter of Clement Attlee to James Griffiths
14. Philip Williams, *Hugh Gaitskell*, p. 487.
15. NLW Huw T. Edwards Papers.
16. NLW, Cliff Prothero Papers, *Biographical Notes*, p. 137.
17. Hansard, vol. 564,11 February 1957, col. 982-3.
18. James Griffiths, *Pages from Memory*, p. 149.
19. Ibid., p. 149.
20. Ibid., pp. 151-156.
21. NLW, Deian Hopkin Papers, *Douglas Hughes Collection*, No. 31-108.
22. Greg Rosen, ibid., p. 193.
23. Greg Rosen, ibid.
24. NLW James Griffiths Papers ibid., This was the motivation to co-operate with Jirí Hájek, the Czechoslovak ambassador to Britain so that Llanelli's Hywel Girls' Choir could hold concerts in Czechoslovakia. Griffiths wanted his agent Douglas Hughes and his wife, Councillor Loti Rees Hughes, to travel with the choir. It was a tour to promote goodwill between the nations.
25. Greg Rosen, ibid., p. 193.
26. Ibid., p. 194.

27. John Campbell, ibid., p. 340.

28. John Campbell, ibid., pp. 328-9. Aneurin Bevan was a member of a sub-committee of the NEC, but he hardly ever attended, to the disappointment of Ian Mikardo and Barbara Castle, who expected his guidance. The Tribune could not support him. See *Tribune*, 19 July 1957.

29. Janet Morgan (Editor), *The Backbench Diaries of Richard Crossman* (London, 1981), p. 604.

30. Greg Rosen, ibid., p. 197.

31. Ibid., p. 198.

32. Ibid. 33. Ibid. 34. Ibid.

35. Ibid.

36. Philip Williams, ibid., p. 474.

37. Lord Cledwyn of Penrhos, *Wales in Both Houses* (Aberystwyth, 1991), p. 10.

38. Ibid.

39. Ibid.

40. NLW, James Griffiths Papers B 6/27. Letter of Hugh Gaitskell to James Griffiths, no date. In his diaries the only politician who gets a clean bill of health from Gaitskell is James Griffiths. This is what he wrote on Callaghan: 'He is a most talented Parliamentarian and a man of considerable charm but he seems to me to have no philosophical basis. He is far too inclined to take a demagogic line, though admittedly every now and then, he will swing to the opposite. He is not really particularly intelligent; not nearly as intelligent as George Brown. On the whole, of the five or six leading people he is the least satisfactory at the moment, though, of course, he may improve'. Of his comrade on the NEC this is his opinion: 'I must record my anxieties about the appalling lack of people with both courage and intelligence. When one looks around the executive it is hard to see anybody apart from Jim Griffiths (Deputy Leader) who has both these qualities. Harold Wilson has plenty of intelligence and a little courage but when we get beyond him, frankly, most of the rest are either just incapable of making good speeches – that is true of the best trade unionists – or just entirely lacking in courage, with only one idea, namely to get as many cheers from the left wing as possible'. See P. M. Williams, *The Diary of Hugh Gaitskell, 1945-56* (London, 1979), p.540 and p. 617; Peter Shore, *Leading the Left* (London, 1993), pp. 161-2.

41. James Griffiths, *Pages from Memory*, p. 164.

42. Ibid.

43. Beti Jones, *Etholiadau Seneddol yng Nghymru 1900-75*, p.129.

44. A useful analysis on the Election, see P. J. Madgwick, D. Steele and L. J. Williams, *Britain since 1954* (London,1983), pp. 200-203.

45. Martin Johnes, *Wales Since 1939*, p. 445. 'James Griffiths was instrumental in leading the Labour Party to create the post of Secretary of State for Wales, that he was the first holder, while Wyn Roberts was a tireless persuader for the Welsh language within the Conservative Welsh Office. Wales thus did not survive by accident. The history of the nation after 1939 was not an inevitable march towards devolution and perhaps beyond. Wales survived because people fought for it. James Griffiths received a wonderful tribute in the *Guardian* in October 1959. This is a portion of it: 'Some were surprised when he became Colonial Secretary in 1950, after having been Minister of National Insurance from 1945. In fact it was a logical step: the idealism of social justice apply to the world scale too; and having helped to build the Welfare State inside Britain, he wanted to expand it overseas'. Then they mention his role as reconciler: 'His position in the party's hierarchy is a tribute to a loyalty and selflessness rare in politics. Even when the party was almost torn in pieces with suspicion and hatred, no one could accuse him of belonging to any faction, he at least stood incontestably for the ideals on which the party was founded. He still does; and we must hope that he is able to serve them for years to come'. See Jim Griffiths, *Guardian*, 19 October 19 1959, p. 6.

# 16

## A Spokesman for Welsh Affairs

After the 1959 general election Griffiths felt that the time was ripe for him to transfer his responsibilities as deputy leader to another politician.[1] He had enjoyed working with Hugh Gaitskell: this was not easy task, as a number of Welsh MPs could not contemplate any sort of partnership with Gaitskell.[2] The Labour Party in the period 1957 to 1959 had been run/by of five politicians: Hugh Gaitskell, a lonely leader, James Griffiths, a popular deputy leader, Aneurin Bevan, the darling of the left and a Stormy Petrel, Harold Wilson, an able Oxford graduate and clever spokesman on foreign affairs, and George Brown, a solid trade unionist and a forceful spokesman on defence.

They were known as the Central Labour leadership. It is fair to admit that Gaitskell had a number of other political friends who gathered regularly at his home in Hampstead to discuss national and international politics. This group included four politicians of distinction besides Gaitskell. They were loyal to Gaitskell. The leader had four intellectuals as well as the Central leadership team to consult. To him there were nobody better than James Griffiths, Roy Jenkins, Douglas Jay, Tony Crosland and Patrick Gordon Walker.[3] Gaitskell was never tempted to bring the Hampstead friends with him to discuss important issues for the party, as he knew that Aneurin Bevan and Harold Wilson would not be happy. Griffiths though was on excellent terms with every one named as well as each one of the Four.

There was one topic which united the intellectuals who met in Hampstead and that was the need to delete a clause in the Constitution of the Labour Party which has been introduced in 1918. This was Clause IV which called for nationalisation of key industries, and Griffiths knew of the importance of it for so many rank and file members. He also knew that any Labour leaders who tried to delete the clause were asking for serious trouble. But before that storm came, Griffiths decided to resign the post of deputy leader.

On 19 October 1959 the editorial of the Manchester Guardian praised the popular politician.[4] This was also the theme of the pro-Labour Party newspaper the *Daily Herald*, which thanked him for his wise stewardship as a deputy to Gaitskell. *The Daily Herald* said:

> *No man served the Labour movement better than Jim Griffiths. Now, quietly, generously and without fuss, he steps down from the deputy leadership.*[5]

The NEC met on 28 October 1959 and expressed its gratitude for all he had done as deputy leader and for his loyalty over the years. This is the official statement prepared by Morgan Phillips, a long-term friend of Griffiths:

*The National Executive Committee puts on record its appreciation of his long years of devoted service and its gratitude for his outstanding loyalty and wise judgements in all its deliberations.*[6]

Gaitskell was sincere in his appreciation of the solid, unwavering support given to him by his loyal friend. On 25 November 1959 Griffiths received a letter from one of the most long-serving leaders of the Labour movement in the USA, Norman Thomas, who was disappointed that he was relinquishing his role as deputy leader, and sending his brotherly love as a fellow international socialist.[7] The Labour Party soon appreciated the loss of Griffiths's influence on Gaitskell. W. Neville Hall and Frances Noel-Baker, who were friends of Gaitskell, recognised the loss.[8] They were afraid that Gaitskell's burning ambition to be prime minister would destroy him. By the Annual Labour Party Conference at the beginning of October 1960 there were even voices calling for Gaitskell's resignation.[9] Tony Benn admits that the protest outside the hotel in Scarborough, where the NEC met on 2 October, was enough to frighten the friends of Gaitskell. This is what Benn wrote in his diary: 'It almost drowned our proceedings and introduced an element of mob violence into our affairs.'[10]

They heard the chant: 'Ban the Bomb! Gaitskell must go!'[11] There was an emotional debate with Sam Watson, leader of the miners in the Durham coalfield, presenting the argument on behalf of the NEC, while Frank Cousins, the trade unionist, Emrys Hughes, the Welshman who represented a Scottish, seat, and Michael Foot, editor of Tribune attacked all nations, including Britain, which possessed weapons of mass destruction.[12] But the conference also heard three powerful contributions for keeping nuclear weapons: first from Jim Griffiths, then from Denis Healey, and finally from Hugh Gaitskell.[13] Griffiths reminded the Conference that he had been, since his youth, a committed pacifist, but he had had to change his stance before the Second World War :

> *By temperament, by upbringing I was a pacifist. Circumstances compelled me to change, and I remember the time when I changed… for a problem of how to prevent aggression and war, pacifism is not enough. Friends, we failed to stop aggression in the thirties. We sacrificed Abyssinia. We killed the League, which was our greatest hope. Non-intervention did not save the Spanish Democrats from being crucified. And appeasement did not prevent, but led to, the Second World War…*[14]

Denis Healey gave a large number of examples of socialists who had to defend the civilised values through the possession of armaments. He referred to Fritz Erler, the spokesman for the Social Democratic Party of Germany, who was present at the conference.[15] Gaitskell had the last word, but he had realised that he could not carry the delegates with him. He promised them all that he would not abandon the commitment to defend his people:

> *There are some of us, Mr Chairman, who will fight and fight and fight, to save the Party we love. We will fight and fight again to bring back sanity, and honesty and dignity, so that our Party with its great past may retain its glory and its greatness.*[16]

He sat down with two-thirds of the delegates appreciative of his bravery while the rest sat quietly dismayed. One of those who sat stubbornly was Harold Wilson, later his successor.[17]

But within a fortnight, a new manifesto was published under the banner of the CDS, Campaign for Democratic Socialism.[18] The CDS called for a renewed debate about neutrality and unilateral disarmament. The leaders of this campaign were three disciples of Gaitskell: Dick Traverne, Bill Rodgers and Denis Howell. But there were a large number of MPs who felt dismayed with Gaitskell's leadership. According to Stephen Swingler, an MP in the Stoke-on-Trent area, Gaitskell was an 'unfortunate leader' and at least sixty MPs agreed with him.[19]

Aneurin Bevan was the Deputy Leader as successor to Griffiths, but tragically his period of office was short. On 6 July 1960 Bevan died of cancer, and the world lost a colourful politician. Griffiths had lost a friend from his college days, and he prepared a number of tributes to Bevan. He compared Nye Bevan to David Lloyd George in his parliamentary career, and how both had 'derived their inspiration from the Democratic Radicalism, which was the rich inheritance bequeathed to us by the religious and social reformers of the Wales of the nineteenth century.'[20]

On 7 July in the House of Commons Griffiths paid tribute to Bevan along with Harold Macmillan, Hugh Gaitskell and Clement Davies.[21] The tributes of the leaders were excellent but it was Griffiths's contribution which captured the hearts and minds of the arliamentarians as well as those in the public gallery.[22] One of these was Arthur Lourie from the Israeli Embassy in London, who had met Griffiths on his visit to Israel. 'Your words were so direct from the heart and from the valleys and mining valleys from which Bevan sprung that I, and I am sure all who listened, found them deeply moving.'[23] Griffiths's niece from Ammanford, May Harris, was proud of her uncle's contribution on television. 'I thought that in it, as in the talk on the evening of his death, you were at your best. And your Welsh was excellent – top marks!'[24] Then she told him of the impact he had created: 'All sorts of people agree that it was by far the best. Dr Gwenan Jones, who is shrewd and often critical, and who is very "*Blaid*" said it was the best of its kind she had ever heard.'[25]

The Treasurer of the Welsh Baptist Union, T. J. Evans of Carmarthen, wrote a splendid letter on the same lines as many others:

> *It was a magnificent tribute, spoken with such rich eloquence, of such transparent sincerity… You have never spoken like it before: that does not belittle your great oratorical gifts, but on this occasion, there was a tear in your voice as there was in the eyes of all of us at Southern Hay [the name of his home in Carmarthen] who looked and listened in. And today's article in the Western Mail was on the same high level.*[26]

Griffiths could deal with Bevan as well as anyone could, and as we have seen he was pivotal to the agreement on the proposal to have a Secretary of State for Wales.

Another important decision took place in the autumn of 1960, when Harold Wilson decided to stand against Gaitskell for the leadership of the Labour Party.[27] The election took place on 3 November and Gaitskell received 166 votes from the MPs while Wilson got 81, which gave Gaitskell a sizeable majority. In the election for deputy leader three stood: Fred Lee, James

Callaghan and George Brown. Brown won, with 118 votes, against 72 for Lee and only 55 for Callaghan on the first vote. On the second vote held on 10 November, George Brown won well, with 146 votes, against 83 for Fred Lee.[28] Callaghan took over from Griffiths as the Opposition's spokesman on the Colonies in December 1956. The colonies were one of the few issues, where Labour MPs were of one accord. The atrocities of the apartheid government of South Africa in the Sharpeville massacre on 21 March 1960 were events which brought Callaghan and Griffiths together in their condemnation. This was reinforced at the annual conference in October 1960 in a memorable debate.

One has to mention an unfortunate incident which happened in the spring of 1961 between Griffiths and his constituency political agent, Douglas Hughes. On 6 March Hughes had been disturbed by an address given by Richard Crossman during a visit to Wales. In the same month a real storm broke out between Griffiths and Hughes. In a letter to the agent on 19 March 1961 Griffiths mentions the chaos which had taken place the day before, largely because the agent had not informed him of the protest march that was to take place in Llanelli arranged by the Llanelli Trade Union and Labour movement on Saturday, 18 March.[29] Griffiths complains that Hughes had not called on him on the phone for a conversation on that Saturday morning. The MP had tried to get through to the agent by telephone but unsuccessfully. Griffiths had come out of the town hall in Llanelli and realised that there was a protest march against the policies of the Tory government.[30] Naturally he was concerned as he had not been forewarned. as the protestors expected to hear him that afternoon. Indeed he felt that the Labour Party locally should have organised the protest rather than the Trades and Labour Council. Griffiths had been kept in ignorance because of the apparent lack of communication with his agent. This is the sentence which explains his frustration with Douglas Hughes his long-serving agent: 'I am not fussy but I was annoyed at the seeming discourtesy of not being informed about the details of yesterday's arrangements.'[31]

Hughes's response is not in the James Griffiths papers, but the veteran MP sent another stinging letter to his agent on 25 March 1961.[32] He goes over the same territory as the earlier letter, complaining bitterly about the failure of his agent to inform him of the protest march considering he was visiting his constituency. Hughes in his reply told him not to complain to him, but to the local trade unionist, Dai Charles, who had organised the march. 'Why should I?' was the unusual response from Griffiths, which was quite out of character. 'After all, I am the Member of Parliament and you are the Agent, and after all we saw each other the night before in the meeting held at Coleshill School in town. It is obvious that you knew all along of the arrangements, and you could have warned me of them at the school.'

Then Griffiths tells Hughes:

> *I must say, however, that I regret that you should bring hate into this correspondence between Member and Agent. Since you have done so I must say that I am not conscious of having (as you say in your letter) shown any discourtesy to Loti.*[33]

216

Hughes had blamed Griffiths for ignoring his wife, Loti. He also used the phrase, 'snubbed her'. Griffiths responded by saying that Loti Rees Hughes was the first person  he saw outside the town hall . He also greeted the people who were on the march before accepting without prior notice the opportunity of addressing them that afternoon.  With his long experienced as a powerful orator he had no difficulty in speaking in a relevant and convincing way.

At the end of the meeting he walked to the far end of the town hall square to his car and shook hands with Councillor Loti Rees Hughes and wished her well. He does not mention that he spoke with anyone else, but it is quite obvious that he had been badly wounded as we can fathom in this paragraph to his agent:

> *I may have many failings – but discourtesy is – I hope – not one of them – and this is the first time in my life, I have even been charged with being discourteous to anyone. In a half century of public life I have had to meet and converse with thousands of people – in my constituency and outside – and I have always shown consideration and courtesy to everyone.*[34]

We cannot disagree with his statement. This was the period, through editorship of the socialist magazine called Aneurin (in memory of Nye Bevan), that the author came into personal contact with Griffiths, and received kind and supportive letters, as well as financial support for his efforts. In 1959 I also came to know Douglas Hughes and to visit him as well as Loti Rees Hughes in their home in Llanelli, and I worked very hard for her in the general election of 1959. I had a great deal of empathy and respect for the three of them as leaders of the Labour Party in west Wales. Griffiths mentions in his letter to Douglas Hughes his own contribution as a reconciler within the Labour Party:

> *I have – all my life – 20 years on the NEC – 22 years as a Front Bencher – striven to promote unity within the Party. I have never once attacked a colleague on the public platform and my influence in the Party has been built up on loyalty to comrades.*[35]

 We have seen many examples of him as a reconciler in this biography. He walked the middle path and refused to be tempted to criticise his fellow leaders in public. He mentioned to his agent that one reason that he was called upon to address political meetings was that he was a man of unity. He mentioned a by-election held in the Small Heath constituency in Birmingham, and added: 'And they asked for me because I could be relied upon to speak on principles and policy, and not to indulge in personalities.'[36]

Douglas Hughes was a very influential politician in Llanelli and on the County Council of Carmarthenshire. He and his wife Loti Rees Hughes were two local politicians in the 1950s who attracted a great deal of publicity as they were extremely hard working as councillors. The Welsh actress Sharon Morgan in her Welsh language autobiography mentions that Carmarthenshire was in the hands of the Labour Party and their leaders, Loti Rees Hughes and her husband Douglas, and they had a great deal of input into any public appointments.[37] Griffiths refers at the end of his letter to the long relationship between them: 'As you say –

we have worked together for 25 years on Monday 26 – for the by-election was on 26 March 1936. I am grateful for your help.'[38]

Then he mentions that this would be the last letter on the subject and he kept to his word. It is unfortunate that the letters of Douglas Hughes to Jim have not been kept, remembering that it was he who has kept the replies in his archives. Otherwise we would know nothing of this disagreement and the apparent cooling of relationship between them. Both worked together for the next few years for the Labour cause in the constituency which was more important than either one of them.

The letter of 25 March 1961 helped to clear the air of suspicion between two remarkable working class people, a miner and steelworker, who became notable politicians, one in his community in Carmarthenshire, and the other of national and international prominence. But we must ask was the trust of the politician and the agent as co-workers beginning to unravel after such a long partnership? We must also ask the question of what motivated Douglas Hughes to write the first of the two letters? Had there been a mistake or misunderstanding on behalf of Douglas Hughes and Loti Rees Hughes? Or is that letter a sign of a lack of trust between the experienced agent and the loveable politician who had won so must praise and admiration within the British as well as the Welsh Labour Party? We do not know. I decided to bring to the fore the unedifying quarrel which was not mentioned in Pages from Memory but the fact that the Griffiths letters had been preserved by Douglas Hughes suggests that at least one of them was quite willing for the whole affair to be looked at in the light of half a century and more. I believe that one must give as full a picture as possible of the personalities and characteristics of these two men who had worked together successfully for so long. Griffiths did not support the first Welsh CND rally in Aberystwyth on Whitsun Saturday in 1961.[39] Over two thousand people came together to the rally, and three Labour MPs attended, but Griffiths kept away as he had shown quite clearly where he stood on nuclear weapons in the debates on the issue at the Labour Party conference.

Nevertheless, he was very willing to give his support as a vice president to the Lord's Day Fellowship in Wales, in particular, to the referendum that was to be held in the autumn of 1964.[40] Griffiths backed the campaign conducted by Sabbatarian and Temperance leaders who were opposed by the brewers on the issue of opening public houses on Sundays. The referendum was held on 8 November 1961, and the Welsh heartland remained staunchly in favour of keeping the public houses closed and safeguarding what was called the 'Welsh Sunday'. The closure of the public houses on Sunday in Wales derived from an Act of Parliament from 1881, and for eighty years the taverns of Wales had been closed on Sundays. The more Anglicised counties of Wales — Breconshire, Flintshire, Glamorganshire, Monmouthshire and Radnorshire — as well as in Cardiff, Swansea, Merthyr Tydfil and Newport voted for Sunday opening. [41] But the public houses of Llanelli and Aberystwyth, Caernarfon and Holyhead were still closed. The support given by the Welsh politicians James Griffiths, Gwynfor Evans, Goronwy Roberts, George Thomas and Cledwyn Hughes was extremely important in safeguarding the Sabbatarian Temperance heritage.[42] Griffiths took a leading role in his constituency as well as in west Wales.[43] One of the successful meetings was held at Tabernacle Welsh Independent chapel in Llanelli on Friday 21 April 1961 when

Sir Cyril Black, the Conservative MP for Wimbledon, and James Griffiths shared the platform. Griffiths criticised the Archbishop of Wales, Dr John Morris, for his decision to support the brewing interests. Alderman T. Glanville Williams presided at this historic and well-attended meeting. The chairman praised the two politicians, stating that: 'Two men of outstanding character were fighting for the best traditions of Wales.'[44]

Griffiths was well pleased with the result in his constituency – a turn out of 58 per cent. The result was 22,439 voted against and 14,031 for Sunday opening, a majority of 8,408. The result in Carmarthenshire was also encouraging with 48,557 against and 23,633 for, a majority of 24,934. It was the highest majority in the whole of Wales.[45]

A. G. Gibby of Llanelli, a leading Liberal, criticised Griffiths for supporting the campaign over Sunday closure and his reluctance to support CND. He wrote to the local weekly, the *Llanelli Star*:

> *Now that the great campaign over Sunday closing is over, can we expect the same oratory and emotion in support of the ban-the-bomb project… Surely he will not stand by and see our children die from the H-Bomb fall-out of Strontium 90. This then, Mr Griffiths, which is more important: Sunday opening or the death roll of the future?*[46]

While Griffiths was the defender of the Welsh Sundays, his Labour MP colleagues Iorrie Thomas and Elfed Davies took the initiative in leading the campaign for opening the public houses. Iorrie Thomas was very much anti-nonconformist and rebelled against his religious upbringing at Salem Welsh chapel in Cwmparc in the Rhondda. He regarded nonconformity as a spent force, a negative movement on the Welsh scene. On most issues to do with Wales and nonconformity, Thomas and Griffiths disagreed.[47] However Griffiths received a large number of letters, including one from Gwilym Prys Davies, who praised him as well as the Bishop of Bangor for his leadership in the referendum.[48]

The Labour Party, and Gaitskell in particular, was glad to have the support of Griffiths on the Opposition Front Bench as the spokesman for Welsh Affairs. Gaitskell had promised him before the 1959 General Election that if Labour won, then he would be given the post of Minister of State for Welsh Affairs. But Griffiths was getting older and he suffered a great deal of ill health for twelve months. He was determined to do his best though, realising that Labour had a good chance of gaining power in the next general election.

The decision of a Plaid Cymru councillor in his home village of Betws, Gwynfor S. Evans, to present his nomination papers for the County Council election in the Welsh language in 1961 brought a swift response from the election officer, W. S. Thomas, who refused to accept them. Through the effort and generosity and expertise of a Welsh barrister, Dewi Watkin Powell, the High Court in London ruled in favour of Evans. Labour-held Carmarthenshire County Council was not allowed to appeal against the decision. It fell to Griffiths to put the claim before the Home Secretary and urge him that steps should be taken to have the nomination papers in the Welsh language.[49]

There is no doubt that this basic right was a catalyst, as was the the long, drawn out struggle of Eileen and Trefor Beasley in Llangennech to persuade Llanelli District Council to issue a bilingual demand for the Council Tax.[50] Their struggle was highlighted in the famous lecture of Saunders Lewis, Tynged yr Iaith (The Fate of the Language) on 13 February 1962, which will be discussed in more detail in the next chapter.[51]

The failure of Tryweryn and the the struggle for bilingual nomination papers and a bilingual Council Tax demand, indicated the unsatisfactory situation of the language in the communities in Wales. Out of this national crisis, new societies came into existence, the most important being the Welsh Language Society (Cymdeithas Yr Iaith Gymraeg) in August 1962, under the influence of the philosopher J. R. Jones. This organisation, as well as more mainstream pressure groups, such as the interdenominational Welsh Language Society, were the direct result of the call to action emanating from Saunders Lewis's lecture.

A letter sent by Cledwyn Hughes to Gwilym Prys Davies a few days before the formation of the Welsh Language Society did as much good as any other deed in this period of Welsh history.[52] It was an invitation to prepare a briefing paper for him and James Griffiths on the reorganisation of local government, suggesting that he could consider the argument in favour of an elected assembly for Wales. This briefing paper would then be discussed in the sub-committee on local government set up by the Welsh Council of Labour and chaired by Griffiths. Prys Davies, a solicitor from Pontypridd, did not take long to complete his task, and in 1963 Undeb Cymru Fydd published two pamphlets, one in English under the title A Central Welsh Council, and the other in Welsh under the title Cyngor Canol i Gymru.[53] The proposed Central Welsh Council would provide a forum for a united Welsh view on the most important issues in the public life of the nation. Griffiths was invited to prepare a preface to the pamphlets in both languages, and he did so, giving the impression to all those who read the pamphlets that the most notable and influential member of the Labour Party in Wales was at least willing to consider (if not support) all the arguments put forward in support of establishing an elected Council to serve the whole of Wales.

There was no doubt in the minds of those who had been involved with the student magazine Aneurin that these pamphlets were ensuring that the Labour Party was giving guidance to the Welsh nation.[54] To act on the lines of A Central Welsh Council would undermine the generalisations uttered by the President of Plaid Cymru on the anti-Welshness of the Labour Party. The Labour leaders in local government were reluctant to be enthusiastic, but a nucleus of Welsh Labour leaders, in particular James Griffiths, Cledwyn Hughes, John Morris and Goronwy Roberts were convinced that the nation needed a combination of a Secretary of State of Wales and a Welsh Elected Council as well as a new Language Act. In the eyes of these four Labour politicians this combination would be the most important political development in the history of Wales since the Act of Union. Furthermore the four of them believed that this goal was possible in the present period.

Griffiths was the eldest of the politicians and he was being reminded that life at its best is short. The death of Aneurin Bevan was a stark reminder, and then on 18 January 1963 came the death of Hugh Gaitskell at the age of 56. The loss of both these remarkable politicians at comparatively early ages was a dismal loss to the Labour Party. An election for a new leader was therefore on the horizon. Harold Wilson was immediately supported by the left wingers, and it was obvious that the choice on the right would be between George Brown and James Callaghan, though Frank Soskice who represented a Welsh constituency was also mentioned as a possible contender.[55] In the first ballot, Wilson received 118 votes, Brown 88 and Callaghan 41. Callaghan withdrew. On 14 February 1963 Harold Wilson was elected as the new leader of the Labour Party. He received 144 votes compared to Brown's 103. Among those who supported Brown was Griffiths, as well as Roy Jenkins, Bob Mellish, Charlie Pannell, Patrick Gordon-Walker and Desmond Donnelly, MP for Pembrokeshire. Griffiths decided to support Brown as he represented the trade unions, one of the foundation stones of the Labour edifice from the beginning.

Considering all the intellectual prowess of Gaitskell, the pundits realised from the beginning that Wilson had the advantage of the common touch which his predecessor did not have, and he was extremely popular with the rank and file members. The government of the day was in deep trouble, with the Profumo scandal, the failure to persuade De Gaulle that he should support the application of Britain to join the Common Market, and the failure of the economic policies pursued by the Chancellor. Callaghan summed it up:

> *Wilson caught the mood of the British people, and even elected a hearing from industry and commerce, they were ready to listen because they had become impatient with successive balance of payment crises in the Tory years of 1955, 1957 and 1961.*[56]

Wilson 'caught the mood of the British people' with the central theme of the manifesto, Labour in the Sixties: that is, the importance of science and technology for the future of Britain. One can agree with the verdict of one of his biographers, Philip Ziegler, when he said that the most important contribution of Wilson to his party was 'to transfer its main thrust from the scorched earth of nationalisation and Clause Four to the brave new world of science and technology.'[57]

At the annual Labour Conference on 2 October 1963 in Scarborough, Wilson spelt out before the country his reason for New Britain, and he did so with panache, even winning over the pundits, like the Welshman from Ammanford, Alan Watkins, and Bernard Ingham, who later became the righthand man of Margaret Thatcher, but who on that day represented the Guardian.[58] Ten days after Wilson's masterful address, Harold Macmillan was expected to address the faithful Tory activists at their conference in Blackpool.[59] He failed to turn up. Macmillan had been taken into hospital. He resigned and a few men in grey suits elected a Scottish laird in his stead: Alec Douglas-Home. The contrast between him and Wilson was glaring and gave added motivation to the activists of the Labour Party.

The general election of 1964 was held on 15 October and James Griffiths was optimistic. He sent a letter in Welsh to his young friend Gwilym Prys Davies at the end of September 1964. To him it was a 'battle… This battle is extremely important to the Labour Party. I honestly believe that we will win – and I hope by enough majority, but the battle will be hard.'[60] His prediction was spot on. By 1964 he had vast experience of campaigning in general elections.

He was invited to campaign in south east England and in the Midlands, and he sensed how hard the battle was. One of his friends, Patrick Gordon Walker, lost his seat to the Tories on a swing of 7.2% against Labour. The struggle in Smethwick had been racial, where the slogan was heard often: 'If you want a nigger for your neighbour, vote Labour.'[61]

In his home county of Carmarthenshire there was no change. The Carmarthenshire seat had Megan Lloyd George as the Labour candidate, and her charisma and oratory was a great help in returning her to parliament.[62] The barrister and Welsh patriot Alun Talfan Davies came second for the Liberals, and the third candidate, with 5,495 votes, was Gwynfor Evans who received fewer votes for Plaid Cymru than Jennie Eirian Davies had done seven years earlier in the by-election. The Conservative candidate, A. E. P. Beynon, gathered 4,996 votes.

In Llanelli the story was as usual, triumphant Griffiths had to campaign against four candidates, the only constituency in Wales where this happened. But even then, he had the largest majority of any MP within Wales, at some 26,246 votes. Five Labour MPs in south Wales had majorities over 23,000: Arthur Probert, Aberdare, Neil McBride, Swansea East, John Morris, Aberavon, W. E. Padley, Ogmore, and H. J. Finch in Bedwellty. Labour had tremendous support in Wales, with twenty-eight MPs, to just six for the Conservatives and two mid-Wales constituencies, Cardiganshire and Montgomeryshire, for the Liberals. In Llanelli Griffiths came to admire the Plaid Cymru candidate, a fellow Welsh Independent polymath, W. T. Pennar Davies, poet, theologian, and one of the most charming personalities of his day. For the first time the Communist Party had a candidate in the person of R. E. Hitchon, who lived in the town of Llanelli.[63] These are the statistics:

| | |
|---|---|
| James Griffiths (Labour) | 32,546 |
| P. A. Maybury (Conservative) | 6,300 |
| E. G. Lewis (Liberal) | 6,031 |
| W. T. Pennar Davies (Plaid Cymru) | 3,469 |
| R. E. Hitchon (Communist) | 1,061 |
| Majority | 26,246 |

After being returned as the government of Britain, it seemed plausible that the Wilson administration would consider adopting the vision of a Welsh Elected Assembly as well as a new Welsh Language Act. This would be an inspiration to the Welsh nation as it considered a framework for a new constitution. But there would be a great number of problems, inevitably, on the way to implementing James Griffiths's vision.[64]

**Notes and References**

1. *James Griffiths and his Times*, p. 137.

2.  E. H. Robertson, *George: A Biography of Viscount Tonypandy* (London, 1992), p. 158. 'It was fairly obvious that George Thomas neither liked nor approved of Hugh Gaitskell. This dislike, it seems was mutual.'

3.  John Harris and Herbert Bowden, the Chief Whip, came occassionly, see, Philip Williams, *Hugh Gaitskell* (London, 1979), pp. 537-8.

4.  *Manchester Guardian*, October 19, 1959, Editorial.

5.  *Daily Herald*, October 19, 1959.

6.  NLW, James Griffiths Papers. B3/22.

7.  Ibid., B3/45. Letter of Norman Thomas, New York, to James Griffiths dated 25 November 1959.

8.  Ibid. This was a letter dated 25 October 1960 from W. Nevill Hall and Frances Noel Baker pleading Griffiths to stand again for the post of Deputy Leader: Dear Jim, Like very many of our colleagues in the Parliamentary Party, we would far rather see you as Deputy Leader again than anyone else. Will you allow us to nominate you? Please do! Yours ever, W Nevill Hall, Frances Noel Baker.

9.  One of these was Michael Foot, candidate in the by-election, as successor to Bevan, in Ebbw Vale. He told eight million viewers of the BBC, in the Panorama programme, that he would like to see Gaitskell resign as leader. See, Geoffrey McDermot, *Leader Lost* (London, 1972), p. 186.

10. Tony Benn, Years of Hope, Diairies 1940-1962 (London, 1994), p 347.

11. Ibid.

12. Greg Rosen, *Old Labour to New: The Dreams That Inspired, The Battles That Divided* (London, 2005), p. 224.

13. Ibid., 225.

14. Ibid., 225.

15. Ibid., pp. 225-6.

16. Ibid., p. 228.

17. Brian Brivati, *Hugh Gaitskell* (London, 1997), p. 374.

18. John Grant, Blood Brothers (London, 1992), p. 19.

19. Stephen Haseler, *The Gaitskellites*, pp. 209-236.

20. Geoffrey McDermont, *Leader Lost*, p. 201.

21. NLW. James Griffiths Papers. B10/7. *Outline of James Griffiths talk on Nye*.

22. James Griffiths, *Pages from Memory*, pp. 137-8. See also *Hansard*, Volume 626 No 141 Col 702-711. 7 July 1960.

23. NLW. James Griffiths Papers. B10/22. Arthur Louire, Embassy of Israel, London to James Griffiths dated 11 July 1960. George Phippen, Labour College Residential Student Association, of Margate wrote to James Griffiths on 6 July 1960 stating: 'We watched both ITV and the BBC programmes on Nye but did not think anyone was able to express our feelings as you did.'

24. NLW. James Griffiths dated 6th July 1960. See also B10/27. Also undated letter Florence Williams, Kidsgrove, Stokeon-Trent to James Griffiths who was glad of the tribute Griffiths had paid to Bevan. 'Until tonight you were merely a name to me but tonight you became a very real sincere person. It was a wonderful tribute, so beautifully spoken'.

25. Ibid, Dr Gwenan Jones stood as Plaid Cymru candidate for the University of Wales constituency in the 1945 General Election.

26. NLW. James Griffiths Papers. BL10/21. Letter of T. J. Evans, 50 Myrddin Crescent, Carmarthen to James Griffiths dated 8 July 1960. See also James Griffiths, 'World figure still remained a true son of the Valley', *Western Mail*, 8 July 1960.

27. James Griffiths gave full support to Hugh Gaitskell. Philip Williams names him, 'other respected and influential figures supporting Gaitskell included Jim Griffiths whose career was almost over,

and Philip Noel-Baker whose life had been devoted to disarmament.' Philip Williams, *Hugh Gaitskell*, p. 627.

28. Ibid., p 682.

29. NLW. Deian Hopkin Papers. Letter of James Griffiths to Douglas Hughes dated 18 March 1961.

30. MP forecast "erosion of Welfare State", *The Star*, March 25, 1965. 'Earlier Mr Griffiths had joined 150 strong procession and protest march from Town Hall (organised by the Llanelly Trades Council)'.

31. NLW Deian Hopkin Papers, ibid.

32. Ibid. James Griffiths to Douglas Hughes dated 25 March 1961.

33. Ibid.

34. Ibid.

35. Ibid. At the meeting Griffiths said the Welfare State was not a luxury, 'but a necessity in the civilised community. When we regain power, we will restore it and improve it.' Cyril Parry, a miners' leader, presided at the meeting. 'MP forecasts "erosion of Welfare State".' *The Star*, March 25, 1961, p. 5.

36. NLW. Deian Hopkin papers, ibid.

37. Sharon Morgan, *Hanes Rhyw Gymraes* (Talybont, 2011), p. 96.

38. NLW. Deian Hopkin papers. Letter of James Griffiths to Douglas Hughes dated 25 March 1961.

39. The speakers at the rally included E. D. Jones (Librarian of the National Library of Wales), Dr Glyn O. Phillips, Mervyn Jones (London), Elaine Morgan, Reverend Gwilym Bowyer and Dick Beamish, Abercrave.

40. H. Carter and J. G. Thomas, The Referendum on the Sunday opening of licensed premises in Wales as a criterion of a Culture Region, Regional Studies, April 1969, Vol. 3, pp. 61-71.

41. Ibid., p. 64.

42. James Griffiths and George Thomas shared the same platform at Cardiganshire. See 'MP wants Drinks Secret Revealed', *Llanelli Star*, March 25, 1961, p 7.

43. A constituent of James Griffiths, A.M. James, Llanelli wrote a letter to the local weekly criticising him for identifying himself with the Fellowship of the Lord's Day in Wales, *Llanelli Star*, April 8, 1961, p.8.

44. 'MP calls Sunday opening demand "phoney"' *Llanelli Star*, April 29, 1961, p.7.

45. 'How Division Voted', *Llanelli Star*, 11 November 1961, p.1.

46. Letter of G. Gibby, Bigyn-Road, Llanelli, *Llanelli Star*, 11 November 1961, p 6. 47. Geoff Rich, 'Why do parsons push people around and tell them how to live', *South Wales Echo*, 27 March 1961, p. 6. According to Iorrie Thomas, the Drinking Club of Tynewydd, Treherbert in his constituency had 1,400 members in 1961; no Nonconformist chapel came near in membership to the popular club.

48. NLW. James Griffiths Paper. D1/3. Letter from Gwilym Prys Davies to James Griffiths dated 17 November 1961. He also mentions that he discussed the results with T. I. Ellis, Secretary of *Undeb Cymru Fydd*. He was also proud of the enlightened leadership given by James Griffiths in the 1961 referendum campaign.

49. NLW. James Griffiths Papers. *Member for Llanelli* D3/15.

50. Trefor Beasley was a miner and his wife Eileen, a teacher, who lived in Llangennech, within the Llanelli constituency. We have no record that James Griffiths took up their struggle as he did with Gwynfor S. Evans.

51. Saunders Lewis, *Tynged yr Iaith, with an introduction in Welsh by Ned Thomas* (Llandysul, 2012), pp. 7-79.

52. Gwilym Prys Davies, *Cynhaeaf Hanner Canrif*, p.48. Letter dated 30 July 1962 from Cledwyn Hughes to Gwilym Prys Davies.

53. *Cyngor Canol i Gymru: A Central Welsh Council* (Aberystwyth, 1963).

54. 'Aneurin: Reinventing Labour, The Voices of a New Generation', *Llafur*, Vol. 9 No. 1 (2004), pp. 71-84.

55. Ben Pimlott, *Wilson* (London, 1992), pp. 247-249.

56. James Callaghan, *Time and Chance* (London, 1987), p .150.

57. Philip Ziegler, *Wilson* (London, 1993), p .142.

58. Ben Pimlott, *Wilson*, p. 305.

59. 'Supermac: Harold Macmillan (1894-1986), in Nicholas Comfort, *Brewer's Politics: A Phrase and Fable Dictionary* (London, 1995), pp. 592-4. Wilson said of him: 'He had an expensive education – Eton and Suez', ibid, p. 593.

60. Gwilym Prys Davies, *Cynhaeaf Hanner Canrif*, p. 51.

61. Lord Wigg, *George Wigg* (London, 1972), p. 313 'I knew that Gordon Walker was not a strong candidate; he was a neighbour at Smethwick and I had seen at first-hand how he had handled the race issue, first by pretending it did not exist and when that line was played out by shying away from the problem.'

62. Rhys Evans, *Gwynfor: Rhag Pob Brad*, p. 250.

63. Bob Hitchon was an engineering worker in the motor industry. See NLW Bert Pearce Papers/Welsh Communist Papers WD5/2.

64. Ned Thomas has argued that Wales in 2012 had achieved the level of self-government that Saunders Lewis hoped for in 1962. The same could be said of James Griffiths. See Saunders Lewis, *Tynged yr Iaith*, p 18.

Jim addressing the National Eisteddfod of Wales in Llanelli, August 1962

**17**

## The First Secretary of State for Wales

To the Jewish people, Moses is a hero because his leadership of the exiles in Egypt brought them from bondage to the freedom of the land of Canaan. The Welsh never had a Moses in the twentieth century, but of all the Welsh leaders, James Griffiths is the politician who came closest, for he is largely responsible for setting the scene for what led, ultimately, to the establishing of the Welsh Assembly in 1999.[1] After a century of discussing the possibility of a Secretary of State of Wales, the difficult years of two world wars and the depression, the people of Wales could thank the Labour Party for the new chapter that was beginning. In 1964 the Secretary of State for Wales was to have a seat in the Cabinet.[2]

The Welsh Office had been established to a large extent on the model of the Scottish Office, which had been in existence since 1885. From the beginning, full responsibility had been given for local government, housing and planning, roads, forestry, economic planning, clearing land which had been polluted by industry, and later for tourism and health, as well as responsibility for agriculture jointly with the Minister of Agriculture. After giving the full list, one realises that the responsibility of the Welsh Office was significantly limited.[3] It did not correspond with the responsibilities noted in the policy document Signposts to the New Wales, which had been published by the Labour Party in 1962. We know that the new Secretary of State was concerned that the responsibility for the Welsh Board of Health, a body which had been in existence since 1919, had been completely under the control of the Department of Health in Whitehall, unlike the Scottish Board of Health.

But one has to give a very special tribute to Harold Wilson. He was an extremely clever politician, as I realised when I enjoyed fellowship with him in Bangor in 1974. Wilson could have chosen another Labour politician for the Secretary of State post.[4] The name that was on the lips of people of every political party was Cledwyn Hughes and a large number of leaders in Welsh life expressed their disappointment to him in private letters that he had not been chosen. The Labour activist in Bangor, Frank Price Jones, (who was at all times quite critical of James Griffiths) once named Cledwyn Hughes as the best choice for the new venture. Harold Wilson could not have given the post to Ness Edwards as he was lukewarm and occasionally hostile to devolution. Sometimes he saw the need but he could not acknowledge that Wales was a nation, and for that reason he struggled on the issue. Wilson realised two things. First, that he wanted to honour Griffiths for his contribution to the miners of south Wales, to the Labour Party, and to the public life of Wales.

In the period 1957-64, they would often meet and share the same hopes with regard to the Labour Party. Though it was for George Brown, because of his strong links to the unions, that Griffiths voted in the election of a Labour leader, Wilson did not show any resentment, but rather gave Griffiths a beautiful greeting the day after the general election at 10 Downing

Street, making him 'Charter Secretary of State for Wales'.[5] This was a big surprise to Griffiths, as Wilson had not promised him any ministerial responsibility before the election.[6]

Second, Wilson realised that Griffiths was an elderly statesman; indeed he was seventy-four years of age. But he was quite certain that nobody was better suited to the post than the 'old miner from Betws'. The Secretaryship of State for Wales would mean a great deal of travelling within Wales, but he had a comfortable car for his official duties. One has to remember that the Welsh Office had very few friends within the government. In the words of Cledwyn Hughes:

> *The other Departments of the Government, like Agriculture and Education, were not willing to lose control of some of their responsibilities, they were extremely stubborn. One could understand: who wants to lose his own empire when he is a Minister in the Department. Very few in any country.*[7]

Another factor in favour of Griffiths was that he was one of the few Labour politicians who had the experience of being a successful minister in a Government as well as having served in the Cabinet. The first cabinet meeting was held on 19 October 1964. Besides Wilson, only two others of the twenty-three had been members of a Labour Cabinet, namely Patrick Gordon Walker and James Griffiths.[8] Both had been members of the Cabinet from February 1950 to October 1951. Wilson spelt out parameters in the first meeting, largely along the same lines as Attlee between 1945 and 1951. Firstly he emphasised the importance of being punctual. Secondly that the briefing papers should be sent in plenty of time. Thirdly a minister could smoke if he wanted around the cabinet table.[9] Winston Churchill allowed it in the war cabinet, but Attlee did not agree with such informality. But as Wilson had a pipe in his mouth as often as he could, even on television, in 1964 the ministers were allowed to smoke. I saw Griffiths smoking occasionally, but today smoking in a committee or Cabinet would be disallowed.

Besides Griffiths, seven other politicians from Wales were invited to be ministers. Neither in 1945 or 1950 had Attlee been supportive of politicians who represented Welsh constituencies. James Callaghan was made the Chancellor of the Exchequer, Sir Frank Soskice would be in charge of the Home Office, Cledwyn Hughes became a minister in the Commonwealth Office, Walter Padley was a minister in the Foreign Office, George Thomas served in the Home Office, John Morris became Parliamentary Secretary in the Ministry of Power, and Eirene White was given the honour of being the first woman from Wales to be a junior minister in the Commonwealth Office.[10]

There was a need for a team of ministers in the Welsh Office to support the Secretary of State. Two were appointed, which was generous of the prime minister, as the task was not that exacting. Goronwy Roberts was appointed minister and Harold Finch appointed a junior minister. Griffiths was extremely contended with his two colleagues. He had known Goronwy Roberts from his days as a lecturer at the University College of Wales, Swansea, and he was regarded as a man of utmost integrity, idealistic in his values, able to reason cleverly in debates in the House of Commons. He was also a cultured Welsh speaker, who could write poetry in the strict metre, creating englynion, and he had been a distinguished columnist for years in the Welsh language weekly *Y Cymro* (The Welshman) on current affairs.

Since the 1920s Griffiths had regarded himself as a sincere friend to Harold Finch. It was he who was responsible, as a miners' leader, for inviting Finch from Pontllanffraith (Blackwood) to the Miners' Office in Cardiff to work on the Compensation Act for Workers. Finch not only became an expert in  the world of compensation within the coalfield, but in every industry, and he also had an extensive knowledge in the world of social security. According to one source, he was one of the most successful ministers in the 1964-66 Government.[11] Tudor Watkins was invited to an unpaid post as Private Parliamentary Secretary to the three Ministers of the Welsh Office. Every region of Wales was represented by the four of them: north Wales by Goronwy Roberts, mid-Wales by Tudor Watkins, south-east Wales by Harold Finch, and south-west Wales by James Griffiths.

There were a number of cabinet ministers who believed that there was no need to transfer responsibilities to the new department. Its main function was to be a focus for Wales within government. Griffiths agreed and when he received a letter from someone who had been a Permanent Secretary to him in the 1950-51 government in the Department of the Colonies, Sir Thomas W. Phillips, he knew he was certainly on the right course. This is a portion of Sir Thomas Phillips's letter:

> *You must be, of course, a watchdog for Wales as a whole, but in order to do this effectively you ought to have a department of your own with a competent civil servant staff. This will help to give you the professional assistance you will need and avoid the risk of being regarded as a tiresome busybody who is always interfering with other people's business  without having any business of your own.*[12]

This letter inspired the Secretary of State for Wales to prepare an important letter to the Prime Minister on the need to transfer responsibilities to the Welsh Office, in accordance with the promise made in the manifesto for "New Wales". The Prime Minister as well as the minister knew that the success of the department and the ministry depended to a large extent on the civil servants. Griffiths was extremely fortunate in having Goronwy Hopkin Daniel as a Permanent Under-Secretary in the Welsh Office.[13] They had much in common. Goronwy Daniel, the son of a colliery manager, came from Ystradgynlais, the town where Griffiths had lived for years. Both were from a mining background in the anthracite coalfield, both were nurtured in the Welsh Independent denomination and both were known as people who appreciated sermons. The Reverend Derwyn Morris Jones has mentioned the attentive listening of Griffiths on his visits to Christian Temple chapel in Ammanford, and I remember how Sir Goronwy Daniel attentively listened to sermons in two services that I conducted in the Welsh Independent chapel in Minny Street, Cardiff. The Welsh language meant a great deal to both and they spoke it as often as they could.

Griffiths sent a letter to Douglas Hughes on 20 October 1964 to thank him 'very warmly for his message' on Griffiths's appointment as Minister of State for Wales.[14] He explained to his agent that he was laying the foundation of the department, and that entailed a great deal of planning and implementation. He described the task as a 'tough job'. It came to his attention that a number of south Wales Labour MPs had written to the Prime Minister requesting him not to transfer administrative powers to the Welsh Office and he realised that a handful of Welsh MPs harboured negative views. But he was annoyed that they had written to the Prime Minister behind his back, without sending a copy of their letter to him as courtesy demanded. He called on Ifor Davies, the Welsh whip, to ask him to call a meeting of the Welsh Labour MPs.[15] He met them and told them in no uncertain terms that they had acted in an unbrotherly manner. Griffiths knew of the anti-devolutionist views of a number of MPs from Monmouthshire and east Glamorganshire. There were a few exceptions such as S. O. Davies, Michael Foot and Llywelyn Williams. He acknowledged to himself later: 'There were fundamental clashes of views as to what Labour's attitude should be to Welsh demands and aspirations.'[16]

The minister emphasised to his fellow labour MPs that they had to understand that the battle in favour of Welsh devolution had been fought when Aneurin Bevan was alive, and that the promise to appoint a Minister of State for Wales had been clearly stated in the Labour Party manifesto for Wales in the general election of 1959 in the booklet Forward with Labour.[17] There was no debate or disagreement voiced in the meeting, and the information on the gathering was sent immediately to the Prime Minister. The minister left the meeting content that he had settled one problem for the time being at least.

But there was another problem, to which we have referred already, the reluctance of the departments to transfer responsibilities which had been agreed upon by the Welsh Office. There was a great reluctance among the civil servants to agree with the original intention. The first to agree was the minister in charge of Transport, Tony Fraser, a proud Scotsman. It is possible that agreement was given as Fraser and Griffiths were great friends, both from a mining background. Another fact to take into consideration is that John Morris was a Parliamentary Under-Secretary in that Department and he also used his influence with Fraser. Whatever the reason, Tony Fraser told his Permanent Secretary to transfer responsibilities for transport in Wales to the new Welsh Office. Griffiths then wrote a letter to the Prime Minister stating that he could not stay in the post of Secretary of State for Wales if the responsibilities that had been promised were not transferred to the Welsh Office.[18] He showed the letter to Goronwy Roberts as well as Harold Finch, and both were in full agreement with him. Within a week he was invited to the Prime Minister's room in Westminster. Wilson showed him a copy of a statement that he intended to read in the Commons defining the powers of the Welsh Office.[19] The minister left the Prime Minister quite content that he had been able to achieve his aim, which would strengthen the Welsh Office.

James Griffiths gave himself three tasks as minister. The first was to build a 'new town' in midWales. Second, to support further work at the feasability of setting up an elected Welsh Council. And third, to strengthen the legal status of the Welsh language. The 'new town' in mid Wales was to be named Treowen as an acknowledgement of the incredible influence of Robert Owen (1771-1859), the pioneer of British socialism and a progressive Welshman born in Newtown.[20.]Treowen with its centre in Caersws and stretching to Newtown on the northern side and from Caersws to Llanidloes on the south side was a special concern to the minister.[21] He saw the proposed new town in the same light as the only town built in Wales under the New Towns Act in 1946, Cwmbran in Monmouthshire.

Griffiths was enthusiastic about building a new town in Montgomeryshire. He appointed a team of experts to prepare a detailed plan under the watchful eye of Tim McKitterick who he knew through the Fabian Society.[22] A detailed plan was produced which, it was hoped would help answer some of the problems of mid-Wales. Griffiths knew that Goronwy Roberts saw the possibility of being able to attract Welsh speakers who had migrated to Birmingham, Coventry, Rugby and Wolverhampton to return to the new town. They estimated that between 60,000 and 100,000 Welsh people (Anglo-Welsh and Welsh speakers) had migrated for work to the West Midlands. The Welsh language chapels of Birmingham, Coventry and Wolverhampton testified to their presence. But one must admit that the majority of Welsh people did not accept that Goronwy Roberts's wishes would be fulfilled this time.

It is also true that to speak of a Welsh town of 70,000 inhabitants was not very practical when one remembers that the population of Cwmbran was only 35,000, fifteen years after its inception. If Griffiths had been content with a town of twenty thousand inhabitants, it is possible that he would have been given a hearing by his fellow Welshmen. But the supporters of the Welsh language were not at all supportive of his policy, for they believed that such a town would weaken the Welsh life of Montgomeryshire and north Ceredigion as well as south Merionethshire. Griffiths explained himself clearly in a comprehensive letter to Iorwerth C. Peate, a native of Llanbryn-mair, and a poet and folk culture historian. [23] In his Welsh letter, Griffiths noted the problems of mid-Wales in particular, as communities there were slowly dying. The young people were drifting mainly to England, agriculture was changing due to mechanisation, and there was a need for a new centre to keep the population from migrating. The chief reason for the existence of a new town was to save the Welsh language. He reasoned in his letter to Peate, that 'we cannot keep our people without providing work and a living as well as an opportunity to have a home for their family'.[24]   In his opinion, the Labour Party had done its best to prepare a plan which would be sustainable. He asked Peate a question: 'What will the situation be in the year 2000 if we do not have a courageous plan to stop the depopulation and undermine the strength of society in Mid-Wales?'[25] His promise to Peate was this: 'We will do our utmost to preserve the language and Welsh traditions but the parlances of depopulation will destroy everything.'[26]

It is possible that his prophetic vision was true, but he did not have other politicians similar to himself who were willing to support the vision. There is no doubt that his failure to establish Treowen was a bitter personal blow to him. He admits it: 'One of my disappointments was that I failed to build my "dream" New Town in mid-Wales.'[27] He adds: 'My successor (Cledwyn Hughes) had to be content with a plan to double in a decade or so the population of Newtown. I am glad to hear of the progress of the scheme and even yet hope it may spread to include the boundary of the original plan.'[28]

The truth is that Cledwyn Hughes, as he admitted, was opposed to the plan to establish Treowen. He said: 'In a debate in the Grand Committee I made a statement that I did not accept the plan of a large town from Newtown to Caersws – "linear new town"– as I believed it would have been a spearhead to the heart of Wales. I decided on a plan to strengthen Newtown and other towns in the area and on this was established the present Development Corporation.'[29]

A great deal of useful work was achieved by the Mid-Wales Corporation to strengthen Newtown. Grifiths's second task was to support a study to see if Wales could consider an elected Welsh Council. The desire for an elected Council to discuss the problems of Wales had been discussed by the movement called Cymru Fydd, established by Tom Ellis, David Lloyd George and other progressive Liberals at the end of the Victorian era. Others had expressed a similar need, in particular the Liberal cum-socialist-nationalist, Edward Thomas John. In 1914 when he was Liberal MP for East Denbighshire he presented a measure on the Government of Wales to Parliament. Though he had strong convictions, he was without much support among his fellow Welsh MPs. Griffiths established a working party within the Welsh Office, chaired by Goronwy Daniel, to research the reorganisation within local government.[30] The report was presented to Griffiths on 16 January 1966 under the title Working Party on Local Government Reorganisation in Wales, Interim Memorandum. The report was not published, but if favoured the establishment of a Welsh elected Council described in the document as the Greater.

The third task Griffiths set himself was to strengthen the legal status of the Welsh language; this was a priority for the Secretary of State.[31] The key role played by the dramatist Saunders Lewis in the debate on the Welsh language is well known, but we must place Griffiths on the same pedestal. Before Saunders Lewis delivered on BBC Wales his lecture on 13 February 1962 on Tynged yr Iaith (The Fate of the Language), Griffiths had spoken the same message to the Welsh broadcaster Aneirin Talfan Davies in a television series known as Dylanwadau (Influences). It was recorded on 11 February 1962 but it was not released until 21 March.[32] Aneirin Talfan Davies asked the question: what is the chief problem of Wales today? The reply 'There is the problem of finding work, the problem of sustenance is important.'
It was quite a surprise to many who saw the programme to hear him say: '*Prif broblem Cymru heddiw yw achub yr iaith – rwy'n credu mai dyna'r brif broblem dros y deg, ugain mlynedd nesaf.*' ['The chief problem in Wales today is to save the language – I believe that this is the main problem for the next ten, twenty years']. I agree with what Gwilym Prys Davies wrote about the answer:

> *It was a revolutionary answer by one of the leaders of the Labour Party. I believe that one can claim that not one Labour leader had said anything like this ever before… Griffiths spoke for himself, but his answer indicates the change of mood and direction that he wanted to see as far as Labour was concerned from 1962 onwards.*[33]

Griffiths was a product of one of the heartlands of the Welsh language: the Amman Valley. It can be said that the valleys of Gwendraeth and Amman in Carmarthenshire was as much a heartland of the language as Penllyn in Merionethshire and Pen Lleyn and Dwyfor in Caernarfonshire. I believe that the decline in the number of Welsh speakers in his constituency was to a large extent due to the reluctance and inability of parents to teach their children the Welsh language at home. I would not be surprised if he realised this himself for he was one of thousands upon thousands of Welsh parents who failed to transfer the language to his own children, and perhaps he felt some guilt himself.

If he did, he did a good deed to the Welsh nation. In November 1963 the Welsh Council produced a report, under the chairmanship of the philosopher R. I. Aaron, setting out recommendations to the government on ways to strengthen the legal status of the Welsh language.[34] Earlier in the year, on 30 July 1963, the Minister for Welsh Affairs, Sir Keith Joseph, had announced in Parliament the setting up of a committee under the chairmanship of Sir David Hughes-Parry, to explain the legal status of the Welsh language. The other two members of the committee were the Swansea-based Professor Glanmor Williams, a staunch supporter of the Labour Party, and one of the most accomplished Welsh historians of post-war Wales, and K. Williams Jones, the clerk of Merionethshire County Council and highly regarded in local government circles. On 25 October 1965 Hughes-Parry presented the report, The Legal Status of the Welsh Language, to Sir Keith Joseph. The report recommended a new Act to acknowledge the principle of equal status for Welsh and English and to delete ten Acts from the statute book. The report supported 'equal status': that is, any action or correspondence in Welsh within Wales had the same legal power as if it was in English. This version was included, though greatly weakened, in the Welsh Language Act of 1967.

Hughes-Parry's report was encouraging to all Welsh speakers within every political party, and Griffiths promised to act as soon as he could.[35] The Welsh language to him should flourish rather than being in a state of constant decline.[36] One politician who found himself in no man's land was the President of the Welsh nationalist Gwynfor Evans. His biographer states that he could not praise too highly the younger zealots of a disrespectful generation, but he also knew that he could not praise any Labour government.[37]

There is a tendency for Welsh historians to forget the unique contribution Griffiths's in influencing the Welsh Labour MPs to support the Hughes-Parry recommendations and prepare the way for the Welsh Language Act. His voice and personality had a great deal of influence among Welsh Labour MPs. Welsh historians were delightfully surprised to realise this as we read the classic volume of Gwilym Prys Davies, *Cynhaeaf Hanner Canrif: Gwleidyddiaeth Gymreig 1945-2005* [The Harvest of Half a Century: Welsh Politics 1945-2005] (Llandysul, 2008) and be reminded of how how massive a figure he was. Davies quotes his friend Sir Goronwy Daniel:

> *Mr James Griffiths and Mr Goronwy Roberts devoted much time to the language problem. But they found it hard to get the support of their colleagues for the Hughes-Parry proposals.*[38]

One of these colleagues was the Labour MP for Pontypool, Leo Abse, who had very little interest in the language and culture of Wales. Abse ferociously attacked the recommendation that prominent civil servants should have a grasp of the language. He played skilfully what is called the 'Gwent card'. Abse argued that the important administrative posts would go to people in north and west Wales, not because they were capable of doing the work, but because they were Welsh speakers. He secured support from Monmouthshire County Council as well as the town council of Newport. To them, there was no need at all to change the legal situation. Goronwy Daniel also admitted that Griffiths, as well as Goronwy Roberts, found it difficult to persuade the Lord Chancellor's Department. He states:

> *...the Department was reluctant to see the costs of court proceedings increased and had limited understanding of the depth of support for the language among Welsh speakers and writers who had devoted themselves to the materially unrewarding task of sustaining it.*[39]

Griffiths persisted in reconciling the opponents, and in November 1965 he announced to Parliament that the government was accepting the principles of equal validity. A minister of the Crown is not without duties and responsibilities to his own political party in his constituency. The Interdenominational Welsh Language Committee in Carmarthenshire was lobbying him, as well as his fellow Labour MP, Megan Lloyd George, who was keen to discuss the place of the Welsh language in the schools of the county. On 13 June 1964 a meeting was held in the Welsh League of Youth premises in Llanelli between Griffiths and leaders of the Interdenominational Committee, especially important as the agenda included an exposition by the Chairman of the Committee, Dr Mathew Williams, ex-Inspector of Schools and a brother to the Welsh scholar, Griffith John Williams. Another meeting was arranged. This was chaired by the Labour Councillor Glanville Williams and another splendid address was given by Dr Mathew Williams. James Griffiths informed them that he would follow up the matter further, as he believed that there was an opportunity of having Welsh medium schools in the Amman Valley.

In December 1964 Griffiths received from his agent a report on the future of the headquarters of the Labour Party in the town of Llanelli, namely Garth Hywel, which had been owned by Labour since the 1930s. Griffiths replied on 8 December 1964 that he was in favour of adapting it as a social centre, but he warned Douglas Hughes that he did not support the idea of turning it into a social club with a licence to sell alcohol.[40] He reminded his agent that such a move would annoy the Temperance movement as well as his nonconformist friends in the Free Church Council of Llanelli. However, he believed that a social centre without a licence to sell alcohol was a splendid idea, meeting the needs of every age group in the town.[41]

Griffiths knew that Douglas Hughes did not support keeping Garth Hywel as an asset of the Labour Party, and he also knew that the financial position was difficult especially since the party had to meet the cost of employing a full-time political agent. Griffiths realised that there were three options before them; firstly to try and persuade the trade union movement to adopt Garth Hywel, or part of it, as an office or a meeting place for its committees and meetings; secondly, to organise a group from the town who supported the Labour Party to consider the future of the building; and thirdly, to consider having a social centre which would be open daily. He believed sincerely that the town of Llanelli had enough drinking clubs to meet its demands, and that there was no need to add to the provision. Garth Hywel was sited at 4 Queen Victoria Road in the heart of Llanelli. In the end, after eighteen months of discussion with Griffiths, the Labour Party sold it to the Amalgamated Engineering Union (AEU) for

£3,000. The estate agents reckoned the building was worth £4,000 to £4,500, but on the open market on 1 February 1966 Garth Hywel was sold for at least £1,000 less that it should have fetched.

A number of other difficult issues arose in 1965 within Griffiths's constituency; matters to do with the libraries, education, and individuals. When one reads the correspondence between him and his agent, the historian is well aware of the wisdom shown time and time again by the Secretary of State. He was afraid that some of the issues which involved local Labour councillors could become irritating, but he made every effort to ensure that everything would work well so as to keep the good name of his party. On the issue of the libraries, he arranged to see Turner Evans, Chief Librarian of the County, for his guidance. He kept in close contact with Selwyn Samuel, Clerk to the Llanelli Town Council, and he called on the local mayor whenever he came to town.

The strength and vitality of the local Labour Party branches was a special concern to the seasoned campaigner and he had a respect for the faithful supporters who came together to listen to councillors' reports on local issues and to prepare for town, county and constituency elections. Two of the strongest branches were situated in Llanelli and Cwmaman. At least 76 members belonged to Branch Ward 1 in Llanelli; 38 of the members were men and the rest women. Among the membership, one sees the name of the Reverend W. Esger James, a minister with the Welsh Independent denomination in Llanelli. He was a loyal supporter of James Griffiths, and so were the Reverend J. S. Williams, the Welsh Baptist minister in Tumble, and Reverend Oswald R. Davies, minister of the Welsh Independent chapel in Garnant. Oswald R. Davies was one of 65 who belonged to the Labour Party branch of Cwmaman, 41 men and 24 women. In the Llangennech Labour Party the number was small; only fifteen members belonged to the branch.

In 1965 a great change took place in the leadership of the Labour Party in Wales when Cliff Prothero decided to retire as the General Secretary. He was a strong character, a determined personality who had been hugely influential on Labour Party strategy for eighteen years. He had clashed and disagreed with Griffiths and Goronwy Roberts on the issue of devolution. He defined his standpoint on devolution clearly and briefly in his autobiography:

> *I am a loyal member of the Labour Party and more convinced than ever that the setting up of an Elected Assembly would be detrimental to the Labour Party in Wales.*[42]

Some Labourites reckoned that the Deputy Secretary of the Labour Party in Wales, Hubert Morgan, a Welsh speaker, would be appointed to follow Prothero. But Griffiths wanted J. Emrys Jones, a native of Penrhiwceibr in the Cynon Valley, and a non-Welsh speaker to fill the post.[43] In 1965 Jones served as the Labour Party organiser in Birmingham, and Griffiths gave him every support in his application for the key post. He was chosen, to the disappointment and possibly bitterness of Hubert Morgan. J. Emrys Jones performed much better than any had expected by being in the forefront on Welsh issues and a staunch devolutionist, which did not please George Thomas or Leo Abse.

The Labour Party was ably led to a positive position. Emrys Jones persuaded the Welsh Labour Council and its annual Conference to support the call to consider setting up, as Griffiths hoped for, a Welsh Elected Council. Panels were established to prepare policies which would give respect and status to the Welsh language in the field of education as well as the mass media, in particular television.Jones approached his tasks quietly and without fuss, arguing with logic and winning most political battles.[44] Griffiths at last had a party official who was on the same wavelength as he was. Most of the leaders of public opinion in Wales saw Griffiths's leadership of in the Welsh Office as positive. Suddenly on the Thursday of the National Eisteddfod of Wales in Newtown in 1965, the news broke that one of the outstanding politicians of Plaid Cymru, Elystan Morgan, who had represented the nationalists four times in Parliamentary elections, was joining the Labour Party.[45] He was joining a party which had a number of politicians with similar values and convictions as himself, in particular Cledwyn Hughes, Goronwy Roberts, John Morris, his school friend from Ardwyn Grammar School in Aberystwyth, John Morris and James Griffiths. Griffiths was naturally delighted to welcome Elystan Morgan to the Labour ranks as a possible future minister.

At the Labour Party Conference in October 1965, Griffiths was invited by the Prime Minister for a private conversation in his room at the hotel where all the members of the NEC stayed. Wilson raised the inevitable question of how Griffiths saw his position and for how long he would like to stay in the important ministerial post he held.[46] Wilson added that this conference would be the last before the general election.[47] Griffiths thanked the Prime Minster for his support and trust in him, pledging that he would continue in post until the general election in 1966.

Griffiths felt that in the short period he had served in the Welsh Office he had laid a sure foundation for the future. But he still fretted that all the responsibilities still had not been transferred to the jurisdiction of the Welsh Office. Before he left the Welsh Office, on 4 April 1966, he prepared a memorandum to the Prime Minister calling for the immediate transfer of the responsibilities for health, education, and agriculture from Whitehall to Cardiff.[48] The question arises: could Griffiths have been more ambitious as Secretary of State for Wales? And it seems that the answer must be yes, he could have been, but one has to remember that he had to cope with the stubbornness of the Civil Service, the ambition of other ministers, the small majority held by the Wilson administration, and his own health at the age of seventy-four when he started in the Welsh Office. When one takes all these considerations into account, we must admit that he succeeded brilliantly in laying the foundation for successive ministers.

He received hundreds of letters thanking him for his wise stewardship, his Welsh orientated programme and his visits to Cardiff, mid-Wales, north Wales and to his own constituency. In his meeting with J. Emrys Jones on 23 February 1966 it was decided, as this was the first general election after the establishment of the Welsh Office, that he should travel to every one of the thirty-six constituencies in Wales. This would allow him only three days to spend in his own constituency. He struggled with the decision to stand for another general election. But he was persuaded by his own Executive and the Central Office in Cardiff, so he could help ensure that the Labour Party gained a better result than it did in 1964.This was asking a great deal from a politician of his age, remembering that Douglas Hughes, his agent since

1935, had retired at the end of 1965, and he would not be at hand for the forthcoming general election. They had to have a new secretary and agent, and the combination of skills needed to fill Hughes's shoes was found in the person of Councillor W. J. Davies. There was tension among Labour councillors in Llanelli, between some who represented the party in the town council and those who served on the county council. Education, and particularly comprehensive schools, had been a hot topic dividing the councillors into two camps. Griffiths made a personal appeal in a letter to the councillors, the branches, the trade union officials, and the ordinary Labour Party members, in view of the fact that he would be absent for most of the time before polling day. He received an encouraging letter from Dai Charles, one of the important trade unionists in Llanelli, saying that he would personally ensure that all the trade unions would be heavily involved in canvassing. This was a promise he could depend upon; after all union members were the backbone of the Labour Party at election times.[49] Same 617 miners were employed in Cynheidre colliery in the Gwendraeth Valley. To have 150 of them to work for the Labour candidate would make a world of difference, as Dai Charles realised. Even with the comforting words of Dai Charles, a Labour councillor in Llanelli, J. G. Hill wrote a more abrasive letter suggesting that some of the councillors would lose their seats in the local elections, and he then added: 'I do not think there was any implied threat to you personally. At least that is my view.'[50]

Griffiths enjoyed his campaigning throughout Wales and he received a warm welcome in every constituency. In every political meeting Griffiths mentioned the need to extend the responsibilities of the Welsh Office to include agriculture and health in particular. It was a joy for him on the threshold of the election to read the statement of Margaret Herbison, the Minister for Pensions and National Insurance, announcing that National Assistance was to be abolished and replaced by new allowance.

Harold Wilson explained the importance of the minister's announcement to the election campaign:

> *When the Election came I found the abolition of the two-book system to be one of the most popular of all of our reforms. Hundreds of thousands of people so hated the indignity of 'going on assistance' that wrongly, but understandably, they failed to claim help to which they were entitled. One result of the reform was that 450,000 of the least well-off members of the community now claimed their rights.*[51]

The campaign began on 11 March 1966, Wilson' fiftieth birthdays Griffiths was seventy-six. At the count in Llanelli on the last day of March 1966, Griffiths received a huge approval from the electors:

| James Griffiths (Labour) | 33,674 |
| J. C. Peel (Conservative) | 7,143 |
| Dr Pennar Davies (Plaid Cymru) | 5,132 |
| R. E. Hitchon (Communist) | 1,211 |

Griffiths won a majority of 26,531, slightly less than Walter Padley received in Ogmore with 26,673, the largest majority in Wales.[52] The other two ministers in the Welsh Office also did well. Goronwy Roberts had a majority of 10,678 over the Conservative Party while Harold Finch had a majority of 24,984 over the Conservative candidate.[53] The number of electors in Wales who supported the Labour Party went up from 58% in 1964 to 61% in the 1966 general election, the largest percentage in the history of the Labour Party.

Labour won 32 out of the 36 Welsh constituencies, and in 27 of them had large majorities. Ednyfed Hudson Davies, son of a minister of religion and who had a high regard for Griffiths, won Conwy for Labour by beating Peter Thomas, the Tory MP, by a majority of 581. D. Elystan Morgan gained Cardiganshire from Roderick Bowen, the long-standing Liberal MP, by a majority of 523 votes. The third young man was Ted Rowlands who won Cardiff North with a majority of 672. The majority of Donald Anderson in Monmouth was 2,965 over one of the heavyweights of the Conservative Party, Peter Thorneycroft.

Two were extremely important constituency results in Griffiths's view, namely Cardiganshire and Carmarthenshire. In Cardiganshire, Elystan Morgan had gained the upper hand for Labour in a seat where the Liberals had been in power for over a century. He was the great favourite of the President of Plaid Cymru, Gwynfor Evans, for years. Evans increased the Plaid Cymru vote in Carmarthenshire from 5,045 in 1964 to 7,416 in 1966, a sizeable increase in a constituency where the Labour candidate was not present, even on the morning of the declaration of the result in Carmarthen. The candidate, Megan Lloyd George, because of ill-health, failed to leave her home in Cricieth.[54] Her nephew, Benjy Carey-Evans represented her in the campaign. He depended a great deal, because of his inability to address people in Welsh, on Gwilym Prys Davies, who came to assist at James Griffiths's request.[55] Megan Lloyd George's majority increased substantially, which suggested that the political tide was flowing strongly in favour of Wilson and Griffiths. In April 1966 Sir Ifan ab Owen Edwards, founder of the Welsh League of Youth, wrote a congratulatory letter to Cledwyn Hughes:

> *Among the other lessons that the latest General Election has taught us, we were taught that the Nationalist Party under present circumstances can never succeed as a political party, and that the Labour Party now is the national party of Wales.*[56]

To Griffiths the result of the general election of 1966, after the establishment of the Welsh Office and his term as Secretary of State for Wales, was a 'magnificent vote of confidence'.[57] On his way back to London after the result in Llanelli, he spoke with his wife Winnie about his decision to relinquish his responsibilities as Secretary of State for Wales, and after another term, he would retire as an MP in a constituency which had been ultra-loyal to him. He had now achieved his political ambition of being the Welsh Secretary. [58]   The generalisation of the historian, Ioan Matthews, has a great deal of truth:

> *Under Griffiths' leadership, the Labour Party in Wales came close to becoming a genuine national movement that would be accepted as such in Welsh-speaking rural areas.'* [59]

## Notes and References

1. Emyr Price, *Lloyd George Y Cenedlaetholwr Cymreig: Arwr ynteu Bradwr?* (Llandysul, 1997), pp. 75-93.

2. On 17 November 1964 Harold Wilson told the House of Commons: 'the interests of Wales are now represented in the Cabinet by my Right Hon. Friend the Secretary of State. My Right Hon. Friend will have a Welsh Office in Cardiff, and a small Ministerial Office in London', *Hansard*, DCCII, 17 November 1964, pps 623-4.

3. 'They had established the nucleus of a Welsh Department at Cardiff with just a few civil servants forming a secretariat. I could see that Dame Evelyn was afraid that I would steal her Welsh corner', James Griffiths, in 'Welsh Politics in my lifetime', *James Griffiths and his Times* (Ferndale, 1979), p 45.

4. Wilson told Griffiths that '… he had been canvassed for the post by MPs younger than myself, some of whom had been very pressing. However, he said "I told them what I now say to you, our Party and Wales have made up their minds that you are the one person for this post, and that is my view." Ibid, p. 44.

5. Griffiths admits that he had not always agreed with Wilson 'We had not always seen eye to eye.' Ibid.

6. Anthony Shrimsley, *The First Hundred Days of Harold Wilson* (London, 1965), p. 17: 'Jim Griffiths, for one, took office on the clear understanding that he would give way gracefully when the time came.'

7. *Yr Arglwydd Cledwyn, Cymry yn y Ddau Dŷ* (Aberystwyth, 1990), p. 9.

8. Harold Wilson, *The Labour Government 1964-1970: A Personal Record* (London, 1971), p 17.

9. Ibid.

10. Ibid., pp. 12-15.

11. A conversation with Gwyn Jenkins on 20 July 2011. This was the opinion of the civil servant John Clements.

12. James Griffiths, *Pages from Memory*, p 166.

13. James Griffiths mentions Goronwy Daniel's considerable talent, ibid., p168. David Rosser, 'New £5,800 post in the Welsh Office', *Western Mail*, 25 November 1964, p.1.

14. NLW. Papers of Deian Hopkin, *Douglas Hughes Collection*, No. 31-128. Letter from James Griffiths to Douglas Hughes, dated 20 October 1964.

15. *James Griffiths and his Times*, p.46.

16. Ibid.

17. James Griffiths, *Pages from Memory*, p.164.

18. 'His prestige within the Labour Party allowed him to do this when others may well have failed, and it has been claimed that Griffiths in contrast to his usual caution threatened resignation if he did not get his way.' See Ioan Matthews, 'Turning Labour Around', *Planet* 142 August/September 2000, p. 86.

19. The statement is on *Pages from Memory*, p 167. Raymond Gower was concerned: 'But there would appear to be a much stronger case for putting education under Mr Griffiths than giving him responsibility for housing – if only because of the importance of the Welsh language'. See Raymond Gower, 'The Political Scene', *Western Mail*, 27 November 1964, p.7.

20. James Griffiths was not the only Welsh politician concerned with a new town in mid Wales, See Emlyn Hooson and Geraint Jenkins, *The Heartland: A Plan for Wales* (London, 1965), pp. 1-22. The two Liberals argued for the extension of Aberystwyth (p. 15) and to strengthen as well as extend towns such as Machynlleth and Lampeter (p.17).

21. *James Griffiths and his Times*, p. 52.

22. Ibid.

23. NLW. The papers of Iorwerth C. Peate A1/5. Letter of James Griffiths to Iorwerth C. Peate dated 30 April 1963.

24. Ibid.

25. Ibid.

26. Ibid.

27. *James Griffiths and his Times*, p.52.

28. Ibid.

29. *Yr Arglwydd Cledwyn, Cymry yn y Ddau Dŷ*, p.11.

30. James Griffiths, *Pages from Memory*, p.175.

31. Ibid, 183. James Griffiths had 'no hesitation in accepting the principle of equal validity', ibid., p 184.

32. Aneirin Talfan Davies (Aneirin ap Talfan; 1909-80*), Cydymaith i Lenyddiaeth Cymru* (Editor: Meic Stephens) (Cardiff, 1986), p.137.

33. Gwilym Prys Davies, *Cynhaeaf Hanner Canrif: Gwleidyddiaeth Gymreig 1945-2005* (Llandysul, 2008), p.57.

34. Gwilym Prys Davies calls it a 'radical document', ibid., p.58.

35. 'The consequences have been extraordinary' as the historian Dr Gwyn Alf Williams admits: 'In response to a militant campaign whose hunger is by definition insatiable, the British state, ruling a largely indifferent or hostile Welsh population, has in a manner which has few parallels outside the Soviet Union, countenanced and indeed subsidized cultural Welsh nationalism. Wales is now officially visibly and audibly a bilingual country. The equal official status of Welsh is nearing achievement.' See Gwyn A Williams, *When was Wales? A History of the Welsh* (London, 1985), pp. 292-3.

36. To James Griffiths the task of 'statesmanship' was to 'foster the growth of the Welsh Language'. ibid., p 184.

37. Rhys Evans, *Gwynfor, Rhag Pob Brad* (Talybont, 2005), p. 267.

38. Gwilym Prys Davies, *Cynhaeaf Hanner Canrif*, p. 58.

39. Ibid., pp. 58-9.

40. NLW Deian Hopkin Papers, Douglas Hughes Collection, No. 31-128 Letter from James Griffiths to Douglas Hughes, 8 December 1964.

41. Ibid.

42. Cliff Prothero, *Recount* (Ormskirk, 1982), p 76.

43. For J. Emrys Jones, see NLW. *Biography on Line, a biographical note* by Dr J. Graham Jones. 44. Gwilym Prys Davies said of him: 'Emrys Jones was a devolutionist by conviction', *Cynhaeaf Hanner Canrif*, p 64.

45. Rhys Evans, *Gwynfor: Rhag Pob Brad*, pp 260-1.

46. *James Griffiths and his times*, p. 52.

47. Ibid.

48. Ibid., p.53.

49. NLW. Papers of James Griffiths D2/10. Letter from Dai Charles to James Griffiths, 21 November 1966.

50. Ibid. Letter of Councillor J. G. Hill to James Griffiths, 21 November 1966.

51. Harold Wilson, *The Labour Government 1964-1970: A Personal Record*, pp. 216-17.

52. Beti Jones, *Etholiadau Seneddol yng Nghymru 1900-75*, pp. 144-45.

53. Ibid, pp. 142-43.

54. The local newspaper, *Carmarthen Journal*, 8 April 1966 had announced that Megan Lloyd George would turn up in the last week of the campaign.

55. Gwilym Prys Davies, *Llafur y Blynyddoedd* (Denbigh, 1991), p.53.

56. Rhys Evans, *Gwynfor: Rhag Pob Brad*, p 270.

57. *James Griffiths and his times*, p 53.

58. Ibid., 'I had reached Wales.' James Griffiths had achieved a miracle since his early days in the ILP in Ammanford in 1908. T. H. Lewis (Penarth) in a letter to the Western Mail reminds us of his commitment: 'There would never have been a Labour Party in the first place had not the ILP blazed the unpopular and difficult trail' See, T. H. Lewis 'Letters to the Editor: Labour's survival', *Western Mail*, 5 February 1965.

59. Ioan Matthews, 'Turning Labour Around', *Planet*, 142 August/September 2000, p.87.

Jim Griffiths celebrating the success of a choir at the National Eisteddfod of Wales

Celebrating choral music

Three patriotic Welshmen, Hywel D Roberts, Jim Griffiths and Ifor Bowen Griffith at a
National Eisteddfod

Cliff Prothero preparing the microphone for
the orator Jim Griffiths

Jim delievering a memorable speech at the National Eisteddfod of Wales

# 18

## Farewell to the House of Commons

On the invitation of the Prime Minister, on 4 April 1966 Griffiths went to have a conversation at 10 Downing Street. There he informed Wilson that he was going to retire, and he thanked the premier sincerely for his wholehearted support in giving him the opportunity to establish the Welsh Office.[1] Later that day Harold Wilson sent him a kind letter stressing his huge debt to Griffiths for being so conscientious regarding the needs of Wales both within the Cabinet and within Wales.[2] 'As I said in Cardiff last week, you have brought to our counsels at every level of Government the needs of the Welsh people.'[3] He also expressed an appreciation of Griffiths's vision, faith and wisdom.

> *But more – you have brought to all our discussions, even those going far beyond the problems of Wales, the imagination and vision which have carried you throughout a great political career, to the sagacity and experience which you have accumulated in all your many years of public services.*[4]

Wilson was glad that Griffiths was staying on as an MP due to his experience, his talent for reconciliation and his ability to get others working for the good of the Labour Party. But before the end of this parliament, due to the civil war in Nigeria, Wilson would find Griffiths a difficult comrade within parliament. According to convention and desire, Griffiths called to see his fellow ministers in the Welsh Office, the secretaries, and to welcome his successor Cledwyn Hughes. He could welcome him as they shared the same idealism towards Wales and its people, the Welsh language and its culture, the religious and social traditions. All this meant a great deal to both of them.

A question which is worth asking is who did James Griffiths have in mind to succeed him? Was it Cledwyn Hughes or Goronwy Roberts? We have the impression that Griffiths tended to favour Goronwy Roberts and one can be quite sure that he more or less expected Harold Wilson to select him as the Secretary of State for Wales. It is quite clear that Griffiths did not envisage a politician who was fiercely apposed to the Welsh nationalists to follow him.at any time.[5]

Griffiths was entrusted with a duty by his fellow parliamentarians when the new House of Commons met that gave him personal delight. He was honoured with the task of proposing the name of a new Speaker of the House of Commons in the person of Dr Horace King, a personal friend, and indeed the first Speaker from among Labour Party politicians. King was a very likeable person – I spent an evening in his company at a dinner in Liverpool organised by the National Union of Teachers (NUT) in 1969. It was a pleasure to converse with him and he referred often to James Griffiths after he realised that I knew him. On 14 May 1966, a few weeks after the opening of Parliament, the news broke of the death of the Labour MP for Carmarthenshire, Megan Lloyd George. Griffiths and Goronwy Roberts were mainly responsible for persuading her to join the Labour Party after she lost Anglesey as a Liberal MP in 1951. She had been steadfast in safeguarding the Welsh heritage and in supporting constitutional reform. She had been re-elected in March 1966 with a majority of 9,233, though she had not been near the hustings or inside the constituency of Carmarthen because of her illness. The constituency seemed a safe Labour seat. There was a need to have a candidate with similar values to her, and there were two who stood out, namely Gwilym Prys Davies who had represented Labour in the general election a few weeks before, and Denzil Davies, another legal brain, and a native of the county, as well as being an up and coming politician. Prys Davies was chosen as the Labour candidate, and he campaigned with determination, addressing large meetings in the Labour heartland of Cefneithin and Pontyates, though he had a different experience in the rural areas within the Vale of Towy and villages such as Llanwrda. In a short period, the atmosphere changed and there was a challenge even in the Gwendraeth Valley where the coal industry was itself under threat. A large number of the inhabitants turned against their own party. The attitude of the Labour group on the county council was another factor which cannot be ignored, especially their announcing the deadly news during the by-election campaign that a large number of rural schools were under threat of closure.[6]

The crisis of the pound, the decision of a large number of Conservatives to vote for Plaid Cymru, economic stagnation, and all the young people from all over Wales who were attracted to work for Gwynfor Evans were also authentic reasons for the unexpected result. Gwynfor Evans, the Plaid Cymru candidate, was a county councillor who had gained a great deal of publicity, and was extremely well liked among the largest nonconformist denomination in the constituency, namely the Welsh Independents. James Griffiths had a high regard for him as a man, and he described the leader of Plaid Cymru in these words: 'He is not a dreamer but a successful business-man, a pillar of nonconformity and a pragmatic politician. His first important decision was to change the name of the party, discarding 'Nationalist' for Plaid Cymru. He has built up the membership of the party by an appeal to three sections of the Welsh community: the traditional Liberals who must, with the decline of their own party, find a new home; the young people who are products of the "all Welsh schools"; and those others who see in "Plaid" the only hope of defeating Labour. It was by mobilizing the votes of all three elements, together with those of the discontented among Labour's traditional supporters, that Plaid gained its electoral successes'.[7]

But such an appraisal did not deter Griffith from campaigning for Gwilym Prys Davies who he wanted to see on the Labour benches in Parliament. But, on 14 July 1966, before a rowdy crowd, the Returning Officer in Carmarthen announced that Gwynfor Evans had won with a majority of 2,436 over the Labour Party candidate.[8] The victory of Gwynfor Evans in the eyes of a number of Labour Party leaders was an obvious barrier to further devolution for the time being. Labour councillors in Carmarthenshire decided not to support the proposed elected Council. The biographer of Gwynfor Evans, Rhys Evans, states in his Welsh version:

*From a political standpoint, Gwynfor was responsible for destroying the hopes of Cledwyn Hughes and creating such paranoia. Ironically the cause of devolution was destroyed till 1973, and that was due to the rise of nationalism.*[9]

Griffiths soon realised the dilemma. Gwynfor Evans never did. He was blind to many of the factors responsible for the Labour calamity. He believed that the Labour Party had been seriously harmed. Unfortunately he made as much fun of devolutionists within the Labour Party as he did of George Thomas and those politicians who opposed the need for Welsh devolution.[10]

The new MP took his place in the House of Commons on 21 July. Gwynfor Evans was presented by two Labour MPs, James Griffiths and S. O. Davies, both proud of their Welshness.[11] One understands on reading correspondence in the Griffiths archives that there was a convention in existence that one of the promoters should be an MP for a next-door seat. It is obvious that Llanelli was a next-door seat to Carmarthenshire but so was Cardiganshire, where Elystan Morgan had been the Labour MP since the general election of 1966. Their friendship was not so evident after Elystan Morgan was made a junior minister in the Home Office. But it is obvious that Gwynfor Evans had chosen Griffiths rather the Elystan Morgan to present him to the House of Commons. Gwynfor Evans naturally decided to make his vows to the Queen bilingually. His plea to do so was refused by Horace King, the Speaker, who explained that the vows had to be sworn in English in the House of Commons; a number of left-wing MPs were annoyed with his ruling.[12]

One of the politicians who would have wished for the result of the by-election to have been different was James Griffiths. But he had enough understanding to realise that the result was not an accident. The nationalists had taken over from the communists as effective opponents to Labour's domination in Wales. He saw this again in the by-election held in Rhondda West in 1967. Plaid Cymru did extremely well, and as one who campaigned in the by-election, I was quite aware of the weakness of the Labour Party machine and the lack of enthusiasm of the Labour Party councillors in the Rhondda, who should have done much more campaigning.One has to remember the disappointment among Welsh speakers who supported the Labour Party at the negative attitude of the ex-Labour MP Iorrie Thomas who was not only anti-Welsh but also anti-Welsh nonconformity. If the Labour Party had not chosen a strong local candidate in the person of Alec Jones the vote would have been even closer. Alec Jones received 12,373 votes as against 10,067 for Victor Davies. Griffiths, as I well remember, canvassed and addressed meetings in Pentre and Treorchy. Alec Jones after his victory served in the Welsh Office under John Morris and he did well as a minister.

He saw a large number of enthusiastic Welsh students from the University of Wales congregate in the Rhondda to support the Plaid Cymru campaign. One of the safest Labour Party constituencies in Wales was nearly lost to Plaid Cymru. Indeed Victor Davies and Plaid Cymru did extremely well, better statistically than they had done in Carmarthenshire. Victor Davies received 40% of the vote, much more than Gwynfor Evans had in his remarkable victory. To Griffiths there were no safe Labour seats left in Wales except his own, and a year later another blow was delivered to the confidence of the Labour Party, this time in the anglicised constituency of Caerphilly. We have to remember that this by-election was taking place because of the death of Ness Edwards, who had been as aggressive in his attitude towards Welsh speakers in the Labour Party as Iorrie Thomas had been in the Rhondda. But Ness Edwards had much more panache and intellectual ability and influence that Iorrie Thomas; indeed we are told that Harold Wilson at one time was seriously considering him as the first Secretary of State for Wales. Wilson, a few days after being elected leader of the Labour Party in 1963, asked John Morris, MP for Aberavon, on a train journey from London to Cardiff, what his opinion was of Ness Edwards as a possible Secretary of State for Wales.[13] If Edwards had been selected to that post, devolution would have suffered and been postponed even far longer that it was.  In the by-election at Caerphilly, Plaid Cymrus elected a very able candidate in Dr Phil Williams, who had been born and bred in Bargoed in the middle of the constituency and was a brilliant scientist at the University College of Wales in Aberystwyth. Meanwhile the Labour Party chose Fred Evans, the son of a miner who also had very close links to the constituency as a schoolmaster and then headmaster of a famous school in the Rhymney Valley. On 4 July James Griffiths addressed three public meetings in the Caerphilly constituency. After the by-election was over, he expressed his dissatisfaction at the huge change in loyalty among the voters and of the apathy of a large number of Labour Party supporters. They had forgotten the campaigning spirit which had been a characteristic of the Labour Party from its inception. He expressed himself in a biting sentence: 'The Party is in the grip of a death wish.' The Labour machine for which he had been responsible in the Ammanford of his youth had perhaps become contented and apathetic, believing that the electorate of Caerphilly was going to support Labour at all times. The leaders of the Labour Party in its headquarters had been shaken by the vote, with Plaid's Dr Phil Williams only 1,874 votes from winning a seat which had a majority of 21,148 for Labour in the general election of 1966. It is obvious that campaigning  Phil Williams of Plaid  had  made an impact d was a warning to Labour never to take the valley seats for granted. While the mining community had sustained the Labour Party nationally, in the by-election the loyalty had been slackened for once. The three by-elections of Carmarthen, Rhondda West and Caerphilly had shown to a politician of the experience of James Griffiths that one had to take positive steps. He believed that three factors had come together to provide the nationalists with sensational results in the byelections.[14] Firstly, the protest vote. The main reason for the protest vote between 1966 and 1968 was the dissatisfaction of a large number of voters with the programme and the implementation of the policies of the Labour government. In England the protest was expressed through the Liberal Party, but in Wales and Scotland in the 1960s, Plaid Cymru and the SNP were the chief means. Secondly, the importance  of language and culture to the Welsh-speaking voter in particular. Griffiths realised that an obvious decline had taken place in the number of people who spoke the language even within its heartland such as the Amman Valley. He believed that the activities and protests and the sacrifice of young members of the Welsh Language Society were going to bear fruit for the nationalists in the future. He saw the tactics and sacrifice of these young protestors very much like the women who used to call for the vote when he was young: 'The Suffragettes won the vote, and Plaid may also eventually win. Therefore I would not, as a Labour man, neglect the possible implications.'[15]

Griffiths believed the third reason for the increase in support for Plaid Cymru was a feeling of frustration that the central government was so far from the ordinary person in the urban and rural areas of Wales.[16] But this was true for the whole of the British Isles. The government seemed uninterested in the individual and his community. It did not seem to be on the same wavelength. One of the reasons for the nationalisation of industry was the hope of a better working environment for the worker. If everyone in the industry worked for the good of society instead of profit for a few owners, the bitterness would disappear under the new order. But such an argument had its weakness. The managers still carried on as in the old order and the workers in many places felt as if nothing had changed. The disagreements as well as the disillusionment were poisoning the atmosphere. Griffiths was hugely worried about the chasm that he saw appearing between central government and the citizen in the political world, and between the manager and the workers in the world of industry.[17]

Griffiths did not rest on his laurels. He was still an inspirational figure even though the Labour government was stumbling. In November 1967 he asked his friend Gwilym Prys Davies to prepare a memorandum on the political situation in Wales in the light of the by-elections at Carmarthen, Caerphilly and Rhondda West.[18] He sent the memorandum to Richard Crossman and to Labour Chief Whip, John Silkin. Crossman was influential in the Labour government of 1964 to 1970. He had responsibility for local government in the Labour governments of 1964-1966, and he was the Lord President of the Privy Council with responsibility for the constitution from August 1966 until April 1968. He knew of the opposition among some Welsh Labour MPs towards James Griffiths and Cledwyn Hughes. Ness Edwards sent a letter to Crossman dated 25 June 1967 stating:

> *Every concession to the 'Nats' only increases their appetite. As you probably know, the majority of us in the Welsh Labour Group are against this tendency, and certainly would be against the idea of a Welsh body outside of Parliament.*[19]

Then comes the knockout blow.

> *So far we have acquiesced in the silly steps that were initiated by Jim Griffiths, now being followed up by Cledwyn.*[20]

Crossman was very different to Ness Edwards, for he was one of the few devolutionists within the cabinet. He was extremely critical of Cledwyn Hughes and of the idea of an Elected Council as he believed that Wales deserved a 'Mini Parliament', and he argued against the establishment of a Commission on the Constitution. Crossman invited Gwilym Prys Davies to London to discuss the memorandum in his room at the House of Commons.

The conversation went on for an hour and then the rest of the evening was spent around the dinner table discussing the implications. There were three others at the dinner besides Crossman and Davies, namely John Mackintosh, John Morris and Tam Dalyell. Crossman gave strong support to Mackintosh and Davies to proceed to develop the concept of the 'Mini Parliament', believing that an Elected Council was not worthy of a proud Celtic nation.

The following morning in the Welsh Office in the presence of Cledwyn Hughes and Goronwy Daniel, the implications of the discussion the previous night were set out. Then a full report was sent to Griffiths. Gwilym Prys Davies also sent a full report to Emrys Jones at the Labour Party offices in Cardiff. In this discussion between Prys Davies and the organiser of the Labour Party in Wales, after hearing of the support of Richard Crossman on the principle of a Mini Parliament with the right to prepare legislation, Emrys Jones showed for the first time an interest in the idea, within bounds.The idea of a mini parliament was extremely attractive to Gwilym Prys Davies but he knew that the Labour Party in Wales would not accept it. The idea was excellent in principle, but the principle was not practical as far as the Labour Party Wales was concerned. Cledwyn Hughes and James Griffiths knew this better that anyone. Indeed James Griffiths argued strongly against Wales adopting an assembly on the pattern of Stormont, because he knew very well the reactionary conservatism which had belonged to that institution since its establishment in Belfast in 1921.[21]

Griffiths was greatly upset at this time with the small militant wing of the nationalist movement, which had used violence in pursuit of its cause within his constituency. After severely criticising their action, he warned the Welsh nationalists: 'If the leaders of Plaid Cymru continue to use such  emotive terms as the "London Government" or "The English" or to refer to their opponents as "enemies of Wales" they will reap the whirlwind of nationalist frenzy.' His immediate response, and his appearance on television condemning the violence, dispelled the rumour that had spread in west Wales with regard to his health. It was rumoured that he would be resigning soon and that a byelection would be held in Llanelli after Christmas 1968 with Carwyn James, a hero on the rugby field, doing well and creating another stir like Gwynfor Evans by winning the constituency outright for Plaid Cymru. Griffiths was prepared to soldier on for a number of years, and indeed he secured one of the most remarkable achievements of his life as a politician in this period: his peace mission to Biafra and Nigeria, which deserves a chapter of its own. He celebrated his golden wedding in 1968, and he and Winnie had a party for the immediate members of his family in the House of Commons, and another party for the whole family and close friends in the Amman Valley, held in Ammanford. The following year his autobiography, *Pages from Memory*, appeared from the publishers, J. M. Dent of London. *Pages from Memory* gives an account of his life up to 1966 and the election of the Labour government.[22]  In his acknowledgements, he names four people who had been of great help in the task of writing the book: his friend Gwilym Prys Davies, his son Harold Griffiths, his niece May Harris of Ammanford and his wife, Winifred Griffiths. To her he presented the volume for fifty years of married life, 1918-1968. He had been preparing the volume for some years before the election of 1964.[23] Indeed, he was very near to completing the task by the summer of 1964, when he put the typescript aside so he could concentrate on being the Secretary of State for Wales. In his archives there are letters praising the autobiography, four of them from Welsh nonconformist ministers, including one from the Reverend D. Eirwyn Morgan who stood against him on four separate occasions in the Llanelli constituency for Plaid Cymru. Lord John Morris, who admired him greatly, told me: 'His autobiography, besides the first chapter, was quite disappointing, for he could not say a bad word of anyone.'[24]

One has to admit that such a verdict is regarded as a weakness to many reviewers, but it is an honour for him. He had a good word for everyone. After reading the volume carefully I must admit that it is difficult to appreciate his tremendous contribution to the life of Wales, Britain and the Commonwealth. I hope this biography will underline his contribution to a new era. His humility was a barrier stopping him from blowing his own trumpet. He deserves to be given a very special place, and Welsh historians in the main are quite ready to acknowledge the key role he played, and to recognise the barriers he had to overcome.Professor Gwyn A. Williams saw this, perhaps more clearly than anyone else, when he claimed in his praiseworthy volume, *When was Wales? A History of the Welsh*, published in 1985:

> *While James Griffiths supported by Cledwyn Hughes and like-minded people within the Labour Party, had pressed for a further measure of self-government, they had run into intransigent resistance from most south Wales Labour MPs committed to the centralist drive of traditional Labour vision and accurately reflecting a profound sense of alienation from what had become official Welshness, centred on the language, among their constituents.*[25]

And perhaps the most controversial historical event of 1969 was held at Caernarfon Castle when Charles of Windsor was made the Prince of Wales. On 1 July that year Charles, the eldest son of Queen Elizabeth II, became Prince of Wales, an event which was given huge publicity by the media, and was welcomed by the majority of the Welsh people. Even then, there were a number of religious and cultural movements that were completely divided on the issue. The Welsh League of Youth was split on the question of the investiture, and so were the religious denominations. Gwynfor Evans sat on the fence by staying away from the ceremony at Caernarvon but earlier he had welcomed the prince to Carmarthen. He lost his seat a year later to Gwynoro Jones (Labour) for a number of reasons, but in his own opinion because of his stance on the investiture.[26]

He was in Aberystwyth for one term so he could in the company of Ted Millward and Dr Bobi Jones receive tuition on the history and the language of Wales so that he could utter a few sentences when needed at the Investiture. However a tragedy took place to two members of the Movement to Safeguard Wales in Abergele on the night before the ceremony at Caernarfon Castle. They were both killed when a bomb they planted exploded at the Even then the Welsh and the English Establishment were able to hold a pageant for the Royal Family and the guests within the walls of the ancient castle. Most of the Welsh MPs were invited to the ceremony, but James Griffiths failed to go because he had to have further medical care.[27] He had been a member of the committee which had been preparing for the investiture. But 1969 as well as 1970 had been difficult for him and his wife as far as their health was concerned.

She had been ill early in 1969 and he had been in and out of Westminster Hospital a number of times. The influence of James Griffiths was still to be seen quite obviously on the devolution question. When George Thomas was appointed Secretary of State for Wales in April 1968, many observers felt that there was no hope of implementing Griffiths's vision while Thomas was at the helm in the Welsh Office. But George Thomas decided to keep faithfully to the initial policy which had been prepared by James Griffiths, Cledwyn Hughes and Goronwy Daniel, so as to enlarge the responsibilities of the Welsh Office and to establish an Elected Council for Wales to be largely responsible for nominated bodies. The fact that he The new Minister accepted this policy, which could have been a hindrance to him, does not make George Thomas a principled devolutionist. Most probably he adopted this policy because of his respect for Griffiths and secondly he had come to realise that this was the best answer to the electoral threat from Plaid Cymru. The worries with regard to the new minister for Wales disappeared. He was not going to be as reactionary as most Welsh devolutionists expected. This is how it is in politics. Sometimes the unexpected happens.

**Notes and References**

1. James Griffiths, *Pages from Memory*, pps.1 91-2. Also see Ben Pimlot, *Harold Wilson* (London, 1993), p. 403.
2. Ibid., *Pages from Memory*, p.191.
3. Ibid.
4. Ibid., p.192
5. Ibid., NLW Manuscript 23091E, Letters to Graham Thomas. In a letter to Graham Thomas, 21 February 1965, Griffiths commented: 'Thought Goronwy Roberts would succeed him. He thought Cledwyn was destined for other things and had a wider-stout'.
6. Gwilym Prys Davies, *Llafur y Blynyddoedd* (Denbigh, 1990), pp. 52-58.
7. James Griffiths, *Pages from Memory*, p. 200.
8. Arnold J. James and John E. Thomas, *Wales at Westminster*, p. 173.
9. Rhys Evans, *Gwynfor* (Talybont, 2005), p. 296.
10. Leading Labour politicians in Westminster were well aware of the Nationalist threat to Labour's hegemomy especially after Gwynfor Evans arrival in Parliament. See *Pro Prem* 13/2151, Richard Crossman to Harold Wilson, 13 November 1967.
11. Rhys Evans, Ibid., p.284.
12. Emrys Hughes, A Welshman who represented a Scottish seat for Labour, gave encouragement to Gwynfor Evans in Westminster. NLW Huw T. Edwards papers A1-927. Letter of Cledwyn Hughes, Minister of State for Wales, to Huw T. Edwards, dated 18 July 1966 maintains that he wanted to present Gwynfor Evans, but it was ruled out as impractical as it would convey the impression that the Labour Government had given its blessing to Plaid Cymru's victory in the by-election. That is how James Griffiths and S. O. Davies, two elder statesmen, were invited to present him.
13. Lord Morris of Aberavon, *Fifty Years in Politics and the Law*, p 50.
14. James Griffiths, 'Welsh Politics in My Lifetime', in *James Griffiths and His Times*, pp. 54-55.
15. Ibid., p 54-5.
16. Ibid., p.51.
17. Ibid.
18. Gwilym Prys Davies, ibid., p.93.
19. NLW Ness Edwards Papers. Letter of Ness Edwards to Richard Crossman, 25 June 1967.
20. Ibid.
21. A conversation with Gwilym Prys Davies, 5 May 2004.
22. Ibid. D1/4 A letter of Gwilym Prys Davies to James Griffiths.when he asks him: 'Is the style sometimes too modest.?' Then in D1/14 GPD mentions that he is not happy with what

Griffiths had written, suggesting the need to 're-write the first six chapters.' This was in the summer of 1964.

23.     Gwilym Prys Davies was a great encourager for the book. See NLW James Griffiths Papers D1/2. Letter to James Griffiths from GPD dated 14 November 1961: 'What I must stress is that this is your Book and what you want included must be included. It is your view of things, your assessment of events which matters: your instinct must, therefore, be the final arbitrator'.

24.     Personal letter of Lord John Morris to me dated 6 December 2011.

25.     G. A Williams, *When Was Wales? A history of the Welsh* (London, 1985), p.291.

26.     Rhys Evans, ibid., p 300.

27.     His wife was a proud royalist. See Mrs James Griffiths, *One Woman's Story*, p.162.

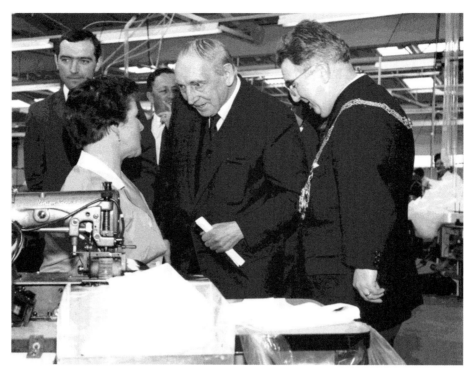

Jim at the opening of a new factory in his constituency

Clledwyn Hughes who followed Jim as Secretary of State for Wales.

# 19

# Peace Mission to Biafra and Nigeria

Of all the important activities of James Griffiths as a reconciler and politician, there is no doubt that his sincere concern for the civil war that took place in Nigeria between 1967 and 1970 is awe inspiring. Nigeria was created in 1900 by the British Empire. It brought together two countries, North Nigeria and South Nigeria, but left out the territory of Lagos. In 1906 Lagos became part of South Nigeria and in 1914 the North and South were united to form the largest colony belonging to Britain on the African continent.[1]

It was not an easy task to keep the different tribes together as the 'Islamic leaders' of the Fulani tribe dominated in the north over members of the Hausa tribe. In the west the Yoruba tribe was powerful, and in the east the Ibo race was influential. Under the constitution of Nigeria in 1954, of which Griffiths was well aware, the Nigerian Federation came into existence, namely the north, east, the west as well as the Trust territory from (Northern Cameroons) and the Lagos territory. In 1960 the Federation became an independent country within the Commonwealth, and in 1963 it became a Republic.[2]

Oil was discovered in the new port of Harcourt in the eastern territory and soon a movement was formed calling for independence for the Ibo race who lived in the area known as Biafra. By 1963 Nigeria was in deep political crisis.[3] Every attempt to come to an agreement failed. When a national election was held on 11 January 1965, the result triggered more strife, in the course of which the military took power on 19 January 1966. Unfortunately, this made the situation worse still because the terrorists, identified mostly as Ibo, were accused of killing the prime minister and other northern political leaders. A northern-led coup took place.[4]   In the wake of this coup, members of the Ibo communities in the north were viciously attacked; many died, and the rest fled to their homeland and decided to fight for secession and independence.

The eastern region of Nigeria, renamed the Republic of Biafra, declared its independence on 30 May 1967, with Lieutenant Colonel Chukwuemeka Odamegwu Ojukwu as head of state. He welcomed back to their homeland around 1.5 million Ibos from the north.[5]

The Federal Government was supported with arms and diplomacy from the Soviet Union, the Arab countries, the United States and Britain. Biafra received international recognition and support from France, four African states (Gabon, Côte d'Ivoire, Tanzania and Zambia), China, Israel and the whitecontrolled southern African states.[6] Mercenaries from all over Europe were drawn to the war on both sides. The civil war became a burning topic within British politics. Movement for Colonial Freedom was concerned with the dire situation, which was fuelling ethnic rivalry and violence. It established a Peace in Nigeria Committee which was chaired by a well-loved socialist, Lord Fenner Brockway. Griffiths was invited to join the Executive Committee in the spring of 1968. The Committee had members from every political party, and its aim was the ending of the war and the cessation of arms sales. Within the parliamentary Labour Party there was a great deal of uneasiness, and Griffiths shared this concern for Nigeria. There were two reasons for the uneasiness.

First, because the Labour government supported the Federal Government rather than being neutral, and second because the Labour Government allowed arms suppliers to sell weapons to the Nigerian Federal Government which were turned on men, women and children Biafra.[7] Harold Wilson realised that one of the most influential politicians within the Labour Party in parliament was completely opposed to the policies of the Labour government on Nigeria. The Prime Minister called him 'the highly respected Colonial Secretary'.[8]

James Griffiths wrote regularly to the Minister of State to persuade him to be even-handed in the conflict, rather than supporting one side in the civil war. He spoke passionately on 12 June 1968 in parliament urging both sides to cease the conflict.[9] By then, after early successes, Biafra was encircled and cut off from the sea and had lost control over oil production. [10] Griffiths was supported in the debate by two Labour members, Michael Barnes and Frank Allaun, both bitterly concerned that Britain was selling armaments to the Nigerian army.[11] Griffiths prepared another speech for the parliamentary debate on 27 August 1968, emphasising that this civil war was a blot on humanity. His message to both sides was 'stop it now'. He felt that a message should be sent to General Gowon, the head of the Nigerian government: humanity did want to be part of the conflict and that Britain should cease immediately providing armaments to the Federal government.[12]

Griffiths received a valuable and detailed report dated 12 November 1968 from Ottawa, the work of three Canadian politicians, Andrew Brewin, David Lewis and Harold Finch from the New Democratic Party.[13] They disagreed with the report which had been prepared by their party on the civil war. Andrew Brewin had visited Biafra and, like Griffiths, had real empathy with the inhabitants of that region in the conflict.[14] Griffiths also wrote to the prime minister about the Nigeria-Biafra civil war. In the Griffiths archives there is a letter he received in the summer of 1968 (there is no date) from Harold Wilson, where Wilson reminds his long-standing friend of what the government had done:

We have indeed used our influence with the Federal authorities and will continue to do so. We had discussed with them the need for observers in the fighting lines to ensure that relief for Ibo civilians followed closely behind the military operations and to reassure world opinion about the fate of the civilian population. Then he states categorically:

> *We certainly do not believe that a 'final solution' in the form of genocide or a planned massacre of Ibo civilians is the Federal intention. If we did, as Michael Stewart said in the House on June 12, we would reconsider our policy.*[15]

The all-party Committee for peace in Nigeria invited James Griffiths and Fenner Brockway to visit Nigeria as peace ambassadors to try and persuade the leaders of both sides to reconcile their differences over the Christmas period. These two veteran politicians accepted the challenge. On Wednesday night, 3 December 1968, both flew from Heathrow Airport to Amsterdam on a Dutch airline. The idea was to fly from there to the island of San Tome and then on Thursday night, fly in the darkness to Biafra.[16]

When they arrived at Amsterdam airport at 7.30 a.m. the plane which was to take them to Africa had already left for Frankfurt. Fenner Brockway phoned the British Embassy in Holland and arrangements were made for the two politicians to stay overnight at the embassy in the Hague. Brockway had brought a medical practitioner, Dr John Wallace, an experienced person who had served in Biafra, to be on hand to assist them.[17] It seems that James Griffiths had not consulted his own doctor with regard to the hazards of the journey and we have no details if both had been briefed by the Foreign Office before they left for Nigeria. Yet the Foreign Office knew of their journey. They had to fly the following morning on a plane coming from Venezuela which took them over Paris, Madrid and to Lisbon. There they disembarked and were taken to the British Embassy for food and were given a room at the Tivoli Hotel where they could relax before travelling to Lisbon. The three of them were flying on a Portuguese airline to Luanda in Angola. This plane carried 160 passengers. They had a comfortable flight and arrived at 9.30 a.m. at Luanda airport. A member of the British Embassy staff was there to meet them and to welcome them to his home on the outskirts of Luanda.

That Thursday night, December 5 at 11 o'clock, they flew out of Luanda for the island of San Tome in a Douglas DC6 aeroplane. This was a small plane which could carry only fifteen passengers and which had been bought second-hand by the Catholic charity Caritas to fly to Biafra from Uganda. The pilots hailed from Canada, Sweden and Finland. Griffiths greatly admired the courage of these pilots, for night after night they flew on flights of mercy. They could easily lose their lives. In his note he calls them the 'Mission of Mercy'. He never forgot climbing the steel  ladder to the little aeroplane. Memories of his time as a miner in Betws overwhelmed him. The aeroplane had no lights to help the passengers. They had to tread carefully as the floor of the plane had sacks of soya beans. He managed to locate his seat, full of fear, in complete darkness. Then the pilot started the engine and the steward used his flash lamp to see that all of them were safely in their seats. Griffiths experienced great fear: as he said:

*At first I was scared stiff and then a strange thing happened; my imagination transformed the dark cavern into the coal mine and I found a profound relief at being back at the coal face.*[18]

The light of the plane came on when they were climbing in the sky. After two hours, the light went off, and fortunately they landed safely.[19] They were encircled with the darkness of the African continent. Griffiths wrote how they were helped without any ceremony into a waiting car at the San Tome island airport.[20] But before they left, they were welcomed by Father Byrne who was in charge of the Caritas charity. Byrne had his colleague with him. Both were elderly Irish priests, old in years but young in heart and in their demeanour.[21] John Dunwoody, a well-known peace campaigner, was also present. A Briton, he worked for the independence of Biafra. They had a journey of forty miles from the airport on the island to the town of Umuaha, and from the light of the car, Griffiths saw a contingent of women, some twenty of them, carrying baskets on their heads, so that they could reach the market by 5.30 a.m. They reached the State House in Umuaha by 4.30 a.m. so that they could have some rest.[22] Fenner Brockway and Dr John Wallace shared a room while Griffiths had his own room. He was given a double bed with a net over it to keep out the mosquitos. James Griffiths fell to sleep without much trouble and he was woken by the woman who looked after the State House. They were provided with a simple breakfast, a boiled egg, and they were introduced to Michael, who was to be their guide, and Isaac, their bodyguard.

They knew that a meeting had been arranged for Friday morning, 6 December for 10.30 a.m. in the Court House with Sir Louis Mbafeno, Chief Justice of Biafra. Both politicians knew a great deal about him: they had met Mbafeno when he visited London in the summer of 1968.[23] Mbafeno had brought condemnation on himself from the Federal Government supporting independence for Biafra. Imprisoned for a while, he was then released. In his welcome and introduction, the Chief Justice told them that the civil war had influenced the inhabitants of Biafra. It had made them into a nation.

They knew that they belonged to a particular nation, which had suffered immensely at the hands of the rest of Nigeria. In this meeting there were a number of other Biafran leaders present, and two of them made an important impact on Griffiths. They were Dr Coakie and Dr Eke, who had graduated from Princeton University and was now the minister of communications for Biafra. They were invited to dinner, which comprised meat from a tin, an apple each, and some wine. Due to his temperance convictions, Griffiths was provided with orange juice.[24]

In the afternoon, the deputation met General Philip Effiong, the military leader of the Biafran Army, and a dozen of the most important army officers. Effiong had been trained at Sandhurst and had served with the military leaders of Nigeria. In his presentation he mentioned how the Wilson government had embittered him and had not provided the support he expected. Lord Brockway and Griffiths asked him three questions. Firstly, why did he object to the planes flying on missions of mercy during the day? He gave the answer: for military security. Secondly, what was the danger of flying in the daylight, and he answered by stating that it would open the way for the enemy to have easy access to the heart of Biafra. To the third question, 'Where do you get your armaments?', the Effiong replied: 'We can produce twenty per cent of the arms, then we confiscate forty per cent of the arms from the Nigerian army, and we buy the rest from Britain and Russia.' These armaments came to them through France, the Portuguese islands, through Gabon and the Ivory Coast.[25]

That evening a dinner was organised for them so that they could meet the Secretary of the Administration, Mr U. N. Akpan, and have further talks with the leader Ofakwu and Effiong. Most of the ministers came as well as the civil servants.[26] The deputation heard the cry that the West should recognise Biafra as a separate country. They should organise a truce, bring both sides of the conflict together, and create a country with its borders corresponding to the borders of Biafra. The United Nations should monitor the peace till they came to a final arrangement. The suffering, the violence, the loss of lives were all underlined. Every family in Biafra had suffered in the civil war and were hard pressed in every way. The message came clear to James Griffiths that the Biafrans were not going to give in easily. They were ready to die for their independence.[27]

The following morning James Griffiths and Fenner Brockway were welcomed to breakfast in the home of distinguished medical missionary Dr Akanu Ibiam. Griffiths had met him when he was minister for the colonies. Christian Ibiam knew Lord Brockway well and had met him regularly over the years. A devout Ibiam insisted on praying to God before their deliberations to ask for guidance. He prayed in terms of "our brothers and friends who have come to our midst in the name of peace".[28]

The discussion took two hours and Ibiam listened attentively, giving his full backing to the programme of a truce and peace to follow – after all they had fought a war to ensure justice. During the discussion a protest took place outside. The protestors had banners condemning the Labour government in Westminster. An effigy of Harold Wilson was burnt by the protestors.[29]

That night, Michael, who had been their guide, as well as two representatives of the Red Cross, came to visit them. Griffiths took an instant dislike to the Red Cross representatives because they were abrasive and extremely critical of Wilson and supported more fighting. Indeed Griffiths felt that he and Brockway were regarded by many of these people as spies for the British government. He wrote:

> *Indeed Fenner and I both felt that they (the rank and file) regarded our visit with some suspicion, they feared that we were representatives of the British government in Biafra to try and induce their leaders to accept some compromise.*[30]

This suspicion was completely unfounded. As they emphasised, the purpose of the journey was to seek reconciliation and a truce over Christmas. The next day, 7 December, was a Sunday. The deputation spent the afternoon visiting a hospital and a hospice in Umnala, which were in the care of medical missionaries who belonged to the Council for World Mission. There were 800 patients in the hospital under the care of a husband and wife team, Dr and Mrs Middlethorp. To Griffiths they were the true heroes of Biafra.[31] He respected their commitment as well as that of the other members of the staff.

The sick were seen everywhere in the corridors, rooms, as well as the wards. It was a tormenting scene: men, women and children who had been injured in the civil war. He also praised the efforts of their companion, Dr John Wallace, in his efforts to get the hospital more drugs and medical equipment. At 5.30 p.m. Griffiths attended the evening service at the hospital. It was a service in the Presbyterian mould and conducted by a Biafran. Griffiths said: "It was a very moving service".[32]

Two well-known hymns were sung, namely, 'O God our help in ages past' and 'Abide with me'. That night they were entertained by an historian who had been a lecturer at the University of Ibadan, Dr Coakie. He had left his post to support his people. Life was hard for him economically and he pleaded for a referendum on the future of Biafra.[33]

On Monday morning, December 8, they had to get up early to travel to Nguru, thirty miles away, to visit the Holy Rosary nunnery. They arrived at 4.30 a.m. and they were met by the Mother Superior, the nuns, priests as well as some two thousand women, and around three thousand children singing:

> *'We are Biafrans*
>
> *Fighting for our freedom*
>
> *In Jesus' name*
>
> *We shall conquer.'* [34]

Every morning at 6 a.m. the mothers and their children would receive their breakfast, made up of porridge and a few other goodies to keep them alive. I remember seeing a photo of the mothers and children, with Fenner Brockway and Griffiths in their midst, in the Guardian.[35] It made a deep impression on me, seeing these two elderly politicians in the middle of the hungry thousands who were waiting for some sustenance from the Catholic Church.

The deputation then met the Roman Catholic bishop of the diocese, Bishop Welland, a native of Ireland who gave both politicians a warm welcome. The meal provided was simple, a boiled egg, some biscuits and a weak cup of tea. After finishing their breakfast, a Mass was arranged and though he had a Welsh nonconformist background, Griffiths appreciated the religious service in the Catholic tradition.[36] They were expected to spend the morning in the Court House in the company of some farmers, women and young people. Outside the building another protest took place: this time the union flag as well as an effigy of Harold Wilson went up in flames.

After a spartan dinner, an opportunity was given to journalists to interview the two politicians. A journalist who had won the admiration of James Griffiths was Freddie Forsyth, today a notable novelist but at that time working for the BBC.[37] He had been won over to the Biafran cause became a strong advocate for Biafran independence. At the end of that day James Griffiths felt grateful for the press coverage and the sharp mind and commitment of Freddie Forsyth.

On Tuesday 9 December the two peace ambassadors were given a session with Colonel Chukwuemeka Ojukwu.[38] This meeting took place in the State House at 9 a.m. with all military splendour. They all had to be searched. The security found a small penknife in Griffiths's pocket, which they confiscated. The Ibo were not taking any risks. A large number of TV companies, including some from France, were allowed in but no TV crews from Britain. The colonel and his soldiers were dressed in the Mao Tse Tung uniform. The colonel expressed his sincere appreciation that two experienced politicians from the British Labour Party had taken the trouble to complete a difficult journey, full of personal risk, from London to Biafra. He turned to Griffiths to tell him that among the 'most happy memories that he had he ever  had was to visit  the town of Aberystwyth'.[39] The colonel felt very sad that the Wilson government had been used by the Nigerian government to support the federal setup, morally as well militarily. Then the opportunity was given to the two socialists to address the gathering. Brockway spoke first, followed by Griffiths.

They both emphasised that they were peace missionaries who had come, not in the name of the Labour Party, but in the name of the Committee for Peace in Nigeria. They emphasised their programme for Biafra and Nigeria. It meant:

(i)   truce at once
(ii)  arrange a Peace Corps
(iii) present a plan to oversee the suffering masses
(iv) a period of six months for discussion and reconciliation  After two hours of discussion

    Colonel Ojukwu agreed with the following  recommendations:

(i)   the truce to be overseen by soldiers from Biafra, Nigeria and the United Nations

(ii)  to co-operate fully

(iii) the period of six months to be extended to a year

(iv) the plan to be presented and accepted by Western Governments and the United Nations

(v)  to inform Gowan of the recommendations, hoping that they would be acceptable.[40]


The colonel and his fellow leaders believed that their recommendations were positive. Fenner Brockway, Dr Wallace and Griffiths spent the rest of the day in the company of the colonel. Griffiths described him as a 'strong character'.[41] The following day would be their last in Biafra but they were unable to carry on to Lagos. The Federal government insisted that they flew back to London, which made it extremely difficult for the two elderly politicians.[42] It would have been easier to fly from San Tome to Lagos.[42] On Thursday morning, 10 December, they motored around San Tome before travelling to the airport. A Boeing 707 was waiting for them. The first part of the journey, with twelve other passengers, was to Accra, the capital of Ghana. [43] From there they would travel to Amsterdam, change and then fly the final part of the journey to Heathrow airport.[44]

The following day in London was full of activity a press conference was arranged for them. Both were busy with their radio and TV interviews before they went to the Foreign Office to give a full account of their activities and the recommendations that had been agreed. They had only five days before they returned on their mission to Nigeria. This time the arrangements were in the hands of the Nigerian embassy in London, and the intention was to present to General Gowan and the Federal government the same agreement that they had presented to the leaders of Biafra.[45] They were informed on Monday 16 December that they would be flying with Nigerian Airways, leaving Heathrow on Wednesday morning, 18 December at 8.30 a.m. They were to fly first class and they were to be looked after in a special lounge before departure. So on Wednesday morning Brockway and Griffiths were walking to a plane for the second time that month for a long flight to war-torn Nigeria-Biafra in the name of peace.[46]

Their flight would take them to Frankfurt Airport, then to Kano and finally Lagos airport. They were met in each of the named airports by journalists with their questions. As they were very experienced politicians there was no danger that they would give an answer which would have created a storm or upset those waiting for them in Lagos. Griffiths slept for most of the journey as he was extremely tired but determined to complete his peace mission.[47]

When they landed in Lagos they were met by officials of the Federal government. Griffiths knew that it would be a long journey from the airport to the Federal Palace Hotel where they were staying as guests of the government. The situation was entirely different to the last time he had been in Lagos in 1962 at that time at the invitation of Dr Benjamin Nnamdi Azikiwe (1904-1996), a leading figure of Nigerian nationalism. The Federal government had arranged a fine room, number 505, for Griffiths and Brockway.[48] It was a double room with every convenience and was cool and sheltered from the blazing sun of Lagos. But they had no time to relax. Journalists clamoured to see them, and radio correspondents were keen on interviewing them both. The BBC had arranged for an experienced journalist, John Osborne, to keep in touch with them over their stay in Lagos.

The two politicians soon realised that a number of other politicians and leaders were staying at the same hotel. There were two senators from the United States (a Republican from Ohio, and a Democrat from Indiana). Harold Wilson had sent an observer, the distinguished military man, Sir Bernard Fergusson (1911-1980), and in the hotel Griffiths came across Colonel Caerus who was keeping company with Fergusson. That evening they spent the time in Ikaye, a district of Lagos, with Chief Justice H. O. Davies QC, and Louis Ainhenfo.[49]

In the morning after breakfast, Griffiths spent some time with the BBC radio correspondent, John Osborne. They liked each other and they got on well. Dr Arepko (the Commissioner for External Affairs) came to see him, and Griffiths acknowledges in his notes that this man was the most capable officer that he had met up till then. He also admitted that the two American senators had tried to persuade him to reveal what Dr Arepko had discussed with him but he had refused. At midday, arrangements had been made for them to meet General Gowan, and the journey that morning to the barracks brought back a lot of memories of his visit when he was Secretary of State for the Colonies.[50] On that occasion he had met the Governor, John Macpherson, and his deputy Sir Hugh Foot, and they had prepared a constitution for the Federal Government as well as the constitution for the regions. Gowan was a young man of thirty-two years of age, who had succeeded in getting the Hausa tribe in the north and the Yoruba tribe in the west under his banner. Griffiths had gathered he was a Christian, a shy person and difficult to communicate with. But it turned out to be an entirely different experience.

He welcomed them in a friendly manner, stating that it was an honour to meet two British politicians 'of your eminence'. He spoke fluently for forty minutes. He felt that the British press, in particular The Times and The Guardian, television and the BBC, had been influenced by the propaganda of Colonel Ojukwu and Biafra. He also mentioned that he had been informed that Ojukwu intended to attack Nigerian forces on Christmas Day, the day of truce between them. Then Chief Anthony Enharo (1923-2010), foremost anti-colonial campaigner within Nigeria, turned to Gowan and stated that he should remember that Brockway and Griffiths were totally wedded to the Biafran cause. He attacked Brockway, and Griffiths could not allow this, and he cut across the surprised outburst of Enharo's by by reminding him that the Labour Government had supported the Federal government of Nigeria. Both were surprised at the venom that came from the lips of Enharo, indeed Brockway and Griffiths left the barracks somewhat hurt.[51]

A dinner was arranged for them at 3 o'clock in the company of Sir David Hunt, Chief Commissioner for Britain in Nigeria, in Lagos. The dinner was not without its controversy as Sir David supported the Federal government and condemned the deeds of the Biafran leaders. Both also met Bernard Fergusson the observer Harold Wilson had sent. Ferguson had not visited Biafra. Griffiths felt uncomfortable that Wilson had sent an observer steeped in the life of New Zealand rather than Nigeria. Brigadier Fergusson had no experience of the African continent.[52]

On Sunday 21 December, the plan was to take them to Port Harcourt, but they had to postpone everything as one of the engines of the aeroplane was not in working order.[53] As it was the Christmas holiday period, there was no way it could be repaired. This meant a wait of four hours and the two politicians had a further opportunity to enjoy each other's. It was a strange partnership: Griffiths first saw Fenner Brockway at the Independent Labour Party Conference in Merthyr Tydfil in 1912. He knew of his involvement in the peace movements in the 1914-1918 war and his support of the freedom movements in the colonies. When Griffiths was appointed Secretary of the Colonies he was in contact with Brockway. In his volume Towards Tomorrow, Brockway mentions returning from Kaba to London in 1950:

> *When I returned to London I submitted a report of all I had seen to James Griffiths, the Colonial Secretary, whom I admired for his humanity. He could not make all the changes I suggested, but much was done.* '[54]

Griffith always admired the way Brockway chaired the Peace Committee of Nigeria. He kept the Committee united, in particular in the arguments that took place between James Griffiths who was supportive of Biafra and two other MPs, John Tilney (Conservative) and Jim Johnson (Labour) who were pro-Nigerian. James Griffiths was saddened the attitude of the Labour government which he supported. The reconciler and conscientious Labourite was annoyed at what was happening. He wrote :

> *'Our own Government had made a big mistake in agreeing to supply arms to the Federals. In Biafra; we had found a Wilson Government regarded as an enemy and*

*as Labour Party members, it was an experience to find friends we had met in happiest days in Nigeria, burning effigies.*'[55]

On Monday, 23 December, they were on their way back to London from Lagos on a VC10 belonging to Nigerian Airways. As soon as the aeroplane left Lagos, Griffiths experienced violent pains in his intestine and for at least an hour he was poorly. The term he himself used was 'desperately ill'. Fortunately, on the plane there was an African doctor and he was called to assist the politician in his pain and distress. He gave him some tablets which helped him, and within a short period he was sleeping. He slept for the rest of the journey until the plane arrived at Heathrow. He knew that he had a heavy day on the Tuesday. Early in the morning there was a press conference and seventy-one journalists, radio and television presenters came to make notes and ask questions. Following the conference, he moved from one interview to another, appearing on 'Today', a new programme on the BBC, and the independent television channels before going to visit the ministers in the Foreign Office, Lord Shepherd and Maurice Foley. Then Griffiths and Fenner Brockway visited the Prime Minister at No.10 Downing Street to present their report on the peace mission. That night both spoke at a public meeting in Conway Hall, a building which was familiar to both.

Griffiths had aged a great deal. He was never the same after his ordeal in Biafra and Nigeria, and he knew that he would not be able to visit foreign lands in the future. He realised that he should not have ventured on this journey at the age of seventy-eight, but he could not forget his loyalty, his support to the Ibo nation and the land of Biafra. It was a huge disappointment for him that they achieved so little after all the effort both had made. Gowan agreed to a truce but only for two days, Christmas Eve and Christmas Day, instead of the eight days for which Brockway and Griffiths had pleaded. One can hear the note of disappointment in this sentence from Griffiths: 'So all we had to show for our efforts were two days of truce at Christmas 1968.[56]

But the peace mission made a huge impact on his constituents, supporters, peace organisations and churches of all traditions. Naturally, details of his visits to Biafra and Nigeria appeared in the local press. Just before Christmas, details appeared in the Llanelli Star, where Griffiths mentions that they were able to have two days of truce. He also referred to the incredible courage of the pilots flying in the darkness in and out of the airport on San Tome:I flew in one of these mercy aircrafts and will never forget the experience.[57]

He also expressed his admiration for the World Council of Churches, the Red Cross, Caritas and those friends he had among the leaders of Biafra and Nigeria. A fortnight later he mentioned the need to conquer the hunger of humanity before spending on special research and travel. He saw hunger on a vast scale in Biafra. Children who looked like elderly people. Women worrying for the future of their families. Griffiths enjoyed a pleasant Christmas with plenty of luxuries, but he remembered young children who only had one meal a day, from the hands of Catholic nuns at 6 o'clock in the morning.

Fenner Brockway mentioned more than once his huge debt to James Griffiths. He wrote of him not in terms of a friend but of a brother:

*We had always been friends, though sometimes differing, but during the experience we became brothers, not only in the comradeship of what we were seeking to do, but in our oneness of attitude to it. Jim had been a Cabinet Minister, with responsibility for much of Africa, and it would have been natural for him to take the leadership. He declined, insisting that I was the Chairman of the London Committee. He supported me unfailingly in the negotiations and his advice was wise in our evening discussions.*[58]

When the autobiography of James Griffiths appeared in March 1969 without a reference to his efforts for the ordinary people of Biafra to reconcile both sides in the conflict, Brockway expressed his disappointment in his review for the Western Mail that there was no reference to his courageous adventure:

*My one regret is that the autobiography has been written before Jim retired. What a chapter in his recent journey to Biafra and Nigeria would have made.*[59]

Fenner Brockway expressed it well. One could have postponed publishing Pages From Memory for two years so that the chapter of his peace pilgrimage could have been included. The physical, mental and emotional stress and strain though were horrendous, as his wife testified:

*The mental and physical strain of the two journeys, together with the differences with our own Labour government about their policy in Nigeria, took their toll.*[60]

This was the only time in his long parliamentary career that he had disagreed with a Labour Government. He had been so dependable and loyal, but he was now, on his quest for justice for Biafra, among the rebels. One could suggest that he was reverting to his earlier pacifist convictions. As a patriotic Welshman he was able to empathise with the aspirations of the Ibo people for devolution. In this involvement he had inherited once more the nonconformist or dissenting voice towards war. Harold Wilson mentioned how the dissenters were united in their opposition to the civil war in Nigeria. Wilson does not mention Griffiths, but he must have thought of him when he wrote this paragraph in his memoirs:

*The Nonconformists all, bar a few, condemned us and placed the guilt for the prolongation of the war and for every single death through military action or starvation at our door. One remains silent, or quietly urges the case, without heat, in Parliamentary debate, but in the life of a Prime Minister, these are things that hurt.*[61]

At 1968, Griffiths received letters from a number of well-known people in the life of Wales. The President of the Welsh Gas Board, Mervyn Jones, told him:

*How admirable all you have been – for what a single tribute it was to you that the mission was ever possible – and all you have done – and clearly this is the first breakthrough of humanity and sanity – for no man of any age could have any assignments be tougher and yet more supremely worthwhile. Blessing upon your*

*noble, kindly hand – sung they will be all by the choirs you love the most – of little*
*children.*[62]

Another who was inspired to send greetings and to thank him for the effort was the Reverend
E. Curig Davies, a well-known Welsh Independent minister who had been influenced by
James Griffiths. Griffiths's courage had moved him to write:

> *Edmygwn eich ysbryd a'ch dewrder yn wynebu'r daith bell â'i holl*
> *enbydrwydd. Y mae'n amlwg fod y sefyllfa'n druenus.*
> [I admire your spirit and courage facing the long journey with all  ts
> difficulties. It is obvious that the situation is desperate.][63]

Two politicians sent him greetings after his return from Lagos: the first was Tam Dalyell, a
young politician who had great admiration for him. At the end of 1968 he him thanked for his
leadership with regard to the civil war, and his dedication to the task of bringing the enemies
to act as friends, and for his values in his witness for justice and peace in Nigeria:

> *I would like you to know how much I admire your efforts to bring the tragic war in*
> *Nigeria to a close.*[64]

The second politician to greet him was his close neighbour Gwynfor Evans, and his letter is
one of the most symbolic of all the correspondence I have read. The letter opens in a
characteristic manner:

> *Er bod gwahaniaeth go fawr rhyngom ynghylch dyfodol Cymru, eto hoffwn eich*
> *llongyfarch yn galonnog a diolch yn gynnes am eich cenhadaeth ddiweddar i*
> *Nigeria a Biafra. Y mae'r arweiniad a roddwyd gennych chi a'r Arglwydd Brockway*
> *yn ardderchog iawn ac yr ydym oll yn eich dyled o'i achos. Mae'r radd o lwyddiant*
> *a gawsoch eisoes yn llawenydd mawr i mi a dymunaf â'm holl galon eich llwyddiant*
> *cyflawn.*

> [As there is quite a difference between us with regard to the fortune of Wales, yet I
> would like to congratulate you and to thank you warmly for your recent mission to
> Nigeria and Biafra. The leadership given by you and Lord Brockway is very special
> and we are all in your debt because of it. The degree of success you have already
> had is of great joy to me, and I wish with all my heart your complete success.] [65]

One can see Gwynfor Evans at his best in this letter. Yet I believe that his first sentence is
misleading. He maintains: 'There is quite a difference between us with regard to the future of
Wales'. Gwynfor Evans loved to believe that. But James Griffiths had, by 1968, become as
much a devolutionist as Gwynfor Evans. Both were alike, battling effectively for Wales and
its future. But for the rest of the letter it is a classic, sincere tribute, which was well deserved,
from one Welsh leader to another. Peace issues were important to both, and our hearts are
warmed when hearing the tribute instead of reading critical appraisal. Evans said it in a
nutshell: 'We are all in your debt from your splendid peace mission.'[66]

During these difficult times Griffiths received another sincere letter from Councillor Brinley Owen from Llanelli, Secretary of the Labour group on Carmarthenshire County Council. It is important that his letter is printed as it expresses respect to James Griffiths by one who worked for him in the constituency. The theme of Brinley Owen was James Griffiths, the reconciler, from his early days in the anthracite coalfield to his effort to reconcile brothers and sisters in Nigeria:

> *Your recent visit to Biafra and Nigeria as a peace mediator was of particular concern to us; to enter territory where active hostilities were taking place, where conditions for travel were difficult and dangerous, and where the activities of the belligerents were unpredictable, was an undertaking which naturally made us apprehensive – particularly so in that you were undergoing these dangers as an elder statesman and no longer as a young man. Although no public meeting for prayer was organised on your behalf, all your friends were praying privately for success in your negotiations and for your safe return.*[67]

Their prayers were partly answered. The man of faith returned safely to his people to carry on his campaign to persuade his government to use its influence for the sake of peace in Nigeria. He spoke with his usual sincerity when he wrote:

> *I have no regrets, indeed I feel some pride that in spite of my age – and already some sign of my impending illness, I ventured on the journey with all its attendant dangers and heart rending experiences. There are poignant memories, I shall take them when I cross the Great Divide. And I shall go happy that the brave people of Biafra – the Ibos – and their allies will some day find the security and peace they deserve. Nigeria needs the skills, enterprise and courage of the Ibos. I hope their future governments will find a place for them and opportunities for the service which they can render to Nigeria and Africa.*[68]

That was the testament of James Griffiths and a clear expression of his support of the Ibo people, of their abilities and vision. He believed that these articulate individuals that he knew would be of service to the Nigerian Government. They did not deserve to be ignored. But Griffiths did not stop campaigning throughout 1969 and he led some seventy Members of Parliament in revolt. They were the conscience of the House of Commons. He tried in February to revive the nonconformist conscience. Among the politicians of Welsh background he received support from Fred Evans (Caerphilly), Gwilym Roberts (Cannock), Emrys Hughes (South Ayrshire), Roy Hughes (Newport), Gwynfor Evans (Carmarthen) and a Welsh Conservative, Sir Brandon Rhys Williams (South Kensington, London).[69]

When a Labour conference for the Llanelli constituency was held on St David's Day 1969 in Ammanford, he concentrated in his address on his peace mission of December 1968.[70] He called on the United Nations to intervene at once so as to stop the bloodbath. On 13 March 1969 in the House of Commons, Griffiths spoke passionately about the situation in Nigeria. The editorial in The Times called it the 'moving speech of James Griffiths.'[71] He again led his fellow rebels in the vote at the end of the debate. The government had the support of 232 MPs while Griffiths mustered 62 to vote with him.[72]

A result of this vote was that the prime minister decided to visit Nigeria to discuss the situation.[73] Wilson as well as the Foreign Secretary Michael Stewart and all members of the Cabinet knew of the strong conviction of James Griffiths on the civil war. In a letter to him in the summer of 1969, Michael Stewart told him: 'I know your strong and dedicated feelings about the situation.'[74]

Before he had received the letter from the Foreign Secretary, Griffiths had sent a letter to *The Times* under the heading, 'A Time for World Action'. He said in his letter:

> *If famine returns to Biafra and countless millions starve and die, we shall carry a terrible responsibility.*[75]

Griffiths knew of the attitude of some of the leaders of the Nigerian army. He believed that a soldier such as Colonel Adekule would be quite willing to commit genocide against the Ibo race.[76] A number of journalists believed that Griffiths, throughout 1969, was giving hope to humanity by his emphasis on the priorities of reconciliation and peace. This was the standpoint of Geoffrey Tribe of London. In his letter to James Griffiths that summer, he said:

> *We have watched with admiration all that you have done. It is splendid work.*[77]

The Foreign Office received constant correspondence from Griffiths statesman. Michael Stewart decided to call and see him when he (Griffiths) was spending a few days at the Adult Education Centre in Huntercombe Manor on the invitation of the warden, Graham Thomas, and his wife, Ismay. Griffiths admired greatly an article in the Sunday Observer by the novelist and journalist, Freddie Forsyth. Forsyth called for three things to settle the dispute:

(i) A truce;

(ii) There was no way for them to settle the dispute through military means;

(iii) The need for self-government for Biafra.

Griffiths responded to the visit of Michael Stewart and the recommendations of Forsyth in a letter dated 9 November 1969 to Stewart.[78] His priority was to see order being restored to Nigeria after its violence and suffering. One can sense his frustration at the sad situation and his great desire for reconciliation:

> *This is my last Parliamentary Session and I would like, before I bid good-bye to Westminster, to see our Government succeed in bringing this tragic war to a peaceful end.*[79]

Stewart responded on 25 November in a detailed letter, but the crux of the letter was to put the blame for the Civil war on the shoulders of Biafra's Colonel Ojukwu. Stewart stated:

> *I am sure that a peaceful conclusion could be obtained if Colonel Ojukwu would change his objectives from sovereignty to security.*[80]

Griffiths was not convinced by the Foreign Secretary. He was determined to attend the debate in the House of Commons on 9 December, even though he was not at all well. He was seen resting on his walking stick as he argued that the civil war in Nigeria meant that the natives were killed by the bullets of the white man.[81] To him the three powers that had to be condemned were France, Russia and Britain, all of them ready to sell arms to fuel the civil war. Once again, in the vote at the end of the debate Griffiths opposed his government. The number of the rebels was much smaller. Only he and 8 other Labour MPs defied the government.[82] Each one of them voted in the hope of persuading their government to change its approach. But there was no way of convincing Wilson and Stewart. The Labour Government had a majority of 170 in the Commons.[83] But James Griffiths and Fenner Brockway had not lost their dynamism. Better news came through at the beginning of 1970. They knew that Judge Louis Mbanefo and Colonel Philip Effiong, both noble characters, were at the helm in Biafra. When Effiong was given authority in Biafra on 8 January, he decided immediately that there was no purpose to continuing the conflict which was wrecking Nigeria.[84] So on Monday 12 January 1970, Biafra ceased its hostilities, and on 16 January a team of eight observers was sent to Biafra to oversee the situation. Among them was Colonel Douglas Cairns from Britain, whom Griffiths had met when he was in Lagos. Though the civil war was at an end, Griffiths reminded his party of the glaring mistakes that had taken place. In March 1970 a letter of his appeared in the journal Socialist Commentary.[85] He stated again that the civil war had created disunity and a big problem for the Labour Party. He felt that the Wilson government had lost an opportunity to be a force for reconciliation:

> *It is my view that we can serve as a mediator and reconciler. Our decision to supply arms to one side made it impossible to fulfil the role in the Nigerian Civil War.*[86]

He reminded the readers that eight nations had contributed to the tragedy of the Nigeria-Biafra civil war:

> *I note General Gowan's statement that there should be an end of foreign intervention in the affairs of Nigeria. I hope he follows it up with the cancellation of arms from London and Moscow.*[87]

Griffiths was unable, due to his physical weakness, to be as active by the beginning of 1970 as he had been in the autumn of 1968 when he began his involvement.[88] Maurice Foley, a minister in the Foreign Office, noticed his absence from the House (something very unusual for him) in a letter dated 31 March 1970:

> *Sorry that we have not seen you at the House in present weeks.*[89]

Foley informed his friend that the Labour government was making a determined effort to alleviate the desperate situation and had already sent 3,750 tons of food to be distributed in Biafra and Nigeria by the middle of March. They knew that much more needed to be done, but Griffiths took comfort that his government was in constant and close contact with the government of Nigeria. Fenner Brockway sent him a letter on 9 April 1970 expressing his regret that he was unable to travel around as he had always done. He referred sensitively to Griffiths's loving nature:

*With you I am always thinking about the children and mothers whom we saw in Biafra. It is very difficult to judge how far relief for the hungry is being given effectively.*[90]

He was also grieved that they could not depend on the truth of the reports of the situation in Nigeria. Then Fenner Brockway expresses his greatest frustration with regard to the ministers within the Foreign Office. He thought each one of them as individuals were decent people. Then he explains:

*One of the difficulties of politics is that unsatisfactory decisions have to be made by people who are fundamentally nice.*[91]

He was referring in particular to politicians like Maurice Foley. James Griffiths had to remember that it was he who had been an inspiration to both Brockway and Foley.[92]

Thousands of Labour Party members had been inspired by their campaign and the courage and determination of James Griffiths and Fenner Brockway. A socialist from Dumfries, Dorothy Usher, reminded Griffiths:

*My father would have been shocked by the present Labour Government's attitude to the whole issue; we thought they believed in human rights.*[93]

To Mabel English of Aigburth, Liverpool both of them were brave politicians who had shown the way forward for the cause of peace on the African continent. It was one more appreciative letter among many that James Griffiths received.[94]

At the end of his career in parliament, James Griffiths achieved a notable contribution. It was so very different to what he had done in his long career. He indicated that human rights, violence and a civil war were matters that forced one politician to rebel against his Party and Government. We have described him as a faithful and loyal politician, always supportive of the leadership, but in 1968 and 1969 Griffiths was without a doubt a rebel with a cause, the need for justice for the ordinary people of Biafra. When he heard at the beginning of 1970 that Colonel Ojukwu was submitting to General Gowan, he admitted: 'When I heard the news I had a mixed feeling of relief and regret.'[95]

He believed that Biafra should have what Wales should also have, namely devolution. That was the real need of his own nation as well as the need of the Ibo nation in Biafra. Throughout 1970 and 1971 his efforts for peace and reconciliation in Nigeria and Biafra were constantly in his thoughts. He wrote his final notes on the subject in his own handwriting on 8 August 1971 when he admits: 'In the interval have re-lived those days in Biafra and Nigeria.'[96]

He could not escape from his courageous adventure. The Nigerian authorities had made it so difficult for these two elder statesmen. Fenner Brockway wrote: 'An MP who wished to go to Biafra, was discouraged, those going to Nigeria were given every assistance.'[97] But he and Brockway had achieved so much in this peace mission. We can only admire his resilience, courage, vision and love of humanity.[98] But we must also acknowledge his sincere commitment and his inspiration to a generation of young as well as older politicians at the beginning of the 1970s.

## Notes and References

1      Fran Alexander, 'Alun Isaacs, Jonathan Law, Peter Lewis (eds.), *Oxford Encyclopaedia of World History* (Oxford, 1998), p. 478.

2      Ibid.

3      Ibid.

4.     Ibid.

5.     Ibid., p.76.

6.     The story is in Frederick Forsyth, *The Biafra Story: The Making of an African Legend* (Barnsley, 2007).

7.     Harold Wilson, *The Government 1964-1970: A Personal Record* (London, 1971), p. 556. 'Had Britain not been the traditional arms supplier we could have taken a more detached line, without facing the charge that every death in Nigeria must be laid at our door'.

8.     Ibid., p. 557. He adds 'who with others, embraced the Biafra cause.' James Griffiths never explains why he supported the people of Biafra. Was it because of what Philip Weeks of the NCB in south Wales said? He wrote in the early 1970s: 'The miners of the Valleys, and I am one, remind me most of the Ibo miners (the Biafrans in the Eastern sector of Nigeria), and of the Ukranians – warm and friendly, emotional, difficult to manage but capable of responding to sensitive and intelligent leadership, an outrageously sly sense of humour, fiercely proud of being Ukranian, Ibo, Welsh – and all quite emphatic that they are not Russian, Nigerian or English; mixed blood; great talkers and debaters'. See Paul H. Ballard and Erastus Jones (eds.) *The Valley Call* (Ferndale, 1975), p. 82.

9.     NLW, James Griffiths Papers B11/16, namely, the article, 'Biafra's terrifying dilemma', *Western Mail*, June 13, 1968, p. 8.

10.    Ibid.

11.    Ibid., B11/26 James Griffiths, *Notes*.

12.    Ibid., 'Tell General Gowan now that we can have no part in the crime and stop at once a supply of arms to the Federal Government... Let our message be to both sides, "Stop it Now". He received a letter from George Thomson, Foreign Office, dated 29 August 1968. See B11/27, and the words of Thomson: 'You will know from my statement that, after the most anxious consideration, we still feel that in present circumstances the policy we have followed in this most difficult and harrowing situation remains the right one'. James Griffiths sent a letter to the *Llanelli Star*, August 10, 1968 calling for unity, see, ibid., B11/23. Letter on 19 August to Lord Malcolm Shepherd.

13.    Ibid. B11/30. Letter Andrew Brewin to James Griffiths, 12 November 1968. The report was dated 6 November 1968.

14.    Ibid.

15.    Ibid., B11/28 Harold Wilson to James Griffiths (no date).

16.    NLW, James Griffiths Papers B11/44 *Biafra and Nigeria*.

17.    Fenner Brockway, *Towards Tomorrow* (London, 1977), p. 252.

18.    NLW, James Griffiths Papers B11/44 *Biafra and Nigeria*.

19. Fenner Brockway, *Towards Tomorrow*, p. 253. As they neared the airport in the dark Brockway says: 'As we neared the mainland, lights were put out and Jim gripped my hand whilst John turned his portable recorder to music'. Why fly by night? Harold Wilson gives the answer, *The Labour Government 1964-1970: A Personal Record*, p. 558. 'Later, when the relief organisations sought to fly the food in, he (Colonel Ojukwu) rejected day flights, because under the cover of night relief, he could fly in the French arms he so sorely needed to carry on the war'.

20. NLW, James Griffiths Papers B11/48. *Night flight to Biafra.*

21. Ibid.

22. Ibid.

23. NLW, James Griffiths Papers B11/44.

24. Ibid. 25. Ibid. 26. Ibid. 27. Ibid. 28. Ibid. 29. Ibid.

30. Ibid.

31. NLW, James Griffiths Papers B11/46.

32. Ibid. 33. Ibid.

34. Ibid.

35. *Guardian*, December 17, 1968. ibid., B11/43.

36. NLW, James Griffiths Papers B11/46.

37. Ibid.

38. Ibid.

39. Ibid.

40. Ibid. 41.

41. Ibid. 42

42. Ibid.

43. Ibid.

44. Ibid.

45. Ibid.

46. Fenner Brockway, *Towards Tomorrow*, p.181.

47. NLW, James Griffiths Papers, B11/46.

48. Ibid.

49. Ibid.

50. Ibid.

51. 'MP in Biafra Mercy Flight', *The Llanelli Star*, December 21, 1968, p. 10.

52. Ibid.

53. James Griffiths, 'We need to Conquer Hunger before Space', *Llanelli Star*, 4 January 1969 p.5.

54. Fenner Brockway, *Towards Tomorrow*, p.254.

55. NLW James Griffiths Papers B11/46.

56. Ibid.

57. Ibid.

58. Lord Brockway, 'The Life and Times of James Griffiths', *Western Mail*, 8 March 1969.

59. Ibid.

60. Winifred Griffiths, *One Woman's Story* (Ferndale, 1979), p. 74.

61. Harold Wilson, *The Labour Government 1964-1970: A Personal Record*, p. 558.

62. NLW, James Griffiths Papers, B11/50. No date on a letter of Mervyn Jones to James Griffiths.

63. Ibid., B11/55.

64. Ibid., B11/49. Letter from Tam Dalyell, MP, dated 30 December 1968 to James Griffiths.

65. Ibid., B11/64. Letter from Gwynfor Evans, Llangadog to James Griffiths.

66. Ibid.

67. Ibid., B11/65. Letter from Brinley Owen, Llanelli to James Griffiths dated 31 December 1968.

68. Ibid., B11/66. James Griffiths Notes on Nigeria-Biafra.

69. Ibid., B11/68. Peace Initiative in Nigeria, 24 February 1969. Those named are Stanley Henig, David Crouch, Hugh Fraser, James Davidson, Frank Allaun from the Labour Party as well as those of Welsh descent.

70. Ibid., B11/69. Labour Conference in Ammanford 1969.

71. Ibid., B11/70. *Times* Editorial 14 March 1969.

72. Ibid.

73. Ibid., B11/72. Harold Wilson visiting Nigeria, April 1969.

74. Ibid., B11/77. Letter Michael Stewart to James Griffiths 8 July 1969.

75. Ibid., B11/76. A Time for world Action.

76. Ibid.

77. Ibid., B11/74. Letter from Geoffrey Tribe dated 27 June 1969.

78. Ibid., B11/79. Letter James Griffiths to Michael Stewart dated 9 November 1969.

79. Ibid.

80. Ibid., B11/81. Letter Michael Stewart to James Griffiths dated 25 November 1969.

81. Ibid., B11/83. *Western Mail*, dated 10 December 1969.

82. Ibid.

83. Ibid.

84. Ibid., B11/83. See letter of Fenner Brockway to James Griffiths, February 1970 where he re-lives the journey to Biafra.

85. Ibid., B11/84. Letter in *Socialist Commentary*, March 1970.

86. Ibid.

87. Ibid.

88. Ibid., B11/85. Letter M. Foley to James Griffiths, 31 March 1970.

89. Ibid.

90. Ibid., B11/86. Letter Fenner Brockway to James Griffiths dated 9 April 1970.

91. Ibid.

92. Ibid.

93. Ibid., B11/56. Letter from Dorothy Usher to James Griffiths.

94. Ibid., B11/59. Letter Mabel English, dated 11 January 1969. He also received letters from: B11/60. A. J. Snowbutts, Llangennech, 22 December 1968 (B11/52); Harold Henemy, Falmouth, 30 December 1968 (B11/53); J. V. Harries, Secretary Presbyterian Church of Wales (English Association), Llanelli, 31 December 1968 (B11/54); Shade Brown, 30 December 1968 (B11/57) and Islwyn Griffiths, Newport 25 December 1968 (B11/58).

95. Ibid., B11/46. A note dated 8 August 1971.

96. Ibid.

97. Fenner Brockway, *The Colonial Revolution* (St Albans, 1973), p. 170.

98. NLW, James Griffiths Papers, B11/46.

# 20

## End of the Pilgrimage

James Griffiths was in the ranks of the veteran politicians when he retired from the House of Commons in 1970. He was eighty years of age. As a Cabinet Minister, a former Secretary of State, he could have accepted the invitation to enter the House of Lords. He did not follow the usual convention, one of the few politicians who declined the perceived elevation.One could argue that his health was an important factor in his decision not to accept the opportunity to serve further in the political sphere. But it would be unfair on him to emphasise his health as the only reason why he refused the attraction of the House of Lords. A large number of his friends from working-class backgrounds had accepted, as a badge of honour, the opportunity to serve in the House of Lords. The House of Lords had been for centuries the bastion of hereditary principle, confined exclusively to men of the upper class. The Life Peerage Act of 1958 had changed the situation.

Some coalminers were very attracted to the pomp of the House of Lords. Bernard Taylor, who had served as James Griffiths's Parliamentary Private Secretary accepted the offer of becoming Lord Taylor, Bill Blyton, another coalminer, became a Life Peer. So did T. W. Jones, the MP for Merionethshire who became Lord Maelor and who was proud of the honour and also proud that James Griffiths had come to see him being introduced to the House of Lords. I believe on the basis of my conversations with him that it was not ill health which made Griffiths reluctant to wear the robes and to sit with comrades from every walk of life: the professions, the academic world, industry, particularly mining, the trade unions and the bishops of the Church of England. It was a matter of principle. On the basis of a conversation which he had with Gwilym Prys Davies and knowing of his proud regard for the working class, it was obvious that he would find it most difficult, on principle, to enter the House of Lords. The life story of Lloyd George indicates how an able politician can do strange things in his old age, and Lloyd George's decision to accept the trappings of the House of Lords completely baffled James Griffiths. He was very proud to prepare the way for a young politician to follow him as member of parliament for Llanelli. He travelled to Llanelli on 25 May 1968 to present his successor to the stalwarts in the Labour movement. Griffiths greatly admired Denzil Davies, a young man of twenty-nine who had graduated with distinction from the University of Oxford. It was he who was choosen to represent the Labour Party for Llanelli.[1] Then in June 1970 Denzil Davies won with a similar majority to his predecessor , even against the rugby idol of Llanelli, Carwyn James, who stood  with  huge confidence for Plaid Cymru.[2]  The verdict of Griffiths on Plaid Cymru was still relevant (even considering their failure to keep Carmarthen in 1970) for the overall vote of the nationalists increased from 61,007 in 1966 to 175,016 in 1970.[3]

 Griffiths met the members of the Welsh Labour Parliamentary Group in a dinner organised after the election to recognise the contribution of the parliamentarians who had retired.[4]

These were James Griffiths, Eirene White, Arthur Pearson and Harold Finch. In their place Denzil Davies, Barry Jones, Brynmor T. John and Neil Kinnock had been elected. Two of the new MPs were from the legal profession and the other two were educationalists. There were no manual workers to succeed them. Of all the Welsh Labour MPs there were only three left who had been involved in the mining industry: Elfed Davies (Rhondda East), Tom Ellis (Wrexham) and S. O. Davies (Merthyr). The leader of the Labour Party, Harold Wilson, came to the dinner to offer a toast to the four who had retired as parliamentarians, though Eirene White had accepted the invitation to serve in the House of Lords. Griffiths was invited to respond on behalf of the four who were retiring. In accordance with his usual practice he had a few notes, but in the friendly atmosphere he forgot his prepared response and spoke from the heart in a highly emotional atmosphere. He was absolutely stunning and Harold Wilson regarded his speech as one of the half dozen best speeches he had ever heard.[5] Griffiths was asked for a copy of his speech, but he admitted it was an impossible request. What he did was to remember his pilgrimage from Betws in the days of Keir Hardie to the days of Harold Wilson and the Labour governments of the 1960s. Wilson had high regard for him though he had proved a difficult MP on the issue of the civil war in Biafra. Griffiths thanked him for one of his  consideration in presenting to the Queen his name for the highest honours in the land at the end of his period as Secretary of State for Wales. James Griffiths received from the Prime Minister a letter on 6 May 1966:

> *I am writing to confirm that I propose to submit your name to the Queen with the recommendation that Her Majesty will be graciously pleased to approve that you be appointed a Member of the Order of the Companion of Honour.*[6]

This is one of the most important honours that a politician or any British citizen can receive, and by the recommendation of Harold Wilson, James Griffiths was given an unexpected and unique honour.  His retirement brought him an opportunity to read widely, to listen daily to the radio, to watch television, to welcome friends from the world of politics and to receive the loving care of his wife and family.[7] He did not neglect his lifelong habit of corresponding with his friends, and one of those who wrote regularly to him was Graham P. Thomas, warden of the Adult Education Residential College in Taplow, Buckinghamshire. The pair had corresponded and regularly met each other over a period of thirty years.[8]

At the beginning of 1971 he was informed that the Adult Education College at Harlech called Coleg Harlech, which he had supported since the 1930s, was going to call one of its rooms the James Griffiths Room. He expressed the wish that the testimonial, which had been organised in his constituency in the capable hands of Councillor W. J. Davies from Glanaman to recognise his sterling service of thirty-four years, should be presented to Coleg Harlech.

By September 1971, this had been realised and the institution at Harlech had been remembered.[9] He had visited his old constituency in May 1971. It was good to see his friends and his family in Ammanford and to call in Llanelli. It was an honour to unveil a tablet to recognise his huge service to the Amman Valley. He experienced a great deal of pain in his legs on this nostalgic journey.[10] The doctors informed him that he was suffering from rheumatism as well as diabetes. He could not escape from these for the rest of his days.

He felt in his retirement that what he called the Welsh Agenda was proceeding favourably. To him the most important event was the publication of the Report of the Commission on the Constitution, the socalled Kilbrandon Report, which would recommend that Wales and Scotland should have Assemblies in Cardiff and Edinburgh.[11] It was a great joy for him that the Welsh Labour Party was ready to respond positively and it was gratifying that his standpoint was being supported by four able politicians: Cledwyn Hughes, Goronwy Roberts, John Morris and Michael Foot, as well as the Welsh organiser of the Labour Party, Emrys Jones. In the summer of 1973 he prepared a valuable chapter on 'Welsh Politics in my Lifetime' which was subsequently published in James Griffiths and His Times. This volume was produced through the efforts of Emrys Jones and others within the Labour Party and published in 1979.

Emrys Jones also suggested that a Memorial Lecture should be held in Llanelli and Professor J. Beverley Smith of the University College of Wales, Aberystwyth, should deliver the lecture. While this was being organised the chapter written by James Griffiths came to the attention of his admirers and it was decided to include the lecture as well. In this chapter he included one small paragraph on a question that he had been a key player on the Welsh scene. One comes across a sentence which reflects his awareness of the reality of British politics:

> *If the Commission recommends a Parliament for Wales and Scotland, it will also have to make a recommendation for a federal system and this might destroy the chance of securing a measure of self government which Labour can support at the Election and in Parliament. I hope the Commission will, in view of the change in Northern Ireland from a Parliament to an Assembly, recommend a National Assembly for Wales and for Scotland.*[12]

The Commission decided against independence for Wales and Scotland as well as rejecting a federal system. The majority voted for a legislative devolution, an Assembly for Wales and Scotland to deal with their own matters within a constitutional framework. The current debate centres on moving to a federal system which James Griffiths foresaw forty years ago. He had a talent for reading the signs of the times, and one can claim that his suggestion is among the most important of his ideas, and that the politicians of tomorrow will have to debate again what James Griffiths suggested in 1973.[13]

This is a question that neither Labour nor the Conservatives are willing to discuss at the time of this biography's publication. In fact they refuse to even consider it as a topic for discussion. Griffiths prepared the valuable article when he was unwell, and he had to face a surgical operation in the summer of 1973.[14] He came through the ordeal and resumed his reading and writing his intriguing study on 'Welsh politics in my lifetime'. Then at the beginning of 1974 his wife fell and broke her hip. The eldest daughter who had settled in Sweden came home to look after her father until her mother was well enough to take charge of the domestic chores. The children suggested that both their parents should move, as there was a bungalow on sale nearby in Teddington. They had very little option but to move, and they did, to 72 Elmfield Avenue, Teddington. After a year in the new address Griffiths's health deteriorated and by the middle of April 1975 he could not leave his home without the assistance of his family.[15] The presence of his son Harold and his family living in a nearby street was a great comfort to both James and Winifred.[16]

 James Griffiths did not welcome spending weeks in a hospital. The eldest daughter and her husband stepped in, and through their efforts, the family doctor and the community nursing service, he was well cared for in his home, to his delight. His political friends, John Morris and Denzil Davies, came to see him and he made an effort to welcome them to his living room. The last words he uttered in Welsh to his successor Denzil Davies was to ask him to 'garco'r ofalaeth', an idiomatic phrase for caring for the constituency.[17] Both Davies and Morris were pleasantly surprised at how sharp his mind was, and how he followed current debate and issues on the Welsh radio channels and Radio Four. At the beginning of August 1975, he slowly fell into a deep sleep, and for the last eighteen days of his life he struggled hard for his breath. As his youngest son, Arthur, was at hand, he was able to stay with him and his mother on the last night of his life. On 7 August 1975 one of the most endearing and influential politicians of the twentieth century died peacefully at his home, surrounded by his loved ones.[18]

The following day an obituary appeared in *The Times*, underlining his greatness, his contribution to the Welfare State and his desire for the whole world to enjoy these benefits. It gives a glimpse of a parliamentarian who embodied sincerity:

> *Cynics might sneer when Jim Griffiths, hand on heart in that familiar gesture, poured out a flood of Celtic emotion. In highest flight of Welsh flavour he could be prolix, repetitive, often obscure, but real sincerity shone through the welter of words. 'Let me say this, Mr Speaker' recurred endlessly in his speeches. Such tricks could irritate but the House constantly found itself swept into the current of his eloquence and beguiled by his utter lack of guile, much more than by what he said – and he said a great deal – Jim Griffiths commanded respect and affection by what he was, a man who enriched and sweetened political life with rare qualities of heart and mind.*[19]

The only deficiency in this valuable obituary in the pages of The Times is that the anonymous author does not deal in detail with the important leadership and support he gave to the idea of Secretary of State for Wales. All this is forgotten in this matter-of-fact note:

> *The crown of his political career was his appointment (1964-66) as the first Secretary of State for Wales with a seat in the Cabinet and a department to which Whitehall had transferred the most important Welsh responsibilities.*[20]

The obituary prepared by John Osmond in the Western Mail was entirely different. He wrote these important insights:

> *When he relinquished the post of Secretary of State in April 1966 he had set the guidelines for what were to become Welsh policy preoccupations to this day – the Welsh economy and the fight for full employment, rural depopulation (he advocated*

*building a new town in mid Wales) and the expansion of education. By the time he became Secretary of State he was also committed to the idea of a directly elected Welsh Assembly and was instrumental in this being adopted by the Welsh Labour Party in 1965.*[21]

John Osmond suggested that James Griffiths had transferred his vision of devolution to three individuals whom he greatly admired, namely John Morris, Secretary of State for Wales, Emrys Jones, Secretary of the Welsh Labour Party, and Gwilym Prys Davies, political advisor to the Welsh Office at that time. These three men always acknowledged the inspiration of James Griffiths.

His funeral was arranged for Wednesday, 13 August 1975 in Gellimanwydd Chapel, Ammanford. The mourners came from far and near and filled the large chapel, and a notable nonconformist service was held under the guidelines of the minister, Reverend Derwyn Morris Jones. Two hymns were sung, a Welsh hymn written by Elfed 'Rho im yr Hedd' ('Give Me the Peace'), and the hymn 'Abide With Me' in English. On the funeral leaflet was printed the prayer of John Henry Newman. It was a prayer uttered by the politician and his wife at the end of the day:

> *May He support us all the day*
> *long, till the shades lengthen,*
> *and the evening comes, and the*
> *busy world is hushed and the fever*
> *is over, and our work is done.*

A tribute was given by the minister, and it is a very fine eulogy. It is appropriate to translate some of the sentiments found in the eulogy. Reverend Derwyn Morris Jones spoke of him as a Welshman:

> *We, his fellow Welshmen, will remember his love for his own people – our language and traditions and our national life. There was nothing more appropriate than for him to be chosen as the first Secretary of State for the Welsh Office which he fought for a long time to get established. Very few men in his Party have struggled with such determination and conviction on these first steps that the Labour Party implemented in its relationship with Wales.*[22]

He emphasised his humanity.

> *This is a man of great humanity, an emotional person, with a warm heart, kind and loving. Many of us knew of his voluntary work as the first Treasurer of War on Want, which was established by Oxfam and Christian Aid to fight hunger and poverty and to relieve suffering.*[23]

He referred to his Christian idealism as one who had been nurtured in the doctrines and principles of the faith. 'The Christian faith was the faith which was sheltered in his heart and

Christ was the locator of Hope in his eyes.' Then the minister gave a glimpse of his relationship with the church of his childhood and adolescence. He added:

> *We thank God for James Griffiths, for the honour of knowing him, and for the delight of remembering him before God in the church where he was brought up, and where he returned regularly to worship.*

In the cemetery of Christian Temple Welsh Independent chapel he was laid to rest, near his ancestors and his fellow Welshmen. A service of Thanksgiving was held in the City Hall, Cardiff, on Friday night, 5 December 1975. The Secretary of State for Wales, John Morris, presided and tributes were paid to his memory by James Callaghan, T. Glanville Williams, a Labour leader in Llanelli, and Glyn Williams from 'the Fed', the miners' union.[24] Reverend Derwyn Morris Jones offered the prayer and the benediction, and two hymns were sung, '*Rho im yr Hedd*' which had been sung at his funeral and a hymn from the Welsh Methodist Revival, 'Guide me, O Thou Great Jehovah'. The Llanelli Male Voice Choir took part and on the leaflet were found the words 'We Want Bread and Roses Too' from his autobiography *Pages from Memory*, where he acknowledges his longing for a better, cleaner and more perfect world, a world which was more righteous than had been seen in the twentieth century. He mentions in *Pages from Memory* the story of a strike in a factory in the United States. It was not a strike about more wages. The leader of the strike carried a large banner beasing the words, 'We Want Bread and Roses'. He adds: 'Bread and Roses, the symbols of the ideal society which inspired me in the morning of life – and still beckons me on at close of day.'[25]

James Griffiths had fought and campaigned from his youth for the Kingdom of Light, for righteousness, for the rights of the miners, the dignity of the underprivileged on five continents, for extending the priorities of the Welfare State of which his fellow Welshmen Robert Owen and David Lloyd George had dreamt of and laid the foundations of in Britain. He sincerely believed that the banner he had flown for bread and roses belonged to every age. The Reverend W. J. Griffiths from Llanelli (a Temperance worker par excellence), who attended his funeral in Ammanford and his memorial service in Cardiff adds: 'Our debt to James Griffiths remains for everything he did to preserve our most important values'.[26] Two other fellow Welsh Independent ministers added similar tributes. The Reverend Dr E. Lewis Evans from Pontarddulais said:

> *besides his obvious talents, he is a very likeable person to whom you could approach and an inheritor of the old Welsh radicalism, with its emphasis on righteousness between human beings and his emphasis on good and sober living.* [27]
> The Reverend E. Curig Davies said: 'His interest to the end of his life was the condition of people and in particular the good of Wales in language and culture'.[28]

I believe that E. Curig Davies brought together in that sentence the message and the emphasis of this biography. Christopher Harvie emphasised the same theme when he wrote in 1995:

> *The early Independent Labour Party espoused much of the gwerin values of radical liberalism, including home rule, supported by Keir Hardie at Merthyr and James Griffiths at Llanelli.*[29]

279

As the years go by, more and more Welsh politicians and Welsh historians realise the unique contribution of James Griffiths. Donald Anderson says: 'In him can be seen most perfectly the specific Welsh input to the British socialist tradition.'[30] Peter Hain, a Welsh Office Minister, meanwhile says: 'Jim Griffiths was the man who converted Labour to the concept of Welsh devolution.'[31] When Carwyn Jones was the first Minister of Wales, was is proud that he stood in the tradition of the Welsh devolutionists within the Labour Party, in the tradition of E. T. John, Huw T. Edwards, James Griffiths, Cledwyn Hughes, David Thomas, John Morris, S. O. Davies, Goronwy Roberts, Huw T. Edwards and Gwilym Prys Davies. James Griffiths would agree with his progressive views on Welsh identity. This is an example:

> *Where the [Labour] Party presents itself as a Welsh party it will succeed. The vast majority of the people of Wales are happy with an inclusive Welshness that does not follow the nationalist path of independence.*[32]

And again:

> *To be seen as taking a position hostile to the Welsh language in a Wales where the clear majority of people either speak Welsh or have a great deal of goodwill towards the language is tantamount to an electorate suicide.*[33]

Carwyn Jones is right in suggesting that James Griffiths would be very happy with such a standpoint. For he was delighted when Harold Wilson invited John Morris to be Secretary of State for Wales in 1974 and not George Thomas who had not embraced fully his idealism. John Morris then appointed Gwilym Prys Davies as a Special Advisor which pleased Griffiths in his old age. He knew that Harold Wilson took the Kilbrandon Report seriously; indeed he was convinced of the need for devolution. In a letter a few months before his death to John Osmond, Griffiths spoke with confidence of the next decade. He believed in all sincerity that the Welsh Assembly was on the horizon. 'I feel,' he said, 'real regret that I shall be out of it all'.[34] If he had lived he would have been so disappointed with the result of the referendum which was held on St David's Day 1979 when the majority of the Welsh people refused to support the concept of a Welsh Assembly in Cardiff. Of the total electorate, 11.8% were in favour of an Assembly and 46.5% were against. Another 42% did not vote.

The British element within the Welsh Labour Party had won convincingly, those led by the so-called Gang of Six, namely Leo Abse, Neil Kinnock, Donald Anderson, Ioan Evans, Ifor Davies and Fred Evans. The most vociferous of the six MPs was Neil Kinnock. To him Wales did not deserve an Assembly, the cost would be excessive and all the arguments from the James Griffiths camp were irrelevant. From the members of the Cabinet, John Morris, Michael Foot and David Owen at least indicated some enthusiasm, though James Callaghan came very late in the day to urge the Welsh electorate to vote Yes, and so possess power in their own country. Leo Abse, MP for Pontypool, argued that the English-speaking people of Wales would be dominated by the Welsh-speaking minority.[35] It was a sad time and the 'Gwent card' of Abse fed into the 1979 Labour No Assembly campaign day and Wales had to wait another eighteen years before implementing one of the most desired policies of James Griffiths. The next referendum was held on 18 May 1997, and supporters of devolution had to wait till the very last moment to receive the result of the County of Carmarthenshire, the county which meant so much James Griffiths, to tip the tide in favour of a yes vote. After counting over a million votes, the majority was only 6,721 in favour of the Yes vote. The No Assembly camp had done exceedingly well.

The most important 'No' figure in 1997 was Llew Smith, MP for Blaenau Gwent. Gwent and Glamorganshire were still in the 'No' camp. Cardiff and Newport were against, though Neath and Swansea were for the proposed Assembly. The valleys of Glamorganshire, Rhondda, Cynon, and Taff were in favour, so was Gwynedd in north-west Wales and Dyfed in west Wales, except for Pembrokeshire. The biggest difficulty was to encourage the electorate to vote. Only 50.3% of voters went to the polling booths, much less than in Scotland where turnout had been 61.5%. But one cannot but agree with the claim of Carwyn Jones: 'The National Assembly is Welsh Labour's greatest creation'.[36] We can also rightfully claim that James Griffiths was the architect of the Welsh National Assembly; it was he who made the dream of Keir Hardie a possibility by the time he became the Secretary of State for Wales. Thirty-three years later, in 1997, that dream came true.

**Notes and References**

1.  For David John Denzil Davies (1938-2018 ), see *Welsh Hustings 1885-2004*, compiled by Ivor Thomas Rees (Llandybïe, 2005), p. 61.

2.  The results for the Llanelli constituency on 18 June 1970: Denzil Davies (Labour) 31,398; Carwyn James (Plaid Cymru) 8,387; Miss M A Jones (Conservative) 5,777; D.J. Lewis (Liberal) 3,834; R.E. Hitchon (Communist) 603; Majority 23,011. Beti Jones, Etholiadau Seneddol yng Nghymru 1900-75, p.152. Denzil Davies was following a politician who had left his mark as Dr Kenneth O. Morgan admitted, 'a career which embraced the Secretaryship of the Colonies and for Wales marked a signal personal achievement, made possible by the success of the moderate constitutional Labour Party he helped to fashion in the 1920s.' See Kenneth O. Morgan, 'Welsh Politics 1918-1939' in Trevor Herbert & Gareth Elwyn Jones (editors) *Wales Between the Wars* (Cardiff, 1988), p.127.

3.  Conversation of the author with Tam Dalyell on Friday, 3 February 2012. He stated that James Griffiths understood the appeal of nationalism in Scotland better than the Scottish MPs did. You could compare his understanding with that of Willie Ross, who had also been Secretary of State for Scotland and had no sensitivity in dealing with the Scottish nationalists.

4.  *James Griffiths and His Times*, p.56.

5.  Ibid., 'News of the oration spread through Labour circles in the House and Harold Wilson said that it was one of the half dozen finest speeches he had ever heard and he regretted that it had not been recorded'.

6.  NLW, James Griffiths Papers C7/44, A letter of Harold Wilson to James Griffiths, dated 6 May 1966.

7.  NLW, Manuscript 23091E. The letters of Graham F Thomas. James Griffiths, in a letter dated 20 November 1970 to Graham F. Thomas .Then Griffiths states  that he  listens to the radio and that Fred
    Peart and Jim Johnson had called and that he was uncomfortable with the standpoint of Tony Benn who was in favour of referendum on every issue.

8.  Ibid.

9.  Ibid., Letter of James Griffiths to Graham F. Thomas, dated 5 January 1971.

10.     Ibid., Letter of James Griffiths to Graham F. Thomas, dated 18 May 1971.

11.     *James Griffiths and His Times*, p.56.

12.     Ibid., pp.56-7.

13.     The presence of James Griffiths was greatly missed in the Welsh Parliamentary Labour Party. By the summer of 1974 when Labour was beginning to look again at the question of devolution the Welsh Parliamentary Labour Party was split by a small number of parliamentarians under the leadership of Neil Kinnock which called for a referendum. Through the careful stewardship of J. Emrys Jones and the existence of a Welsh Trade Union Congress (since 1972), devolution had become a possibility. See John Osmond, *Creative Conflict: The Politics of Welsh Devolution* (Llandysul, London, Boston, 1978), pp. 124-5. After the publication of the booklet, Democracy and Devolution Proposals or Scotland and Wales (London, 1974), pp.1-24. James Griffiths could claim that he had read it carefully. See NLW, James Griffiths Papers.

14.     NLW, Manuscript 23091E. Letters to Graham F. Thomas. A letter from James Griffiths to Graham F. Thomas, dated 24 August 1973 where he mentions the task of writing the chapter, on his surgical operation, and how his wife was enjoying reading the large volume, *Anatomy of Britain* by Anthony Sampson.

15.     Ibid. Letter of James and Winifred Griffiths to Graham F. Thomas dated 15 April 1975. It was his wife who wrote the letter on his behalf. He was too weak to do what he had done day after day since his adolescence. Both admitted: 'Our health is declining with age, and we are confined to the house except for occasional car rides with the family'.

16.     Ibid.

17.     A personal conversation with Denzil Davies on 3 February 2012. NLW James Griffiths Papers. A letter from Denzil Davies to James Griffiths 25 September 1974. This letter has a great deal of information on the political situation in Wales. Griffiths received a letter from John Morris, after the October 1974 General Election, that is written on 20 November 1974. The Secretary of State for Wales had read the letter written by James Griffiths and published in the *Times*, dated 20 October and his important comments on devolution. 'Your concept of an Annual State of Nation Convention is an interesting one'. Morris admits that the relationship of the Welsh Assembly and national as well as local government is extremely important and entails a great deal of discussion. He was personally very grateful for his views and agreed that it was presented in the public forum so they could be studied.

18.     Editor, Meic Stephens, *Cydymaith i Lenyddiaeth Cymru* (Cardiff, 1980), p. 233.

19.     Obituary, *The Times*, 8 August 1975.

20.     Ibid.

21.     John Osmond, 'James Griffiths' *Western Mail*, 8 August 1975.

22.     Derwyn Morris Jones, 'James Griffiths', *Y Tyst*, August 1975.

23.     Ibid.

24.     The tribute by James Callaghan has been published in James Griffiths and his Times, pp. 9-15. It is a fine tribute, and in particular when he brings together the qualities which was responsible for the greatness of the politician 'He was never a ruthless or self-seeking man. He gave himself to the people. He worked for them: and it was because of this that they responded to him'. (p.14).

25.     James Griffiths, *Pages from Memory*, p. 208.

26.     W. J. Griffiths, 'Remembering Jim Griffiths', *Amrywiaeth Llanelli*, Number 11 (Llanelli), p.56.

27.     E. Curig Davies, 'Remembering James Griffiths', *Y Tyst*, August 29, 1975, p.2.

28.  Ibid.

29.  Christopher Harvie, 'Wales and the Wider World', in *Post War Wales* (editors, Trevor Herbert and Gareth Elwyn Jones) (Cardiff, 1995), p. 165. Harvie said of him in this essay: 'Effectively, the Welsh Office created by and for James Griffiths reflected both his "Lib-Lab" *gwerin* outlook, and the equation that he had made between self-government and the colonies which he sought to usher towards freedom while Colonial Secretary, 1950-1. (p.168).

30.  Donald Anderson, 'Socialism and Community' in John Osmond (ed.) *The National Question Again* (Llandysul, 1985). Donald Anderson maintained: 'There was no conflict between his Welshness and his socialism, both of which derived from his roots in the vital Amman Valley community of his early years'.

31.  Peter Hain, *A Welsh Third Way* (London, 1999) p. 20.

32.  Carwyn Jones, *The Future of Welsh Labour* (Cardiff, 2004) p. 9.

33.  Ibid., p. 11.

34.  John Osmond, 'James Griffiths' *Western Mail*, 8 August 1975.

35.  John Osmond, *Creative Conflict*, p. 127.

36.  Carwyn Jones, *The Future of Welsh Labour*, p. 15.

# 21

## Appreciating the Politician

It is a difficult task to sum up the life and work of a unique politician such as James Griffiths. There is so much romance belonging to his early life in west Wales, as well as amazement that he became a major figure in the life of Britain. After all he had very little formal schooling; he left the primary school in Betws at the age of thirteen. Very few of his contemporaries from the same working-class background became as prominent as him within the Labour movement. He was a remarkable propagandist on the platform of the trade union movement. Indeed he could claim that in his period as a miners' leader he addressed meetings in every mining village and town in the south Wales coalfield. From 1925 to 1936 he would spend at least one Saturday in every fortnight addressing miners' meetings, and in every general election from 1929 to 1966 he travelled throughout Wales, England and Scotland to address usually well-attended public meetings on behalf of the Labour Party.[1]

He fulfilled thousands of invitations from all over Britain between 1936 and 1959 and dedicated two weekends a month on travels to address political meetings in different constituencies to his own.[2] At the end of his career as a politician, Charles Pannell, a Member of Parliament for one of the Leeds constituencies, spoke of him as a sincere and outstanding communicator. But if you really did need to hear Jim at the high noon of his powers to see a great conference of over a thousand delegates hanging on to his every word, and what he liked to call 'my own immense sincerity'.[3]

James Grifitths's emphasis on brotherhood and sisterhood extended to all his fellow human beings .It was a prominent aspect of his background and his personality, and it was always so attractive to people who struggled for dignity, human rights and full-scale independence in different parts of the world. This was without doubt the strength of his stewardship as Minister for the Colonies in 1950 and 1951. Within the concept of "brotherhood of man" as propounded by the Reverend R. J. Campbell, Griffiths saw the best hope for these colonial countries and their leaders, who sought selfgovernment. He said:

> *But all our efforts will be in vain, unless these people feel we think of them as brothers, whose fate is always our concern.*[4]

He added:

> *There is no security for any of them in domination. Neither white domination or black domination. That way is bitterness and strife. The only way forward is partnership.*[5]

Griffiths became an important figure to the leaders of the freedom movements in the colonies. They corresponded regularly with him, came to London to see him, and invited him to their celebrations and special occasions throughout the fifties and into the sixties. He was well loved and respected, and he saw the possibility of a better, more affluent, world for the developing nations. It was a process of converting countries which had been exploited and under the domination of British Imperialism to enjoy freedom and responsiblity. He was glad that these countries were willing to exist in a new organization called the the Commonwealth. He was highly thought of at the international conferences he attended, and he stood firm in solidarity with Nelson Mandela and in his opposition to the policy of apartheid in South Africa. His attitude was simply:

> *There is no place in Labour's Colonial Policy for any doctrine of racial superiority.*
> *Socialism and Apartheid are utterly incompatible.*[6]

As we evaluate the life of James Griffiths, we have to emphasise his skill as well as his ability to have people of different tribes and diverse views to co-operate for the good of the the community and the nation. One can see his flair and charisma in his early life in Ammanford as one of the early socialists who, in 1908, formed a branch of the Independent Labour Party. We then saw his successful efforts over the next few years to increase the membership of the branch and to motivate his fellow members to canvas and gather support in local elections as well as within the constituency of East Carmarthenshire. This he achieved in the face of the obvious opposition from the majority of his fellow miners as well as those who attended, like he did, Christian Temple Welsh Independent Chapel, who still clung to the Liberal Party. He succeeded in creating a community of fellow socialists who were willing to support unpopular causes such as the suffragette movement, and to plead the cause of pacifism during the First World War.[7] As a young political agent he persuaded a number of other young men to support his publication, Llanelli Labour News, and by doing so assist the Labour Party to elect its first Labour MP, Dr. J. H. Williams. There is no doubt that without his ability to lead and co-ordinate others in campaigning the Labour Party would not have kept the Llanelli constituency in the 1923 general election. After he was appointed as a miners' agent in 1925, one could see the same characteristics at work in his effort to strengthen 'the Fed' and further on to sustain a strenuous campaign in Monmouthshire and Glamorganshire against the existence of the socalled Spencer Union which had its base in the Nottinghamshire coalfield. He campaigned with courage on this issue, and successfully, during his term of office as Vice-President, and later as President of 'the Fed'. He kept 'the Fed' as a powerful force during a critical period and in the end won the bitter struggle with the Spencer Union in a few collieries where they had a foothold. When he was elected an MP for Llanelli in 1936 this fulfilled an ambition which he had nurtured since his youth, though he found it difficult to cut his ties as an officer of 'the Fed'. At Westminster his humility, ability, oratory and sincerity made an impact on his fellow parliamentarians. He soon became a member of the National Excutive of the British Labour Party, as well as Secretary of the Welsh Parliamentary Party. He a very effective parliamentarian for nearly forty years. It was there in Parliament that he made lasting contributions as Minister of Insurance, Minister for the Colonies, and the first Minister of State for Wales.

Soon others realised that he had the statesman's gift for compromise, a desire to co-operate with politicians of left-wing as well as and right-wing views within his beloved party, and he had a natural respect for his opponents in every other political party. These were important characteristics in his life as a politician; indeed it was to be seen from his early days as a trade unionist and as a pioneer of the Labour movement. Between 1919 and 1920 when he was undergoing his training at the Central Labour College in London, a well-known Marxist-orientated college, the ideology of his early hero, Keir Hardie, was still extremely relevant. His Christian socialism was reflected by a number of his fellow students. To Hardie, socialism was steeped in the Sermon on the Mount, a desire for welfare from cradle to the grave, and not class warfare as the Marxists proclaimed. The way to achieve a Socialist State was by education and co-operation and constitutional means as well as by the laws prepared for Parliament, rather than by a bloody revolution. Griffiths's wife, Winifred, expressed her opposition to the philosophy which dominated the Central Labour College, though her husband as one of the students had been inspired by the communist revolution of Russia in 1917.[8] He returned to Ammanford with different views from those he had before he entered the college, but he soon realised that he had to find the common ground with people. Griffiths saw this immediately in adult education. It had become a bitter struggle between the Workers Educational Association (WEA) and the National Council of Labour Colleges (NCLC). It was the NCLC which received the financial support from Carmarthenshire County Council. Griffiths was regarded as a most competent lecturer, but to those who propagated the Marxist faith in the Amman Valley he was not steeped enough in the ideology of Karl Marx. The most hardline of them, Glyn Evans of Garnant, was not content with the spirit of reconcilation and compromise as exemplified by James Griffiths. A small group of miners in the anthracite coalfield felt that those adults who came to the evening classes needed more Marxism than James Griffiths could supply.[9] He was not in the same league, according to these local Marxists, as another socialist lecturer, D. R. Owen of Garnant. These miners felt that the NCLC evening classes should encourage the students to oppose the values and even the existence of Welsh language nonconformist chapels.[10] According to D. J. Williams, who later became Labour MP for Neath, some of these NCLC educational classes were held on Sunday so as to upset the ministers of religion and the officers of the different chapels. The WEA on the other hand resisted such an outlook. These Marxists of the Amman Valley were even suspicious of the leaders of the White House in Ammanford such as James Griffiths and his brother D. Rees Griffiths known as Amanwy.[11] Glyn Evans knew that Griffiths was too ready to see the best in both camps (the WEA as well as the NCLC movements), and always worked as hard as he could for the common ground. Griffiths believed that some of the most enthusiastic supporters of Dr. J. H. Williams in the newly-formed Llanelli constituency had lost the seat for him and Labour in the 1918 general election. These were ideologists whom we call today the hard Left.

During his time with 'the Fed', he came to realise that the miners needed a better vehicle to overcome the confrontation with the owners than reverting to strike action. He saw the danger of people from the same background as him opting out of union activities and the local lodge meetings being in the hands of a handful of left-wingers. He sounded the trumpet for the sake of the Welsh Anglican and nonconformist church and chapel trade unionists.For Church and Chapel members of the anthracite to absent themselves on the excuse of attending big meeting or prayer meetings is only to bury their heads like ostriches in the sand and to give the left wingers the very opportunity they want to manipulate the lodge machinery.[12]

Griffiths, who himself had been a left-winger in his days as a miner in the Amman Valley had, by the time he became a MP for Llanelli, realised that for the sake of winning an important victory, a politician has to compromise. It is the only way to achieve one's goal or win an argument. By the beginning of the Second World War he was pleading as a politician for the Labour Party to act positively. It was he who took the initiative in the crusade within the Parliamentary Labour Party for implementation of the far-reaching Beveridge Repor [13]. As soon as the war was over he was critical of the coalition government for its lack of vision with regard to Beveridge. The historian Stephen Brooke has written extensively on his role in parliament during the Second World War, and his eloquent attacks on the coalition government.[14] He believed sincerely that the coalition government, led by Winston Churchil, had lost a 'golden opportunity'. Like Laski, Strauss and Bevan, Griffiths argued that the coalition had a responsibility to win the war, but at the same time they needed to prepare for a better world at the end of the conflict. Though Griffiths had created a political storm and forced the House of Commons to vote on the Beveridge Report, his wise leadership and action was so important. Ninety-seven Labour MPs out of a total of 150 voted against the coalition government at the end of the Beveridge Report debate. Griffiths had stood his ground, and his rebellious action had created quite a stir among the Labour leaders in coalition. Ernest Bevin, for example, was furious – he even threatened to resign from the Cabinet.[15] It did not happen because Clement Attlee was able to reason with him, and Bevin had a great deal of ambition. Griffiths had another opportunity at the annual conference of the Labour Party in December 1944 to emphasise once more their responsibility to promote social reform and to assist the coalition government to consider, after a great deal of debate, the implications of an ambitious political programme. He was listened to. There was a need to confront the coalition government which he did, and then a need to convince the British public to consider a far-reaching programme to revitalise the economy and improve living conditions.[15]

Another instance of him standing on a matter of principle took place at the end of his parliamentary career, when he received the invitation to intervene with Lord Fenner Brockway in the NigerianBiafra civil war. Britain, as well as Wales, saw a heavyweight politician who had received the highest accolade of being made a Companion of Honour, at the end of a remarkable political career, ready on a matter of Christian and socialist principle as well as common humanity to rebel against a Labour government; a government and a party of which he had been such a loyal member all his life had to be sincerely rebuked because to him it had forgotten its idealism. In the circumstances of Biafra, he was not willing to compromise, even to a prime minister, Harold Wilson, for whom he had such a regard. He could not ignore the cry of the hungry children of Biafra, and this is why he involved himself for years as treasurer of the charity, War on Want.

I am one of those historians who believe that every outstanding politician, at some time or other, disagrees with his or her political party. David Lloyd George rebelled and so did Aneurin Bevan (in his case a bit too often), Winston Churchill, Harold Wilson and James Griffiths. Bevan and Lloyd George were always politicians that he greatly admired.[16.]

Griffiths had two characteristics that are true of all politicians who achieve prominence namely loyalty as well as courage. One sees time and time again examples of his loyalty to his family, his community, to nonconformity and its values, and to the Labour movement. He was a politician who never forgot his roots. When you read the pages of the local press, say the Amman Valley Chronicle, one is conscious of his close connection with those comrades in his early life who against all odds struggled for socialism. Though one of his early comrades, Edgar Bassett, became an adherent of Marxism-Leninism, that did not affect their deep friendship. When Bassett died, Griffiths paid him a fitting tribute and shared the memorial service with the Communist leader, Arthur Horner.

His loyalty to the leaders of the Labour Party, to George Lansbury, Clement Attlee, to Hugh Gaitskell and Harold Wilson has been well documented.[17] He had a key role in the 1950s as the deputy leader of the Labour Party. The situation demanded, in his eyes, total loyalty against the threat of destruction to his party from Bevanism. It was difficult for Attlee, but even worse for Gaitskell. Griffiths stood his ground. This can be gleaned in the correspondence with the prominent Welsh Nationalist, Elwyn Roberts, in 1954. Roberts was the secretary of the Campaign for a Welsh Parliament. They exchanged a number of letters, but in the end Griffiths felt that he had to be loyal to the resolutions of the Labour Party. These are the words which underline his loyalty, indeed he uses the word in his reply to Roberts, written in Welsh:

> *I feel that this is not a personal matter to me anymore as I have taken part in the discussions of my party on the issue from the very beginning, till our adoption of a Welsh policy. I am sure your Committee will recognise that to accept the honour of belonging to any Party preserves loyalty to its original decision.*[18]

In this letter to Roberts, Griffiths gave an important reason for his reluctance to lead the campaign for home rule for Wales. But on the other hand, one can understand those like Roberts who accepted Griffiths's pre-eminence in Wales but wanted to meet him to discuss the campaign for a Welsh Parliament. Though he saw the necessity of recognising the privilege of membership of the Labour Party, and the need to show loyalty to the party that had given him so many opportunities, especially at a time when there were a sizeable group of MPs who were disloyal, it is difficult for many of us, who supported the standpoint of Cledwyn Hughes and others within the Parliament for Wales campaign, to understand why Griffiths didn't give the same emphasis at this time to his obligation to Wales. But the situation did change due to the friendship of Griffiths and Gaitskell.

The leader realised that he had a Deputy who he could utterly trust with his last penny; a politician whose sole aim was to work for unity within the Party. He achieved his purpose by the time Harold Wilson took over as leader and led the Labour Party to victory in 1964. It was not a decisive victory but at least there was a Labour Government for the first time since 1951. With this electoral victory James Griffiths succeeded in laying the foundations for something that meant so much to him. This is the reason that James Griffiths is called an 'architect of Welsh devolution'. He was the politician who shaped modern Wales, but to achieve his vision, his loyalty had been a key factor. This can be seen in the way that he kept unity among the Labour MPs in Wales. Without his powerful influence Aneurin Bevan would have been thrown out of the party on at least two occasions. He argued for him, and always was on good terms with Bevan having a very high regard for the ability and influence of the rebel. Bevan himself at times was so outrageous as to criticise the loyalty of his old college friend, but Griffiths never responded. He was the same to old college friend, Ness Edwards. So we must recognise that loyalty played in his contribution another.

Humility as an important element of his personality key role. With all the attention he received within Wales, in the British and Commonwealth context, he never lost his working-class awareness was also. In the Second World War, many an historian argues that he should have led the Labour Party as the party of opposition. Due to his humility he never for a moment thought that he should be the leader. The two leaders were H. B. Lees-Smith and Frederick Pethick-Lawrence that Attlee installed to represent the Labour Party in Parliament during the Second World War.[19] Griffiths however was the politician who gave Labour the leadership they wanted on a number of issues and he was a key figure in their landslide victory of 1945. It was he who took the reins in the crusade within the Parliamentary Labour Party for the Beveridge plan and he received a great deal of support from rank and file Labour MPs.[20] He strove for nationalisation of key industries, such as the coal industry. Again he received support from a large number of MPs, some of whom were well versed in the mining industry, such as George Dagger and Rhys Davies.

Education was another of his priorities, and he argued within the NEC that education needs should not be in the hands of politicians, but should be dictated by the needs of the children. He sowed the seed that later became an integral part of the Labour Party education policies.[21]

An example of his humility is the fact that he refused the opportunity to receive one of the most important positions in government, namely to be the Minister for Foreign Affairs. His wife mentions the choice before him during Attlee's second Labour government:

> It came as a complete surprise to be offered one of the highest posts in the Government. It appeared that Ernest Bevin had expressed the wish that Jim should follow him. Gratifying as such an offer was my husband's immediate reaction was to refuse. We talked it over and we decided it would not be right to accept.[22]

The first reason was an obvious one, that he was fully content with his responsibilities as Secretary of State for the Colonies. His wife underlines this:

> Moreover he had grown keenly interested and deeply involved in the affairs of the Colonies and would hate to break the connection.[23]

But according to Mrs Griffiths, the real reason for turning it down, was that his colleague Herbert Morrison was so keen on the position:

> He was a senior colleague and one to whom the Labour Movement, and indeed the country, owed much and Jim could not bring himself to stand between Herbert and what he most desired.[24]

Griffiths did not want to upset Morrison. I cannot think of any other politician within the Labour Party or any other party these days who would decline such an opportunity. I am certain that Aneurin Bevan would never have refused such an honour. Griffiths's Pages From Memory is a testament to his innate humility. I was time and time again surprised at the way he left out so many of his achievements which should have been mentioned. Among the autobiographies of twentieth-century politicians his memoir ranks as one of the most unassuming records that has been published.

His Welsh patriotism was another important characteristic. The language at the hearth in Betws was Welsh, as it was on the playing fields in the village, in the chapel in Ammanford, in the colliery and the union, and the language of his early political involvement. He pleaded within the Labour Party for the language to be given status, but there was very little support. In his Llanelli Labour News, he includes news items in Welsh, and some of his friends were among the most committed Welsh speakers possible, such as Iorwerth Cyfeiliog Peate, Alwyn D. Rees and Gwilym Prys Davies. The exchange of letters between them on the Welsh language, University of Wales, devolution and pacifism is a proof of this bond. He succeeded beyond all expectations with the hierarchy of the Labour Party in the days of Clement Attlee and Herbert Morrison (who was so negative) to the days of Hugh Gaitskell and Harold Wilson. The memoirs of Cledwyn Hughes in his conversation with Dr. R. Merfyn Jones are worth reading.[25]

James Griffiths was the incarnation of a Welsh patriot at his best, as was his brother D. R. Griffiths, known as Amanwy in the Amman Valley and Welsh literary circles. I believe that the innate Welshness of Amanwy and his passionate concern for Welsh poetry and language was an important influence on the patriotism of his younger brother. Amanwy was nearer to the large circle of poets which attended the local eisteddfodau in the anthracite coalfield than James was, and therefore he depended a great deal on his brother for his opinion on the fate of the language and his interpretation on the standpoint of the Welsh-speaking public as discussed in his weekly column in the Amman Valley Chronicle. One should refer to the esteem he had for the opinion of his niece, May Harris, who was so enthusiastic for the Welsh Christian heritage. She would often thank him for his contribution in Welsh on radio and later on television, and would refer to prominent members of Plaid Cymru who were impressed with his steadfast views. James Griffiths understood the standpoint of Plaid Cymru much better than any other Labour Party politician. He always had a high regard for Saunders Lewis (much more than his brother) and also for Gwynfor Evans, and he analysed the nationalist victory in the Carmarthen by-election in a most readable memorandum. We know of his support for D. J. Williams of Fishguard during the 'Fire in Lleyn' when he went to see R. A. Butler to argue that Williams should have his teaching post back.[26] To Griffiths the preservation of the language was more important than condemning people who were doing creative, positive work for the language. He was easily upset when some Welsh speakers criticised Welsh people who did not speak the language. The task was to win the Anglicised Welsh to support the language and its needs.[27]

Another of his strong points was his support for other politicians. In his archives one glimpses his support for a large number of Labourites who deserved a word of praise or a word to encourage them in their political career. In the papers of the Welsh sociologist, D. Caradog Jones, we have examples of Griffiths's support and his keenness for the able university lecturer to have a better constituency as a Labour candidate than Montgomeryshire. He tried to persuade Jones to consider letting his name appear before the Executive of the Carmarthenshire Constituency Labour Party for the 1955 general election. It was Griffiths who finally got Lady Megan Lloyd George to join the Labour Party. He gave the task of contacting her in the first place to his colleague, Goronwy Roberts, for Megan was reluctant to move from the Liberal fold. But it was Griffiths who succeeded in having her as his neighbour. He was also keen to see Gwilym Prys Davies as a Member of Parliament. Prys Davies admits that Griffiths had 'been such support to me. I will never forget this' were his words to me.[28] Another Welsh politician who had extensive support from Griffiths was Tudor Watkins. Griffiths had lived in the Brecon and Radnor constituency and had seen the ability of Tudor Watkins, especially his contribution as a councillor and an officer of the Labour Party. When Tudor Watkins stood as a parliamentary candidate, he received total support from Griffiths and kind words which could be used on his election leaflets.[29]

Another well-known politician who had full-blooded support from James Griffiths is John Morris. His autobiography Fifty Years in Politics and Law is full of evidence to James's influence. He admits: 'He was my principal mentor.'[30] Then he adds:

> *There is no doubt in my mind that Jim Griffiths is the father of Welsh devolution, based on this and his personal encouragement to me at a time when it was politically very lonely to be a devolutionist in the Labour Party in Wales. He was the political compass which was to guide me for the future, and there was no doubt that he was one of the outstanding South Wales industrial MPs sharing all our interests.*[31]

Griffiths used to send a note to a new Member of Parliament after he had taken part in a debate in the House of Commons. Cledwyn Hughes and Elwyn Jones (a native of Llanelli) did the same. Tam Dalyell mentioned to me how he received a word of commendation from Griffiths for his contribution in a debate on the coal industry and the plight of miners in the Scottish coalfield who suffered from silicosis. He did likewise to most of the Welsh MPs. He supported MPs from different parts of Britain, and by doing so, endeared himself as a great parliamentarian and a robust debater. Tom Sexton, Labour MP for a constituency within the Durham coalfield, said:

> *If I had been possessed of the oratory of a Demosthenes or the rhetoric of a golden mouthed St Chrysostom, I would have been unable to pay the tribute to the Hon. Member' speech which it deserved.*[32]

Those were his strong qualities. He had his weaknesses, but I must admit that it is not easy to underline them as I have been greatly impressed by his life and contribution. I agree wholeheartedly with the verdict of the Welsh historian, Emyr Price:

> *I have no doubt that James Griffiths was one of the giants of the Labour Party in the twentieth century – the politician who created the concern that the chief political party of Wales must walk hand in hand with the Welsh Nationalist desires, and to give to Wales the means to control its industrial and economical life.*[33]

The time has come for us to consider James Griffiths as one of the architects of Welsh devolution, one of the most important in his generation. He had taken his time to give the leadership that was badly needed within the Labour Party. I would not be surprised that it was during the period between the death of his brother Amanwy in 1953, and the frustration involved in the drowning of the Tryweryn Valley a few years later that he became determined to act.

One has to be fair and acknowledge that Wales and its politicians have been very apathetic on the question of devolution. The bitter truth is that most of the Welsh MPs did very little for the cause of devolution or self-government. Though Lloyd George showed a great deal of interest early in his career one cannot claim that he did a great deal after he became Chancellor of the Exchequer. Devolution was again on the political agenda at the end of the First World War, but nothing came from the conference or the report published by the committee of thirty-three individuals who considered the issue. E. T. John, who served as a Liberal MP from 1910 to 1918, was a convinced devolutionist and he spread his influence to three political parties: the Liberals, the Labour Party and the Welsh Nationalist Party. He could not do more than he did as a backbencher because Lloyd George detested him for his pacifism. The politician who could have achieved a great deal for devolution if he took it seriously was Lloyd George.[34] Griffiths could have theoretically been in the vanguard of devolution much earlier, but one must realise that he was heavily involved in the creation of the welfare State.

Another weakness which I stressed in this volume was the Tryweryn issue, but one could argue that he could not do more than support the Welsh Labour MP for Merionethshire, T. W. Jones. He was the leader of the delegation, in the name of the local committee, which met the leaders of the Liverpool Corporation. But personally I would have expected Griffiths to have taken part in the debate in the House of Commons, and to have given a much clearer and definite leadership. I cannot but admit that he lost a golden opportunity in this sad episode in the history of Wales. For after all his word was greatly appreciated within the House of Commons. Another difficult issue was the way Gwynfor Evans was treated as a councillor on Carmarthenshire County Council. Perhaps one sees in this episode that his loyalty to his party was responsible for his silence. In a private conversation, May Harris admitted that her uncle knew of the harm done by the Labour Party councillors and he promised to do what he could to bring civility to the foolish antics displayed often in the Council Chambers.[35] But this indicates weakness Griffiths's in not speaking out and allowing the insults and the bickering to fester for years. One could see in the quarrel between him and his agent, Douglas Hughes, a reflection of the tension with one of the foremost leaders of Labour on the Council.

Unfortunately Gwynfor Evans did not help the situation for he could not in any way support the Labour Party on the County Council. He often went out of his way to upset them, and he identified himself with the Independents who were in the main pseudo-Conservatives. Like Evans, Griffiths was in the peace movement, a pacifist in the First World War and in the 1920s.

He had great admiration for the blind preacher Puleston Jones when he was the political agent for Llanell and for all similar pacifists within the Labour Party, in particular Lansbury. Of the outstanding characters within the Labour Party who he came to admire, George Lansbury was the greatest. He admitted a 'close friendship in my days as President of the South Wales Miners' Union'.[36] He regarded Lansbury as one of the greatest men he knew. He came under the influence of Lansbury's pacifism when Lansbury visited the White House in Ammanford in 1918, and he became a supporting speaker at the by-election in Llanelli in 1936 and welcomed Griffiths to the House of Commons. There is evidence that Lansbury shared many of the experiences of his travels with Griffiths.

Early in 1939 Lansbury came to Llanelli to speak to a Labour meeting, and during this visit both of them spent hours in each other's company in Pendine discussing the reasons why Griffiths was supporting the "just war" approach rather than espousing his well-known pacifism. It was obvious that James Griffiths, like many others, had been disillusioned with the failure of the League of Nations to fulfil its mission, and the response of British, and other European leaders to the threat of the Nazis and the fascists in Germany, Italy and Spain. The behaviour of Mussolini and Italy towards Abyssinia (Ethiopia of our day) drove Griffiths to re-consider his beliefs as a pacifist, and this was reinforced by his experiences on the continent of Europe, in Prague amongst the miners, in Danzig as well as in Spain.

He saw the threat from Hitler to the values of the civilised world, and the peril to the Christian heritage. Griffiths was convinced that he had no choice but to reconsider the foundations of his pacifism. To some of us in the peace tradition he turned his back much too soon on his long-held pacifist views. But we must reluctantly acknowledge that it was through his decision to turn his back on pacifism that he became very popular with his electorate in the Second World War.

Another weakness in his character was a weakness constantly discerned in other politicians, the tendency to say yes to every invitation. He was so willing to please everyone that he could not refuse any invitation to address a rally, a meeting, or a conference. He was extremely fortunate that his wife, Winnie, was so supportive. He pays her a fine tribute, acknowledging that she had to shoulder so many responsibilities for the children and the family on her own. He knew that he was doing what all prominent politicians are expected to do but Griffiths pays her a wonderful tribute:

> *She has some of the qualities I lack – real tenacity and courage, and the ability to live within herself and let the rest of the world go by, completely untouched by the lure of 'Society': she has always fought shy of it. She has the deep strength of her Dad.*[37]

An attempt has been made to evaluate James Griffiths as one of the most significant politicians in the history of twentieth-century Welsh politics. In the 1930s he was the leader of the south Wales miners. During the Second World War he exerted his influence and then he became a minister in the Labour government of 1945-1950 and 1950-51, and 1964-66. Following on from this he became deputy leader of the Labour Party and undertook a peace mission to Nigeria. He was imbued throughout all this with a spirit of mutual regard and frankness as well as the instincts of a progressive politician. He won the admiration of people from every political party as he was a politician who had sincere convictions, who fought without fear for the miners and their communities, and was a leading light in the struggles of what can be called 'moral minorities' within Britain, such as the temperance movement and within his own nation, the Lord's Day Fellowship in Wales. He also had great respect for those who campaigned for independence in every part of the world. He involved himself against colonialism and apartheid, gave leadership on the Beveridge Report, and on the Sir David Hughes Parry Report on the Welsh language. Griffiths supported wholeheartedly the Welsh language and its culture. In an article in *Alliance News* (the magazine of the Temperance Movement) during the summer of 1969 they emphasised correctly that he was a politician of strong convictions and principles; a man who often could be more emotional than most of his fellow MPs, and who could, now and again as he indicated in one of his visits to Africa, lose his temper but yet win commendation at the same time. The Alliance News piece underlined that he was a man of principle.[38]

Griffiths is shown to be a man of strong convictions, and there is no doubt where he acquired his lifelong beliefs. They came to him from the early influences of his parents and the Welsh nonconformist tradition in which he was brought up in Betws annd Ammanford. Among these principles was one which this journal Alliance News encouraged, namely total abstinence.

There is no doubt that he stands in the tradition of the powerful politicians nurtured in Welsh nonconformity such as Henry Richard, David Lloyd George, Mabon and S.O. Davies. In August 2000 on the threshold of the National Eisteddfod of Wales held in Llanelli (a town where James Griffiths had been an icon), the television company HTV for S4C prepared a Welsh language film under the title, '*Jim y Gwleidydd Coll*', (Jim the Lost Politician). The historian Emyr Price who was involved with the programme wrote an article to the weekly Welsh language magazine Golwg, under the title '*Y Gwleidydd ga'dd ei wrthod*' (The Politician who had been refused). I believe sadly that Emyr Price was near the mark when he generalised and said that Wales 'had chosen to forget the most important politician of the last century'. I can add the words of the poet David James Jones better known as Gwenallt which are so relevant:

> *Er yr holl ganmol a fu arnat ti werin Cymru, yr wyt tithau yn gallu bod mor oriog â'r gwynt, ac mor greulon â Nero wrth dy gymwynaswyr'*
>
> (Though all the praise that's been bestowed upon you, the working class of Wales, you also can be as fickle as the wind, and as cruel as Nero towards your benefactors).[39]

It is a great loss that this endearing and humble politician had not arranged in his later years after retiring from parliament to establish a society to develop his views on devolution. I am sure that this would have been foreign to his nature on a number of counts, but by now I am convinced that he should be honoured with a statue in Cardiff, the capital of Wales. One can see statues to two of the outstanding twentieth-century politicians, David Lloyd George and Aneurin Bevan. Emyr Price told the truth in 2000 on the absence of a statue to James Griffiths:

> *The biggest scandal is that there is no worthy statue to him in the capital city though there is one to Aneurin Bevan. There is a great need for such acknowledgement, and it should be done as soon as possible.*[40]

Nearly twenty years have passed since that sentence was written on this lost opportunity and none of our contemporary leaders are mentioning the need for such a statue. As far as I am concerned, the situation can be rectified very quickly. But we can say without fear of contradiction that we owe the existence of Y Senedd, the National Assembly for Welsh in Cardiff, above all to James Griffiths. The Wales of today would not be what it is without his dedication, inspiration and his valuable contribution to our life as a nation.

**Notes and References**

1.     NLW, James Griffiths Papers, D3/14. Member for Llanelli.
2.     Ibid.
3.     Charles Pannell, 'The Man from the Valley', *Yorkshire Post*, 6 March 1969.
4.     NLW, James Griffiths Papers, B6/8.
5.     Ibid.
6.     Ibid. B6/11. The Report of the Treasurer of the Socialist International Congress in Stockholm 15-18 July 1953. He was one of 6 who represented the Labour Party. Griffiths was chosen as Chairman of the Committee that was to prepare the resolution on Colonialism. He was regarded in the same light as the three outstanding Socialists, Guy Mallet, Henri Rolin and Norman Thomas.
7.     D. Gwenallt Jones, 'Credaf' [I Believe] in J. E. Meredith, *Gwenallt: Bardd Crefyddol* (Davies Lecture) (Llandysul, Gomer Press, 1974), pp. 58-9.
8.      Mrs James Griffiths, *One Woman's Story*, p.89.
9.     Ioan Aled Matthews, *The World of the Anthracite Miner*, PhD Thesis, University of Wales, 1995, p. 326.
10.     NLW, James Griffiths Papers, D3/2.
11.     Ioan Matthews, 'Maes y Glo Carreg ac Undeb y Glowyr (1872-1925)' in *Cof Cenedl* VIII, editor Geraint H. Jenkins (Llandysul, 1993), pp. 133-64.
12.     NLW, James Griffiths Papers, D3/2.
13.     13. Stephen Brooke, *Labour's War* (Oxford, 1992), p. 67.
14.     NLW, James Griffiths Papers, D3/20-1. A draft of his autobiography, *Daily Herald*, 17

February 1943; minutes of the Parliamentary Labour Party 17 February 1943; Brooke, *Labour's War*, p. 173.

15. Ibid. A typical statement of James Griffiths: 'I think the Government have missed a glorious opportunity'. See, Alan Bullock, *The Life and Times of Ernest Bevin, ii Minister of Labour* (London, 1968), pp. 231-2; 'The Beveridge Report', *Amman Valley Chronicle*, February 2, 1943, p. 4; *Hansard* 5th series, vol. cdv, 8 March 1945, col. 2285.

16. In his study of Aneurin Bevan, Kenneth O. Morgan states, on p.108, that James Griffiths was 'the main architect of the Welfare State'. See Kenneth O. Morgan, 'Aneurin Bevan 1897-1960', in *Founder of the Welfare State* (London and Portsmouth, New Hampshire), pp.105-113. James Griffiths had a high regard for Aneurin Bevan. See James Griffiths, 'World figure still remembered as a true son of the Valley', *Western Mail*, July 8, 1960, p. 6.

17. David Rubenstein, The Labour Party and British Society 1880-2005 (Brighton, 2006) p. 80.

18. NLW, D. Caradog Jones Papers. Letter of James Griffiths to Elwyn Roberts, dated 28 December 1954.

19. Stephen Brooke, *Labour's War*, pp. 73-4.

20. Ibid., pp. 85-6; *Hansard*, vol ccclxxviii, 24 February 1942, col. 55.

21. Ibid. 22. Mrs James Griffiths, *One Woman's Story*, p. 143.

23. Ibid.

24. Ibid.

25. R. Merfyn Jones and Ioan Rhys Jones, 'Labour and the Nation' in *The Labour Party in Wales 1900-2000* (editors Duncan Tanner, Chris Williams, Deian Hopkin) (Cardiff, 2000), p. 255.

26. Lord Morris of Aberavon, *Fifty Years in Politics and the Law*, p. 50, 'He told me that as a constituency MP he had gone to see R. A. Butler, then minister for education to get D. J. Williams, one of the convicted Lleyn bombers, re-instated as a teacher. Whether anyone knew of his actions, I don't know. Jim added, rather sadly, "it was never acknowledged."'

27. Remember his analysis of Aneurin Bevan's attitude: 'he was impatient of nationalism which divided peoples and enslaved nations within their narrow geographical and spiritual frontiers'. See John Osmond, *Creative Conflict: The Politics of Welsh Devolution* (Llandysul and London, 1977), p. 102.

28. NLW, James Griffiths Papers, D1/4. Letter of Gwilym Prys Davies to James Griffiths, dated 26 January 1962. G. Prys Davies was on the short list for nomination to the Swansea West constituency. He said: 'I would like to do a good day's work for Labour – though I am quite nervous when I think of the selection conference at Swansea'.

29. NLW, Lord Tudor Watkins Papers, File 1/4/13/2. An election address by James Griffiths on behalf of Tudor Watkins for the 1950 general election.

30. Lord Morris of Aberavon, *Fifty Years in Politics and the Law*, p. 50.

31. Ibid.

32. NLW, James Griffiths Papers, D3/20. *Second World War*.

33. Emyr Price, 'Y Gwleidydd ga'dd ei wrthod', *Golwg*, volume 12, No. 47, 3 August 2000, p.11.

34. John Pennant, 'Could "LG" have done more for Wales?', *Western Mail*, 2 October 1943, p. 2. Pennant argued on these lines: 'Probably he [David Lloyd George] thought that in the long term he could do more for Wales by dedicating himself to the great tasks with which his name will always be associated, the protection of the millions of Britons against poverty and want, infirmity and old age, ill-health and unemployment'. For Tryweryn, see Watcyn L. Jones, *Cofio Tryweryn* (Llandysul, 1988).

35. In a private conversation with Lord Gwilym Prys Davies, 27 April 2013.

36. James Griffiths, *Pages from Memory*, pp. 52-3.

37.     Ibid., p 146.
38.     NLW James Griffiths Papers D6/1-55 (reviews of his book *Pages from Memory*).
39.     J. E. Meredith, *Gwenallt: Bardd Crefyddol* (Davies Lecture) (Llandysul, 1974), p .22.
40.     Emyr Price, *Golwg*, Volume 12, no. 47, 3 August 2000, p11; Carwyn Fowler, 'Nationalism and the Labour Party in Wales, *Llafur*, Volume 8, No 4, 2003, pp. 97-105.

# Bibliography

**Manuscript Collections**

Personal Papers

University of Wales,Bangor

Bala-Bangor Collection, Principal Thomas Rees Papers, Principal John Morgan Jones Papers, Bangor collection (General), Revd T.E. Nicholas Papers, David Thomas Papers, R. Silyn Roberts Papers.


**National Library of Wales (NLW)**

NLW  Amanwy (David Rees Griffiths) Papers

NLW  Leo Abse Papers

NLW  Aneurin Bevan Papers

NLW  D.R. Coleman Papers

NLW  Idris Cox Papers

NLW  Cassie Davies Papers

NLW  Ithel Davies Papers

NLW  R. J. Derfel Papers

NLW  Desmond Donnelly Papers

NLW  Huw T. Edwards Papers

NLW  Gwynfor Evans Papers

NLW  Deian Hopkin Papers.

NLW  Cledwyn Hughes Papers

NLW  E.T. John Papers

NLW  D. Caradog Jones Papers

NLW  Frank Price Jones Papers

NLW  Iorwerth Jones Papers

NLW  Frederick Elwyn-Jones Papers

NLW  James Griffiths Papers

NLW  W. J. Gruffydd Papers

NLW  Labour Party (Cardiganshire) Papers

NLW  Labour Party (Llanelli) Papers

NLW  Labour Party (Wales) Papers

NLW  John Morris Papers

NLW  Elystan Morgan  Papers

NLW  Islwyn ap Nicholas Papers

NLW  T. E. Nicholas (Niclas y Glais) Papers

NLW R.  Williams Parry Papers

NLW  Bert Pearce (the Papers of the Welsh Communist Party)

NLW  Iorwerth C. Peate Papers

NLW  Alwyn D. Rees Papers

NLW   Brinley Richards Papers

NLW Goronwy O. Roberts Papers

NLW  David Thomas Papers

NLW  George Thomas Papers

NLW  Graham F. Thomas Papers

NLW  Tudor Watkins Papers

NLW  John Lloyd Williams Papers

Conversations with: Densil Davies;Tam Dalyell; Lord Gwilym Prys Davies; Lord John Morris; Lord Elystan Morgan; Lord Ted Rowlands; Dr Huw Walters; Dr John G.Williams; Dr J.Graham Jones; Sir Deian Hopkin and correspondence with Nick Thomas- Symonds, David Griffiths, Emyr Williams .

1. **Books, pamphlets and articles written in English and Welsh by James Griffiths**

Griffiths, Jim, *Whither Mankind* (Ystalyfera, 1937), 16 pp.

Griffiths, James, *Coal* (London, Labour Party, 1942), 24 pp.

*idem., Glo*, Cyfres Pobun (ed. E. Tegla Davies) (Liverpool,1945), 45 pp.

*idem., Call to Labour Women* (Labour Party, 1949), 4 pp.

*idem., The Labour Government* (London, 1951), Introduction by Sir William Lowther, 12 pp.

Griffiths, James; Jones, Arthur Creech; Hinden, Rita *The Way Forward*, (London, Fabians, 1950) 40pps.

Griffiths, James, 'The Road Back', *Socialist Commentary*, Vol. 15, December 1951, pp. 272-3.

*Idem.*, *Protest Rally and March: Speakers James Griffiths and others* (Spanish Democrats Defence Fund, 1960), 2pps.

*Idem.*, An Anniversary, *Socialist Commentary*, Vol. XVIII, September 1954, pps.240-1

*Idem.*, 'Yn Syth o'r Swyddfa', *Barn*, No 29, March 1965, p 124.

*Idem.*, 'Glo Carreg: Memories of the Anthracite Coalfield', *Carmarthenshire Historian*, 1968, 5, pp. 7-16

Griffiths, James, *Pages from Memory* (London, 1969), 222 pp.

*Idem.*, Memories of the Miners', *Radical Cymru*, No. 8, June 1971, p. 7

Griffiths, James, 'Welsh Politics in my Lifetime', in *James Griffiths and his Times* (Ferndale, 1979), pp. 16-57.

Fabian Society, *What Labour Could Do* (Routledge, 1945), pp. 111. Contributions from Lord Latham, J. S. Clarke, James Griffiths, Kingsley Martin, L. Barnes and R. H. Tawney.

**1(a)**      **A volume of memoirs by his wife, Mrs Winifred Griffiths**

Mrs James Griffiths, *One Woman's Story* (Ferndale, W T Maddock & Co., 1979), pp. 1-169.

**1(b)**      **The background of James Griffiths in Betws and Ammanford**

Amanwy, *Gweinidog fy Ieuenctid: Canmlwyddiant Geni y Parchedig Isaac Cynwyd Evans (1845-1945)* (Ammanford, Christian Temple, 1945), 24 pp.

Bevan, Hugh, *Morwr Cefn Gwlad* (Llandybie, 1971), pp. 1-231

Brennan, T., 'The White House', *Cambridge Journal*, Vol. VIII, 1953-4, pp. 243-8.

Davies, D. Tegfan (ed.), *Cyfarfodydd Dathlu 150 mlynedd o Jiwbili yr Eglwys* [Gellimanwydd], Christian Temple, October 24-27, 1932 (Ammanford, 1932), 30pps.

Francis, Hywel, 'The Anthracite Strikes and the Disturbances of 1925', *Llafur*, 1973 1(2), pp. 15-28.

Matthews, Ioan, 'The World of the Anthracite Miner', *Llafur* 6 (1), 1992, pp. 96-104

Jones, Graham, A Bettws Boy, Amman Valley History Society Newsletter, No. 18 (1996), pp. 7-9.

Idem., 'Cwmaman and the port of Llanelli', *Amman Valley History Society Newsletter* No 13 (1991), pp. 1-2.

*Minister at the White House* [Revd John Griffiths, Ammanford], *Amman Valley Chronicle*, 21 March 1918, p.4.

Murphy, Carol and Dixon, Chris, *Betws Mâs o'r Byd* (Betws, 2000), 220 pp.

Thomas, D. Trumor, *Hen Gymeriadau Plwyf y Bettws* (Ammanford, 1912), 72pp.

Walters, Huw *Canu'r Pwll a'r Pulpud: Portread o'r Diwylliant Barddol Cymraeg yn Nyffryn Aman* (Swansea, 1987), 275 pp.

Williams, D. J., *Yn Chwech ar Hugain Oed* (an autobiography) (Llandysul, 1959).

Williams, Mari A., 'Glanaman' yn Gwenfair Parry and Mari A. Williams (eds.) *The Welsh Language and the 1891 Census* (Cardiff, 1999), pp. 217-236

**1 (c)      Studies on James Griffiths**

Davies, Gwilym Prys, *Cynhaeaf Hanner Canrif, Gwleidyddiaeth Cymreig 1945-2005*, (Llandysul, 008), pp. 1-180.  See the second and third chapters pp. 30-65.

An HTV production in the Welsh Language for S4C, Saturday, August 5 2000 entitled '*Jim, y Gwleidydd Coll*' (Jim the Lost Politician).

Mabon, 'Dylanwad James Griffiths', *Barn*, No 26, December 1964, p. 50.

Morgan, Kenneth O., *Labour People: Leaders and Lieutenants, Hardie to Kinnock* (Oxford,1987), especially on James Griffiths, pp. 197-203.

Price, Emyr, 'Y Gwleidydd ga'dd ei wrthod', *Golwg*, Volume 12 No. 47, August 3, 2000, pp. 10-11.

Rees, D. Ben, *Cofiant James Griffith, Arwr Glew y Werin* (Talybont, 2015), 352 pp.

Nicholas Timmins, *The Five Giants: A Biography of the Welfare State*, (London 1996), pp. 1-606+13. See the seventh chapter 'With a song in my heart'- *Health and social Security*, pp. 127-138.

Matthews, Ioan, 'Turning Labour Around', *Planet* 142, August-September 2000.

Smith, J. Beverley, 'James Griffiths: an appreciation' in *James Griffiths and his Times* (Ferndale, W T Maddocks and Co., 1978), pp. 58-119.

**1 (d)      Biographical entries and obituaries**

Brockway, Lord, 'The Life and Times of James Griffiths', *Western Mail*, March 8 1969.

Callaghan, James, 'Memorial Address' in *James Griffiths and his Times* (*ibid.*), pp. 9-15.

Davies, E. Curig, 'Cofio James Griffiths', *Y Tyst*, August 29, 1975, p.2

Jones, Derwyn Morris, 'James Griffiths: Coffâd' (Obituary), *Y Tyst*, August 24, 1975.

Morgan, Kenneth O., 'Griffiths, Jeremiah (James: 1890-1975)', *Oxford Dictionary of National Biography* (Oxford, 2004).

Stephens, Meic (ed.), 'James Griffiths', *Cydymaith i Lenyddiaeth Cymru* (Cardiff, 1986), p. 233.

*The Hutchinson Encyclopaedia of Modern Political Biography* (Oxford, 1999), 527pp. The entry on James Griffiths is on page 171.

**1 (e)    The Anthracite Coalfield and the Life of the Miners of South Wales**

Arnot, R. Page, *South Wales Miners: Glöwyr De Cymru: A History of the South Wales Miners Federation 1898-1914* (London, 1967), pp. 390.

David, Davies, M. P., 'The Coal Position in South Wales', *Welsh Outlook*, Volume 16 No. 2 (Febuary 1929), pp. 38-40.

Davies, T. Alban, 'The Distress in the Rhondda Valleys', *Welsh Outlook*, Volume 16 No. 1 (January 1929), p. 10.

Davies, W.H., 'The South Wales Miner', *Welsh Outlook*, Volume 16, No. 2 (February 1929), pp. 40-6.

Davies, Paul, The Making of A. J. Cook, *Llafur*, 1978 2(3): pp. 43-63.

Desmaris, Ralph H., 'Charisma and Conciliation: A Sympathetic Look at A J Cook', *Societas* (USA), 1973, 3:1 pp. 45-60.

Edwards, Hywel Teifi, *Arwr Glew Erwau'r Glo: Delwedd y Glöwr yn Llenyddiaeth y Cymraeg 1850-1950* (Llandysul, Gwasg Gomer, 1994), pp. 1-254.

Edwards, Ness, *The History of the South Wales Miners* (London, 1926), pp. 1-122.

Evans, Neil and Jones, Dot, 'A Blessing for the Miner's Wife: the campaign for Pithead Baths in the South Wales Coalfield 1908-1950', *Llafur*, 6 (3), 1994, pp. 1-28.

Francis, Hywel, 'Welsh Miners and the Spanish Civil War', *Journal of Contemporary History*, 1970, 5 (3) pp. 177-191.

Idem.,'The secret world of the South Wales Miner: the relevance of oral history' in David Smith (ed.) *A People and a Proletariat: Essays in the History of Wales* (London,1980) pp. 166-80.

Francis, Hywel a Smith, David, *The FED: A History of the South Wales Miners in the Twentieth Century* (London, 1980), 550 pp.

Felstead, Richard, *No other way: Jack, Russia and the Spanish Civil War: A Biography* (Port Talbot, 1981), 115 pp.

Griffiths, Ieuan Lloyd, 'Changes in the South Wales Anthracite Industry', *Geography*, 1959, 44 (2), pp. 118-120.

*idem.*, 'The New Welsh Anthracite Industry', *Geography*, 1962, 47 (4), pp. 38-40.

Griffiths, Thomas Hughes, 'The South Wales Anthracite Coal Industry', *Welsh Outlook*, 1927, 14: 132-135, 163-166, 248-250.

Harries, P. H. G., 'Cwmllynfell Colliery: An Early Attempt to form a Workers Co-operative', *Llafur*, 7/2, 1997: pp. 81-93.

Hanley, James, *A study in Humbug and Misery in South Wales* (London, 1937) pp. 1-230.

Hartshorn, Vernon, 'Mr Baldwin attacks miners' hours and wages' (London, 1926), 12 pp.

Matthews, Ioan, 'Maes y Glo Carreg ac Undeb y Glöwyr 1872-1925', in Cof Cenedl ( ed.) Geraint H Jenkins *Cof Cenedl*, VII (Llandysul, 1993), pp. 133-164.

*idem.*, 'Hen Arwr Maes y Glo Carreg: John James 1869-194 in Hywel Teifi Edwards (ed.), *Cwm Aman* (Llandysul, 2000), pp. 320-49.

Phillips, G. A., 'The Labour Party and the General Strike', *Llafur* (1977) Vol. 2 No. 2, pps. 458.

*Phillips, E. W., The Ammanford and District Anthracite Strike of 1925*, BA Thesis (unpublished) University of Wales, 1977.

Walters, Huw, 'Cerddetan: Golwg ar Ryddiaith Amanwy', in *Cynnwrf Canrif: Agweddau ar Ddiwylliant Gwerin* (Swansea, 2004), pp.318-71.

*idem.*, 'David Rees Griffiths (Amanwy) 1882-1953', *The Carmarthenshire Antiquarian*, 35 (1999), pp. 89-102.

**1(f)      James Griffiths and his Pacifism**

Eirug, Aled, 'Agweddau ar y Gwrthwynebiad i'r Rhyfel Byd Cyntaf yng Nghymru', *Llafur*, Vol.4, No. 4, (1987) pp. 58-68.

Gruffydd, Ioan W., 'John Puleston Jones (1862-1925)' in *Herio'r Byd* (ed: D. Ben Rees), (Liverpool and Llanddewi Brefi, Modern Welsh Publications, 1980), pp. 93-103.

Hopkin, Deian R., 'Patriots and Pacifists in Wales,1914-1918', *Llafur*, Vol.1 No.3 (1974), pp. 27-41.

Jones, J. Graham, 'Lloyd George, W. Llewelyn Williams MP and the 1916 Conscription Bill', *National Library of Wales Journal*, Vol.31, No. 2 (Winter 1999), pp. 137-187.

Mor-O'Brien, A. '"Conchie": Emrys Hughes and the First World War', *Welsh History Review*, Vol. 13, 1986-7, pp. 328-9.

Mainwaring, M. R., 'John Morgan Jones (1861-1935)' in *Herio'r Byd* (ed. D. Ben Rees), *ibid*, pp. 61-69.

Pritchard, Islwyn, 'Thomas Evan Nicholas' (1879-1971) in *Herio'r Byd*, (ed D. Ben Rees) *ibid.*, pp. 16-22.

Rees, D. Ben, 'George Lansbury', in *Oriel o Heddychwyr Mawr y Byd*, (ed. D. Ben Rees), (Liverpool and Llanddewi Brefi, 1983), pp.70-75.

Robbins, Keith, 'Morgan Jones in 1916' *Llafur,* Vol.1 No.4 (Spring 1975), pp. 38-43.


**1(g)    Religion**

Bryant, Chris, *Possible Dreams: A Personal History of British Christian Socialists* (London 1996), 351 pp.

Edwards, Huw, *Capeli Llanelli: Our Rich Heritage* (Cyngor Sir Gâr, 2009), 560 pp.

Gibbard, Noel, 'Pastors in Public 1868-1918', *Carmarthenshire Antiquary*, Vol. XXII, 1986, pp. 59-78.

Inglis, K S., *Churches and the Working Classes in Victorian England* (London, 1963), 358 pp.

Jones, Geraint Ll., 'Rhai Traddodiadau Diwinyddol yng Nghymru Heddiw', *Yr Efengylydd*, Vol.XXIV No. 4, April 15, 1932, pp. 64-65.

Jones, P. d'A., *The Christian Socialist Revival 1877-1914: Religion, Class and Social Conscience in late Victorian England* (Princeton, 1968), 517 pp.

Mayor, S., *The Churches and the Labour Movement* (Independent Press, 1967), 416 pp.

Morgan, D Densil, *Cedyrn Canrif: Crefydd a Chymdeithas yng Nghymru'r Ugeinfed Ganrif*, (Cardiff, 2001), 282 pp.

Owen, D Huw, 'Chapel and Colliery: Bethel, Cross Hands 1907-1982', *Carmarthenshire Antiquary*, Vol.XVIII, 1982, pps. 55-68.

Pope, Robert, *Building Jerusalem: Nonconformity, Labour and the Social Question in Wales 1906-1939* (Cardiff, University of Wales Press, 1998), 269 pp.

Rees, D. Ben, *Chapels in the Valley: A study in the Sociology of Welsh Nonconformity*, (Upton, 1975), 222 pp.

Rees, D. Ben, *Pregethu a Phregethwyr* (Denbigh, 1997), 192 pp.

Robbins, Keith, 'The Spiritual Pilgrimage of the Rev R. J. Campbell', *The Journal of Ecclesiastical History*, XXXX/2 (1979), pp. 261-76.

Roberts, John R., *Canrif o Bregethu Cymraeg 1850 hyd 1950*, (Davies Lecture) (Caernarfon, 1978), 45 pp.

Shaw, Jane and Kreider, Alan (eds.), *Culture and the Nonconformist Tradition* (Cardiff, 1999), 187 pp.

Thomas, M. Wynn, *In the Shadow of the Pulpit: Literature and Nonconformist Wales* (Cardiff, 2010), 372 pp.

Williams, C. R., 'The Welsh Religious Revival, 1904-5', *British Journal of Sociology*, III/3 (1952), pp. 242-59.

**1(h)    Educational background of James Griffiths**

Brennan, T., 'The White House', *Cambridge Journal*, Vol.11 No 4 (1952-1954), pp. 243-48.

Craik, W. W., *The Central Labour College* (London, 1969).

Chushichi, Tsuzuki, 'Anglo-Marxism and Working-class Education' in Jay Winter (ed.), *The Working Class in Modern British History: Essays in Honour of Henry Pelling* (Cambridge, 1983), pp. 187-199.

James Griffiths NLW Papers A1/15, a hard back notebook with the title, 'Labour College,1922' on the spine.

Lewis, Richard, *Leaders and Teachers: Adult Education and the Challenge of Labour in South Wales,1906-1940* (Cardiff,1993), 271 pp.

Rees, D. Ben., *Adult Education 1945-1970: Preparation for Crisis*, (Ormskirk, 1981), 389 pp.


**2(a)    Welsh History**

Eames, William, 'Brithgofion Newyddiadurwr', *Y Genhinen*, Vol. XIV No. 1, Winter 1963-4, pp. 36-7.

Earnshaw, Eric, *Modern British History for Schools in Wales* (Denbigh, 1979), 556 pp.

Evans, Gwynfor, *Aros Mae* (Swansea, 1971), 325 pp.

Davies, John, *Hanes Cymru* (London, 1990), 725 pp.

Herbert, Trevor and Jones, Gareth Elwyn, *Wales between the Wars* (Cardiff, 1998), 296 pp.

Hughes, Dewi Rowland ,' Y Coch a'r Gwyrdd : Cymru Fydd a'r Mudiad Llafur Cymreig (1886- 1996 )', *Llafur* (6) , 60-79.

James, Arnold J and Thomas, John E., *Wales at Westminster: A History of the Parliamentary Representation of Wales 1800-1979* (Llandysul, 1981), 284 pp.

Jones, Aled Gruffydd, *Press, Politics and Society: A History of Journalism in Wales* (Cardiff, 1993), 317 pp.

Jones, J.Graham, *A Pocket Guide to the History of Wales* (Cardiff,1990), 140 pp.

Idem, Wales and the ''New Socialism'' 1926-1929, *Welsh History* Review. Vol. 11 No. 4 (December 1982), pp. 173-199.

Jones, R. Merfyn, *The North Wales Quarrymen, 1874-1922* (Cardiff, 1981), 359 pp.

Jones, Iorwerth, *David Rees: Y Cynhyrfwr* (Swansea, 1971), 317 pp.

Jones, Watcyn L., *Cofio Tryweryn* (Llandysul, 1988), 283 pp.

Jones, Bill & Thomas, Beth, *Teyrnas y Glo* (Cardiff, 1993), pp. 1-48.

Johnes, Martin, *Wales Since 1939* (Manchester, 2012), 465 pp.

Jenkins, Gwyn (Editor), *Llyfr y Ganrif* (Talybont, 1999), 448 pp.

Morgan, K. O., *Rebirth of a Nation: Wales 1880-1980* (Cardiff and Oxford, 1981), 420 pp.

Osmond, John, *Creative Conflict: The Politics of Welsh Devolution* (Llandysul and London, 1977), 305 pp.

Parry, Cyril, *The Radical Tradition in Welsh Politics: a study of Liberal and Labour politics in Gwynedd 1900-20* (Hull, 1970), 100 pp.

Philip, Alan Butt, *The Welsh Question: Nationalism in Welsh Politics 1945-1970*, (Cardiff, 1975), pp. 1-367.

Price, Emyr, *Cymru a'r Byd Modern ers 1918* (Cardiff, 1979), 233 pp.

Trevor, Herbert and Jones, Gareth Elwyn, *Post-War Wales* (Cardiff, University of Wales Press, 1995), pp. 1-94.

Wallace, Ryland, *The Women's Suffrage Movement in Wales* (Cardiff, 2004), pp. 1-350.

Williams, Gwyn A., *When Was Wales? A History of the Welsh* (London, 1985), 341 pp.

**2(b)**    **Welsh Politics**

'Cymru 71' in D. Ben Rees (ed.) *Arolwg*, Vol. 7, 1971 (Liverpool and Pontypridd, 1972), p. 15.

Davies, Gwilym Prys, *Llafur y Blynyddoedd* (Denbigh, 1991), 192 pp.

Davies, Gwilym Prys, 'Wedi'r Is-Etholiadau', *Barn*, July 1967, pp. 224-5.

Evans, Gwynfor, 'Hanes Twf Plaid Cymru 1925-1995', in *Cof Cenedl: Ysgrifau ar Hanes Cymru* X (Llandysul, 1995), pp. 154-184.

Griffiths, Robert, *Turning to London, The Labour Party's attitude to Wales, 1893-1956*, (Abertridwr, 1983.)

Gildart, Keith, 'Mining Memories: Reading Coalfield Autobiographies', *Labor History* Vol. 50 No. 2 (May 2008), pp. 139-61.

Harries, David Marsden, *Carmarthen Politics: The Struggle Between Liberals and Labour 1918-60*, MA Thesis (unpublished) University of Wales, 1980.

Jones, J. Graham, Rift and conflict within the Labour Party in the 1950's, *Llafur*, Vol.7 No. 2 (1997), pp. 31-40.

Jones, Thomas, *Lloyd George* (London, 1951), 330 pp.

Jenkins, Clive, *All against the Collar: Struggles of a White Collar Union Leader* (London, Methuen, 1990), 243 pp.

Lord Morris of Aberavon, *Fifty Years in Politics and the Law* (Cardiff, 2011), 261 pp.

Parry, Ted, *The Pathologies of Centralism: The Labour Party and Wales to 1957*, University of Wales ( Aberystwyth ) PH.D Thesis 2005 ( unpublished ), 315 pages.

Prothero, Cliff, *Recount*, (Ormskirk, 1982).

Lord Roberts of Conwy, *Right from the Start: The Memoirs of Sir Wyn Roberts* (Cardiff, 2006), 341 pp.

Rees, D .Ben, *Cofiant Cledwyn Hughes: Un o Wyr Mawr Môn a Chymru*, (Talybont, 2017), 320 pp.

McAllister, Laura, *Plaid Cymru: The Emergence of a Political Party* (Bridgend, 2001), 224 pp.

McAllister, L., 'Gender, Nation and Party: An Uneasy Alliance for Welsh Nationalism', *Women's History Review*, Vol. 1 No. 1 (2001), pp .51-64.

Melding, David, *Political Parties and the Welsh Nation* (London, 1987), 24 pp.

Morgan, Kenneth O., 'Gwleidyddiaeth Cymru yn 1970' in D Ben Rees (ed.), *Arolwg*, Vol. 6, 1970 (Liverpool and Pontypridd, 1971), pp. 27-31.

Morgan, Derec Llwyd (ed.), *Adnabod Deg*,(Denbigh, 1977), 153pp.

O'Leary, Paul, 'The Problems of Political Biography: The Lives of George Thomas, Viscount Tonypandy (1909-1997)', *Transactions of the Cymmrodorion Society* 2007, Vol. 14, 2008, pp. 162-174.

Smith, David (ed.), *A People and a Proletariat: Essays in the History of Wales 1780-1980*, (London, 1980), 239pps.

Smith, Robert, 'In the Direct and Homily Speech of the Worker', *Llais Llafur 1898-1915* (Aberystwyth, 2000), 47 pp.

Thomas, Ned, *The Welsh Extremist: a Culture in Crisis* (London, 1971), 127 pp.

Williams, Dafydd, *The Story of Plaid Cymru* (Aberystwyth,1990), 59 pp.

**2(c)** **Welsh Culture and the Welsh Language**

Betts, Clive, *Culture in Crisis: The Future of the Welsh Language* (Upton, 1976), 243 pp.

Chapman, T. Robin, *Un Bywyd o Blith Nifer: Cofiant Saunders Lewis* (Llandysul, 2006), 402 pp.

Davies, Gwilym Prys, 'Statws Cyfreithiol yr Iaith Gymraeg yn yr Ugeinfed Ganrif' in *Eu Hiaith a Gadwant*, (editors: Geraint H Jenkins and Mari A Williams) (Cardiff, 2000), pp. 207-238.

Jones, J. Graham, The National Petition on the Legal Status of the Welsh Language,19381942, *Welsh History Review*, Vol. 8 No.1 (June 1996), pp. 92-124.

Hopkin, Deian, 'Llafur a Diwylliant Cymreig, 1900-1940', in *Transactions of the Honourable Society of Cymmrodorion*, 2001, pp. 128-148.

Lewis, Saunders, 'Tynged', *Barn*, March 1963: p. 143.

Morgan, T. J., *Diwylliant Gwerin ac Ysgrifau Eraill* (Llandysul, 1972), 188 pp.

**2(d)**    **Devolution**

Bogdanor, Vernon, *Devolution* (Oxford, 1979).

Coupland, Sir Reginald, *Welsh and Scottish Nationalism: a study* (London, 1954), 426 pp.

Deacon, Russell, *The Governance of Wales* (Cardiff, 2002), 279 pp.

Evans, Gwynfor, *The Labour Party and Welsh Home Rule* (Cardiff, no date), pp. 1-12.

Evans, John Gilbert, *Devolution in Wales: Claims and Responses, 1937-1979* (Cardiff, 2000).

*idem*, *Devolution in Wales* (Cardiff,2006), 174 pp.

Jones, J. Graham, 'E. T. John and Welsh Home Rule,1910-14', *Welsh History Review*,Vol. 13 No. 4 (December 1987), pp. 453-467.

*idem*, 'The Parliament for Wales Campaign 1950-1956', *Welsh History Review*, XVI/2 (1992).

idem, 'Early campaigns to secure a Secretary of State for Wales, 1890-1939', *Transactions of the Honourable Society of Cymmrodorion*, 1988, pp.153-75.

*idem*, 'Socialism, Revolution and a Secretary of State for Wales', *Transactions of the Honourable Society of Cymmrodorion*, 1989, pp.140-64.

*idem*, 'Y Blaid Lafur, Datganoli a Chymru,1900-1979,' *Cof Cenedl*, 7 (1992), pp. 167-200.

Jones, R Merfyn and Jones, Ioan Rhys, 'Labour and Nation' in *The Labour Party in Wales 1900-2000* (eds. Duncan Tanner, Chris Williams and Deian Hopkin) (Cardiff, 2000), pp. 241-263.

McAllister, Laura, 'The Welsh Devolution Referendum: Definitely, Maybe?' *Parliamentary Affairs*, L/2 (1998), pp. 149-165.

Osmond, John, *Creative Conflict: The Politics of Welsh Devolution* (Llandysul, 1978)

Price, Emyr, *Lloyd George Y Cenedlaetholwr Cymreig: Arwr ynteu Bradwr?* (Llandysul, 1999), pp. 203.

Prys-Davies, Lord Gwilym, *Turning a Dream into a Reality* (Aberystwyth, 2000).

Thomas, David, *Llafur a Senedd i Gymru*, (Bangor, 1954), pp. 1-28.

*idem.*, *Diolch am Gael Byw* (Liverpool, 1968).

Williams, J. Ellis, 'Lloffion', *Y Genhinen*, Winter 1971, pp. 190-1.

## 3(a)    Pioneers of the Labour Movement in Britain

Blatchford, Robert, *My 80 Years* (Cassell, 1931), 303 pp.

Blaxland, G., *J H Thomas: a Life for Unity* (London, 1964), 303 pp.

Cole, G. D. H., *The Life of Robert Owen*, (London, 1965), 372 pps

Davies, Sir Alfred T., *Robert Owen (1771-1858), Pioneer, Social Reformer and Philanthropist* (Manchester, 1948), 84 pps

Glasier, J. Bruce, *The Meaning of Socialism* (Manchester, 1919), 372pp.

Morton, A. L., *The Life and Ideas of Robert Owen* (London, 1969), 240 pp.

Nicholas, T. E., 'R J Derfel: y gwrthryfelwr Cymreig', *Y Genhinen*, xxxii (St David's Festival), pp. 59-62.

Roberts, Arthur Meirion, 'R. J. Derfel 1824-1905', *Y Traethodydd*, clxv (January, 2009), pp. 34-54.

Taylor, Antony, 'The Old Chartist: Radical Veterans on the Late Nineteenth- and Early Twentieth-Century Political Platform', *History*, Vol. 95, No. 320, October 2010, pp. 458-476.

Thompson, E. P., *The Making of The English Working Class* (London, 1964) pp. 1-848.

Ward, Paul and Wright, Martin, 'Mirrors of Wales - Life Story as National Metaphor: Case Studies of R J Derfel (1824-1905) and Huw T Edwards (1892-1970)', *History*, Vol. 95 No. 317, January 2010, pp. 45-63.

Webb, Harri, *Dic Penderyn and the Merthyr Rising of 1831* (Swansea, 1956), pp. 1-16.

Williams, Gwyn A., 'The Merthyr of Dic Penderyn', in *Merthyr Politics: The Making of a Working-Class Tradition* (ed. Glanmor Williams) (Cardiff, 1966), pp. 9-27.

Williams, Gwyn A., 'The Emergence of a Working-Class Movement' in *Wales Through the Ages*, Vol. 2, (ed. A J Roderick) (Llandybïe, 1971), pp. 140-6.

## 3(b)    Pioneers of the Labour Movement in Wales

### Noah Ablett

Bellamy, Joyce a Saville, John, 'Noah Ablett (1883-1935)' in *Dictionary of Labour Biography*, Vol. 3 (Basingstoke, 1961), pp. 1-3.

Egan, David, 'Noah Ablett, 1883-1935', *Llafur*, Vol. 2 No. 3 (1978), pp. 64-80.

### William Abraham

Evans, E. W., *Mabon (William Abraham, 1842-1922): A study in Trade Union Leadership* (Cardiff, 1959), pp. 1-167

*idem.*, 'Mabon and Trade Unionism in the South Wales Coalfield', in *Men of No Property: Historical Studies of Welsh Trade Unions* (ed. Goronwy Alun Hughes) (Caerwys, 1971), pp. 51-8.

### Eleanor Andrews

Andrews, E., *A woman's work is never done: being the recollections of a childhood and upbringing amongst the South Wales miners and a lifetime of service to the Labour movement in Wales* (Rhondda, 1940), pp. 1-51.

### Arthur James Cook

Desmaris, Ralph H. & Saville, John, 'Arthur James Cook (1883-1931) in *Dictionary of Labour Biography*, Vol.3 (Basingstoke, 1976), pp. 38-49.

### John Davies

Davies, John, 'John Davies (1882-1937)', *The Dictionary of Welsh Biography 1941-1970*, Atodiad/ Appendix (London, Honourable Society of Cymmrodorion, 2001), pp. 325-6.

### Arthur Deakin

Allen,V. L.,*Trade Union Leadership based on a study of Arthur Deakin* (London,1957), 339 pp.

### Stephen Owen Davies

Jones, J. Graham, 'S.O. Davies and the Government for Wales Bill, 1955' *Llafur*, Vol. 8 No. 3 (2002), pp. 67-78.

### Huw Thomas Edwards

Edwards, Huw T., *Tros y Tresi* (Denbigh, 1956), pp. 1-133.

Edwards, H. T., *Hewn from the Rock: the Autobiography of Huw T Edwards* (Cardiff, 1967), pp. 1-238.

Jenkins, Gwyn, *Prif Weinidog Answyddogol Cymru: Cofiant Huw T Edwards* (Talybont, 2001), pp. 1-271.

**W J Edwards**

Edwards, W. J., *From the Valley I Came* (London, 1956), pp. 1-271.

**Dai Dan Evans**

Francis, Dai, 'Dai Dan Evans - a Tribute', *Llafur*. Vol. 1 No. 3, May 1974, pp. 3-4

**James Keir Hardie**

Hughes, Emrys, *Keir Hardie* (London, 1956), pp. 1-248.

Morgan, Kenneth O., *Keir Hardie: Radical and Socialist* (London, 1997), pp. 1-343.

**Vernon Hartshorn**

Stead, Peter, 'Vernon Hartshorn: Miners' Agent and Cabinet Minister, in Stewart Williams (ed.) *Glamorgan Historian*, VI, (Cowbridge, 1969), pp. 83-94.

**Arthur Horner**

Horner, A., *Incorrigible Rebel* (London, 1960), 235 pp.

Paynter, W., 'Tribute to Arthur Horner, 1894-1968', *Labour Monthly*, October 1968, 50 (10), pp. 469-70.

David Smith, 'Leaders and Led' in K. S. Hopkins (Ed.), *Rhondda Past and Present* (Ferndale, 1974), pp. 37-65.

**John Gwili Jenkins**

Jenkins, R. T., 'John Gwili Jenkins (1872-1936)', *Y Bywgraffiadur Cymreig hyd 1940*, p. 410.

Smith, J Beverley, 'John Gwili Jenkins', *Transactions of the Honourable Society of Cymmrodorion*, 1974-5, pp. 191-214.

**Edward Thomas Owen**

Jones J. Graham, E. T. John, 'Devolution and Democracy,1917-24', *Welsh History Review*, Vol.14 No.3 (June 1989 '), pps'. 439-469.

**Thomas Jones, CH**

Ellis, E. L., *T .J.  A Life of Dr Thomas Jones, CH* (Cardiff, 1992), 553 pp.

**Thomas (Tom) Jones**

Gildart, Keith, 'Thomas (Tom) Jones (1908-90)', *Dictionary of Labour Biography*, Vol. XI (eds. Keith Gildart, David Howell and Neville Kirk) (Basingstoke, 2003), pp. 159-166.

Pugh, Jane, *A Most Expensive Prisoner. Tom Jones Rhosllanerchrugog's Biography* (Llanrwst, 1988)

### Thomas Gwynn Jones

Jones, T. Gwynn, *Dr T Gwynn Jones: a Great Welshman*, Tributes by Idris Bell, J. Ellis Williams, T. E. Nicholas, Keidrych Rhys, W. J .Rees, D. Gwenallt Jones, Dilys Cadwaladr, D. Tecwyn Lloyd, Idris Cox (Cardiff, The Welsh Committee of the Communist Party, 1945), 24 pp.

Gwyn, Arthur ap, and Jones, Francis Wyn, 'Thomas Gwynn Jones (1871-1949, *The Dictionary of Welsh Biography 1941-195* (London, 2001), pp. 33-4.

Jones, J. W., 'Thomas Gwynn Jones: Atgofion Chwarelwr', *Eurgrawn*, CXIL, 153-6, 186-7.

Thomas, David, 'Nodiadau'r Golygydd', *Lleufer*, XIV, 105-7, and 'Cofio Thomas Gwynn Jones'.

### Thomas Evan Nicholas (Niclas y Glais)

Hopkin, Deian', 'The Merthyr Pioneer 1911-29', *Llafur*, Vol. 2 No. 4 (Spring 1979), pp. 54 64.

Rees, D. Ben, Thomas Evan Nicholas (Niclas y Glais) (1879-1971)', in *Dictionary of Labour Biography*, Volume X111, (Edited by Keith Gildart & David Howell (Basingstoke, 2011), pp. 282-292.

### David  Thomas

Tomos, Angharad Wyn, *Hiraeth am Yfory: Hanes David Thomas a Mudiad Llafur Gogledd Cymru* (Llandysul, 2002).

Rees, D. Ben, David Thomas (1880-1967) 'Labour Pioneer in Wales', in *Dictionary of Labour Biography* Volume X111, *ibid*, pp. 362-372.


### 3 (c). **Contemporaries of James Griffiths in the House of Commons**

### Clement R.  Attlee

Burridge, Trevor, *Clement Attlee: A Political Biography* (London, 1985).

Jenkins, Roy, *Mr Attlee: An Interim Biography* (London, 1948), 274 pp.

### Aneurin Bevan

Brome, V., *Aneurin Bevan* (London, 1953), 252 pp.

Goodman, Geoffrey (ed), *The State of the Nation: The Political Legacy of Aneurin Bevan* (London, 1997), 242 pp.

Edwards, H. T. 'A Pen-Portrait of the Late Aneurin Bevan', *Aneurin: Student Socialist Opinion in Wales*, Vol. 1 No. 2, pp 5-6.

Foot, Michael, *Aneurin Bevan: a Biography, Vol.1: 1897-1945* (London, 1962), 536 pp.

Griffiths, James, 'World figure still remembered as a true son of the Valley', *Western Mail*, July 8, 1960, p. 6.

Krug, M. M., *Aneurin Bevan: Cautious Rebel* (New York, 1961), 316 pp.

Llewellyn, D., *Nye: The Beloved Patrician, Glimpses of the Greatness of Aneurin Bevan* (Cardiff, 1960), 31 pp.

**Ernest Bevin**

Bullock, Alan, *The Life and Times of Ernest Bevin, Vol.1, Trade Union Leader 1881-1940* (Heinemann, 1960), 678pps. *Vol. 2 Minister of Labour 1940-5* (Heinemann, 1967), 421 pp.

Crossman, R H S., 'Ernest Bevin's Loyalty', in *The Charm: Politics and other essays in Political Criticism*,(Hamilton, 1958), pp. 75-7.

Jones, J. Graham, 'Ernest Bevin and the General Strike', *Llafur*, Vol. 8 No. 2 (2001), pp.9 7-103.

Williams, Francis, *Ernest Bevin: Portrait of a Great Englishman* (London, 1952), 288 pp.

**Stafford Cripps**

Cooke, Colin, *The Life of Richard Stafford Cripps* (Londdon,1957).

Dalyell, Tam, *Dick Crossman, A Portrait* (London, 1982).

**Clement Davies**

Jones, J. Graham, 'The reminiscences of Clement Davies, MP', *Journal of the National Library of Wales*, Vol. 28 No. 4 (Winter 1994), pp. 405-417.

*idem*, 'D. Caradog Jones and Montgomeryshire Politics', *Montgomeryshire Collections*, Vol. 92 (2004), pp. 127-143.

*idem*, 'The Political Baptism of E. Clement Davies', *Montgomeryshire Collections*, Vol. 94 (2006), pp. 143-155.

**Desmond Donnelly**

Jones, J. Graham, 'Desmond Donnelly and Pembrokeshire Politics 1964-70', *Journal of the Pembrokeshire Historical Society*, Vol. 12 (2003), pp. 67-102 .

**Walter Elliot**

Coote, Colin, *A Companion of Honour: The Story of Walter Elliot in Scotland and Westminster* (London, 1965), 288 pp.

**Gwynfor Evans**

Evans, Rhys, *Gwynfor* (translated by T.Robin Chapman) (Talybont,2008), 526 pp.

**Michael Foot**

Morgan, Kenneth O., *Michael Foot* (London, 2007), 588 pp.

**David Lloyd George**

Adams, Rufus, *David Lloyd George's Astonishing Career 1863- 1916* (Rhyl, 2006), 24 pp.

Hattersley, Roy, *David Lloyd George: the Great Outsider* (London, 2010), 710 pp.

Jones, J. Graham, 'Every vote for Llewelyn Williams is a vote against Lloyd George,' *Journal of Liberal Democrat History*, 37 (Winter 2002/2003), pp. 3-9.

**William Gallacher**

Knox, William, William Gallacher (1881-1965), in *Scottish Labour Leaders 1918-1939: A Biographical Dictionary*, (Edited by Dr William Knox) (Edinburgh,1984), pp. 113- 121.

*William Gallacher's Speeches in Parliament* (Glasgow, 1938), 54pp.

**Emlyn Hooson**

Jones, J. Graham, 'Emlyn Hooson and Montgomeryshire Politics, 1962-79,' *Montgomeryshire Collections*, Vol. 97 (2009), pp.165-204.

**Emrys Daniel Hughes**

Knox, William, Emrys Daniel Hughes (1894-1969), in *Scottish Labour leaders 1918-1939, A Biographical Dictionary* edited by William Knox (Edinburgh, 1984), pp.144-148.

**Henry Haydn Jones**

Jones, J. Graham, 'Sir Henry Haydn Jones, MP (1863-1950)', *Cylchgrawn Cymdeithas Hanes a Chofnodion Sir Feirionnydd*, Vol. 15 No. 3, (2008), pp. 293-316.

**James Idwal Jones**

Gildart, Keith, James Idwal Jones (1900-1982) in *Dictionary of Labour Biography* Vol.X111 (Edited by Keith Gildart & David Howell) (Basingstoke 2012), pps.180-188.

**Thomas William Jones**

Gildart, Keith, 'Thomas William (Lord Maelor) (1898-1984)', in *Dictionary of Labour Biography* Vol. X111, *ibid.*, pp. 188-198.

Lord Maelor, *Fel Hyn y Bu* (Denbigh, 1970), 122 pp.

**Ramsay Macdonald**

Marquand, David, *Ramsay MacDonald* (London, 1977).

Mc Kibbin, R. I., 'James Ramsay MacDonald and the Problem of the Independence of the Labour Party', *Journal of Modern History*, Vol. 42 No. 2 (June 1970).

**James Maxton**

Marwick, A. J. B., 'James Maxton: His Place in Scottish Labour History', *Scottish Historical Review*, Vol. 43 (April 1964), pp. 25-43.

Orr, Boyd, *The role of the Rebel in History*, Maxton Memorial Lecture (Edinburgh, 1950), 32 pp.

## Ian Mikardo

Mikardo, Ian, *Back-bencher* (London, 1988).

## D. Elystan Morgan

Jones, J. Graham, D. 'Elystan Morgan and Cardiganshire Politics ', *Welsh History Review*, Vol. 22 No. 4 (December 2005), pp .730-761.

## David Llewellyn Mort

Gildart, Keith, David Llewellyn Mort (1888-1963) in *Dictionary of Labour Biography* Vol. X111, ibid, pp. 266-279.

## George Lansbury

Postgate, Raymond, *The Life of George Lansbury* (London, 1951), 332 pp.

## Frederick Elwyn Jones

Jones-Elwyn, Lord., *In My Time: An Autobiography* (London,1983), 319 pp.

## Jennie Lee

Lee, Jennie, *The Great Journey: a Volume of Autobiography, 1904-45* (London, 1963), (published in 1940 under the title *Tomorrow is a New Day*), 230 pp.

## Ness Edwards

David, Wayne, *Remaining True: a Biography of Ness Edwards*, (*Caerphilly Local History Society*, 2006), 118 pp.

## Harold Finch

Finch, Harold, *Memoirs of a Bedwellty MP* (Risca, 1972), pp. 1-206.

## Hugh Gaitskell

Brivati, Brian, *Hugh* Gaitskell (London, 1996), 332pp.

Rodgers, W. T. (ed.), *Hugh Gaitskell 1906-63* (London, 1964), 167 pp.

## William Gallacher

Gallacher, William, *Rise Like Lions* (London, 1951), 253 pp.

Gallacher, William, *The Last Memoirs of William Gallacher* (London, 1966), 320 pp.

## Denis Healey

Williams, Geoffrey and Reed, Bruce, *Denis Healey and the Policies of Power*, (London, 1971), 286pp.

**Hugh Dalton**

Dalton, H., *Call Back Yesterday: Memoirs 1887-1931*,(London, 1953), 330 pp.

Dalton, H., *The Fateful Years: Memoirs 1931-45* (London, 1957), 493 pp.

Dalton, H., *High tide and after: Memoirs 1945-60* (London, 1962), 453 pp.

Pimlott, Ben, *Hugh Dalton* (London, 1985),.

**Tom Driberg**

Driberg, T., *The Best of Both Worlds: a Personal Diary* (London, 1953), 234 pp.

**S. O. Davies**

Griffiths, Robert, *S. O. Davies: A Socialist Faith* (Llandysul, 1983), 312 pp.

**Frank Cousins**

Goodman, C., *Brother Frank: the Man and his Union* (London, 1969), 128 pp.

Stewart, M., *Frank Cousins: a Study* (London, 1968), 210 pp.

**Richard Stafford Cripps**

Cooke, C., *The Life of Richard Stafford Cripps*,(London, 1957), 415 pp.

Estorick, E., *Stafford Cripps: a Biography* (London, 1949), 378 pp.

**Bessie Braddock**

Braddock, John and Bessie, *The Braddocks* (London, 1963), 244 pp.

D. Ben Rees, *A Portrait of Battling Bessie: Life and Work of Bessie Braddock, a Liverpool MP* (Nottingham, 2011), 56 pp.

D. Ben Rees, 'Bessie Braddock AS', in *Cwmni Deg Dawnus* (Liverpool, 2003), pp. 42-61.

Toole, M., *Mrs Bessie Braddock MP: a Biography* (London, 1957), 223 pp.

**Fenner Brockway**

Brockway, F., *Inside the Left: Thirty Years of Platform, Press, Prison and Parliament* (London, 1947), 352 pp.

Brockway, F. *Outside the Right: a Sequel to 'Inside the Left* (London, 1963), 231 pp.

**George Brown**

Brown, George, *My Way* (London, 1971).

Harris, K., *'George Brown 1966', Conversations* (London, 1967), pp. 89-95.

**Barbara Castle**

Castle, Barbara, *The Castle Diaries 1974-76* (London, 1980), 788 pp.

**Eleanor Rathbone**

Pederson, Susan, *Eleanor Rathbone and the Politics of Conscience* (London, 2004), 469 pp.

**George Thomas**

Robertson, Edwin H., *George: A Biography of Viscount Tonypandy* (London, 1992), 352 pp.

**Harold Wilson**

Pimlott, Ben, *Harold Wilson* (London, 1992).

Wilson, Harold, *Memoirs: The Making of a Prime Minister 1916-64* (London, 1986).

Ziegler, Philip, *Wilson* (London, 1993).

**Ellen Wilkinson**

Vernon, Betty D., *Ellen Wilkinson*, (Brighton, 1982).

**The Parliamentary Labour Party**

Brookes, P., *Women at Westminster: an Account of Women in the British Parliament 1918-1966* (London, 1967), 292pps.

Ellis, Tom, *After The Dust Has Settled: The Autobiography of Tom Ellis* (Wrexham, 2004 ).

Hughes, E., 'The Revolt in Parliament', *Labour Monthly*, March 1968, Vol. 50 (3), pp. 11112.

Jackson, R. J., *Rebels and Whips: An Analysis of Dissension, Discipline and Cohesion in British Political Parties* (London, 1968), 358 pp.

Judge, David, *Backbench Specialisms in the House of Commons* (London, 1981).

Miliband, Ralph, *Parliamentary Socialism: a Study in the Politics of Labour* (London, 1964).

Morgan, Janet (ed.), *The Backbench Diaries of Richard Crossman* (London, 1981), 1136 pp.

Morgan, W. Geraint, 'Denbighshire Members of Parliament in the Twentieth Century', *Denbighshire Historical Society Transactions* (1971), pp. 217-37.

Morrison, Herbert, *Government and Parliament: A Survey from the Inside* (second edition) (London, 1959).

Pearce, Robert (ed.), *Patrick Gordon-Walker: Political Diaries 1932-71* (London, 1991)

Punnett, R M., 'The Labour Shadow Cabinet 1955-64', *Parliamentary Affairs*, Winter 1964, Vol. 18 (1), pp. 61-70.

Sharp, Evelyn, "Politicians", *The Listener*, 88/28, 28 September 1971.

**3(e)** **Trade Unions**

Allen, V. L., *Power in Trade Unions: a Study of their Organisation in Great Britain* (London, 1954), 332 pp.

Chaloner, W H., 'The British Miners and the Coal Industry Between the Wars', *History Today*, June 1964, Vol. 14 (6), pp. 418-26.

Gregory, R., *The Miners and British Politics 1906-14* (Oxford, 1968), 218pp.

Gildart, Keith, *North Wales Miners, A Fragile Unity 1945-1996* (Cardiff, 2001).

Pelling, H., *A History of British Trade Unionism* (London, 1966, first edition 1963), 299 pp.

Pugh, Sir Arthur, *Men of Steel: by One of Them, a Chronicle of Eighty-Eight Years of Trade Unionism in the British Iron and Steel Industry* (London, 1951), 624 pp.

Zweig, F., *Men in the Pits* (London, 1948), 183pp.

**3(f)** **Movements within the Labour Party**

**Fabian Society**

Cole, G .D. H.; Bevan, Aneurin; Griffiths, Jim; Easterbrook, L. F.; Beveridge, Sir William; Laski, Harold J.; *Plan for Britain: A Collection of Essays* (London, Fabian Society), 127 pp.

Cole, Margaret, *The Story of Fabian Socialism* (London, 1963), 371 pp.

Healey, Denis, "A Natural Belt in Europe" *Fabian Tract 311* (London, 1958).

Milburn, J. F., 'The Fabian Society and the British Labour Party', *Western Political Quarterly*, June 1955, Vol.11 (2), pp .319-39.

Shaw, George Bernard (ed.), *Fabian Essays in Socialism* (London, 1889).

**Independent Labour Party**

Dowse, R. E., *Left in the Centre: the Independent Labour Party 1893-1940* (London, 1966), 224 pp.

Marwick, A., 'The Independent Labour Party in the Nineteen Twenties', *Bulletin Institute of Historical Research*, May 1962, Vol. 35 (91): pp. 62-74.

McKinlay, Alan and Morris, R.J (eds), *The ILP on Clydeside 1893-1932: From Foundation to Disintegration* (Manchester, 1991) 249 pp.

Parry, Cyril, 'The Independent Labour Party and Gwynedd Politics 1900-20', *Welsh History Review*, June 1968, Vol. 4 No. 1, pp. 47-66.

**4(a)** **The Labour Party**

Abrams, M and Rose, R., *Must Labour Lose?* (London, 1960), pp. 1-127.

Adams, W S., 'Lloyd George and the Labour Movement', *Past and Present*, February 1953, Vol. 3, pp. 55-64.

Attlee, C R., *Mr Attlee Replies to Lady Megan Lloyd George* (London, 1945), pp. 1-2.

Attlee, Clement R., *The Labour Party in Perspective – and twelve years later*, (Introduction by Francis Williams) (London, 1949), first published under the title *The Labour Party in Perspective* in 1937), pp. 1-199.

*idem., As it happened* (London, 1956), pps.1-256.

Bevan, Aneurin, *In Place of Fear* (London, 1961), pps.1-203. *idem.,*

*The Defence of Our Liberties* (London, 1951), pps. 1-4.

Cole, C. D. H., *A History of the Labour Party from 1914* (London, 1969), pp. 1-527.

*idem.,* 'The Labour Party and the Trade Unions', *Political Quarterly*, January-March, 1953, Vol. 24 (1), pp. 18-27.

Cronin, James E., *New Labour's Pasts: The Labour Party and its Discontents* (London, 2004), pp. 1-497.

Crossland, A., *Can Labour Win?* (Fabians, 1960), pp. 1-24.

Davies, A. J., *To Build a New Jerusalem: The British Labour Party from Keir Hardie to Tony Blair* (London, 1996), 578 pp.

Davies, Mary, *Comrade or Brother? The History of the British Labour Movement 1789-1951* (London, 1993), pp. 1-226.

Dagger, George, *Has Labour Redeemed its Pledges?* (Abertilery, 1949), pp. 1-35.

Davies, S. O., 'Labour and the War', *Labour Monthly*, September 1950, 32 (9), pp. 400-4.

*idem.,* 'Labour and Re-armament', *Labour Monthly*, June 1951, 33 (6), pp. 253-6.

Durbin, Elizabeth, *New Jerusalem, The Labour Party and the Economics of Democratic Socialism* (London, 1985), 341 pp.

Dutt, R. Palme, 'Crisis of the Labour Party', *Labour Monthly*, April 1955, 37 (10), pp. 433-446.

Dowse, R E., 'The entry of the Liberals into the Labour Party 1910-20', *Yorkshire Bulletin of Economics and Social Research*, November, 1961, Vol. 13 (2), pp. 78-87.

Donnelly, Desmond, *Gadarene '68: the Crime, Follies and Misfortunes of the Wilson Government* (London, 1968), pp. 1-192.

Gupta, Paratha Sarathi, 'Imperialism and the Labour Government of 1945-51' in Jay, Winter (ed.), *The Working Class in Modern British History: Essays in Honour of Henry Pelling* (Cambridge, 1983), pp. 99-121.

*idem., Imperialism and the British Labour Movement 1914-1964* (London, 1975), pp. 1-454.

Jeffreys, Kevin, *Labour Forces from Ernest Bevin to Gordon Brown* (London, 2002), 256 pp.

Jeffreys-Jones, T. I., 'The Rise of Labour' in A. J. Roderick (ed.). *Wales Through the Ages*, Vol. 2 (Llandybïe, 1971), pp. 201-8.

Jones, Gwynoro, *The Record Put Straight: Labour's Record in Wales 1964-70* (Carmarthen, 1973), Preface by the Rt. Hon. James Griffiths, C.H., 54 pp.

Howard, Christopher, 'Expectations Born to Death' in Jay, Winter (ed.), *The Working Class in Modern British History: Essays in Honour of Henry Pelling*, *ibid.,* pp. 65-81.

Saville, John, Morgan Phillips, *Dictionary of National Biography*, Supplement. 1961-70 (Oxford, 1971).

Lapping, B., *The Labour Government 1964-70* (London, 1970), pp. 1-219.

Miliband, Ralph, 'The Labour Government and Beyond', *Socialist Register*, 1966, Vol. 3, pp. 11-26.

*idem.*, *Parliamentary Socialism: A study in the Politics of Labour* (London, 1979), pp. 1-384.

McAllister, Ian, 'The Labour Party in Wales: The Dynamics of One-Partyism', *Llafur*, Vol. 3 No. 2 (1981), pp. 79-89.

Prothero, Cliff, *Recount* (Omskirk, 1982), pp. 1-118.

Saville, John, 'Labourism and the Labour Government', *Socialist Register,* 1967, Vol. 4, pp. 43-7.

Schneer, Jonathan, *Labour's Conscience: The Labour Left 1945-51* (London, 1988).

Thorpe, Andrew, *A History of the British Labour Party* (Second edition, Basingstoke, 2001).

Vickers, Rhiannon, *The Labour Party and the World: Volume 1: The Evolution of Labour's Foreign Policy 1900-51* (Manchester, 2003)

Wright, Anthony, *British Socialism: Socialist Thought from the 1880s to 1960s* (London, 1983).

*idem.,* 'British Socialism and the British Constitution', *Parliamentary Affairs* 43/3, July 1990.

*idem., Socialisms: Old and New* (Second Edition, London, 1996).

**4(b)**     **The Labour Party in Wales**

Hain, Peter, *A Welsh Third Way* (London, 1999), pp. 1-28.

Hain, Peter, *A Road Map for Labour* (Aneurin Bevan Memorial Lecture) (Tredegar, 2003), pp. 1-16.

Hopkin, Deian, 'The Rise of Labour: Llanelli, 1890-1922', in *Politics and Society in Wales 1840-1922*, (eds., Geraint H. Jenkins and J. Beverley Smith) (Cardiff, 1988), pp. 161-82.

*Labour is Building a New Wales* (Cardiff, date unknown), pp. 1-16.

Jones, Carwyn, *The Future of Welsh Labour* (Cardiff, 2004), pp. 1-41.

Morgan, Kenneth O., 'Post-war Reconstruction in Wales, 1918 and 1945', in Jay Winter (ed.), *The Working Class in Modern British History: Essays in Honour of Henry Pelling* (Cambridge, 1983), pp. 82-98.

Parry, Jane, *A History of the Labour Movement in Neath* (Neath, 1996), pp. 1-52.

Pelling, Henry, 'The Politics of the Osborne Judgement', *Historical Journal*, 25 (1982), pp. 889-909.

Stead, Peter, 'The Labour Party and the Claims of Wales' in John Osmond (ed.), *The National Question Again: Welsh Political Identity in the 1980s* (Llandysul, 1985), pp. 99-123.

*idem.*, 'Working Class Leadership in South Wales 1900-1920', *Welsh History Review*, Vol. 6 No. 3 (1973), pp. 329-53.

*idem.,* 'Establishing a Heartland: The Labour Party in Wales' in *The First Labour Party 1906-1914*, ed. K D Brown (Beckenham, 1985), pp. 64-88.

Tanner, Duncan, Chris Williams a Deian Hopkin (eds.), *The Labour Party in Wales 19001920* (Cardiff, 2000), pp. 1-324.

Turner, Christopher, 'Conflict of Faith: Religion and Labour in Wales, 1890-1914' in *Class Community and the Labour Movement: Wales and Canada, 1850-1930*, (ed. Deian R. Hopkin and Gregory S. Kealey) (Aberystwyth, 1989), pp. 67-85.

**4(c)**     **The Labour Party and Welsh Socialists**

Davies, D. L., 'Watkin William Price (1873-1967)', *The Dictionary of Welsh Biography 1941-1970*, (London, 2001), pp. 211-12.

*idem*, 'Edmund William Stonelake (1873-1960)', *ibid.*, pp. 197-8.

Davies, John, 'George Daggar (1879-1950)', *ibid.*, p. 26;

*idem.*, 'Ness Edwards (1987-1968)', p.57.

Hopkin, Deian, 'Y Werin a'i Theyrnas: Ymateb Sosialaeth i Genedlaetholdeb 1880-1920', in G. H. Jenkins (ed.), *Cof Cenedl: Ysgrifau ar Hanes Cymru*, VI (Llandysul, 1991), pp. 63-192; *idem.*, Gordon Macdonald, 1888-1966, *The Dictionary of Welsh Biography 1941-1970*, p. 179.

James, Mary Auronwy, 'David Thomas (1880-1967)', p. 254,

*idem,* Morgan Walter Phillips (1902-63), *ibid*, p. 208.

Jones, David Gwenallt, 'Robert Jones Derfel, 1824-1905', *Dictionary of Welsh Biography* (London, 1959).

Jones, Evan David, 'Llywelyn Williams (1911-65)', *The Dictionary of Welsh Biography* (London, 1959), pp. 302-3

Jones, John Graham, 'Stanley Stephen Awbrey (1888-1969)' *The Dictionary of Welsh Biography 1941-1970,* p.7.

*idem,* 'Arthur Deakin (1890-1955)', *ibid.,* p. 50.

*idem.,* 'Huw Thomas Edwards (1892-1970)', *ibid.,* p. 55.

*idem,* 'Emrys Daniel Hughes (1894-1969)' *ibid.,* p.98.

*idem.,* 'Thomas Isaac Mardy-Jones (1879-1970)', *ibid.,* p.148.

*idem.,* 'Ronald Cavill Mathias (1912-1968)', *ibid.,* pps1 80-1.

*idem.,* 'Iwan James Morgan (1904-1966)', *ibid.* p.185.

*idem.,* 'Percy Morris (1893-1967)', *ibid.* pp.189-90.

*idem.,* 'David Emlyn Thomas (1892-1954)', *ibid.,* p.245.

*idem.,* 'Iorwerth Rhys Thomas (1895-1966)', *ibid.,* p.258.

*idem.,* 'Edward John (Ted) Williams (1890-1963)', *ibid.,* p.291-2.

D. Ben Rees, *Cymry Adnabyddus 1952-1972* (Liverpool and Pontypridd, 1978), There are, in Welsh, entries on a number of Welsh socialists; Sir John Bailey, p.18; Aneurin Bevan, pp .22-4; David Jones Davies, p .33; Stephen Owen Davies, p. 40; Huw Thomas Edwards, pp. 47-9; John Evans, p. 64; Lady Megan Lloyd George, pp. 74-5; David Rhys Grenfell, p. 83; David Rees Griffiths (Amanwy), pp. 84-6; Thomas Hudson-Williams, p. 90; Emrys Hughes, p. 93; Ronw Moelwyn-Hughes, p. 94; Thomas Ieuan Jeffreys-Jones, pp. 101-2; William John, p. 108, Arthur George Llewellyn, p. 141; Ronald (Ron) Mathias, pp. 153-4; Sir James Frederick Rees, pp. 166-7; Bryn Roberts, p. 170; John Roberts (Cardiff), pp. 172-3; David Thomas, pp. 178-180; John Alun Nicholas Thomas, p.181; David Emrys Williams (Tregarth), p.186; Llywelyn Williams, p. 194; Thomas Nefyn Williams, p. 198.

Roberts, Gomer Morgan, 'David Rees (Amanwy, 1882-1953)', *The Dictionary of Welsh Biography 1941-1970,* p. 84.

*idem,* 'Thomas Williams ('Tom Nefyn', 1895-1958)' *ibid,* pp. 305-6.

Walters Huw, 'Ebenezer Rees (1848-1908)', *ibid.,* p. 368.

# Index

## A

Amanwy (David Rees Griffiths) 3, 4, 9, 10, 19  20, 22, 23, 30, 31, 33, 34, 35, 36, 37, 39, 40, 44, 58, 59, 61, 67, 69, 78, 80, 83, 88, 109-110, 115, 117, 121, 129, 130, 135, 136, 158, 164, 190, 191, 194, 196, 203, 286, 290, 292

Amman Valley 8, 10, 15, 21, 22, 23, 30, 31, 40, 46, 49, 50, 51, 54, 55, 58, 59, 61, 62, 63, 64, 66, 67, 68, 72, 78, 79, 80, 104, 106, 107, 109, 110, 117, 119, 120, 121, 127, 134, 135, 145, 152, 187, 196, 232, 275, 283, 286, 287, 288, 290, 293, 296

Ammanford 3, 4, 6, 8, 9, 15, 16, 18, 20, 21, 22, 23, 24, 25, 27, 30, 33, 34, 38, 39, 40, 41, 46, 47, 49, 50, 53, 55, 56, 59, 60, 61, 62, 63, 64, 66, 67, 72, 73, 76, 77, 78, 80, 82, 84, 88, 89, 91, 93, 99, 103, 104, 107, 110, 115, 117, 118, 119, 120, 122, 127, 144, 152, 157, 164, 171, 186, 187, 189, 190, 195, 196, 200, 203, 215, 221, 229, 241, 248, 250, 267, 273, 275, 278, 279, 285, 286, 290, 293, 294,

Anderson, Donald 238, 280, 283

Anderson, Sir John 130

Andrews, Elizabeth 92, 103

*Aneurin* (a student's socialist journal) 8

Angell, Sir Norman, 181, 193,

Anglican 18, 126, 280

Annibynwyr Cymreig (Welsh Independent Union) 15, 16, 195, 196

Appiah, Joe 172

Ardudwy 160

Armistice (1918) 65

Asquith, H. H. 66

Attlee, Clement 7, 108, 111, 113, 124, 125, 126, 134, 139, 142, 145, 147, 153, 154, 156, 159, 161, 167, 168, 176, 177, 179, 181, 183, 186, 191, 197, 198, 199, 200, 201, 205, 211, 228, 287, 288, 289, 290

Azikiwe, Dr Benjamin Nnamdi 262

Bethesda 15, 39, 115, 123

Bevan, Aneurin  8, 9, 26, 38, 73, 74, 76, 79, 81, 102, 110, 122, 12, 125, 132, 134 136, 138, 139, 143, 144, 145, 147, 151, 155, 158, 159, 161, 163, 164, 168, 177, 180, 181, 182, 183, 184, 193, 194, 198, 199-202, 204-7, 211-13, 215, 217, 220, 225, 230, 287, 289, 290, 295, 296

Bevan, David (Tredegar) 74

Bevan, Evan 64

Bevan, Hugh 23, 68, 104, 115

Bevan, William 63

Bevanism 182, 188, 288

Bevanites 181, 183, 185, 206,

Beveridge, Sir William 130-134, 137, 147, 148, 158, 160, 283, 287, 289, 294, 296

Bevin, Ernest 98, 102, 108, 129, 130, 139, 147, 176, 181, 194, 287, 289, 296

Biafra 250, 255-275, 287

Bickersaff, Mabel 32

Birch, Nigel 144, 146, 156,

Black and Tans 78

Black, Sir Cyril 219,

Blackburn 56

Blackpool 139, 156, 221

Blackstone, Tessa 80

Blackwood 100, 102,

Blaenau Ffestiniog 15, 82, 123,

Blaenau Gwent 281

Blaina 89, 92

Bloomsbury 111

Boer War 18

Chappel, E. L. 57, 63

Charles, Dai (Llanelli) 216, 237, 241

Chicago 18, 22, 136

Christian Temple Welsh Independent Chapel, Ammanford 8, 18, 22, 27, 31, 49, 78, 79, 99, 120, 157, 164, 190, 229, 279, 285

Churchill, Sir Winston 80, 114, 125, 127, 130, 131, 132, 134, 135, 138-40, 142, 143, 145, 149, 178, 181, 187, 191, 199, 228, 287

Citrine, Walter 97-8, 106

Cohen, Andrew 172

Cole, G. D.H. 129, 132, 183

Cole, Margaret 129, 135, 183

Collieries in the Ammanford area

    Betws, No 1 and No 2 15, 24, 29, 34, 61-3, 73, 79, 82, 114-5, 129, 257

    Caerbryn 23

    Emlyn (Penygroes) 17, 23. 107

    Pantyffynnon, 15, 29, 36, 61, 117-18, 190

    Parc 23

    Pencae 23

    Pont –y –clerc 23

    Rhos 23, 63-4

    Saron, 23

Collins, Reverend Canon John 206

Commonwealth 9, 169, 173, 228, 251, 255, 285, 289,

Communism in Britain 93-4, 182, 204

Communism in south Wales 105, 221

Communism in the South Wales Miners Federation 95, 97

Davies, Ifor 230, 280

Davies, Ithel 164

Davies, Jennie Eirian 203, 222

Davies, John (Betws) 24-5, 29, 34

Davies, John (historian) 89, 104, 144

Davies, John Rosser 170-1

Davies, Keith 10

Davies, Reverend O. R. (Garnant) 126

Davies, Rhys John (Westhoughton) 289

Davies, Rose 102

Davies, S. O. 56, 58, 62, 91, 98, 106, 109, 134, 144, 155, 187-90, 194-95, 230, 247, 252, 275, 280

Davies, Victor 247

Davies, W. J. 115, 237, 275

Davies, Reverend Principal W. T. Pennar 164, 222, 238

Davies, Reverend William 54

Davies, William Cathan 37

Davidson, Jock 115

Davison, George 56, 59

Day, Colonel Harry 112

Deakin, Arthur 182, 193, 205

Deputy Leader of the Labour Party 4, 7, 8, 23, 197-199, 207-8, 213-15, 223, 288, 294

Derfel, R J 51

Devolution 38, 74, 137-9, 142, 153 -56, 163, 190-1, 195-6, 201-2, 211-227, 230, 235, 246-8, 251, 265, 270, 276, 278, 280, 282, 288, 290-2, 295-6

*Deyrnas, Y* (Journal of Welsh Pacifists) 62, 68

Dobbie, Bill 115-6, 118

Donnelly, Desmond 220

Driberg, Tom 183

Drummond, Henry 36

Dunn, Clara 75

Dunn, Edward (Rother Valley) 111

Durbin, Elizabeth 112, 120

Freeman, John 181

Fursac, J. Rogues 35, 39

Fyfe, David Maxwell 187, 208

His Life

*Birth*, 13, 15-16; *Christened as Jeremiah by Rev Isaac Cynwyd Evans* 18,33; *Band of Hope and his teacher* 19, 22; *with his parents and family a member of Christian Temple Welsh Independent Chapel, Ammanford* 16, 19, 22-3, 63, 79, 286; *deaths in the family* 36-7, 190; *education* 18, 21, 72-80, 147, 284, 286, *family at Betws* 14 -18, 71, 96-7, 162; *First World War* 60-67; *friends at Betws and Ammanford* 20; *Miner at Betws Colliery* 24-6, 28-30 , 91-98; *Marriage To Winifred Rutley at Overton, Hampshire* 66; *Nonconformists Ministers who supported Jim Griffiths* 41-2, 49, 51, 55, 64,-5, 83, 120-1, 142; *Member of the Labour Party* 47, 164-66; *Pacifist till the Second World War* 60-1, 67, 121, 124-5, 134, 293, *Preaching* 26-7, 31, 67; *Parental Influence* 44; *Political agent to Dr D.H Williams* 82-90; *Participant in the Independent Labour Party ( ILP )* 37-38, 44-6, 53-4, 57-9, 62, 73, 84 ; *Ideology* 28, 80; *Lib Lab members* 46-7, 51; *Miners Agent* 91-106; *President of the South Wales Miners Federation* 88, 99-106, 285; *Religion* 31-35, 66 ; *Religious Revival of 1904-5*, 32-5, 39- 40, 48-9, 66 ; *Republicans in Wales who opposed him* 160-1, 164 ; *Pantyffynnon Colliery tragedy* 36-7 ; *Reading Comics and Books* 20-1, 62, 66, 78 ; *Visit to the USA 132-3,* 136; *Pilgrimage* 255-290; *Farewell to the House of Commons in 1970* 234-253, 284, *White House at Ammanford* 56-7.

His Character and Personality

*Aneurin Bevan and Jim* 24, 289, 295; *Anti -Socialists* 49-50, 54-5; *Approachability* 196; *Belief in the Christian Faith* 196, 279-281. 286-9, 294; *Companion of Honour* 275; *Friendship with political leaders* 20, 37- 8, 39- 58,70, 99-105, 197- 204, 240- 248, 250, 274- 278, 287; *Reconciler and Socialist Revisionist* 181-196, *Sunday School* 80; *Sabbatarian* 294; *Democrat* 191, *His health* 290; *His love of the Welsh Language* 115, 149, 157, 195, 234, 242-4, 290-1.

His Contribution as a Politician

*Contribution to the Constituency of Llanelli* 48-50, 107-115, 118, 135, 150-153, 235-239, 255 ; *Contribution to Spanish Civil War, Beveridge Plan and the Welfare State* 123, 136, 150-1; *Defender of Biafra* 255, 273, 286; *Devolution to Wales* 154, 157, 163, 187, 195-6, 236-8, 283; *Secretary of State*

Hart, Judith 205

Hartshorn, Vernon 49, 50, 60, 97, 102, 105

Healey, Denis 185, 194, 214

Henderson, Arthur 47, 64-5, 137, 176

Henderson, J 115

*Herald, Daily* 57, 114, 116, 127, 197-8, 213, 223, 295

Herbison, Margaret 237

Heycock, Llewelyn 89

Hill, J. G. (Llanelli) 237, 241

Hinden, Dr Rita 167-8, 179, 185, 194

Hird, Dennis 55, 75

Hitchon, R E (Bob) 222, 225, 238, 281

Hitler, Adolf 98, 114, 118-9, 121, 123-5, 127, 293

Hodges, Frank 55, 82, 87

Hooson, Emlyn 40

Hopkin, Sir Deian 10, 40, 68, 88-9, 146, 162-3, 179-80, 211, 224, 239, 240, 296

Horner, Arthur 62, 67, 96, 99, 135, 152, 281, 288

Horrabin, J. F. 75

Howard, Reverend J.  39, 41, 67, 89

Howard, Sir Stafford 54

Huggins, Sir Godfrey 175-6

Hughes,  Cledwyn 5, 7, 163, 178, 188-9, 192, 196, 200, 202, 208, 210, 218, 220, 225, 227-8, 231, 236, 238, 245, 247, 249-52, 254, 276, 280, 288, 290-1

Hughes, Reverend Daniel (Detroit) 41, 135-6

Hughes, Douglas  7, 11, 109, 142, 148, 151-3, 157, 162-4, 170, 177-80, 190, 205, 209, 211, 216-8, 224, 229, 234, 236, 239, 240, 292

Poland 87

Pope, Robert 48, 58, 50, 304

Plaid Cymru (Welsh Nationalist Party) 114-116, 146,  149-150, 156-8, 160-162, 164, 187-191, 195-78, 200, 202-3, 210, 214-215 , 246-250, 252, 318

Plebs League 73

Preaching the Gospel 26

Price, Emyr 292, 294-7, 309

Price, Peter (Dowlais) 32

 Probert, Arthur 191, 196, 210

Prothero, Cliff 142, 146, 154, 163, 188-189, 202, 234, 244

Pryce, Sheila Rose see Griffiths. Sheila Rose

Prys Davies, Lord Gwilym 219-221, 224-5, 232-3, 234, 238, 240, 244, 246, 249-250, 252-3, 274, 277 -8, 280, 290-1, 296, 300, 306, 308

Public Ownership 140-142


R

Rathbone, Eleanor 148, 159, 162-3

Rees, Alwyn D. 290

Rees, Dafydd 4, 10

Rees, Reverend David (Llanelli) 65

Rees, D. Ben 4, 6-7, 9, 31,58,67, 105, 121, 301, 303-4, 30-7, 312, 316, 322

Rees, Ebeneser 51

Rees, James Frederick 151

Rees, Meinwen 6

Rees, Noah 75

Rees, R. O. 107, 117